iSeries and AS/400®

Work Management

About MC Professional Books

Developed by Merrikay Lee, the MC Press line of professional books emphasizes practical solutions, applications-based examples, tips, and techniques for the IBM midrange community of IT professionals.

Merrikay Lee is series editor for the MC Press line of professional books, which comprises more than 75 titles. She has spent more than 20 years as a technical professional in the IBM midrange industry and 15 years in the publishing field. She is the author of four books and has worked with numerous IT technical professionals to develop titles for the IBM midrange community of IT professionals. She is president of MC Press, LLC and can be reached at mlee@mcpressonline.com.

iSeries and AS/400®
Work Management

Chuck Stupca

PRESS

First Edition

Second Printing—May 2002

Every attempt has been made to provide correct information. However, the publisher and the author do not guarantee the accuracy of the book and do not assume responsibility for information included or omitted from it.

The following terms are trademarks of International Business Machines Corporation in the United States, other countries, or both: IBM, AS/400, OS/400, and 400. Other trademarked company names and product names mentioned herein are the property of their respective owners.

Printed in Canada. All rights reserved. No part of this publication may be reproduced in any form without prior permission of the copyright owner.

© 2001 MC Press, LLC
ISBN: 1-58347-019-0

Corporate Offices:
125 N. Woodland Trail
Double Oak, TX 75077 USA
Sales & Customer Service
P.O. Box 4300
Big Sandy, TX 75755-4300 USA
www.mcpressonline.com

For information on translations or book distribution outside the USA or to arrange bulk-purchase discounts for sales promotions, premiums, or fund-raisers, please contact MC Press Sales Office at the above address.

V5R1

To Bev, Matt, and Marissa
for their support and encouragement.

Acknowledgments

iSeries and AS/400 Work Management is the result of years of dedicated effort by many programmers who have produced an extremely valuable part of the system. From the first work-management team led by Tom Schwalen to the current iSeries team led by John Modry, I would like to thank all who have patiently answered all of my questions.

I would especially like to thank Dave Novey, whose thorough and professional review of the material has greatly reduced the number of PTFs that would have been required to correct my errors. And also, I would like to thank Brendan Farragher for his customer review.

Contents

Introduction

Computers are tools that help get work done quickly and correctly. Once you have access to a computer, you potentially have a powerful tool available. Microcode interacts with hardware, operating systems, and applications, all designed to make your use of the computer easier. But just what does all of that support do to help you use the computer? Fortunately, you don't need to do much to get a computer to function.

Start by looking at a PC, a type of computer that most of us use every day. When you first get a PC, it is preloaded with microcode, an operating system, and some applications. Press the power button and the system boots. While the system is booting, it is loading microcode, finding devices attached to your PC, and establishing the runtime environment for the operating system. Eventually, you get to a sign-on screen. After signing on, you have an active desktop that allows you to select applications. Actually, you can have several applications active at once (multiple windows).

An iSeries has many characteristics in common with personal computers. The iSeries system is shipped with microcode called Licensed Internal Code (LIC); it is shipped with an operating system, OS/400; and it is shipped with the applications (licensed products) that you ordered. When you start your system with the Power On switch, the system IPLs (boots). During the IPL, microcode is being loaded, hardware is being located, and the operating system runtime environment is being established. An iSeries machine also presents a sign-on screen. The initial sign-on screen for the iSeries system has a menu of items for you to make selections, similar to the desktop on a PC screen.

In the case of an iSeries system, you can have many displays with sign-on screens inviting users to begin using the system. To get to this stage in an iSeries system, you must make extensive use of work management.

While both PCs and the iSeries system can operate with just the default environment shipped with them, they are usually customized for each installation. In the case of an iSeries machine, customizing means adding applications, modifying the initial menu, allowing a workstation to have multiple jobs active, providing performance-tuning information, and making many more changes that affect how work is started and run on the system.

All of these changes are designed to improve the efficiency and usability of your system, and all involve changes to the default work-management parameters. Unfortunately, there are too many instances in which changes are not done correctly, and the results are less efficient, or even nonfunctioning, systems.

This book explains work management and how to make modifications to the defaults provided by IBM to produce an efficient runtime environment for your workload.

1

The Big Picture

You begin your journey through work management when you start your system. When the system is ready to use, a sign-on screen like the one in Figure 1.1 will appear.

```
                              Sign On
                                        System  . . . . . : TSCSAP02
                                        Subsystem . . . . : QINTER
                                        Display . . . . . : QPADEV0026


           User  . . . . . . . . . . . . .
           Password  . . . . . . . . . . .
           Program/procedure . . . . . . .
           Menu  . . . . . . . . . . . . .
           Current library . . . . . . . .












                         (C) COPYRIGHT IBM CORP. 1980, 2001.
```

Figure 1.1: The sign-on screen is displayed at the console after the iSeries IPL is complete.

You need a user name and password in order to access the system. When you installed OS/400 on your iSeries system, you used the IBM-supplied QSECOFR user profile and changed the password for QSECOFR. Therefore, you should sign on

1

using the QSECOFR user name and this new password. (As a security precaution, re-member to change the passwords for all IBM-supplied user profiles.) After the sys-tem processes your sign-on request, you will see the standard menu display as shown in Figure 1.2.

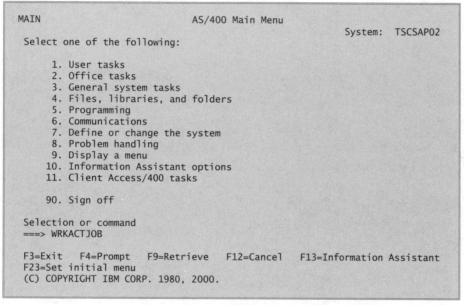

```
MAIN                          AS/400 Main Menu
                                                        System:  TSCSAP02
   Select one of the following:

         1. User tasks
         2. Office tasks
         3. General system tasks
         4. Files, libraries, and folders
         5. Programming
         6. Communications
         7. Define or change the system
         8. Problem handling
         9. Display a menu
        10. Information Assistant options
        11. Client Access/400 tasks

        90. Sign off

   Selection or command
   ===> WRKACTJOB

   F3=Exit   F4=Prompt   F9=Retrieve   F12=Cancel   F13=Information Assistant
   F23=Set initial menu
   (C) COPYRIGHT IBM CORP. 1980, 2000.
```

Figure 1.2: The menu appears after the system operator has signed on to the system. It includes op-tions for some of the most frequently used tasks and allows any OS/400 command to be entered.

Take a look at the jobs that are active on the system. As shown in Figure 1.2, en-ter the Work with Active Jobs command (WRKACTJOB) on the input line, and press Enter. You'll see the jobs shown in Figures 1.3a through 1.3f.

```
                   Work with Active Jobs                    TSCSAP02
                                               02/16/01   07:58:04
CPU %:     .0     Elapsed time:   00:00:00    Active jobs:   184

Type options, press Enter.
  2=Change   3=Hold   4=End   5=Work with   6=Release   7=Display message
  8=Work with spooled files    13=Disconnect ...

Opt  Subsystem/Job  User       Type  CPU %  Function        Status
     QBATCH         QSYS       SBS    .0                     DEQW
     QBASE          QSYS       SBS    .0                     DEQW
       QPADEV0026   JCSTUPCA   INT    .0    CMD-WRKACTJOB    RUN
     QCMN           QSYS       SBS    .0                     DEQW
     QSPL           QSYS       SBS    .0                     DEQW
     QSYSWRK        QSYS       SBS    .0                     DEQW
       QAPPCTCP     QSYS       BCH    .0    PGM-QZPAIJOB     TIMW
       QCQEPMON     QSVMSS     BCH    .0    PGM-QCQEPMON     MSGW
       QCQRCVDS     QSVMSS     BCH    .0    PGM-QCQAPDRM     MSGW
                                                              More...
Parameters or command
===>
F3=Exit   F5=Refresh       F7=Find      F10=Restart statistics
F11=Display elapsed data   F12=Cancel   F23=More options   F24=More keys
```

Figure 1.3a: This is the first display of jobs that are currently active on the system and are started automatically. The "More... In the lower-right corner indicates that additional jobs are active. Press the PageDown key to see those jobs.

```
                   Work with Active Jobs                    TSCSAP02
                                               02/16/01   07:58:04
CPU %:     .0     Elapsed time:   00:00:00    Active jobs:   184

Type options, press Enter.
  2=Change   3=Hold   4=End   5=Work with   6=Release   7=Display message
  8=Work with spooled files    13=Disconnect ...

Opt  Subsystem/Job  User       Type  CPU %  Function        Status
     QECS           QSVSM      BCH    .0    PGM-QNSECSJB    DEQW
     QGLDPUBA       QDIRSRV    ASJ    .0    PGM-QGLDPUBA    SIGW
     QGLDPUBE       QDIRSRV    ASJ    .0    PGM-QGLDPUBE    DEQW
     QIJSSCD        QIJS       BCH    .0    PGM-QIJSCMON    DEQA
     QNEOSOEM       QUSER      ASJ    .0    PGM-QNEOSOEM    TIMW
     QNEOSOEM       QUSER      BCH    .0    PGM-QNEOSOEM    TIMW
     QNEOSOEM       QUSER      BCH    .0    PGM-QNEOSOEM    TIMW
     QNPSERVD       QUSER      BCH    .0                    SELW
     QNSCRMON       QSVSM      BCH    .0    PGM-QNSCRMON    DEQW
     QPASVRP        QSYS       BCH    .0    PGM-QPASVRP     DEQW
     QPASVRS        QSYS       BCH    .0    PGM-QPASVRS     TIMW
     QALERT         QSYS       SYS    .0                    DEQW
                                                              More...
Parameters or command
===>
F3=Exit   F5=Refresh       F7=Find      F10=Restart statistics
F11=Display elapsed data   F12=Cancel   F23=More options   F24=More keys
```

Figure 1.3b: This display shows system jobs that are started automatically. The last job on this display, QALERT, is the first of several system jobs discussed in this chapter.

```
                        Work with Active Jobs              TSCSAP02
                                               02/16/01  08:27:05
     CPU %:   20.8      Elapsed time:   00:29:01    Active jobs:   183

     Type options, press Enter.
       2=Change   3=Hold   4=End    5=Work with   6=Release   7=Display message
       8=Work with spooled files    13=Disconnect ...

     Opt   Subsystem/Job   User       Type   CPU %  Function      Status
           QCMNARB01       QSYS       SYS     .0                  EVTW
           QCMNARB02       QSYS       SYS     .0                  EVTW
           QCMNARB03       QSYS       SYS     .0                  EVTW
           QDBSRVXR        QSYS       SYS     .0                  DEQW
           QDBSRVXR2       QSYS       SYS     .0                  DEQW
           QDBSRV01        QSYS       SYS     .0                  EVTW
           QDBSRV02        QSYS       SYS     .0                  DEQW
           QDBSRV03        QSYS       SYS     .0                  DEQW
           QDBSRV04        QSYS       SYS     .0                  DEQW
                                                                  More...
     Parameters or command
     ===>
     F3=Exit   F5=Refresh       F7=Find       F10=Restart statistics
     F11=Display elapsed data   F12=Cancel    F23=More options   F24=More keys
```

Figure 1.3c: This display shows system jobs that are started automatically.

```
                        Work with Active Jobs              TSCSAP02
                                               02/16/01  08:27:05
     CPU %:   20.8      Elapsed time:   00:29:01    Active jobs:   183

     Type options, press Enter.
       2=Change   3=Hold   4=End    5=Work with   6=Release   7=Display message
       8=Work with spooled files    13=Disconnect ...

     Opt   Subsystem/Job   User       Type   CPU %  Function      Status
           QDBSRV05        QSYS       SYS     .0                  DEQW
           QDCPOBJ1        QSYS       SYS     .0                  EVTW
           QDCPOBJ2        QSYS       SYS     .0                  EVTW
           QDCPOBJ3        QSYS       SYS     .0                  EVTW
           QFILESYS1       QSYS       SYS     .0                  TIMW
           QJOBSCD         QSYS       SYS     .0                  EVTW
           QLUR            QSYS       SYS     .0                  EVTW
           QLUS            QSYS       SYS     .0                  EVTW
           QPFRADJ         QSYS       SYS     .0                  EVTW
                                                                  More...
     Parameters or command
     ===>
     F3=Exit   F5=Refresh       F7=Find       F10=Restart statistics
     F11=Display elapsed data   F12=Cancel    F23=More options   F24=More keys
```

Figure 1.3d: This display shows system jobs that are started automatically.

```
                    Work with Active Jobs                    TSCSAP02
                                               02/16/01  08:27:05
     CPU %:   20.8      Elapsed time:   00:29:01    Active jobs:   183

     Type options, press Enter.
       2=Change   3=Hold   4=End    5=Work with   6=Release   7=Display message
       8=Work with spooled files    13=Disconnect ...

     Opt  Subsystem/Job  User      Type  CPU %  Function      Status
          QQQTEMP1       QSYS      SYS    .0                  DEQW
          QQQTEMP2       QSYS      SYS    .0                  DEQW
          QSPLMAINT      QSYS      SYS    .0                  EVTW
          QSYSARB        QSYS      SYS    .0                  EVTW
          QSYSARB2       QSYS      SYS    .0                  EVTW
          QSYSARB3       QSYS      SYS    .0                  EVTW
          QSYSARB4       QSYS      SYS    .0                  EVTW
          QSYSARB5       QSYS      SYS    .0                  EVIW
          QSYSCOMM1      QSYS      SYS    .0                  EVTW
                                                               More...
     Parameters or command
     ===>
     F3=Exit   F5=Refresh       F7=Find      F10=Restart statistics
     F11=Display elapsed data   F12=Cancel   F23=More options  F24=More keys
```

Figure 1.3e: This display shows system jobs that are started automatically.

```
                    Work with Active Jobs                    TSCSAP02
                                               02/16/01  08:27:05
     CPU %:   20.8      Elapsed time:   00:29:01    Active jobs:   183

     Type options, press Enter.
       2=Change   3=Hold   4=End    5=Work with   6=Release   7=Display message
       8=Work with spooled files    13=Disconnect ...

     Opt  Subsystem/Job  User      Type  CPU %  Function      Status
          Q400FILSVR     QSYS      SYS    .0                  DEQW
          SCPF           QSYS      SYS    .0                  EVTW




                                                               Bottom
     Parameters or command
     ===>
     F3=Exit   F5=Refresh       F7=Find      F10=Restart statistics
     F11=Display elapsed data   F12=Cancel   F23=More options  F24=More keys
```

Figure 1.3f: This display shows system jobs that are started automatically.

Where did all of those jobs come from? Didn't you just start this system?
Actually, you might see even more than these jobs. You're seeing all of the jobs

that the system will start automatically to provide many of the OS/400 services that keep your system running smoothly. Also, the system is set up to allow users to run jobs without any knowledge of work management. Of course, as you will discover in this book, a good understanding of work management can make systems run even better!

You might notice that some jobs are indented under other jobs in the displays in Figure 1.3. You'll learn about the indented jobs in a minute. For now, notice that all of the jobs that are not indented are listed in alphabetical order, which doesn't tell you much of anything.

Figure 1.4 shows a different look at these jobs. Right now, the diagram probably isn't any more meaningful than the alphabetical list. However, the next few paragraphs discuss how these jobs are started and the functions that they provide. At the end of the discussion, the relationship between these jobs and the diagram will become much more meaningful to you.

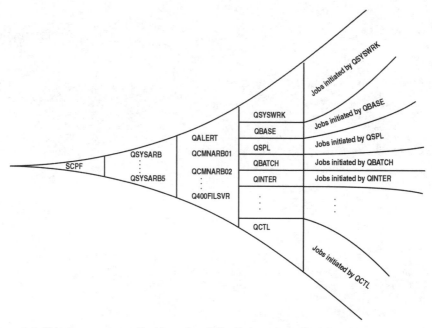

Figure 1.4: This diagram shows the hierarchy of jobs that run on an iSeries system.

System Jobs

As the system starts, it begins with many of the jobs on the left side of Figure 1.4. The first job that gets started is the Start Control Program Function (SCPF). This job is used to run the programs that perform the system functions required to ensure that your system is usable. SCPF remains active at a low priority to handle any long-running system functions that do not need immediate attention. In addition, it will be the last job to end when you power-down your system.

The next set of jobs is referred to as the *system arbiter*. At one time, the system arbiter was a single job, but as systems grew larger and additional functions were provided by OS/400, this job became overloaded. There are now five jobs that are collectively referred to as the system arbiter:

- QSYSARB.
- QSYSARB2.
- QSYSARB3.
- QSYSARB4.
- QSYSARB5.

QSYSARB

QSYSARB performs the following functions:

- Device configuration—When a device is created with the ONLINE parameter set to *YES, it will be varied on by this job.

- Communications—As with devices, any objects that are created with the ONLINE parameter set to *YES will be varied on.

- Device locking—Before any subsystems are started, all devices are owned by QSYSARB. If you view devices as plots of government land that are available for prospectors to receive, QSYSARB is the government—which really owns all the land. When a prospector arrives (a subsystem starts) and stakes a claim for some land (wishes to own a device), the rights to the land (lock) are transferred to the prospector (subsystem). If the prospector leaves (the subsystem ends) and the land (device) is not claimed by another prospector (subsystem), the rights (lock) for the land (device) revert to the government (QSYSARB).

QSYSARB2

QSYSARB2 performs the following functions:

- Security auditing—If security auditing is active, every time an object is created, renamed, changed, moved, or deleted, an event is generated. The event is handled by QSYSARB2 and the information is passed to security.

- System/36 environment configuration—If your system is set up to run the System/36 environment, configuration events are handled by QSYSARB2.

QSYSARB3

QSYSARB3 performs the following functions:

- Temporary job structures—Each job uses several temporary objects. These structures are created each IPL (reboot). The number of structures created is specified by the system value QACTJOB. When all of the created structures are in use, additional structures are created using the setting of the system value QADLACTJ.

- Permanent job structures—In addition to temporary objects, a job will use several permanent objects. Once created, these structures will remain on the system. The number of structures created is specified by the QTOTJOB system value. As for temporary structures, when all of the created structures are in use, additional structures are created using the setting of the system value QADLTOTJ.

QSYSARB4

QSYSARB4 starts and end subsystems, and handles the ENDSYS and PWRDWNSYS commands.

QSYSARB5

QSYSARB5 performs the following functions:

- System test.

- Test request.

- Unsolicited events—Events that are not explicitly handled by the other arbiter jobs are handled by QSYSARB5.

- Machine and LIC events—Events that are generated by the hardware but are not handled by any of the other system arbiter jobs are also handled by

QSYSARB5. Low-level error recording is an example of an event that would fall into this category.

Other System Jobs

The following set of jobs is the remainder of the system jobs (those not indented in Figure 1.3) starting with the job named QALERT:

- QALERT—This is the alert manager job. Certain messages generated in the system have an attribute that identifies them as an alert. When these messages occur, an alert will be generated. All of the alerts that occur in your system are handled by this job.

- QCMNARB*nn*—These are APPC communications arbiters. Even with five system arbiter jobs, there are still situations that could overload the system arbiter. In particular, complex APPC environments that experience a communication failure could tie up the system arbiter for an extended period of time. To alleviate these issues, communications arbiter jobs were created to handle APPC communications events. By default, the system will determine the number of these jobs that need to be started.

- QDBSRVXR and QDBSRVXR2—These are database cross-reference jobs, which maintain a cross-reference of tables (files) and columns (fields) that appear in your database. The cross-reference information helps database efficiency for operations like queries.

- QDBSRV*nn*—These are database server jobs, which recover access paths (keys) used in your database definition. Access-path recovery is a function usually performed only during an abnormal IPL. In addition, these jobs are used whenever you use the access-path protection function provided by the system.

- QDCPOBJN— These jobs provide decompression functions. Portions of the operating system used by a small subset of iSeries installations are shipped in compressed format to conserve disk and media space. When you access a compressed object, it must be decompressed before it can be used.

- QFILESYS1—This is the file system job. As you use files in your system, you are continually making changes to them. To provide maximum throughput of your jobs, the changes are not immediately written from main storage to disk. This job runs in the background (asynchronously) and writes the changed pages to disk.

- QJOBSCD—This is the job scheduler, which waits for timer events to submit batch jobs for processing. Its function is explained in chapter 12.

- QLUR—This job handles logical unit (LU) 6.2 resynchronization. When using remote databases, a function called *two-phase commit* is used to ensure that changes in data made on local and remote systems can be resynchronized. This job provides the resynchronization of one-phase commit operations.

- QLUS—This is the LU services job, used to manage communication devices used on your system and handle any communication-device-related events that occur.

- QPFRADJ—This job handles the dynamic performance adjustment. It is responsible for distributing main storage to help the system run as efficiently as possible. This feature is discussed in detail in chapter 4.

- QQQTEMP1 and QQQTEMP2—These are database parallelism jobs. When you use a distributed database called DB2 Multisystem in your environment, these jobs are used to provide faster response to queries.

- QSPLMAINT—This job handles system spool maintenance. It has a status associated with it that determines the actions taken by the job when it is started:

  0 DLSTSPLF—Whenever a user deletes a spool file, this job will clear the data from an internal file that maintains spool files.

  1 RCLSPLSTG—When members of the internal spool file have gone unused for a specified amount of time, they are deleted. This operation can be used to reclaim space that has gone unused. The QRCLSPLSTG system value can be used to specify the number of days that a member can be unused.

2 SPLCLNUP—The job will perform spool cleanup operations. Most of the operations are performed as the result of an abnormal IPL.

- QSYSCOMM1—This is the systems communications job, which handles certain types of communications and I/O activities.

- Q400FILSVR—This is the remote file system communication job. It performs the APPN or APPC Common Programming Interface Communications (CPIC) operations that are requested on your system.

For the most part, you should not be concerned with these jobs or the actions they perform. Just remember that they are there to make your life a lot simpler.

Now that you've waded through the system jobs, you need to learn about another set of jobs provided by IBM: the *subsystem monitor jobs*. Subsystems are your access to the system. They are responsible for, among other things, locating sources of work, starting jobs, and ending jobs. Finally, past the subsystems, are the jobs that are initiated by the subsystems.

These are the jobs that are indented below the subsystem that initiated them in Figure 1.3. Most of these jobs will be ones that your users are running. There is, however, one subsystem that is an exception: QSYSWRK is an IBM-supplied subsystem used by OS/400 functions to run jobs. These functions need a subsystem that they know exists on every iSeries system and is active when the system is running.

As mentioned in the preceding section, subsystems are the doors to your system, and are defined by a subsystem description. The first subsystems you will use are provided by IBM and are started automatically. When the subsystems are started, a job called the subsystem monitor is started. The subsystem monitor uses the subsystem description to find and initiate work. Also, when a subsystem starts a job, the job will be assigned to a part of main storage called a *pool*. The next chapter covers the basic operations of subsystems in detail.

Storage Pools

Return to the main menu and run the Work with System Status command (WRKSYSSTS), as shown in Figure 1.5. When you press the Enter key, you will see a display similar to Figure 1.6. This display shows the storage pools used to run the jobs on your system. These storage pools can be of two types: shared and private.

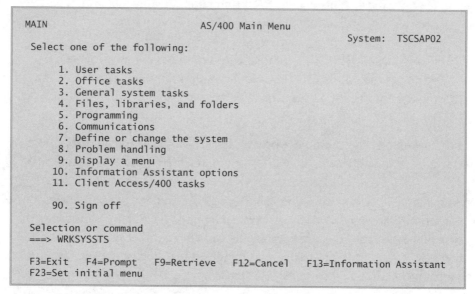

```
MAIN                           AS/400 Main Menu
                                                  System:   TSCSAP02
    Select one of the following:

        1. User tasks
        2. Office tasks
        3. General system tasks
        4. Files, libraries, and folders
        5. Programming
        6. Communications
        7. Define or change the system
        8. Problem handling
        9. Display a menu
       10. Information Assistant options
       11. Client Access/400 tasks

       90. Sign off

    Selection or command
    ===> WRKSYSSTS

    F3=Exit   F4=Prompt   F9=Retrieve   F12=Cancel   F13=Information Assistant
    F23=Set initial menu
```

Figure 1.5: Run the WRKSYSSTS command from the main menu.

```
                        Work with System Status            TSCSAP01
                                              09/18/00  11:08:03
    % CPU used . . . . . . :      86.7   Auxiliary storage:
    Elapsed time . . . . . :   00:05:01     System ASP . . . . . :     95.94G
    Jobs in system . . . . :       305     % system ASP used  . :    29.0611
    % addresses used:                       Total  . . . . . . . :     99.88G
      Permanent  . . . . . :      .009     Current unprotect used :     1850M
      Temporary  . . . . . :      .015     Maximum unprotect . . :      1865M

    Type changes (if allowed), press Enter.

    System   Pool    Reserved   Max    ---DB---   --Non-DB--
    Pool    Size (M)  Size (M)  Active Fault  Pages  Fault  Pages
      1       325.00   190.88   +++++    .0     .0     6.0    7.0
      2      1283.50      .00       4   2.0  257.5     3.0    3.1
      3      2700.00      .00     197   1.0   16.3   122.8  124.6
      4        43.50      .00       1    .0     .0      .0     .0

                                                              Bottom
    Command
    ===>
    F3=Exit    F4=Prompt          F5=Refresh   F9=Retrieve    F10=Restart
    F11=Display transition data   F12=Cancel   F24=More keys
```

Figure 1.6: The WRKSYSSTS command shows status information that can be used to monitor system activity.

Shared Storage Pools

A shared storage pool can run jobs that are initiated by more than one subsystem; that is, the pool is shared by multiple subsystems. Chapter 11 provides several examples of subsystems using the same shared pools. For now, that's not important. What is important is another feature of shared pools: they can be adjusted automatically by the performance adjustment feature of OS/400.

There are 64 shared pools in the system: *MACHINE, *BASE, *INTERACT, *SPOOL, and *SHRPOOL1 through *SHRPOOL60. *MACHINE is a special pool that cannot be used by a subsystem to run any jobs. It will always be the first system pool.

*BASE can be used by any number of subsystems to run jobs. It will always be the second system pool. If you are using the IBM-supplied defaults, *INTERACT will be the third pool and *SPOOL will be the fourth. The pools are assigned system pool numbers whenever a subsystem that can run jobs in the pool is started.

But how does a subsystem indicate that it wants to use a shared pool for jobs that it initiates? When the subsystem description is created, one of its parts is a list of pools that the subsystem would like to use for jobs that it will initiate. The pool is identified by the subsystem using a number and the name of the shared pool that the subsystem would like to use. For example, the IBM-supplied subsystem QBASE has the following description:

```
POOLS((1 *BASE)(2 *INTERACT))
```

As a result, QBASE has two different shared pools that it can use to run jobs. But isn't the first system pool *MACHINE and the second system pool *BASE? Maybe you should use this instead:

```
POOLS((2 *BASE)(3 *INTERACT))
```

Actually, that's not necessary. The number used when you specify the pools refers to the relative pool number in the subsystem description. It does not need to be the same number as the system pool that will be used for the shared pool.

Private Pools

Private pools are different from shared pools in two ways: only one subsystem can use them to run jobs, and they are not modified by the performance adjustment feature of OS/400. If you want to use private pools for QBASE, you could use the following in your subsystem description:

```
POOLS((1 663000 2)(2 12340000 83))
```

Wait a minute! What are those other two numbers that weren't there when you used shared pools? Those two numbers are used to set the size and activity level of the pool. The size is the amount of main storage (in kilobytes) that you would like allocated to the pool. The activity level refers to the maximum number of jobs that can be in main storage trying to get work done at the same time. For interactive jobs, think of this as the number of users who can press Enter at any one time. For a shared pool, these values are set with different commands and/or displays.

Pools as Pools

Usually, when you think of pools, you think of swimming pools. In fact, swimming pools can be used as an analogy to main storage pools. Shared pools are like public swimming pools. People (jobs) from many different neighborhoods (subsystems) can use the public pool. Private pools are like your neighbor's backyard pool. Only the swimmers (jobs) that your neighbor (subsystem) invites are allowed to enter the pool.

In Review

Your long journey through work management starts in this chapter with a look at the system jobs and functions provided for you. This chapter also introduces subsystems, subsystem monitor jobs, and pools. The next few chapters explain more about subsystems, jobs, performance, and pools. Then, you'll have a solid foundation for making work management work for you.

2

Subsystems:
The Heart of Work Management

In chapter 1, you learned the basic job structures of OS/400, and you should now have a subsystem that has allocated storage. At this point, however, the subsystem cannot introduce any work to the system. In order to examine the work-initiation functions of the subsystem, you need to take a closer look at the components of the subsystem that are responsible for finding work and initiating it.

This chapter begins by looking at the default description of QBASE, which is the default controlling subsystem, and is also capable of finding and introducing work. By examining QBASE, you will better understand how an AS/400 or iSeries system works after it has been IPLed. This chapter also discusses the way each of the parts of QBASE is defined within the subsystem. As you will learn, work management has many different ways of controlling the work that is introduced. This chapter doesn't attempt to cover the tremendous flexibility of a subsystem, but does cover each of the basic functions that a subsystem (and the subsystem monitor) performs.

The Parts of a Subsystem

Begin with a simple display of the description of the QBASE subsystem by entering the following Display Subsystem Description (DSPSBSD) command:

```
DSPSBSD QBASE
```

The resulting display is shown in Figure 2.1. Notice the *More...* message at the bottom right corner of the screen, which indicates you can press the PageDown key for additional options. In this case, there is one additional option (30), which can be used to view all of the options shown on this screen. Because you are concerned only with the basic job-initiation functions of work management, it's not necessary to look at all of the options.

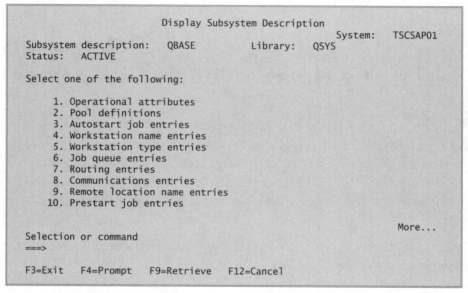

```
                    Display Subsystem Description
                                            System:    TSCSAP01
   Subsystem description:    QBASE        Library:    QSYS
   Status:    ACTIVE

   Select one of the following:

        1. Operational attributes
        2. Pool definitions
        3. Autostart job entries
        4. Workstation name entries
        5. Workstation type entries
        6. Job queue entries
        7. Routing entries
        8. Communications entries
        9. Remote location name entries
       10. Prestart job entries

                                                     More...
   Selection or command
   ===>

   F3=Exit    F4=Prompt    F9=Retrieve    F12=Cancel
```

Figure 2.1: The Display Subsystem Description command shows a menu that allows you to view the parts of a subsystem.

This chapter describes the shipped values for options 5, 6, 7. As discussed in chapter 1, the pool definitions are used by the job-initiation process. The operational attributes are not relevant to job initiation. The remainder of the options are discussed in subsequent chapters.

Option 5—Workstation Type Entries

Select menu option 5 to show the workstation type entry of QBASE, as in Figure 2.2. Clearly, this is not a very interesting display. Before looking more deeply into the two entries shown, however, consider why they are part of the subsystem.

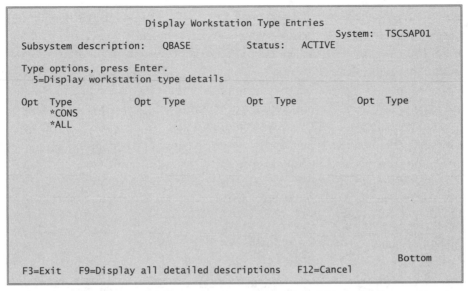

```
                    Display Workstation Type Entries
                                                  System:   TSCSAP01
     Subsystem description:    QBASE          Status:    ACTIVE

     Type options, press Enter.
       5=Display workstation type details

     Opt   Type              Opt   Type          Opt   Type           Opt   Type
           *CONS
           *ALL




                                                                      Bottom
     F3=Exit    F9=Display all detailed descriptions    F12=Cancel
```

Figure 2.2: The QBASE workstation entries are used to locate available workstations and send a sign-on screen to them.

As mentioned earlier, there must be a method for the subsystem to find work that it should initiate. The workstation entries are used to locate displays similar to the one you are using. (If you are using a PC, pretend that you are not.) Once the display has been located, the subsystem can take ownership of it.

Finding and taking ownership of a workstation is much the same as prospecting during the California gold rush. When prospectors arrived in California, they used a map to look for an area that they thought would contain gold. When prospectors found such land, they would try to stake a claim for it. However, if another prospector owned the land, it was not available. Once the claim was filed, the land needed to be mined, or the claim would be considered abandoned and could be taken over by another prospector. Once the land was in the process of being mined, it remained the property of the original prospector until that prospector moved away or retired.

In work management, starting the subsystem is similar to the prospector's arrival in California. The workstation type entry represents the map the prospector used—it guides the subsystem to prospective workstations. If the workstation has not already been claimed by another subsystem, it is available to the new subsystem, which takes ownership of it and sends a sign-on screen to the display.

17

Sending the sign-on screen to the workstation will not guarantee ownership of the workstation; it must be put to use by the subsystem. That is, the claim must be mined. If the workstation has not been used to start a job in the owning subsystem, it is the same as an abandoned claim: another subsystem may be started, find the workstation available, and send a sign-on screen. Once the workstation has been used to run work in a subsystem (the claim is being worked), it remains assigned to the subsystem until the subsystem is ended. In the case of QBASE, once a user has signed on to a workstation, the workstation will remain the property of QBASE until one of the following occurs:

1. The user signs off and a new subsystem with a workstation entry for the device is started.

2. The entire system is shut down.

Now that you know why the entries are there, you need to find out how they got there. In order to create the workstation entry, the Add Workstation Entry (ADDWSE) command in Figure 2.3 was run after the QBASE SBSD was created.

A similar command was run to produce the workstation entry *CONS. Once these commands have been run, the subsystem can acquire devices and initiate work from the devices. The subsystem now has pools in which to run the work that it initiates, and it has ownership of potential sources of work. Since QBASE is active, any device that is powered on and varied on will be sent a sign-on. The diagram in Figure 2.4 represents the result of running the commands.

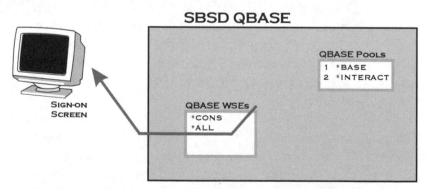

Figure 2.4: A workstation entry of *ALL is used to send a sign-on screen to any device that is powered on and varied on.

```
                  Add Workstation Entry (ADDWSE)

Type choices, press Enter.

Subsystem description  . . . . .  SBSD          QBASE
  Library . . . . . . . . . . .                 *LIBL
Work station name, or  . . . . .  WRKSTN
Work station type  . . . . . .    WRKSTNTYPE    *ALL
Job description  . . . . . . . .  JOBD          *USRPRF
  Library . . . . . . . . . .
Maximum active jobs  . . . . . .  MAXACT        *NOMAX
Allocation . . . . . . . . . .    AT            *SIGNON




                                                         Bottom
 F3=Exit    F4=Prompt  F5=Refresh  F12=Cancel  F13=How to use this display
 F24=More keys
```

Figure 2.3: The Add Workstation Entry command identifies workstations that can receive a sign-on screen from a subsystem.

The *CONS entry refers to the console device for your system AS/400. There can only be one console device. It will have different characteristics from other workstations that are defined by the *ALL entry. These differences will be discussed later. For now, take a closer look at the *ALL by moving your cursor to the line in front of *ALL, typing 5, and pressing Enter. You will be shown the information in Figure 2.5.

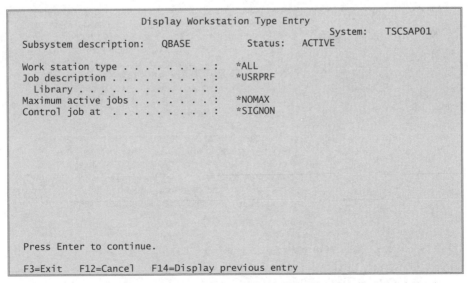

```
                  Display Workstation Type Entry
                                           System:    TSCSAP01
 Subsystem description:   QBASE        Status:   ACTIVE

 Work station type . . . . . . . . :    *ALL
 Job description . . . . . . . . . :    *USRPRF
   Library . . . . . . . . . . . . :
 Maximum active jobs . . . . . . . :    *NOMAX
 Control job at  . . . . . . . . . :    *SIGNON






 Press Enter to continue.

 F3=Exit    F12=Cancel    F14=Display previous entry
```

Figure 2.5: The workstation entry includes information that describes how the workstation is used by the subsystem.

Notice how the parameters specified on the ADDWSE entry are used to define the workstation type entry. The first parameter merely names the subsystem (QBASE). The following parameters describe the characteristics of the entry. Table 2.1 shows each parameter and the resulting characteristic of the workstation ENTRY.

Table 2.1: Keywords for Workstation Entries		
Keyword	Value	Result/Comments
WRKSTN	N/A	This parameter is used when the subsystem uses workstation names to find devices. In the prospecting example, the map would have specific names for each of the potential areas to be mined.
WRKSTNTYPE	*ALL	Any workstation device attached to your system can be acquired by QBASE. You can restrict the device types that a subsystem can acquire by specifying a single device type. If you choose to allow more than one device type (but not *ALL), you must provide an ADDWSE command for each device type.
JOBD	*USRPRF	When the user of a workstation signs on, the subsystem initiates a job. The operational attributes of the job are obtained from a job description. In this case, the job description that is used is specified by the user profile of the person who is signing on.
MAXACT	*NOMAX	This parameter controls the number of jobs that can be initiated using this workstation entry. When *NOMAX is used, there is no limit to the number of jobs that can use this entry. Typically, *NOMAX is the correct value for this parameter. Otherwise, a sign-on screen will appear at the workstation, but an attempt to use the workstation might result in an error of "Routing step terminated abnormally." This is not a user friendly situation or message.
AT	*SIGNON	This value indicates that the subsystem can send a sign-on screen to any workstation that meets the criteria for this entry. In this case, all devices that are varied on and powered on will receive a sign-on screen from QBASE. This parameter has another value, *ENTER, which is discussed in a later chapter.

You now have a subsystem with pools that will accept work, a workstation entry to find and acquire devices, and a sign-on screen at all of the devices that are powered on and varied on. You are ready to accept interactive work! Before accepting any work, however, take a look at another class of jobs: batch jobs.

Option 6—Job Queue Entries

In order for a subsystem to find and initiate batch jobs, several other constructs are involved. Job queues, job queue entries, and batch job submission are discussed here. After the discussion of these constructs, you should understand the basic elements needed to initiate batch work.

The first item to investigate is the job queue. As the name implies, a job queue is an object that holds jobs in a line (queue) until a subsystem is ready to initiate them. Several job queues ship with OS/400, and many of them are available for QBASE to find and initiate batch jobs. This chapter focuses on the job queue QBATCH, which is the most commonly used job queue. Begin by looking at the command that is used to create job queues, Create Job Queue (CRTJOBQ), shown in Figure 2.6.

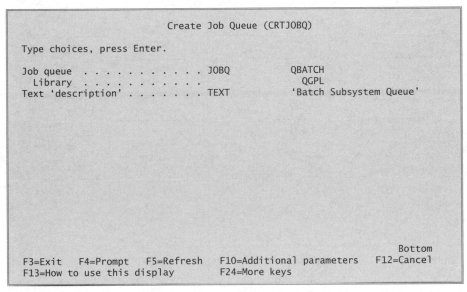

```
                          Create Job Queue (CRTJOBQ)

Type choices, press Enter.

Job queue  . . . . . . . . . . JOBQ          QBATCH
  Library  . . . . . . . . . .                QGPL
Text 'description' . . . . . . TEXT          'Batch Subsystem Queue'




                                                                    Bottom
F3=Exit   F4=Prompt   F5=Refresh   F10=Additional parameters   F12=Cancel
F13=How to use this display        F24=More keys
```

Figure 2.6: The Create Job Queue command creates a queue that will be used for batch jobs.

As you can see, there is not much to this command. The two parameters merely let you name the queue, provide the location (library), and give some descriptive text about the queue. As noted before, many of the shipped OS/400 objects are contained in QGPL. In this case, the default batch job queue QBATCH has been created in QGPL for you.

Now that you have a job queue, you need to find a way to look for and initiate jobs on the queue. Basically, you need to provide a map to enable a prospector to stake a claim and begin to work it. Instead of providing a map using a workstation entry, one is provided by a job queue entry. Add the job queue entry to QBASE so that it can have a place to look for batch work. As you might have guessed by now, the job queue entry is added to the subsystem description with the Add Job Queue Entry (ADDJOBQE) command, as shown in Figure 2.7.

```
                    Add Job Queue Entry (ADDJOBQE)

 Type choices, press Enter.

 Subsystem description  . . . . .  SBSD          QBASE
   Library  . . . . . . . . . .                  *LIBL
 Job queue  . . . . . . . . . . .  JOBQ          QBATCH
   Library  . . . . . . . . . .                  QGPL
 Maximum active jobs  . . . . . .  MAXACT        1
 Sequence number  . . . . . . .   SEQNBR        10
 Max active priority 1  . . . . .  MAXPTY1       *NOMAX
 Max active priority 2  . . . . .  MAXPTY2       *NOMAX
 Max active priority 3  . . . . .  MAXPTY3       *NOMAX
 Max active priority 4  . . . . .  MAXPTY4       *NOMAX
 Max active priority 5  . . . . .  MAXPTY5       *NOMAX
 Max active priority 6  . . . . .  MAXPTY6       *NOMAX
 Max active priority 7  . . . . .  MAXPTY7       *NOMAX
 Max active priority 8  . . . . .  MAXPTY8       *NOMAX
 Max active priority 9  . . . . .  MAXPTY9       *NOMAX
                                                         Bottom
 F3=Exit  F4=Prompt  F5=Refresh  F12=Cancel  F13=How to use this display
 F24=More keys
```

Figure 2.7: *The Add Job Queue Entry command defines queues that a subsystem uses to initiate batch jobs.*

As you can see, there are a few more parameters to deal with when running this command. Once again, the first parameter merely names the subsystem that will become the owner of the job queue, while the second parameter names the job queue. Table 2.2 lists the other parameters and their significance to the subsystem monitor.

Table 2.2: Keywords for Subsystem Monitor

Keyword	Value	Result/Comments
MAXACT	1	This parameter is used to control the number of jobs that can be initiated using this job queue entry. When *NOMAX is used, there is no limit to the number of jobs that can use this entry. However, since batch jobs have a tendency to use more of the system's processing power, *NOMAX is not a good value for MAXACT on a job queue. The default value of 1 states that QBASE will initiate only one job from the job queue, waiting until an initiated job completes before initiating another one. In this manner, the processing capabilities of the system will not be overrun. This value may be adjusted to a higher number if processing capacity is available. Techniques for determining a reasonable value for this parameter are discussed in the next chapter.
SEQNBR	10	This value indicates the order in which a subsystem will search job queues for batch work to initiate. The value can be any number from 1 to 9,999. Each job queue entry must have a unique SEQNBR.
MAXPTY1 MAXPTY2 MAXPTY3 MAXPTY4 MAXPTY5 MAXPTY6 MAXPTY7 MAXPTY8 MAXPTY	*NOMAX *NOMAX *NOMAX *NOMAX *NOMAX *NOMAX *NOMAX *NOMAX *NOMAX	All jobs on a job queue can be assigned a priority. Much the same as SEQNBR, these parameters place the jobs on the job queue in a search order for the subsystem. Each of the nine priorities may specify the number of jobs that can be active (initiated) at one time by QBASE. Now for some more confusion. All of these values specify *NOMAX, so how many jobs will QBASE initiate? If you said one, congratulations! Although these values specify *NOMAX, the MAXACT value for the job queue entry specifies only one. Since the MAXACT for the job queue entry is the more powerful of the values, only one job is started. As you might guess, the combinations of MAXPTY*n* and MAXACT values are unlimited. So, how should these values be used? Unless you are running an S/36 environment, you will most likely not use these MAXPTY*n* values. In an S/36, there was only one job queue for the entire system. The MAXPTY*n* values were used to allow the system to introduce a mixture of batch jobs. In OS/400, there are easier methods of accomplishing the same function. These methods are discussed in a later chapter.

Take a breather! Trying to understand all these MAXACT and MAXPTY*n* relationships can make your head spin. The key thing to remember is that the job queue QBATCH is used by QBASE to introduce batch jobs. Also, remember that the default for QBASE is to initiate only one batch job at a time.

After running the CRTJOBQ and ADDJOBQE commands, the subsystem now has the structure shown in Figure 2.8. Other job queues and job queue entries are included with QBASE. The CRTJOBQ and ADDJOBQE entries were run for each of the other job queues that appear in QBASE. To see all of the job queues available to QBASE, return to the menu shown by the DSBSBSD command. From the menu screen, select option 6, Job Queue Entries, to get the display shown in Figure 2.9.

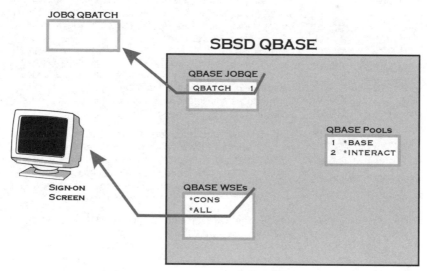

Figure 2.8: QBASE can initiate interactive work using the workstation entries, and batch work using the job queue entry.

```
 Display Job Queue Entries
                                                       System: TSCSAP01
   Subsystem description:    QBASE        Status:    ACTIVE

   Seq  Job                        Max   -----Max by Priority-----
   Nbr  Queue       Library      Active   1   2   3   4   5   6   7   8   9
    10  QBATCH      QGPL              1   *   *   *   *   *   *   *   *   *
    50  QINTER      QGPL         *NOMAX   *   *   *   *   *   *   *   *   *
   100  QCTL        QSYS         *NOMAX   *   *   *   *   *   *   *   *   *
   150  QS36MRT     QGPL         *NOMAX   *   *   *   *   *   *   *   *   *
   200  QS36EVOKE   QGPL         *NOMAX   *   *   *   *   *   *   *   *   *
   250  QBASE       QGPL         *NOMAX   *   *   *   *   *   *   *   *   *




                                                                Bottom
   Press Enter to continue.

   F3=Exit    F12=Cancel
```

Figure 2.9: These job queue entries are included in the IBM-supplied subsystem, QBASE.

As you can see from the display, each of the job queue entries added to QBASE is shown. Notice that the job queues appear in sequence number (*Seq Nbr*) order with the job queue name. This is the order that QBASE uses when looking for batch jobs to run.

Also notice all of the MAXACT (Max Active) and MAXPTY (Max by Priority) values. All job queue entries other than QBATCH have a value of *NOMAX! Isn't that wrong? Well, maybe. It depends on the types of jobs submitted to these queues and the relationship between the MAXACT value on the job queue entry and other controlling values. Typically, jobs that are submitted to these job queue entries are not long-running, CPU-intensive batch jobs. So *NOMAX is usually a good choice.

Finally, in order to put something on the job queue, run the Submit Job (SBMJOB) command. This rather complex command has a large number of parameters that are important to the initiation of the job. Run SBMJOB to put a job on the QBATCH job queue. Figures 2.10 and 2.11 show the parameters for the command—and this is the simple version; there are two more pages of parameters. Table 2.3 describes the parameters and their meanings.

```
                        Submit Job (SBMJOB)

Type choices, press Enter.

Command to run . . . . . . . . .  CMD




...
Job name . . . . . . . . . . .  JOB            *JOBD
Job description  . . . . . . .  JOBD           *USRPRF
  Library  . . . . . . . . . .
Job queue  . . . . . . . . . .  JOBQ           *JOBD
  Library  . . . . . . . . . .
Job priority (on JOBQ) . . . .  JOBPTY         *JOBD
Output priority (on OUTQ)  . .  OUTPTY         *JOBD
Print device . . . . . . . . .  PRTDEV         *CURRENT
                                                        More...
F3=Exit   F4=Prompt   F5=Refresh   F10=Additional parameters   F12=Cancel
F13=How to use this display       F24=More keys
```

Figure 2.10: The Submit Job command has several parameters used to define the job to be run.

```
                        Submit Job (SBMJOB)

Type choices, press Enter.

Output queue . . . . . . . . . .  OUTQ          *CURRENT
  Library  . . . . . . . . . .

                    Additional Parameters

User . . . . . . . . . . . . .  USER           *CURRENT
Print text . . . . . . . . . .  PRTTXT         *CURRENT

Routing data . . . . . . . . .  RTGDTA         QCMDB






                                                        More...
F3=Exit   F4=Prompt   F5=Refresh   F12=Cancel   F13=How to use this display
F24=More keys
```

Figure 2.11: These additional Submit Job command parameters define batch jobs that are to be run.

Table 2.3: SBMJOB Parameters (1 of 2)		
Keyword	**Value**	**Result/Comments**
CMD	Any valid OS/400 command	When the submitted job is initiated, the command that is specified by this parameter will be run. For most batch jobs, this command will be CALL, to start a CL (or other language) program that will control and manage the batch processing to be performed by the submitted job.
JOB	*JOBD	This parameter will provide the name of the job. The job name is assigned when the job is submitted. To check on the status of a submitted job, you refer to it by its job name. You can specify any valid OS/400 name that you like. In this case, the name of the job is the same as the job description specified by the JOBD parameter.
JOBD	*USRPRF	When the batch job is started, the operational attributes of the job are obtained from a job description. In this case, the job description that is used is specified by the user profile of the person submitting the batch job. Whenever a parameter in the SBMJOB command uses the value *JOBD, the actual value will be obtained from the job description specified for this parameter. To avoid being overly repetitious, this statement will not be repeated for any subsequent parameters that specify *JOBD as a default.
JOBQ	*JOBD	As discussed, batch jobs are submitted to a job queue. This parameter names the queue. The value specified must be the name of an existing job queue. OS/400 job queues are first-in, first-out (FIFO). Therefore, when a job is placed on the queue, it generally appears as the last job. The actual position of the job on the queue may be affected by other factors, such as held jobs and the value specified for JOBPTY.
JOBPTY	*JOBD	You saw in the discussion of the ADDJOBQE command earlier in this chapter that nine different priorities can be assigned to a job on the job queue. Jobs are placed on the queue in FIFO order within each of the priorities.
OUTPTY	*JOBD	This parameter is the priority assigned to any printed output produced by the submitted job. Printed output is placed on an output queue (OUTQ) for processing by another job that actually writes the printed material to the printer device. Output is placed on the output queue in FIFO order, within priority.

Keyword	Value	Result/Comments
Table 2.3: SBMJOB Parameters (2 of 2)		
PRTDEV	*CURRENT	This parameter provides the name of the device that will receive printed output. Print devices are obtained and managed by the jobs that actually print the information. When *CURRENT is used for this parameter or any of the next three parameters, the value in use by the job running the SBMJOB command will be copied to the submitted job. Once again, to avoid being overly repetitious, this statement will not be repeated for any other parameter that uses *CURRENT as a default.
OUTQ	*CURRENT	This parameter specifies the output queue that will receive any printed output produced by the submitted job.
USER	*CURRENT	Job names are of the format *jobname.usename.jobnumber.* This parameter specifies the user-name portion of the job name. This is the user profile that the job uses when it starts to run, and it defines the authority that the job has.
PRTTXT	*CURRENT	This parameter holds printed text that appears at the bottom of each page and on page separators.
RTGDTA	*QCMDB	When QBASE selects a job from a job queue, it needs some additional information to initiate the job. The RTGDTA parameter provides the subsystem with the key to this additional information. The default for batch jobs is QCMDB.

As you can see, the SBMJOB command ties pieces of information together that allow a batch job to complete its task. While many of the parameters might appear confusing, the defaults specified are sufficient for most batch work that you will do. Chapter 8 looks at modifying some of these parameters to customize the batch jobs you are running. For now, just run the following Submit Job command:

```
SBMJOB CMD('CALL BATCHCL') JOB(SAMPLE)
```

Take the defaults for everything else. Figure 2.12 illustrates the result of running the command.

There is now a job on the QBATCH job queue and a sign-on screen at your work-station. Although QBASE has pools allocated to run jobs and ways to find and initiate both batch and interactive work, it is still not ready to initiate work. The Routing Data (RTGDTA) parameter will be used as input for the last main ingredient for initiating work: the routing entry.

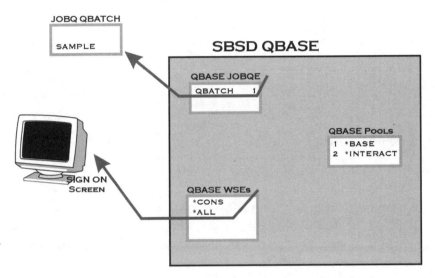

Figure 2.12: *Submit Job commands are used to place the SAMPLE batch job on the QBATCH job queue.*

Option 7—Routing Entries

So far, you have seen how pools, workstations, and submitted jobs are linked to subsystems. Now you need to see how these resources are put to use by the subsystem when initiating jobs. Once again, return to the menu display shown when you ran the DSPSBSD command.

This time, select option 7, Routing Entries to display the screen in Figure 2.13. The following discussion examines how the subsystem uses the RTGDTA information to initiate jobs.

```
                           Display Routing Entries
                                                    System: TSCSAP01
     Subsystem description:    QBASE          Status:     ACTIVE

     Type options, press Enter.
       5=Display details

                                                                    Start
     Opt    Seq Nbr    Program      Library      Compare Value       Pos
              10       QCMD         QSYS         'QCMDB'               1
              50       QCMD         QSYS         'QCMDI'               1
              70       *RTGDTA                   'QNMAPINGD'          37
              80       QNMAREXECD   QSYS         'AREXECD'            37
             100       QCMD         QSYS         'QS36EVOKE'           1
             150       QCMD         QSYS         'QS36MRT'             1
             260       *RTGDTA                   'QOCEVOKE'           37
             300       QARDRIVE     QSYS         '525XTEST'            1
             310       *RTGDTA                   'QZSCSRVR'           37
             320       *RTGDTA                   'QZRCSRVR'           37
             330       *RTGDTA                   'QZHQTRG'            37
             350       *RTGDTA                   'QVPPRINT'           37
                                                                   More...
     F3=Exit    F9=Display all detailed descriptions    F12=Cancel
```

Figure 2.13: QBASE routing entries are used to determine where and how jobs are run.

This time your display presents a lot of information regarding routing entries. To understand routing entries, consider that jobs entering a system are similar to people entering a concert or sporting event. Everyone has a ticket. Some are for the main floor (interactive) and some are for the balcony (batch). The main-floor ticket holders use different gates (workstation entries) to enter the arena than the balcony ticket holders (job queues). Each person's ticket specifies a section and seat number so that the usher can locate the correct seat. When a job enters the system, its routing data is like the seat location, and the subsystem is the usher. Using the routing data, the subsystem will select the runtime attributes (seat location) of the job being initiated.

You're now ready to see how these routing entries become a part of the subsystem. Once again, they are added to the subsystem by running a command. In this case, you run the Add Routing Entry (ADDRTGE) command, as shown in Figure 2.14.

```
                    Add Routing Entry (ADDRTGE)

Type choices, press Enter.

Subsystem description  . . . . . SBSD          QBASE
  Library . . . . . . . . . . .                  *LIBL
Routing entry sequence number  . SEQNBR        10
Comparison data:                 CMPVAL
  Compare value . . . . . . . .                QCMDB

  Starting position . . . . . .                1
Program to call . . . . . . . . PGM           QCMD
  Library . . . . . . . . . . .                  *LIBL
Class . . . . . . . . . . . . . CLS           QBATCH
  Library . . . . . . . . . . .                QSYS
Maximum active routing steps . . MAXACT        *NOMAX
Storage pool identifier . . . . POOLID        1

                                                      Bottom
F3=Exit  F4=Prompt  F5=Refresh  F12=Cancel  F13=How to use this display
F24=More keys
```

Figure 2.14: The Add Routing Entry command defines the routing entries used by a subsystem to initiate batch jobs.

By running this command, a routing entry (seat location) for batch jobs will be added to QBASE. Table 2.4 shows the value and meaning of the parameters of the ADDRTGE command.

Table 2.4: ADDRTGE Parameters (1 of 2)

Keyword	Value	Result/Comments
SBSD	QBASE	This parameter holds the name of the subsystem receiving the routing entry.
SEQNBR	10	This parameter defines the search order that QBASE will use when trying to select a routing entry. Each routing entry in the subsystem must have a unique sequence number.
CMPVAL	QCMDB 1	When the subsystem is searching for a routing entry to use, it compares the routing data to the value specified by this parameter. (This is the tie-in to RTGDTA!) The first routing entry with a compare value that matches the job's routing data will be used. The second part of this parameter indicates the starting position in the routing data. In this case, the subsystem will compare the characters starting in the first position of the routing data with the compare value in the routing entry.

Table 2.4: ADDRTGE Parameters (2 of 2)

Keyword	Value	Result/Comments
PGM	QCMD	QCMD is the system command processing support. Typically, this is the desired program for the routing entry. Once the job is initiated, QCMD will process the command specified on SBMJOB. In most cases, this means QCMD will call the program that you want to run.
CLS	QBATCH QSYS	When a job is initiated, it is assigned runtime attributes. The subsystem obtains these attributes from the class that is specified on the selected routing entry. The QBATCH class, shown below, will assign batch-job runtime attributes.
MAXACT	*NOMAX	As with the other commands in this chapter, there is a MAXACT value. Once again, *NOMAX is specified. *NOMAX indicates that any number of batch jobs may be initiated at the same time using this routing entry. However, recall that the job queue entry, BATCH, specified a value of one. Therefore, only one job will be initiated from QBATCH at a time. However, since *NOMAX is specified for the routing entry, the subsystem may initiate jobs that have been submitted to one of the other job queues that QBASE is using to locate batch jobs you have submitted.
POOLID	1	This parameter identifies the subsystem pool that the job will use. In this case, it will use the first pool of the subsystem, *BASE.

Now that you have a routing entry for the batch jobs, do the same thing for interactive jobs by running the ADDRTGE command shown in Figure 2.15. As you can see, there are only minor differences between this command and ADDRTGE. There is a different sequence number (50), compare value (QCMDI), class (QINTER), and pool identifier (2). Now, when the subsystem processes a sign-on screen, the routing data will match this routing entry, and QBASE will initiate the job in the second subsystem pool (*INTERACT) using runtime attributes obtained from the QINTER class.

On the routing entry display for option 7 on the DSPSBSD menu, notice that not all of the information specified on the ADDRTGE entry command is shown. Type 5 (Display Details) in front of the first two routing entries, to display Figures 2.16 and 2.17. Now, you see all of the information provided on the ADDRTGE command.

```
                    Add Routing Entry (ADDRTGE)

Type choices, press Enter.

Subsystem description  . . . . .  SBSD        QBASE
  Library . . . . . . . . . . .               *LIBL
Routing entry sequence number  .  SEQNBR      50
Comparison data:                  CMPVAL
  Compare value . . . . . . . .               QCMDI

  Starting position . . . . . .               1
Program to call . . . . . . . .   PGM         QCMD
  Library . . . . . . . . . . .               *LIBL
Class . . . . . . . . . . . . .   CLS         QINTER
  Library . . . . . . . . . . .               QGPL
Maximum active routing steps  . . MAXACT      *NOMAX
Storage pool identifier  . . . .  POOLID      2

                                                        Bottom
F3=Exit  F4=Prompt  F5=Refresh  F12=Cancel  F13=How to use this display
F24=More keys
```

Figure 2.15: The Add Routing Entry command defines routing entries that are used by a subsystem to initiate interactive jobs.

```
                   Display Routing Entry Detail
                                          System:    TSCSAP01
Subsystem description:   QBASE        Status:   ACTIVE

Routing entry sequence number . . . . . . . :   10
Program . . . . . . . . . . . . . . . . . . :   QCMD
  Library . . . . . . . . . . . . . . . . . :     QSYS
Class . . . . . . . . . . . . . . . . . . . :   QBATCH
  Library . . . . . . . . . . . . . . . . . :     QSYS
Maximum active routing steps  . . . . . . . :   *NOMAX
Pool identifier . . . . . . . . . . . . . . :   1
Compare value . . . . . . . . . . . . . . . :   'QCMDB'

Compare start position  . . . . . . . . . . :   1


Press Enter to continue.

F3=Exit    F12=Cancel    F14=Display previous entry
```

Figure 2.16: This is detailed, batch job-routing entry information.

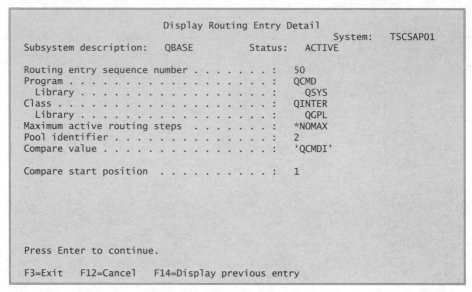

```
                    Display Routing Entry Detail
                                          System:    TSCSAP01
Subsystem description:   QBASE         Status:   ACTIVE

Routing entry sequence number . . . . . . . :   50
Program . . . . . . . . . . . . . . . . . . :   QCMD
  Library . . . . . . . . . . . . . . . . . :     QSYS
Class . . . . . . . . . . . . . . . . . . . :   QINTER
  Library . . . . . . . . . . . . . . . . . :     QGPL
Maximum active routing steps  . . . . . . . :   *NOMAX
Pool identifier . . . . . . . . . . . . . . :   2
Compare value . . . . . . . . . . . . . . . :   'QCMDI'

Compare start position  . . . . . . . . . . :   1




Press Enter to continue.

F3=Exit   F12=Cancel   F14=Display previous entry
```

Figure 2.17: This is detailed, interactive job-routing entry information.

Now you are ready to look at the classes that supply the runtime attributes of the batch and interactive jobs initiated by QBASE. These classes are created by yet another command, CRTCLS (Create Class). The display in Figure 2.18 shows the CRTCLS command used to create the QBATCH class that was shipped with OS/400.

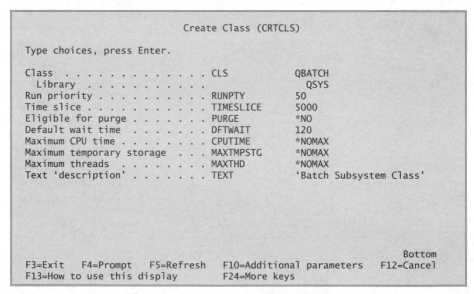

```
                          Create Class (CRTCLS)

Type choices, press Enter.

Class . . . . . . . . . . . . . CLS         QBATCH
  Library . . . . . . . . . .                QSYS
Run priority . . . . . . . . . RUNPTY       50
Time slice . . . . . . . . . . TIMESLICE    5000
Eligible for purge . . . . . . PURGE        *NO
Default wait time  . . . . . . DFTWAIT      120
Maximum CPU time . . . . . . . CPUTIME      *NOMAX
Maximum temporary storage  . . MAXTMPSTG    *NOMAX
Maximum threads  . . . . . . . MAXTHD       *NOMAX
Text 'description' . . . . . . TEXT         'Batch Subsystem Class'




                                                       Bottom
F3=Exit    F4=Prompt   F5=Refresh   F10=Additional parameters   F12=Cancel
F13=How to use this display        F24=More keys
```

Figure 2.18: The Create Class command is used to define the runtime attributes of batch jobs.

While this is not a very complicated command, the runtime attributes specified by it are used to help manage the work being done on the system. Chapter 3 details the runtime management of jobs in the system. For now, take a look at Table 2.5 for the values and what they mean.

Table 2.5: CRTCLS Parameters (1 of 2)		
Keyword	**Value**	**Result/Comments**
CLS	QBATCH QGPL	This is the name of the class being created. Because the routing entry is looking for a class named QBATCH in library QGPL, it is a good idea to use these values as the name and library of the class.
RUNPTY	50	This parameter is used by the system scheduler/dispatcher to determine which job(s) can access one of the systems processors. The lower the value, the higher the job's priority. In general, higher-priority jobs are scheduled before lower-priority jobs. The process of scheduling/dispatching is discussed in the next chapter.
TIMESLICE	5,000	When a job is allowed access to a processor, it will use the processor until it finishes its work, even if it is forced to wait for a resource that is unavailable. On occasion, a job might stay at a processor for a very long time. The TIMESLICE parameter forces an interrupt of a job that is using a processor. The value for this parameter is specified in milliseconds, so 5,000 is five seconds. If a batch job has been using a processor for five seconds without interruption, its time slice will expire, and another job may be given access to the processor.
PURGE	*NO	Jobs that are using a processor are referencing information in order to complete their tasks. The information being used by a job can be shared information, like data, or information that is unique to a job, like program variables. The PURGE parameter determines how the information that is unique to a job is brought into and removed from main storage. The next chapter provides a more detailed description of the objects that are unique to a job and the actions that are taken as a result of the value specified for the PURGE parameter.

	Table 2.5: CRTCLS Parameters (2 of 2)	
Keyword	**Value**	**Result/Comments**
DFTWAIT	120	When resources are not available to a job, the job might wish to wait for them to become available. The Default Wait (DFTWAIT) parameter is used to provide a default wait for instructions or commands that do not explicitly provide a wait time. The value is specified in seconds, so 120 is 2 minutes. If the resource is not available within two minutes, a message will be sent to QSYSOPR.
CPUTIME	*NOMAX	This parameter is the amount of CPU time that a job can use before it is ended abnormally by the system. The default value is *NOMAX, meaning the job can run for days and days and days….
MAXTMPSTG	*NOMAX	When a job is running, it may be allocating space to support itself. Typically, when the job ends, it will delete any of the temporary objects it was using. If the temporary space allocated exceeds the value of this parameter, the job will end abnormally. Specifying *NOMAX will prevent an abnormal end caused by temporary space allocation.
MAXTHD	*NOMAX	Jobs may create temporary "sub-jobs" to assist them in performing a task. The most efficient way to create these temporary "sub-jobs" is by spawning a thread. A thread appears as a subset of the originating job and has the same operational and turn-time attributes. However, the thread is initiated by work management and is scheduled and dispatched the same as other jobs in the system. Threads are covered in more detail in a later chapter.
TEXT	Any valid text	Any descriptive text for this class may be specified in this parameter.

You're almost done! Run another CRTCLS command to create the QINTER class for interactive jobs, as shown in Figure 2.19. Notice that there is very little difference between the two classes. The QINTER run priority is higher (20), its time slice is shorter (2,000, or 2 seconds), its purge is set to *YES, and the default wait time is shorter (30 seconds).

You now have everything you need in the subsystem to initiate batch and interactive jobs, as shown in Figure 2.20. So let's follow the steps of job initiation!

```
                          Create Class (CRTCLS)

 Type choices, press Enter.

 Class . . . . . . . . . . . . . CLS          QINTER
   Library . . . . . . . . . .                QGPL
 Run priority . . . . . . . . . RUNPTY        20
 Time slice . . . . . . . . . . TIMESLICE     2000
 Eligible for purge . . . . . . PURGE         *YES
 Default wait time . . . . . . . DFTWAIT      30
 Maximum CPU time . . . . . . . CPUTIME       *NOMAX
 Maximum temporary storage  . . MAXTMPSTG     *NOMAX
 Maximum threads . . . . . . . . MAXTHD       *NOMAX
 Text 'description' . . . . . . TEXT          'Interactive Job Class'




                                                            Bottom
 F3=Exit   F4=Prompt   F5=Refresh   F10=Additional parameters   F12=Cancel
 F13=How to use this display       F24=More keys
```

Figure 2.19: The Create Class command is used to define the runtime attributes of interactive jobs.

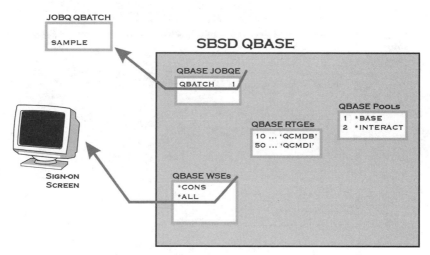

Figure 2.20: The subsystem components necessary to initiate work are workstation entries, job queue entries, routing entries, and pools.

Putting it All Together—Job Initiation

Having covered the functions in QBASE necessary to provide job initiation, you can now tie them all together by simulating the start of a batch job and an interactive job. (Have you ever wonder how you got that sign-on display?)

Starting a Batch Job

So far, you have created the key elements of job initiation, have an active subsystem, and have a job on the job queue. As noted in the discussion on job queues, QBASE knows where to look for potential jobs from the job queue entries. One of the job queue entries is QBATCH. QBASE locates QBATCH and finds a job, SAMPLE, waiting to be initiated, as shown in Figure 2.21. Because no jobs have been initiated from QBATCH, QBASE can select SAMPLE for initiation.

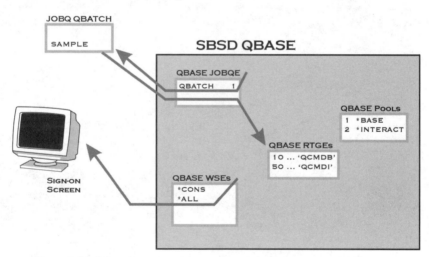

Figure 2.21: QBASE locates SAMPLE on the QBATCH job queue and begins to initiate the job.

Once QBASE selects SAMPLE for initiation, it needs to determine how to initiate the job. Remember that the Submit Job (SBMJOB) command specified QCMDB as your routing data (RTGDTA). QBASE uses the routing data and searches through the routing entries that have been defined looking for a match. As shown in Figure 2.22, it immediately encounters the routing entry at sequence number 10, which has a compare value (CMPVAL) of QCMDB—a match!

The subsystem uses the routing entry to locate the class in order to assign runtime attributes to SAMPLE. Returning to the detail information for selected the routing entry (shown in Figure 2.16), you'll find that the class is QBATCH. QBASE uses the information in the routing entry to locate the class. You now have all of the runtime attributes for SAMPLE.

Finally, the subsystem uses the routing entry to identify the pool that will be used to run SAMPLE. Once again, looking at the detail information of the routing data, it finds that the POOLID value is 1. The subsystem then looks at the pools it can use for jobs, and finds that pool 1 is *BASE.

You're done! SAMPLE is now running in *BASE with runtime attributes obtained from the QBATCH class, as shown in Figure 2.22.

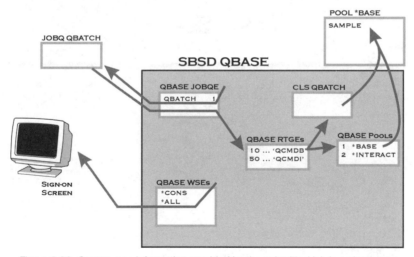

Figure 2.22: QBASE uses information provided by the submitted job in order to complete the job initiation process.

Once SAMPLE has been started, no other jobs that are either already on the job queue or arriving on the job queue will be initiated until SAMPLE completes. Do you remember why? It's because the MAXACT value specified for the QBATCH job queue entry was set to 1. Because SAMPLE is running, no other job can be initiated until SAMPLE finishes its work.

Starting an Interactive Job

All that remains is to initiate an interactive job. From a workstation that has the sign-on screen displayed, enter your user name and password. Unlike jobs that are on a job queue, there is no routing data at the workstation, so how do you find your way? Your user name is the same name as your user profile. When you sign on, the system locates your user profile, validates your password, and finds the job description specified in your user profile. If you recall, the job description for the batch job was specified on the SBMJOB command. Just as with your batch job, the job description contains the routing data (RTGDTA) for the subsystem to use. In this case, the defaults are set up such that your routing data will be QCMDI. These steps are shown in Figure 2.23.

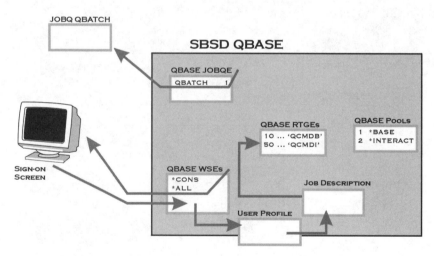

Figure 2.23: The user name is used to locate the routing information for an interactive job.

QBASE now has the routing data and uses it to search for a matching compare value (CMPVAL) in the routing entry. Sure enough, it finds a match with the second routing entry in the table. Figure 2.24 shows how the remainder of the job initiation is performed by the subsystem. Using the matching routing entry, QBASE locates the class containing the runtime attributes for the job. Referring to the detail information of the second routing entry, you see that QBASE will use the QINTER class.

Finally, QBASE uses the routing entry to determine the pool where the new job will run. Once again, the detail information for the routing entry (shown in Figure 2.17) provides the pool identifier (POOLID) that the job will use. For this routing entry, the POOLID is 2. QBASE's second pool is defined to be *INTERACT. When QBASE completes initiation of the job, it will run in *INTERACT with a job name that matches the workstation name, and a user name that matches the user profile name. For the purposes of this example, the workstation name is BOSSWS and the user is JJJONES.

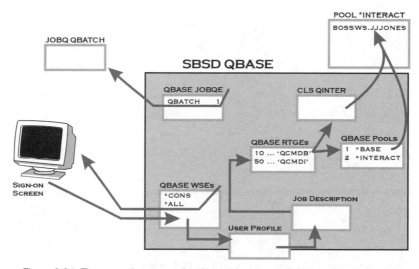

Figure 2.24: These are the steps taken by a subsystem to initiate an interactive job.

All right! You've finished initiating an interactive job. Since the MAXACT parameter of the workstation entry used to find and initiate this job is *NOMAX, QBASE can continue to initiate interactive jobs from the same workstation or other workstations via the same workstation entry used to initiate the BOSSWS job.

In Review

It is important that you understand the aspects of work management presented in this chapter before you begin to customize your environment. Before proceeding, review the following key elements of basic job initiation:

1. Workstation entries and job queue entries are used by subsystems to locate sources of work.

2. Routing entries are used by subsystems to locate such things as runtime attributes and for each job that is initiated.

3. Runtime attributes are stored in classes (object type *CLS).

4. Routing data is used as a key to locating the correct routing entry for a job.

5. Routing data may be specified on the Submit Job command (SBMJOB) or obtained from a job description.

6. The job description used for interactive jobs is specified in the user profile of each user who signs on to a workstation.

Once you understand how jobs are initiated, you can advance to using additional subsystems, separating jobs into different pools, supplying different runtime attributes, and performing other functions to better manage the environment that results from the jobs initiated by work management. Before getting to those features, it's important that you understand the management of simple workloads, consisting only of interactive jobs and batch jobs using the shipped defaults. The next chapter begins with an examination of the methods used to manage the jobs initiated by QBASE and running in the *BASE and *INTERACT pools.

3

Managing Active Jobs:
Runtime Attributes

As described in the preceding chapter, subsystems are responsible for finding and initiating work. So, now that you have these jobs, what do you do with them? The first thing you'll find out is that the subsystem has very little to do with these jobs while they are active.

However, as mentioned, the subsystem did assign runtime attributes to the job and directed each job to one of the pools it owns. Other components of the operating system and AS/400 Licensed Internal Code (SLIC) actually use the runtime attributes to manage the jobs.

The preceding chapter looked at two methods to initiate jobs: workstation entries and job queue entries. Once the jobs have been initiated, you are no longer interested in how a subsystem found the job and initiated it; you are interested only in the jobs themselves, that is, the runtime attributes and the pools. Therefore, the information in this chapter applies only to active jobs, and not the method that the subsystem used to initiate the job.

When a job is running, there are three key runtime attributes: PURGE, TIME SLICE, and RUNPTY. These attributes are assigned to the job by the subsystem and are found in the class used to initiate the job.

PURGE

When an active job is running the instructions of an application, it is in main storage. In order to operate on objects, the objects need to be in main storage. The objects used by a job can be shared by other jobs, or they can be unique for each job. The operating system and licensed internal code use PURGE to determine the method for moving the job-unique information into and out of main storage.

Shared Objects

When jobs are running, many of them may be using the same application, the same database files, the same data queues, and many other objects. These types of objects are shared. There is only one copy of the object in the entire system, and all of the jobs accessing the object will use the same copy. When this copy is brought into and written from main storage, PURGE does not apply. Rather, each object will be read into main storage based on the object attributes, and will be written from main storage when it is not being used by active jobs.

Transfer attributes for an object indicate how to get the object into main storage. The attributes may specify small transfers (one or two pages) or large block transfers. Small transfers are used for large objects that have only a few pages used by jobs (*active pages*). In this case, transferring a large object into main storage just to use a small number of pages is very inefficient. Large transfers are used to move large blocks of information into main storage. Since the blocks that are transferred are likely to all be used at the same time, using one disk access to retrieve a large amount of information is efficient.

Another transfer attribute for shared objects is the pool identifier. The pool identifier tells the operating system which main storage pool should receive the information being read. The object can be read into the machine pool (*MACHINE, or the first system pool) or the requester's pool.

Objects that specify the requester pool will be read into the pool of the job that requested the information. Once the information is read into a requester pool, any job, regardless of the pool it is using, will be able to use the information that is in main storage. It is not necessary to relocate or reread the page into the next requester's pool.

The use of shared objects in an AS/400 is one of the benefits of single-level storage. Since many jobs can take advantage of an object in main storage, many read operations can be eliminated. The transfer attributes for most objects are set by the system and should not be changed. However, one notable exception to this statement is database record blocking, discussed in a later chapter.

Job-Unique Objects

The second class of objects used by active jobs is job-unique objects. As mentioned, many jobs can use the same applications and the same database files. However, not all jobs are at the same position in the application, not all jobs have the same value for variables (fields) used by the application, not all jobs are processing the same data records in a file, and not all jobs are using the database files in the same way—some might only be reading data, while others might be updating it. Similarity is not the same as equality.

To keep these similar but different sets of objects straight, each job has a copy of the objects for its exclusive use. But what are these objects, and how do jobs use them?

All of the job-unique objects are temporary. They exist only as long as the job is active, or until the job is through using them. Then, they are discarded. There are a lot of these temporary objects, but this chapter focuses only on a few of the more important:

- Program invocation stacks.
- Program automatic/static storage areas.
- Open data paths.

The Program Invocation Work Area

Whenever a job is running an application, it is using several different programs. To get from one program to another, it uses a call statement. Each call to a program results in an entry in the invocation work area. Each time a program ends, an entry is removed.

Thus, as Figures 3.1 and 3.2 illustrate, jobs running the same application have totally different-looking invocation work areas. The job-unique invocation work area lets the operating system know where each of the jobs is positioned within an application.

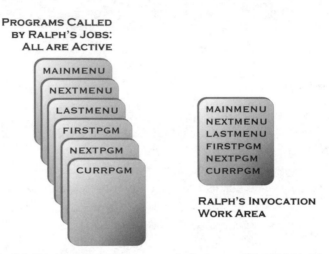

Figure 3.1: This internal structure represents the programs that Ralph's job calls to complete a task.

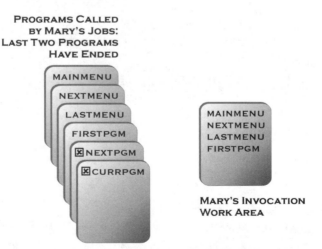

Figure 3.2: When a program ends, its entry in the invocation entry is removed. In this example, Mary's job currently has four active programs and four entries in the invocation area. The two programs that have ended are no longer in the invocation work area.

Program Automatic/Static Storage Areas

Each time a program is called and added to the invocation work area, the variables associated with the application are placed in the automatic or static storage areas. The variables are defined by a program to be either automatic or static, thereby determining which of the two areas contains the variable. A program may have both types of areas. As with the invocation work area, the storage areas for the variable are added whenever a program is called and are removed whenever the program is removed from the invocation stack. If a program appears more than once in an invocation stack, the variable storage areas also appear more than once. Figures 3.3 and 3.4 (very similar to the invocation work area diagrams) show the program static storage areas.

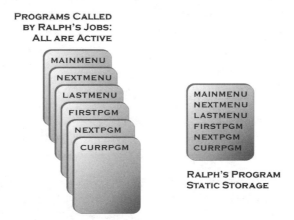

Figure 3.3: Static storage areas are created for each program that is called in a job.

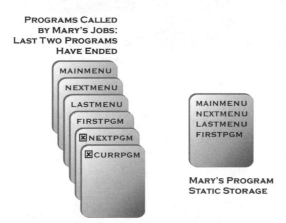

Figure 3.4: When a program ends, the static storage area created for the program is removed.

Open Data Paths

In order for a program to use a file, it must open the file. An open operation may be either FULL or SHARED. Each file is created with a SHARE parameter. If this parameter is *NO, every time an open operation is performed by an application in the same job, an Open Data Path (ODP) will be created in the job unique data. If the SHARE parameter is *YES, an ODP will be created in the job-unique data whenever an ODP for the file is not present for the job. Typically, all files will be opened by the first program in the invocation and will remain in use until the job ends. In this case, there will only be one ODP for each file that a job uses.

Notice that the SHARE parameter does not pertain to the sharing of the data between jobs. Since the file itself is an object shared by all jobs, the data in the file is automatically shared by all jobs. In order to simplify this potentially confusing concept, consider an analogy. Suppose a textbook represent the data in the file, and students using the textbooks are jobs with an ODP to access the data. The textbook might be used in several different classes, but the information in it is the same for all students. This is similar to the data in the file. (The same information is shared.)

Multiple classes using the same book represent multiple programs that have an OPEN for the text; there is only one textbook for all the classes, and there is only one ODP to access a file that has a parameter of SHARE(*YES).

But what is in this ODP? An ODP is to files as the automatic and static areas are to variables. That is, it keeps track of how each job is using the file, where each job is within the file, and what record or records are being processed by the job. Thus, many jobs use the same data, but may be using completely different information.

Returning to the textbook analogy, it's similar to the students using the text for independent study—each student may be at a different place on a different chapter of the textbook (different location in the file) and will be processing different parts of the text (using different records).

Figures 3.5, 3.6, and 3.7 show the effects of SHARE(*YES), SHARE(*NO), and the function provided by the ODP. If programs using FULL open operations are constantly being ended and called again, ODPs are constantly being deleted and created. This is an inefficient use of system resources, and one of the reasons that SHARE(*YES) should be specified.

EACH OF THE THREE PROGRAMS OPENS THE SAME THREE FILES.

CUSTOMER
LINEITEM
SHIPPING

CUSMAST
INVENTRY
ORDERS
CUSMAST
INVENTRY
ORDERS
CUSMAST
INVENTRY
ORDERS

JOB'S ODP STRUCTURE

*Figure 3.5: An ODP is created for every open operation of a file that is specified SHARE(*NO).*

THE LAST PROGRAM ENDS.

CUSTOMER
LINEITEM
☒ SHIPPING

CUSMAST
INVENTRY
ORDERS
CUSMAST
INVENTRY
ORDERS

JOB'S ODP STRUCTURE

*Figure 3.6: Every time a file with SHARE(*NO) specified is closed, an ODP will be removed.*

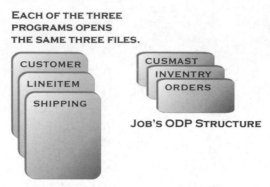

Figure 3.7: *An ODP is created only for the first open operation of a file with SHARE(*YES) specified.*

Collecting the Pieces

The three objects just discussed are representative of many other temporary objects that are unique to each job. While this information might appear unrelated to work management and your job, it isn't. Understanding the objects used by a job can even help you write better applications and set work-management values correctly. As mentioned, whenever a job becomes active, these objects must be brought into main storage. To make transfers of these objects efficient in an iSeries, these objects have been collected into a composite object called a *Process Access Group* (*PAG*). The PURGE attribute is used by the system to efficiently manage the transfer of the PAG into and out of main storage. So, now you're finally to the point of needing to use the PURGE attribute. The two possible values for PURGE are *YES and *NO.

PURGE(*YES)

When PURGE(*YES) is specified, the system will try to bring large amounts of the PAG into main storage at a single time and will try to write information from main storage more quickly than with PURGE(*NO). If you view the transfer function from the perspective of an interactive job, the job will be running whenever data from an input display is processed, and the PAG will be brought into main storage. The job often requests information from the PAG that is currently not in main storage. When this situation occurs, the system will bring in a 32 Kb block of the PAG that contains the requested information. The PAG will be written out to disk when the job displays the next input screen for the user.

PURGE(*YES) is generally preferred when many jobs compete for space in the same storage pool. Since there are often many interactive jobs using the same main storage pool, PURGE for interactive jobs is set to *YES. Figures 3.8 and 3.9 represent the operations performed by PURGE(*YES).

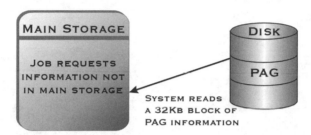

Figure 3.8: Large blocks of information are transferred into main storage when PURGE(*YES) is specified.

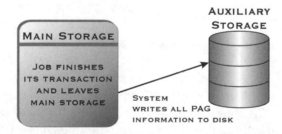

Figure 3.9: Pages used by a job will be automatically written from main storage whenever the job has left main storage to wait for additional work.

PURGE(*NO)

PURGE(*NO) is not as aggressive at transferring the PAG into main storage or removing it from main storage. If you use the interactive example from the previous section with PURGE(*NO) specified, when the job enters main storage, the system will not automatically read any of the PAG into main storage. When the job leaves main storage, the system will not automatically write anything to main storage. If there are large amounts of main storage available for the jobs to run, PURGE(*NO) may be specified. Figures 3.10 and 3.11 illustrate the functions it performs.

Figure 3.10: When PURGE(*NO) is specified, pages remain in main storage after the job has left to wait for additional work.

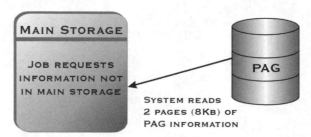

Figure 3.11: Much smaller amounts of data are transferred to main storage when PURGE(*NO) is specified.

Now that you have seen both of these values, another analogy can be used to explain this parameter. Suppose the pool that your jobs are running in represents a playroom. The jobs coming into the pool to run are children coming into the playroom. The PAG is similar to the toys and games that the children will use. The system manages the contents of the pool like an attendant maintains order at the playroom. Finally, the PURGE attribute tells the system (the attendant) how to keep the pool (the playroom) clean.

If the value of PURGE is *YES, the attendant (the system) automatically retrieves all the parts of a game when a child selects one piece from the game. The attendant has anticipated the child's need for more of the game than just one piece, and put them in the playroom. This is similar to the system automatically reading large portions of the PAG whenever a job requests one page that was not in main storage. Similarly, when a child leaves the room, the attendant immediately picks up the things that the child was using and puts them away. This is similar to the system automatically writing the PAG to disk when the job leaves main storage. So, PURGE(*YES) represents a very fastidious attendant who has to deal with a large number of children using the area.

When the value is PURGE(*NO), when a child enters the playroom, the attendant will wait until the child asks for something that is not there. Then, the house-keeper will go to the storage area and retrieve the object. In the system, when a job enters main storage, none of the PAG will be read into main storage. Whenever the job asks for a part of the PAG that is not in main storage, the system will go to disk and retrieve the information. When the child leaves the room, the attendant will leave everything in place, knowing that the child will be in and out of the room at least 100 times a day. Similarly, in the AS/400 iSeries, the system will not write any of the PAG pages to disk because it assumes that the job will return shortly and will want to use the same parts of the PAG that are still in main storage. So, PURGE(*NO) represents either a sloppier attendant or a larger room (or group of rooms) to hold more toys and games.

The End of the PAG

As you might have guessed, the PURGE attribute could be a valuable setting for jobs, depending on the amount of space and number of jobs in the pool. However, it takes system resources to manage the PAG for each job in the system. As the iSeries has grown to large machines with fast processors and disks, the effort to maintain the PAG has become less and less beneficial. Finally, in Version 4, Release 4, released in 1999, the PAG was mercifully put away, making the PURGE attribute obsolete.

So why bother discussing the PAG and PURGE? Because not everything stays put away. If the PAG should have a comeback, it will be valuable to understand PURGE.

Time Slice

The second runtime attribute to investigate is the time slice. This attribute deals with a job that is in main storage and is using a processor to run instructions. Whenever the instructions are being run by a processor, other jobs will wait for an opportunity to use the processor. The time slice value limits the amount of time an individual job can use the processor before the system gives another job a turn to run.

Time Slice Basics

As mentioned in the preceding chapter, the time slice values are obtained from the class specified by the selected routing entry. The default value for an interactive job is 2 seconds, for a batch job 5 seconds. The time slice value only pertains to the amount of processor (CPU) time that a job can use without interruption. If a job is interrupted, when it begins to run again it will be granted another full time slice of 2 seconds. Typically, interruptions are caused by the job waiting for a resource lock held by another job, or the job completing a transaction and sending another input display to the interactive user.

So, does the job reach the time slice in 2 seconds of elapsed time? Typically, no. While the job is running, it is requesting information. If the information is not in main storage, it must be retrieved from disk. While the job is waiting for the information to be retrieved, the wait time adds to the elapsed time of the work being done, but does not add to the processor time used by the job. So, a job will usually be in main storage longer than the amount of time the job spends actually using the CPU.

Compare using the processor (CPU time) and elapsed time (transaction time) to a transaction at a bank teller's window. When you withdraw money from your account, you might be asked for a photo ID. The processor (teller) waits for you to retrieve your ID (a disk operation). Satisfied that your photo ID is at least a facsimile of your appearance, the teller starts processing again by retrieving your account balance. Then, the teller again waits for the information (another disk operation). Satisfied that you have sufficient funds for your withdrawal, the teller begins processing again by entering the withdrawal amount.

Once again, the teller waits, this time for the withdrawal to be deducted from your balance. Finally, the teller begins processing again by giving you the cash, and asking if you have any other business. If you do, the process repeats. When you have completed all your work, you leave the teller's window (the processor) and another customer (job) takes a turn. The amount of time you were at the window (your time in main storage) was longer than the amount of time the teller (processor) was actually busy.

The Benefit of a Time Slice

Imagine that you and several other customers are at a travel agency waiting to talk with an agent. Only one customer is allowed to be in the agent's office (pool) at a time to use the resources of the agent (the CPU). All of the remaining customers are waiting outside of the office until the current customer is through using the agent's services.

Most of the people waiting have simple requests: picking up a ticket, making a vacation deposit, getting a map, etc. However, some of the people have longer transactions. For example, suppose a couple is making travel reservations:

> *Agent: Can I help you?*
>
> *Couple: Yes, we're about to be married and are trying to plan our honeymoon.*
>
> *Agent: Congratulations! What did you have in mind?*
>
> *Couple: We don't know. What have you got?*

This is going to be a very long transaction. Wouldn't it be nice if, after 5 minutes, the agent told the couple to take the information gathered so far, go to the back of the line, and return after all of the simple transactions had been completed?

The act of removing the couple from the agent's office after 5 minutes describes the effects of a time slice in an iSeries. For an interactive job, the system will detect when the job has used 2 seconds of CPU without interruption. When this amount of CPU time has been used, the job has reached *time slice end*. If other jobs that are the same or higher run priority are waiting to enter main storage, the job at time slice end will be removed from main storage, and the first job in line will be allowed to enter. This same principal applies to batch jobs that reach a 5-second time slice end. While waiting in lines in real life, many of us wish that there were more time slice ends!

Extending the Benefit of a Time Slice

Now that you know the benefit of a time slice, you can appreciate a method of improving its effectiveness. This time, consider a classroom (pool) full of students (jobs). While most students are well-behaved and stay within their space (complete their tasks within the time slice value), there is usually one student who will occasionally act up in class (exceed the time slice). When this happens, other students in the classroom are disrupted and cannot do their work efficiently.

A good teacher (system) will have the unruly student removed from the class-room and sent to the principal's office (another pool). The student will eventually return to the classroom to, presumably, behave better (complete the next transaction within the time slice).

This scenario illustrates the function of the QTSEPOOL (Time Slice End Pool) system value. This value can be set to *NONE or *BASE. If the value is *NONE, an interactive job is allowed to stay in the same pool at time slice end (the student isn't removed from the classroom). If the value is *BASE, the interactive job will be moved from its current pool (classroom) to *BASE (the principal's office) in order to finish its work. The QTSEPOOL system value applies only to interactive jobs. Figures 3.12 and 3.13 show the effects of QTSEPOOL.

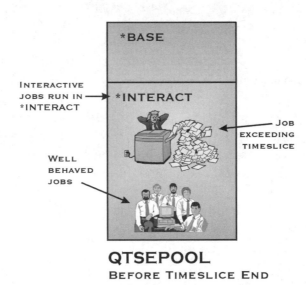

QTSEPOOL
BEFORE TIMESLICE END

Figure 3.12: All jobs running in a pool share the same space. Jobs that frequently exceed the time slice disrupt the contents of the pool.

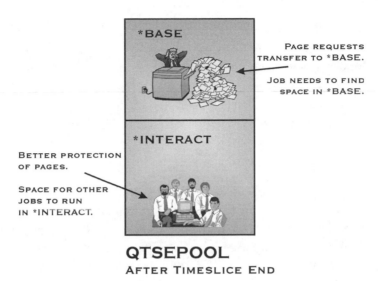

QTSEPOOL
After Timeslice End

Figure 3.13: The system value QTSEPOOL can be used to move disruptive jobs to *BASE.

Setting the Time Slice

For interactive jobs, your time slice value should be sufficient to finish over 95 percent of your transactions. The value of 2 seconds was established a long time ago when processors were much slower. With the processor speeds of today's iSeries machines, 2 seconds is probably longer than needed. However, it is usually not necessary to change the time slice value. If you would like to change it, an easy rule of thumb is to multiply the average CPU time per transaction by three. The resulting time slice should accommodate more than 95 percent of the interactive transactions. For example, if the average CPU time per transaction is 0.12 seconds, the time slice would be 0.36 seconds.

Run Priority

The last runtime attribute to discuss here is the job's run priority. When jobs are waiting to use a processor or are waiting to get into main storage, they stand in line and wait for their turn. Their position in line is determined by their run priority; the higher a job's run priority, the closer it is to the front of the line. Chapter 4 covers the management of jobs entering main storage. For now, just deal with the job's access to a processor.

Whenever a processor completes work for a job, or the job is interrupted, the processor is available for another job to use. The system must then determine which job to assign to the available processor. This function is referred to as *task scheduling/dispatching*. In an AS/400, the selection process can use either fixed- or dynamic-priority scheduling/dispatching. The scheduling/dispatching method is determined by the setting of the system value QDYNPTYSCD.

Fixed-Priority Scheduling

If you select fixed-priority scheduling by setting QDYNPTYSCD to zero, the algorithm is very simple. The system looks at the jobs that are in main storage and are ready to run, and selects the job with the highest priority. If there is more than one job with the same priority, they are generally placed in line in the order they arrive in the system. The system will continue to select high-priority (interactive) jobs until there are no more of them in main storage waiting for a processor, and then low-priority (batch) jobs will finally get their turn to use the processor.

Consider an example from airline check-in counters to illustrate fixed-priority scheduling/dispatching. You might have noticed, when you check in for a flight, that there is a line for first-class passengers and frequent fliers who have attained "super elite" status (system jobs/tasks). Then, there is a line for business-class customers and frequent fliers who have earned some kind of "elite" status (interactive jobs). Finally, there's a line for the rest of us (batch jobs).

If an airline used fixed-priority ticket processing, all agents would work with all the first-class/super-elite customers, then all would work with all of the business-class/elite customers, and, finally, they'd get around to serving the rest. Also, once they began to process customers in a given line, any customer arriving at either of the other two lines would be given access to the next available agent, regardless of how long the first person in line had been waiting. And, since fixed-priority scheduling is being used for the high-priority jobs, these jobs will continue to use the processor even if they reach time slice end many times. As a result, the low-priority customers (jobs) will wait a long time for the agent (processor). They will have poor response time and/or throughput when the agent has a large number of high-priority customers to process.

Dynamic-Priority Scheduling

As you might have guessed, fixed-priority scheduling can lead to performance issues if the workload involves high volumes or high processor utilization. Consider the following examples:

- A high-priority job has a complex transaction that exceeds the time slice multiple times. Since it is a high-priority job, it will continue to use the CPU unless its priority is lowered.

- High-priority jobs are completing transactions within a single time slice, but are using more than 90 percent of the CPU. Low-priority batch jobs do not gain access to the CPU very often.

These two cases and several others require a different method of scheduling. As a result, the iSeries implemented dynamic-priority scheduling, with QDYNPTYSCD set to one. Dynamic-priority scheduling/dispatching is the default algorithm.

The Basics of Dynamic-Priority Scheduling

While many different algorithms can be chosen for dynamic-priority scheduling, all of them have the same principles:

- Distribute the CPU more equitably among the large number and wide variety of jobs running.

- Recognize the length of time that a job has been waiting for the CPU.

- Prevent a high-priority job from monopolizing the CPU.

To implement these principles on the iSeries, the dynamic-priority scheduling is implemented in an algorithm called *delayed cost scheduling*.

As the name implies, delayed cost scheduling calculates the cost for the time that a job is in main storage but has not gained access to the CPU. Since all work in the system is important, costs are calculated for all of the jobs that are running, regardless of their initial priority. When the system is choosing the next job to schedule/dispatch, it uses the job's cost, not its original priority. Figure 3.14 provides a schematic view of this algorithm.

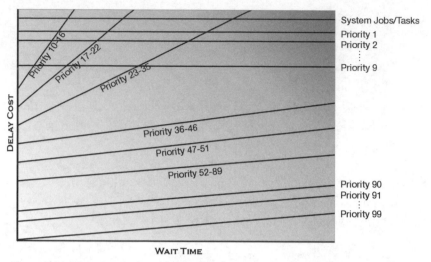

Figure 3.14: Dynamic-priority scheduling uses the delayed cost scheduling algorithm to determine the scheduling and dispatching of jobs to an available processor.

While this diagram represents the algorithm very well, it is not necessarily easy to understand. It needs a fair amount of study to see how the system uses the job's RUNPTY value in this scheduling/dispatching scheme. It's also not very easy to see how this scheme provides the benefits asserted earlier. The next few pages explain how dynamic-priority scheduling works, and how it benefits a large variety of environments. Examples are provided to help explain the algorithm in real situations.

The dynamic-priority scheduling algorithm uses the job's run priority as follows:

1. Each job, as it enters the system, has its run priority converted to an initial cost. The job is then placed on the cost curve (line) that is used to determine its wait-time costs.

2. At the top of the cost chart, there are some solid flat lines for the system jobs and jobs that were assigned a run priority of one through nine when they were initiated. These lines represent fixed-priority scheduling. Jobs in these categories will not have any wait-time costs added to their original priorities, but they will always be scheduled before any other jobs in the system. Clearly, the system jobs need to be scheduled before any user jobs, or the

system will not run well. The assignments with priorities one through nine should only be used for user jobs that are extremely critical; typically, there shouldn't be any.

3. The remainder of the curves on the system represent a range of run priorities. When a job is placed on a cost curve using its initial cost, it is placed on the curve that includes its assigned run priority. That is, a priority-20 job will have a certain initial cost and will be placed on the priority 17-22 curve, while a priority-50 job will be on the priority 47-51 curve.

4. The cost of waiting for a high-priority job is higher than the cost for a low-priority job. This is represented by the slope of each of the cost lines. The curves that are used for jobs with higher run priorities have a steeper slope than the curves used for jobs with lower run priorities.

5. Finally, notice that the cost of a job can exceed the cost of the system jobs and the jobs with priorities one through nine. Although the cost of these jobs might be higher, they will not be dispatched before the system jobs and the jobs with priorities one through nine.

6. The cost-curve priority ranges are designed to separate jobs that use the typical (default) run priority values. Thus, the system console and spool writers are on one curve, interactive jobs on another, and batch jobs on yet another. This helps to preserve the importance of the run priority that you assigned to the jobs.

Using these basic cost calculations, you can now see that a batch job running on the priority-50 curve will eventually increase in cost until its cost is higher than a newly arrived priority-20 job. Remember the airline check-in example? As long as the cost of the wait time of people in the low-priority line (batch) is higher than a customer who has just arrived in the business/elite (interactive) line, the agent will process customers from the low-priority line. However, the customers waiting in the business/elite line will increase in cost faster than those in the low-priority line, so it will not be long before an agent will handle the new arrival in the business/elite line.

That's the purpose of delay cost: to allow lower-priority, but still important, jobs an opportunity to use the processor when they have waited a long time (their cost has increased), while limiting the wait time for higher-priority jobs by assigning a higher cost to their wait times.

Calculating the Initial Cost

Now that you understand the basics of the delayed cost dynamic-priority algorithm, you can begin to look more closely at the first step in this scheme: the initial cost calculation. While the system defaults only use a few priorities, there are 99 priorities available for use in OS/400.

As mentioned in the previous section, there are separate curves for each of the priorities one through nine, and 90 through 99. Since jobs with these run priorities are still dispatched using a fixed cost, there is no need to discuss them; just take a look at the curves that have multiple run-priority values. It is important that the initial cost associated with each priority represent the difference in run-priority values. Figure 3.15 shows the method of determining the initial cost for priorities assigned to the same cost curve.

ASSIGNING INITIAL COSTS

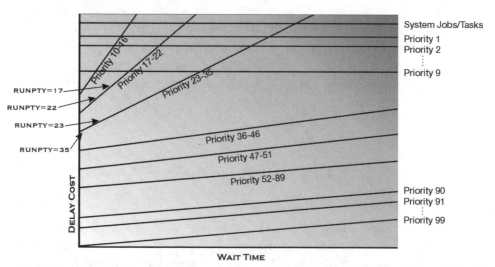

Figure 3.15: The initial cost and the cost curve of a job are based on its run priority.

As you can see, the initial cost is obtained by applying a wait-time cost to a job's run priority when it is placed on the cost curve. In this case, jobs with a run priority of 17 receive the highest initial cost on the cost curve, and jobs with a run priority of 22 receive the lowest initial cost. The same scenario is true for the cost curve for run priorities 23-35. Finally, notice that between the curves, the jobs with run priority 22 have an initial cost that is higher than jobs with run priority 23. The initial cost assignment for the jobs in the system is used to retain the notion that jobs with higher priority should receive preference over jobs with lower priority, regardless of the curve to which they are assigned.

Cost Increases between Jobs on the Same Curve

Although jobs are assigned initial costs based on their run priority, their costs increase independently. A lower-priority job that has been waiting longer than a new job will have a higher cost. This part of the algorithm is shown in Figure 3.16.

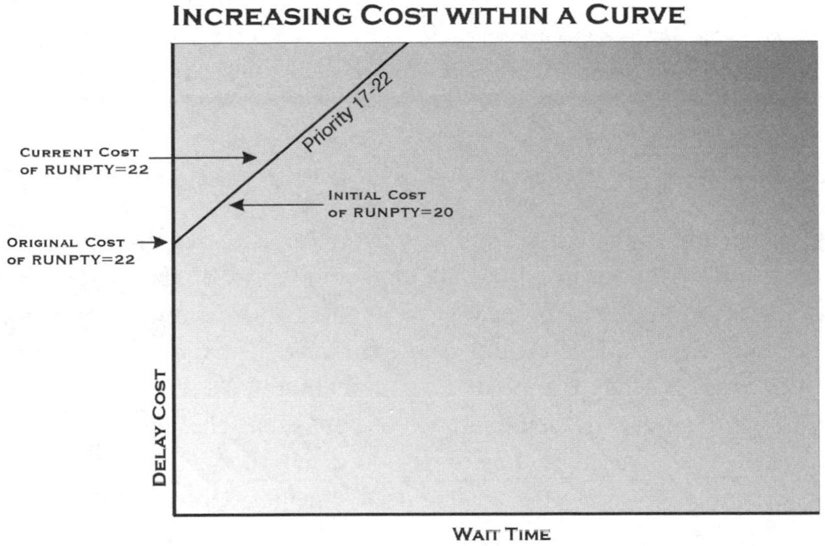

INCREASING COST WITHIN A CURVE

Figure 3.16: The cost of a job may be higher than the initial cost of a job that has a higher run priority.

As you can see, although the initial cost of the job with a run priority of 22 is lower than the job with a run priority of 20, the priority-22 job has accumulated a higher cost and will be dispatched before the priority-20 job.

Return to the airline counter example, this time focusing on the line for the business/elite customers. Assume that the airline prioritizes business/elite customers in the following order:

1. Business class with elite status.

2. Business class only.

3. Elite status only.

In a fixed-priority scheme, new arrivals would be placed in the line at the end of customers having the same status, and in front of all customers with a lower status. The amount of time that someone in a lower-status line has been waiting would not alter the position of the new arrival—the newly arrived higher-priority customer would always be placed closer to the front of the line. With dynamic-priority scheduling, a new arrival would be assigned an initial cost. The initial cost would be used to determine the new customer's position in line. Thus, a customer with lower status who had been in line a while might retain a position closer to the front of the line than a higher-status new arrival.

Avoiding CPU Monopolization

Finally, you need to deal with jobs that try to do too much processing in relation to the other jobs in the system. In an attempt to prevent a single job from monopolizing a processor's time (like the couple at the travel agency), the dynamic-priority scheduler has a built-in penalty clause for jobs that have a run priority of 17-22 and 23-35. Whenever a job exceeds an internal CPU limit without taking a break (similar to a time slice), the job will be penalized. The internal limit is assigned by the system based on the processor's speed; these CPU limits cannot be modified. Figure 3.17 shows the method used to penalize jobs that try to monopolize the processor.

The jobs that have exceeded the CPU limit are moved to the curve below and given the lowest initial cost on that curve. Although the jobs will not be reassigned to a lower cost for any further CPU overuse, they will be reset to the lowest initial cost on the new curve each time they exceed the CPU limit.

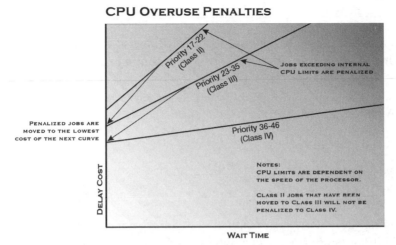

CPU OVERUSE PENALTIES

Figure 3.17: Jobs exceeding CPU limits imposed on the second and third cost curves will be assigned a new cost and placed on the next lowest curve.

So, back to the airline example. Suppose a business/elite customer wants to investigate the schedule possibilities of a 14-day trip to 18 cities. It's going to take a while to get it figured out. In fact, it will take so long that the customer will be holding up customers in more than one line. In a fixed-priority scheme, that would be just too bad for everyone else. In a dynamic-priority scheme, the customer with the complex transaction will have his or her current position in the transaction saved, and will then be sent to the end of the line with the rest of us. (YES!!) In addition, when the customer finally got another turn at the processor, he or she would still be susceptible to a time limit. Failure to complete the transaction in time would have the customer returned to the end of the line again. It sure would be nice to have this algorithm applied to some real-life situations!

Dynamic Priority—Summary

This has been a fairly lengthy and complicated discussion about dynamic-priority scheduling. However, by understanding the workings of this algorithm, you will be better prepared to adjust the run priority attribute assigned to jobs. Just remember that a job's run priority is only one factor in scheduling/dispatching work in OS/400.

In Review

You have made it through a fairly lengthy and complicated chapter. Here are some things to remember from it, about a job's runtime attributes:

1. When jobs are running instructions, they must be in main storage. Also, any objects that they wish to use, whether shared or unique, must also be in main storage.

2. With the elimination of the Process Access Group, the PURGE parameter is obsolete.

3. Time slice values are helpful only to jobs that have the same or a higher run priority than the job that is using the CPU and/or occupying main storage.

4. Setting the QTSEPOOL system value to *BASE can enhance the benefits of time-slice end processing.

5. Dynamic-priority scheduling is very valuable for all OS/400 environments. The CPU is more equitably distributed, CPU-monopolistic jobs are penalized, and response times become more consistent.

The information in this chapter is intended to provide an understanding of the runtime parameters that are assigned to jobs when they are initiated by a subsystem. As you have seen, for many environments, the default values will work fine. However, a better understanding of these values will help you customize work management to do a better job in other environments. These techniques are described in a later chapter.

4

Managing Jobs: Pools

Chapter 3 describes how the runtime attributes translate to the system functions that manage jobs running on your system. These jobs run in divisions of main storage called pools. The focus of this chapter is on the pools. Topics discussed include the activity that takes place in the pools and what you can do to help the jobs run better.

Main Storage Pools: The Basics

As noted in the introduction to subsystems in chapter 1, one of the primary assets of a subsystem is the pools that are defined by the POOLS parameter on the Create Subsystem Description command (CRTSBSD). Main storage is allocated to the pools and becomes available for the subsystem to introduce jobs to the system.

This chapter starts by looking at a basic OS/400 pool configuration that would occur the first time you started your system. To see the pools, enter the command Work with System Status (WRKSYSSTS) at your workstation. You will see the information in Figure 4.1.

```
                      Work with System Status                TSCSAP01
                                                 09/18/00    11:08:03
% CPU used . . . . . . . :       86.7    Auxiliary storage:
Elapsed time . . . . . . :    00:05:01     System ASP . . . . . . :      95.94 G
Jobs in system . . . . . :        305    % system ASP used  . . :    29.0611
% addresses used:                          Total  . . . . . . . . :      99.88 G
  Permanent  . . . . . . :       .009      Current unprotect used :       1850 M
  Temporary  . . . . . . :       .015      Maximum unprotect  . . :       1865 M

Type changes (if allowed), press Enter.

System    Pool    Reserved    Max    ---DB---   --Non-DB--
 Pool    Size (M)  Size (M)  Active  Fault  Pages  Fault  Pages
   1      325.00    190.88   +++++    .0     .0     6.0    7.0
   2     1283.50      .00      4     2.0   257.5    3.0    3.1
   3     2700.00      .00     197    1.0    16.3  122.8  124.6
   4       43.50      .00      1      .0     .0     .0     .0

                                                             Bottom
Command
===>
F3=Exit    F4=Prompt             F5=Refresh   F9=Retrieve   F10=Restart
F11=Display transition data      F12=Cancel   F24=More keys
```

Figure 4.1: *The Work with System Status (WRKSYSSTS) display shows runtime information about your system.*

When using the WRKSYSSTS command, you should refresh (F5) every 5 minutes. At the end of a half-hour of refreshing the display, you should restart (F10) the statistics. As you can see from the display, there is more information that can be shown by simply pressing other function keys. For now, take a look at the information that appears on the first screen.

WRKSYSSTS—The Top Half

The top half of the WRKSYSSTS display provides some general information about the operation of your system. Starting in the upper-left quarter of the screen, the following sections explain the meaning of the different lines of information on the display.

WRKSYSSTS—The Upper-Left Quarter

The first line in the upper-left quarter of the screen shows the percentage of processing power being used by the jobs. This is the total amount of CPU being used by all of the jobs that have used the processor during the elapsed interval. You cannot tell what type of jobs have been using the processor, nor can you tell how many jobs have been using it. However, if your system CPU utilization is 99 percent, you might want to investigate the jobs that are using the CPU. To observe the CPU used by individual jobs, run the Work with Active Jobs (WRKACTJOB) command. (In this book, this command is occasionally used, but methods for using the display to manage system performance are not discussed.)

The next line shows the elapsed time. This is the amount of time spent observing the system status. As you can see, you have been observing the system for approximately 5 minutes. The next use of the F5 key should be at approximately 10 minutes of elapsed time. When your elapsed time reaches 30 minutes, press F10. Many users like to press F10 twice to reset the statistics immediately.

After the elapsed time is a line that shows the jobs in the system. Jobs in the system consist of any job that:

- Is running.
- Is on a job queue waiting to be initiated.
- Has finished running but still has output to print (in a spool file).

Typically, the number of jobs in the system is not very interesting. However, if this number is much larger than the number of jobs that are running, you probably have a lot of completed jobs that have left printed output in the system. When this occurs, it is a good idea to print or delete the spool files and eliminate the jobs from the system.

The next three lines tell you the addresses that have been used on your system. The system assigns an address every time an object is created. Objects may be permanent (lasting until they are deleted by you), or temporary (deleted when the system is IPLed). It is very unlikely that you will see a large percentage of addresses used on your system. In the unlikely event that either type of address reaches 99 percent, stop processing and reboot (IPL) your system immediately.

WRKSYSSTS—The Upper-Right Quarter

The upper-right quarter of the display is probably the least dynamic. It provides information regarding the disk storage on the system. The system's Auxiliary Storage Pool (ASP) will, by default, contain all of the disks attached to your system. When the system ASP becomes more than 90 percent full, the system will send you a warning. Each time another one percent of your disk space is used, you will get another message. When the system ASP is completely full, your system will crash, so please do not ignore these warnings.

WRKSYSSTS—The Pool List

The bottom half of the display provides a list of pools that are currently in use by subsystems and that have storage allocated. The remainder of this chapter focuses on this portion of the display. The pool numbers don't tell you much, but regardless of how you have defined your subsystems, pool 1 will always be the machine pool (*MACHINE). The size of the machine pool is set by the system value QMCHPOOL. This system value is the only way to change the machine pool's size. Changes made to the system value QMCHPOOL take place immediately and do not require an IPL. The machine pool is used to run low-level system tasks, and to hold code and information used by all SLIC and some OS/400 functions (such as scheduling/dispatching and database).

The second pool in the list will always be *BASE. The size of this pool is not set explicitly. Instead, the minimum allowable size for *BASE is set by the system value QBASPOOL. *BASE contains all the storage that has not been claimed by the other pools that are in use. Usually, *BASE is larger than the value specified by QBASPOOL. Should another pool, say, *MACHINE, need more storage, increasing the QMCHPOOL system value would cause storage to be transferred from *BASE to *MACHINE until *BASE is the same size as the QBASPOOL system value. If QMCHPOOL is decreased, storage will be transferred from *MACHINE to *BASE. Transferring storage to or from any of the other pools in the system follows the same principle. Finally, any new pools added to the environment will need to obtain their storage from *BASE. In a default environment, batch jobs, the system console, and the subsystem monitors run in this pool.

Pool 3 is *INTERACT and pool 4 is *SPOOL. In the default subsystem environment, *INTERACT is used to run interactive jobs initiated by QBASE. *SPOOL is used for spool writers that produce printed output from spooled files. Jobs in *SPOOL are initiated by the QSPL subsystem.

Before going on, let's explore this *BASE/main storage transfer by using an example. Suppose *BASE represents a pool of employees who are capable of working in any area of your business. Their usual work assignment is in department 2 (*BASE), but they know that if they are needed elsewhere, they may be reassigned to a different department. Suppose department 1 (*MACHINE), falls behind schedule (does too much paging). You increase the size of this department (increase QMCHPOOL), and temporarily reassign workers to it. However, you don't want to transfer everyone from department 2; this department must always have a certain minimum number of employees (QBASPOOL). When department 2 is reduced to its minimum size (*BASE becomes the same size as QBASPOOL), no transfers from it are allowed. To help out a department that is in trouble, you would first need to look for departments that are currently overstaffed, transfer the employees to department 2, then reassign them.

Similarly, if department 1 has too many members, rather than lay off the employees (decrease the size of main storage), you merely transfer them back to department 2. Direct transfers between any other departments, such as from department 3 to department 4, are not possible. All transfers must first be made to department 2 before they can be reassigned.

Finally, when a new department is created (department 5), it will be staffed by employees currently in department 2. Eventually, your company might need to add more employees (get more main storage) to keep up with all aspects of your business.

WRKSYSSTS—The Pool Information

Interestingly, most of the pool information shown in Figure 4.1 comes in pairs:

- Pool size and reserved size.
- Database fault and pages.
- Non-database fault and pages.

The following sections look at each of these pairs of values, and then at the maximum active value.

Pool Size and Reserved Size

The first pair of values is reasonably self-explanatory. The pool size is simply the amount of storage, in megabytes, that is available for jobs or system functions. As with the discussion of the PURGE runtime attribute, the jobs use the storage to hold shared and job-unique information. The pool size value simply indicates how much storage the jobs have to use.

The reserved size of a pool tells us how much space, in megabytes, is currently tied up with important information. The reserved pages generally contain information that the system would like to keep in main storage for a long time. Many of the reserved pages in pool 1 (*MACHINE) are permanently located in main storage. They represent functions that are done regularly and are critical to performance. Waiting for a disk operation on any of these pages might cause everything running in the system to wait for the disk transfer—not a very productive situation.

Another use of the reserved portion of a pool is to allocate buffers for certain operations that require a lot of disk/media transfer. Typically, a save or restore operation allocates reserved storage for buffers. By reserving the buffers in main storage, these operations perform efficiently without allocating the entire pool as a buffer. At the same time, reserving the buffer space protects the contents of the buffer area from other jobs in the pool that are requesting information.

Database and Non-database Faults

A *fault*, or *page fault*, occurs whenever a job running in main storage requests a page of information that is not in main storage. The job requesting the page stops and waits for the page to be retrieved from disk. When the page has been retrieved and is ready for use, the job may resume processing. Because the job must stop and wait for the page to be read into main storage, keeping the number of page faults low is very important.

Disk operations that force a job to stop and wait for the completion of the operation are called *synchronous I/O operations*. Whenever the system performs a synchronous operation, it tries to keep the pages read to a small number—usually one or two pages per fault. By keeping the number of pages transferred small, there is less overhead reading them into main storage, so the length of time the job is forced to wait is kept to a minimum.

The database fault value shows the number of times per second that the system stopped one of the jobs running in the pool while it retrieved a page from a database object for the job. The database pages value shows the number of pages per second that are being read into the pool.

In the example, you see very little activity except for pool 2 (*BASE). In *BASE, you see a low DB (database) fault value (2.0) and a very high DB pages value (257.5). You just learned that the system brought a small number of pages on a fault, so why is the number of pages per fault more than 125? There is a good explanation for this apparent inconsistency. By analyzing the usage of database objects, the system support for database functions tries to anticipate what records and keys will be needed in main storage. As a good "system citizen," a database starts to read pages into main storage before they are needed. Most of the time, a database's read operations are complete before the job needs the data. Since a job does not need to wait for the disk operation to complete, there is no fault recorded for the I/O operation. These types of disk operations are referred to as *asynchronous I/O operations.*

Another factor that contributes to the large difference between faults and pages is *database blocking.* Whenever a job is processing a database file in the same sequence in which it is stored on disk, the job will run better if the application has implemented record blocking. Record blocking results in the transfer of large blocks of information from disk to main storage, and the system will perform these large block transfers asynchronously. This gives you the best of both worlds: large blocks with a single read operation that take place while your job keeps running. Record blocking is activated by running the Override Data Base File (OVRDBF) command and specifying SEQONLY(*YES *number of records).* The *YES value instructs the system to perform asynchronous operations for the file, while the *number of records* value gives the size of the block to be transferred. This is a great function to implement for files that are read sequentially and not updated. If you use this function, you should set the block size to at least 1 Mb.

So, when you see a low database fault value and a high database pages value, rest assured that the system database functions are hard at work on behalf of the jobs running on your system.

Non-database Fault and Pages

The non-database pair of values represents the same information as the database values, but for non-database objects. As mentioned in the preceding chapter, jobs running in a pool use information that is unique as well as information that is shared by other jobs. Most of the non-database information read into a pool is job-unique. There is usually little asynchronous activity for non-database objects.

As a result, the fault and pages will have values that are close to the same. Once again, it is advantageous to keep the fault value low to reduce the number of times that a job must stop and wait for a disk operation. Later in this chapter you'll learn how to determine a reasonable number for the fault value.

Max Active

The last value on the screen is Max Active (maximum active). It might seem as though you just can't get enough of this maximum activity stuff! This maximum active value, however, has a completely different meaning than the value described in previous chapters. Before, maximum active meant the maximum number of jobs that could be initiated using various parts of the subsystem description. In this case, maximum active does not restrict the number of jobs that can be initiated. Rather, it specifies the maximum number of threads that can be in main storage at the same time. There might be many more threads running on the system than are allowed into main storage.

Another example will help explain maximum active. You are probably familiar with the process of registering for college classes. Consider a course that a large number of students want to take. By accepting their registrations, the registrar (subsystem) has processed their requests (initiated the jobs). Using registration date (priority), the system begins to fill the class (allows jobs into main storage). When the class is full (all activity levels used up), no other students (jobs) are allowed into the class (pool). They are placed on a waiting list (ineligible queue). If a student drops out of the class (a job completes its work or reaches time slice), one of the students on the waiting list is allowed into the class. Figure 4.2 shows this principle.

In Figure 4.1, notice that the value of Max Active for the machine pool is +++++. This means only low-level (Licensed Internal Code) system tasks will run in the machine pool. User jobs and most OS/400 system jobs run in the other pools. These low-level system tasks perform operations that are crucial to the overall performance of the user jobs. Whenever a system task needs to run, it runs. System tasks are allowed immediate access to main storage no matter how many tasks are already in the machine pool. So, the +++++ is merely another way of saying that Max Active is not applicable to the *MACHINE pool.

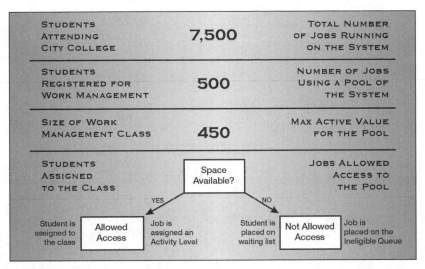

STUDENTS ATTENDING CITY COLLEGE	7,500	TOTAL NUMBER OF JOBS RUNNING ON THE SYSTEM
STUDENTS REGISTERED FOR WORK MANAGEMENT	500	NUMBER OF JOBS USING A POOL OF THE SYSTEM
SIZE OF WORK MANAGEMENT CLASS	450	MAX ACTIVE VALUE FOR THE POOL
STUDENTS ASSIGNED TO THE CLASS	Space Available?	JOBS ALLOWED ACCESS TO THE POOL

YES → Student is assigned to the class | Allowed Access | Job is assigned an Activity Level

NO → Student is placed on waiting list | Not Allowed Access | Job is placed on the Ineligible Queue

Figure 4.2: A pool's maximum active value is similar to the maximum number of seats in a class.

While allowing an unlimited number of tasks access to the machine pool at the same time is acceptable, do not try this in any of the other pools. If too many jobs are running in a pool at the same time, there will be intense competition among the jobs for the space available. In particular, the jobs will be competing to get their unique information into main storage.

As each job brings in more unique information, there is less room for shared information. As a result, there will be an increase in the number of faults for both job-unique and shared information. Finally, if the competition becomes too intense, a situation known as *thrashing* occurs, where the system spends more time doing I/O operations than it does processing work. Thrashing results in horrendous performance!

Clearly, a value of *NOMAX is not good. What is a good value for Max Active? Would making Max Active for pool 3 really small—say five—be a good value? Well, maybe. The Max Active value depends on how frequently jobs want to access the pool. If a large number of jobs are always trying to get into main storage at the same time, setting Max Active too low will result in long waits on the ineligible queue.

Here is a simple method to determine a reasonable Max Active level:

1. Pick a time of the day that represents your typical workload (if there is such a thing).

2. Reduce Max Active by 10 percent.

3. Continue to reduce Max Active by 10 percent until jobs are not allowed access to the pool, that is, they are placed on the ineligible queue.

4. When you see jobs on the ineligible queue, increase the activity level by 10 percent.

5. Monitor the ineligible queue periodically to validate your setting.

Using this simple technique, you will arrive at a reasonable setting for Max Active. To use this technique, however, you need to be able to monitor ineligible-queue activity. How do you do that?

WRKSYSSTS—Transition Data

Now is the time to consider some of the other information that WRKSYSSTS provides. Return to the WRKSYSSTS display and press F11 to show the transition data in Figure 4.3.

```
                     Work with System Status                TSCSAP01
                                             09/19/00       09:33:23
% CPU used . . . . . . . :        1.0   Auxiliary storage:
Elapsed time . . . . . . :    00:00:01    System ASP . . . . . :     95.94 G
Jobs in system . . . . . :        306     % system ASP used  . :    29.1128
% addresses used:                         Total  . . . . . . . :     99.88 G
  Permanent  . . . . . . :       .009     Current unprotect used:    1887 M
  Temporary  . . . . . . :       .015     Maximum unprotect  . .:    1890 M

Type changes (if allowed), press Enter.

System    Pool    Reserved    Max    Active->  Wait->  Active->
 Pool    Size (M)  Size (M)  Active    Wait     Inel     Inel
  1       325.00    190.70   +++++      .0       .0       .0
  2      1283.50       .00       4     2.4       .0       .0
  3      2700.00       .00     197    87.6       .0       .0
  4        43.50       .00       1      .3       .0       .0

                                                            Bottom
Command
===>
F3=Exit    F4=Prompt      F5=Refresh    F9=Retrieve    F10=Restart
F11=Display pool data    F12=Cancel    F14=Work with subsystems    F24=More keys
```

Figure 4.3: *Pressing F11 on the first display shown by WRKSYSSTS provides transition data for running jobs.*

The upper half of this display repeats the information that appeared in the first display. The bottom half of this display gives the information about job transitions in each pool. Let's look at each of the three new columns on this display.

Active-to-Wait

The first of the new columns indicates the number of times per minute that a job made a transition from the active state to the wait state. Each time one of these transitions takes place, the job leaves main storage and waits for a resource to become available. For interactive jobs, most active-to-wait transitions are the result of completing work and requesting additional work (input) from a user. For batch jobs, an active-to-wait transition is the result of a record lock conflict; another job has locked a record that the batch job would like to access (usually to update the record). For spool jobs, these transitions are the result of sending large buffers of output to a printer device and waiting for the information to be printed.

As you might have guessed, a large number of other conditions could also cause these transitions. Most of these conditions are beyond the scope of this book, however, the following are reasonably common:

- *Event waits*—An event is a method of signaling information between jobs and tasks on the system. In some cases, the work you are doing requires your job to use another task. Your job will wait for an event to be signaled by the task doing the requested work. When the task completes its work, it will signal an event to your job.

- *Waiting for a message*—This wait is similar to waiting for an event. Once again, two jobs are performing dependent functions. User jobs do not have access to the event function and must find some other method for communicating with each other. One method is via messages on a message queue. With this method, your job will put a message on a message queue that another job is using. Then, your job will wait for a message to be returned on a different queue. The job processing the queue that has your message will eventually get to your message and handle it. When the job completes processing for your message, it will place a completion message on the queue where your job is waiting.

- *Waiting for an entry on a data queue*—This construct is the same as using message queues, but uses far less system resources. It is the fastest user-job-to-user-job communication vehicle.

- *Mutex waits*—A mutex (mutually exclusive) is a method to synchronize processing between two threads in the same job. It is similar to a switch: when one thread does not want another to proceed, it sets the mutex on; when it is ready for another thread to proceed, it sets the mutex off. This construct will gain in popularity as threads (discussed later) become more prevalent.

- *Display waits*—This wait is the most common for interactive jobs. It appears whenever the job has completed processing a user's input and has sent a display to the workstation requesting the next input.

The WRKACTJOB display indicates the type of wait for each job in a wait state. Typically, it is not important that you know the reason that jobs are making active-to-wait transitions.

Wait-to-Inel

This column tells you the number of times per minute that a job wanted to enter a pool, but found there was no room. When a job is not allowed into the pool, it is placed on the ineligible queue. The job is placed on the queue according to its current cost value, where it will wait until a space becomes available because, for example, one of the jobs in main storage has experienced an active-to-wait transition.

In the discussion about setting the maximum active value earlier in this chapter, you were told to lower the activity level until jobs are not allowed access to main storage. However, you were not told how to recognize this condition. The wait-to-ineligible transition value gives you the information you need. In other words, lower the activity level in a pool until this value becomes greater than zero, then raise it slightly.

Active-to-Inel

The final column shown on this display tells you the number of times that a job was forced to leave main storage to give another job access. Basically, this value represents the number of times that a job reached time slice end while a job of equal or higher cost was waiting to enter the pool. If jobs complete their work in main storage before reaching time slice end, this value will be zero. Typically, the default time slice value and a reasonable Max Active value will result in this value being zero.

Remember the simple example of the travel agency in chapter 3? At last report, there were a number of customers (jobs) waiting (ineligible) to get into the agent's office (pool). The customers were waiting to get into the office because of a complex transaction (the couple planning their honeymoon). The travel agency has now instituted an office use limit (time slice) of 5 minutes. There is no way that the couple in the office will complete their transaction in 5 minutes. Since there are other customers (jobs) that are just as important (have an equal or higher cost), when the couple has been in the office for 5 minutes, they will return to the end of the line (have an active-to-ineligible transition).

When the couple reenters the office, they are given another 5 minutes to finish their transaction. Most likely, they will use up the 5 minutes without completing the transaction. Once again, if someone else is waiting to enter the office, the couple will be placed at the end of the line. If, however, nobody is waiting, they will be allowed to remain in the office and will be given an additional 5 minutes of time in the agent's office (pool). This process continues until the transaction is finished.

Main Storage Pools:
Managing Pool Size and Maximum Active

As you have seen, the WRKSYSSTS display can be used to monitor transitions and paging statistics to determine if pool sizes and activity levels are set correctly. So far, the discussion has focused on managing the pools by controlling the number of jobs in the pool at the same time (Max Active). However, you could also provide assistance to jobs running in the pool by providing more room for them to run. The additional storage would allow more information to be placed in the pool, reduce the page faults, and improve performance.

So, how do you figure out which of the two management methods (storage or activity level) to use? Once you have that figured out, do you really need to continually monitor the activity with WRKSYSSTS? If you're running WRKSYSSTS, how can you do your real job? Is there something to help you with this task? These are all valid questions. Unfortunately, the answers aren't as straightforward as the questions. A number of factors must be considered, including the following:

- What is the most important work?
- Which pools are running the most important work?
- How many jobs are attempting to access the pools?
- How much job-unique information is there for each pool?
- What is a good fault rate for the pools running important work?
- Have you provided any service guarantees?

Fortunately, OS/400 has a function called *dynamic performance adjustment* that can help manage the pools in your environment.

Dynamic Performance Adjustment: The Basics

To make pool management easier, you can activate the dynamic performance adjustment functions of OS/400. Once activated, the dynamic tuner will attempt to balance storage among shared pools. It will also adjust activity levels in shared pools. In the default environment, all pools—*MACHINE, *BASE, *INTERACT, and *SPOOL—will be managed by dynamic performance adjustment. (If you've forgotten the difference between shared and private pools, return to the discussion about pools in chapter 1.)

Dynamic performance adjustment is controlled by the QPFRADJ system value. QPFRADJ can be set to the following values:

- 0—Do not initialize pool sizes, and do not dynamically adjust pool sizes and activity levels.

- 1—Initialize pool sizes when the system is IPLed, but do not dynamically adjust pool sizes and activity levels.

- 2—Initialize pool sizes when the system is IPLed, and dynamically adjust pool sizes and activity levels. This is the default setting

- 3—Do not initialize pool sizes when the system is IPLed, but dynamically adjust pool sizes and activity levels.

The default setting for QPFRADJ is two, so when the system is IPLed, OS/400 will establish the initial size of all four pools. The initial size is calculated by an internal algorithm that analyzes the system resources, main storage size, processor speed, and installed features of OS/400. In addition, when sizing the machine pool (*MACHINE), OS/400 will consider the amount of reserved space that exists. The algorithms are fixed and cannot be adjusted.

Once the pool sizes have been established, the IPL process will continue. When IPL is complete, the subsystems are active and ready to initiate work into the pools. The initiated work will now begin to request information, but some of the requests will result in faults and force the user jobs to wait for the information. In addition the QPFRADJ job will be running. This job, initiated by the system (not by a subsystem), will perform the dynamic performance adjustments.

Dynamic Performance Adjustment: The Mechanics

So, you've got your initial pool sizes and activity levels, and the jobs are off and running. QPFRADJ is started and ready for work. If you run the Work with Active Jobs command (WRKACTJOB) and locate the QPFRADJ job, you will see a display similar to Figure 4.4.

```
Opt   Subsystem/Job   User        Type   CPU %  Function      Status
      QPFRADJ         QSYS        SYS     .0                  EVTW
```

Figure 4.4:The QPFRADJ job information is shown on the Work with Active Jobs display.

Notice that QPFRADJ has a status of EVTW. This is an event wait. In this case, the event being waited for is an indication that a minute has elapsed. At every 1-minute interval, QPFRADJ will wake up from a short nap and collect the fault rate in each pool and the amount of CPU used by each job that is running. These two pieces of information are used to estimate the efficiency of the jobs that are running in each pool.

Without detailed analysis of each job, it is impossible to know just what its performance characteristics are. Analyzing the performance of each running job requires several steps and experience using the OS/400 performance tools, and is beyond the scope of this book. However, QPFRADJ provides an estimate of the performance of the jobs that can be used to help determine reasonable pool sizes and values for Max Active for the workload you are running.

Estimating Machine Pool Efficiency

Now that you have QPFRADJ, initial pool sizes, and data, where do you go next? Focus your attention on the *MACHINE pool. Unlike most of the other pools in the system, you don't need to be concerned about the number of tasks that are running in this pool or the amount of CPU being used. The only thing that matters in *MACHINE is the page fault rate. Every minute, QPFRADJ calculates this page fault rate. If it is less than 10, QPFRADJ is happy. If it is greater than 10, QPFRADJ is disappointed (but not yet unhappy). If QPFRADJ finds the page fault rate of *MACHINE to be greater than 10 for three consecutive intervals, it becomes unhappy. Typically, most of your users will also be unhappy with the performance of their jobs at this rate.

In order to correct the high faulting rate in *MACHINE, QPFRADJ will increase the size of *MACHINE by changing the QMCHPOOL system value. QPFRADJ will increase the value of QMCHPOOL by 10 percent. Once QPFRADJ has started to increase the size of the machine pool, it will make an adjustment every minute until the page fault rate falls below 10.

There are three things to notice about QPFRADJ's management of high faulting in the machine pool:

1. The machine pool is always evaluated and adjusted first. As mentioned earlier, the key components of the operating system are running in this pool. If these components are performing poorly, everything is performing poorly.

2. QPFRADJ waits for three consecutive intervals of poor faulting before any changes are made. Often times, a small burst of transient activity might temporarily raise the faulting rate outside the 10-per-second guideline. It is not advisable to adjust pool sizes when transient activities cause the faulting increase. These activities usually run quickly, and faulting returns to fewer than 10. By waiting for three intervals, QPFRADJ can be fairly certain the higher faulting rate is caused by normal activities.

3. Once QFRADJ has made an adjustment, it continues to adjust every minute. Since QPFRADJ has determined that the machine pool faulting is caused by normal activities, high faulting in any subsequent interval is also considered to be caused by normal activities.

What happens if faulting in the machine pool never gets below 10? Hopefully, this condition will not happen in your environment. If it does, your system should be upgraded with additional main storage. In the meantime, QPFRADJ will try to distribute the main storage you have as evenly as possible. In the case of the machine pool, it sets a maximum size. QPFRADJ will restrict the size of the machine pool to four times the reserved size of the pool. This size restriction prevents QPFRADJ from assigning all of your available main storage to the machine pool.

Up to now, we've been concerned about the situation of insufficient space in the machine pool. But what if there is too much main storage in the machine pool? QPFRADJ will not reduce the size of QMCHPOOL unless there is a need for the storage in another pool. If all other pools in the system have too little storage, storage will be taken from the machine pool and distributed to the others. Once again, QPFRADJ will not make any changes until the faulting condition has lasted for three intervals. Also, QPFRADJ will not reduce the size of *MACHINE below the minimum size of the machine pool, which is 1.5 times the reserved size of *MACHINE.

Other Shared Pools

It would be nice if all you had to do was reduce machine-pool paging to get your jobs to run well. As you might have guessed, however, there is more to getting jobs to run well; you need to manage the fault rates in the other pools as well. So, how does the dynamic performance adjustment function deal with the other pools? (Before continuing, be sure to have a fresh pot of coffee handy!)

In all of the other shared pools, a more complicated evaluation scheme is required. Earlier, in the introduction to this section, several questions were listed regarding what is needed to evaluate paging in these pools. Several of the factors mentioned are used in an algorithm that transforms the raw page-fault numbers into grades. This grading algorithm is used to determine if storage allocations or activity levels need to be adjusted.

Pool Priority

The first factor, pool priority, is used to determine which pools contain the most important jobs. The pool priority can have a value of one (most important) to 14 (least important). In the default environment of a non-server model system, the pool priority for *INTERACT and *MACHINE is one. *BASE and *SPOOL have a priority of two. In a system with a server (batch-oriented) model, *INTERACT has a priority of two and *BASE has a priority of one.

Much as run priority is used to assign an initial cost for each job, pool priority is used to assign an initial grade to each pool. For pools with a priority of one, the initial grade is 10. The initial grade for pools with any other value is zero. You may change the priority of any pool other than *MACHINE by running the Work with Shared Pools (WRKSHRPOOL) command and pressing F11 once. This will show the information in Figure 4.5.

```
                       Work with Shared Pools
                                              System:   TSCSAP01
 Main storage size (M)   . :         4352.00

 Type changes (if allowed), press Enter.

                      ---Size %---  ---Faults/Second---
 Pool          Priority Minimum  Maximum  Minimum  Thread  Maximum
 *MACHINE          1      6.16     100     10.00     .00    10.00
 *BASE             2      4.99     100     10.00    2.00     100
 *INTERACT         1     10.00     100      5.00     .50     200
 *SPOOL            2      1.00     100      5.00    1.00     100
 *SHRPOOL1         2      1.00     100     10.00    2.00     100
 *SHRPOOL2         2      1.00     100     10.00    2.00     100
 *SHRPOOL3         2      1.00     100     10.00    2.00     100
 *SHRPOOL4         2      1.00     100     10.00    2.00     100
 *SHRPOOL5         2      1.00     100     10.00    2.00     100
 *SHRPOOL6         2      1.00     100     10.00    2.00     100
                                                          More...
 Command
 ===>
 F3=Exit   F4=Prompt   F5=Refresh   F9=Retrieve   F11=Display text
 F12=Cancel
```

Figure 4.5: Pool adjustment factors are shown on the Work with Shared Pools display.

Eventually, you'll need to look at all the values on this display. For now, you should only be concerned about the priority. From this display, you can enter the priority you would like for each of the pools that your jobs are using. Assign the more important pools a priority of one and the less important pools a priority of two. You can assign a priority of one to any number of pools.

Page Faults

Now, let's look at the faults in the pools. As mentioned earlier, a fault represents the number of times per second that any job had to stop and wait for information to be transferred from disk to main storage. While the total number of faults in the pool is interesting, you should be more concerned with the number of times each job had to stop and wait. In setting the size of the machine pool, you can just use the raw fault number. For all other pools, you need to convert the fault number into something more meaningful.

To get a more meaningful value for the other pools, the dynamic performance adjustment function will use information from the active jobs in the system. For each 1-minute interval, the CPU seconds for each job in the pool are examined. Any job that has used the CPU during the 1-minute interval is considered to be an actively running job. You now have the two pieces of information you need for this part of the pool's grade. Divide the faults per second by the number of actively running jobs in each pool to get the number of faults per job in the pool. Look up the faults-per-job value in Table 4.1 to find the corresponding value for this portion of the pool's grade.

The dynamic performance adjust now has two of the three values that it needs to produce a final grade for each pool.

Table 4.1: Faults per Job Component of a Pool's Grade	
Faults/Job	Grade
10 or less	0
11-20	10
21-30	20
31-40	30
41-50	40
51-60	50
61-70	60
71-80	70
81-90	80
More than 90	90

Pool Space per Job

As a final factor in determining a pool's grade, the dynamic performance adjust function will determine the amount of space each active job in the pool has available. Once again, using the CPU times for each job assigned to the pool, you can find the number of active running jobs. Divide the pool size by the number of active running jobs to produce the pool space per job. The pool will have 10 points deducted from its score if the result is 3 Mb per job. If the result is 6 Mb per job, the pool loses 20 points, etc. Without this adjustment, you might never be able to get storage back from pools that previously had a large number of jobs, but now have fewer jobs, or from pools with one or two jobs that are faulting heavily. Now you have all the factors needed to determine the final grades of the pools.

Numeric Grades and Letter Grades

To get the numeric grade for each pool, add the pool's priority and fault-per-job values, and then subtract the space-per-job value. Remember, however, that this grade is only one of three that are taken for each pool (once every minute). Average the three grades to derive the final grade for each pool. In this case, a low number represents a good grade, and a high number is a poor grade.

But what is a good number grade? 20? 70? 33? Well, it depends. Just as in school, where a curve might be used to determine which students get each of the five possible letter grades, the numeric pool grades are placed on a curve to determine which pools need help. Instead of using five letter grades, you use a simple pass/fail grading system. You want everyone to pass with approximately the same grade value.

So, as long as all of the pool grades are within 20 points of each other, the dynamic performance adjust will leave the pool sizes and activity levels alone (everyone is getting a passing grade). If there is a 20-point or larger difference between the pool with the best grade (lowest number) and the pool with the worst grade (highest number), you need to adjust the pools to get them within a 20-point spread.

Adjusting the Pools

Finally, you are ready to adjust the pools. You know that you need to help a pool with a poor grade, and you need to get some help from the pools with the better grades. Should you adjust pool size or activity level? The dynamic performance adjust function will try to balance main storage first. But how much storage should you give to the pool with the poor grade? In other words, how much storage should you take from the pools with good grades?

The dynamic performance adjustment feature will start by trying to increase the size of the pool with the poor grade by 10 percent. Next, it needs to determine how much storage to take from the other pools. A sliding scale, shown in Table 4.2, is used. It is based on the amount of storage being used by jobs in the "good" pools. It's now merely a matter of changing the sizes of the pools.

Adjustment Example

An example will help put this algorithm into perspective. Start with the sizes and grades of *BASE, *INTERACT, and *SPOOL, as shown in Table 4.3.

You can see that *INTERACT is failing and needs some help because it has a grade that is at least 20 points worse (higher) than at least one other pool. It is at 2,000 Mb, so a 10 percent increase in its size would be 200 Mb. Assume that the active jobs in *BASE are using an average of 900 Kb each, and the

Table 4.2: Percentage of Storage Taken from Pools with Good Grades	
Amount of Storage per Active Job (Kb)	Percentage of Storage to Take
300 or less	5
301-600	6
601-1,200	7
1,201-2,000	8
2,001-3,000	9

jobs in *SPOOL are using 250 Kb. Using the information in Table 4.2, you can see that you will move 7 percent of *BASE (105 Mb) and 5 percent of *SPOOL (5 Mb), for a total of 110 Mb. The algorithm will not force itself to achieve the 10-percent increment that was calculated from the size of *INTERACT.

At the completion of the adjustment of the pool sizes, main storage is distributed as shown in Table 4.4. In another minute, you will have new grades for each of the pools and can determine if you have given enough storage to *INTERACT. If the

Table 4.3: Pool Sizes and Grades after Three Minutes of Observation		
Pool	Size (Mb)	Grade
*BASE	1,500	20
*INTERACT	2,000	70
*SPOOL	100	30

Table 4.4: Pool Sizes after Adjustments	
Pool	Size (Mb)
*BASE	1395
*INTERACT	2110
*SPOOL	95

next set of grades show that *INTERACT is still 20 or more points worse than at least one other pool, you'll need to move more storage from the pools with better grades. And so it goes, minute by minute, as long as QPFRADJ is set to two or three.

Managing the Performance Adjustment Function

While the dynamic performance adjustment function works quite well on its own for most workloads, there there are two basic methods of influence that you can impose on it:

1. Assign work to a private pool.

2. Use the WRKSHRPOOL display to customize the tuning to better suit your workload.

These methods are discussed in the following sections.

Assigning Work to a Private Pool

Perhaps the easiest way to influence the performance adjustment feature is to assign work to a private pool. As you recall from the discussion in chapter 1, a subsystem can assign work to either shared or private pools. The default subsystem descriptions all use shared pools. To change the pools from shared to private, you need to change the subsystem description, hold all job queues, complete all jobs in the subsystem (interactive users should sign off), and then release job queues and have interactive users sign back on. Once these actions have been completed, work will be running in a private pool.

A private pool's size and activity level can only be changed manually. The dynamic performance adjustment function will not change the attributes of a private pool. In addition to requiring observation and adjustment by an operator, there are several functional shortcomings of private pools. For example, the PAGING option, which is used to provide more efficient disk operations, is not available to private pools. A more detailed explanation of the benefits of PAGING appears later in this chapter.

Using WRKSHRPOOL to Customize Performance Adjustments

The second method for influencing the dynamic performance adjustment feature is to customize the parameters used to adjust the pool sizes. So far, you've only looked at the priority value for the pools in Figure 4.5. Now it's time to consider how the fields on this display can be used to customize the performance adjustments.

Priority

As indicated in the grade calculation, the priority of a pool is used to assign 10 bonus points to it. Currently, the display in Figure 4.5 shows the default values for each of the pools in a non-server model. However, when the system is shipped, there is no way to know what work is important and the pool where it is running. To adjust the bonus points for a pool, merely change the value of the priority to one (high) to assign 10 bonus points to the pool, or two (low) to assign no bonus points. By changing the priority of a pool, you can provide some minor direction to the performance adjustment function.

Size Percent—Maximum and Minimum

The values specified by the maximum and minimum size percent are designed to control the degree of main storage reassignment handled by the performance adjustment feature. First, specify the minimum amount of memory you would like allocated to a pool. This can be an important factor for performance in many situations. Here are two examples of situations where setting the minimum size of the pool will control main storage allocation to one or more pools and provide better system throughput:

- If jobs in the pool are not getting dispatched because higher-priority work is running, they might lose all of their allocated storage. When they finally get a chance to run, they spend all their time trying to get their information back into main storage. As a result, there will be an increase in I/O operations and faults in the pool. Eventually, the performance adjustment algorithm will recover and rebalance the main storage, but it might take a while, and the jobs will not progress very well.

- A pool might be dormant for a period of time, losing all of its main storage, only to return to activity and require all of the information to be reloaded into main storage. For example, a pool that is used by interactive users who perform a large number of interactions with the system might become dormant when the people entering the transactions leave for lunch. When they return and start entering information again, they will experience poor performance until the pool is allocated enough main storage to produce efficient transactions.

In both of these instances, you can preserve some of the information that these jobs were using by establishing a reasonable minimum size percent. As usual, what is reasonable depends on a number of factors, including the following:

- The number of jobs running in the pool.
- The importance of the performance of the jobs.
- The length of time it takes for performance to return to normal.
- The amount of space each of the jobs need.
- The length of the dormant period.

As you might have guessed, each situation will be different. The best approach is to establish a minimum percent that is one-quarter the normal percentage used when the workload is active. If this percent is too small (the jobs don't return to reasonable performance fast enough), increase the value to half the normal percentage used.

Consider an example of a system that has 64,000 Mb of main storage. During a normal workday, an interactive pool has an average size of 32,000 Mb of main storage. This represents 50 percent of the main storage available in the system, so the minimum size percent of the pool would be set to 12.5 (a quarter of 50 percent). Thus, when the interactive pool was dormant or less active, it would never have less than 8,000 Mb of main storage allocated to it. If this didn't work, you would increase the minimum size percent to 25 (half of 50 percent), and try again.

Now that you have the minimum size percent set the way you want it, it's time to look at the maximum size percent. The default value for the maximum amount of storage that can be assigned to the pool is 100 percent—an alarming amount. Assigning all of main storage to a single pool, even the machine pool, would certainly cause trouble in all of the other pools in the system. Remember the test-score example? If you were to allocate all of the available main storage to a single pool, it would be the same as putting students on a curve where one extremely high score (the dastardly curve wrecker) spelled doom for all of the other students. The one pool would eventually run really well, while all of the others had trouble. The dynamic performance adjust function would then need to go back and help the other pools that are in trouble. You can prevent this situation from occurring by setting the maximum size percent to something less than 100.

So how do you determine the correct value? Once again, there can be numerous factors to consider when you set the maximum size percent. You want the value to be larger than the normal workload size in order to handle the peak workloads that occur during the day. Let's set the maximum size percent at 1.25 times the normal size. In the previous example, you would set the maximum size percent to 62.5. This should handle most of the peak workloads likely to be encountered.

Once you have established these values, you should periodically monitor the effects of the dynamic performance adjustment function. If the workload increases, and the amount of main storage used in a normal period grows from 32,000 Mb to 36,000 Mb (56.25 percent of the main storage available) and stays there for several days, you might need to adjust the size percent values to 14 (minimum) and 70 (maximum). Finally, if several attempts fail to produce reasonable results in all of your pools, you might need to consider adding main storage to your system configuration.

Faults per Second—Minimum/Thread/Maximum

The next three values on the display allow you to specify faulting rates for the pools that are used to run your jobs. Before discussing modifications to these values, you should examine the origins of the default values for all of the pools except *MACHINE.

The minimum value represents paging that will occur in a pool no matter how large it becomes. As long as jobs are active, there will be paging. For interactive and spool pools, the minimum or base page-faulting rate is five. For pools that are running batch jobs, the minimum page-faulting rate is 10. In your environment, these base values might be different.

While it can be done, it is not easy to measure the base faulting rate. If you simply must determine what your base faulting rate is, you can do the following:

1. Pick a pool that interests you.

2. Add all available main storage to the pool. (Be prepared to handle calls from irate users in other pools.)

3. Measure the faults per second per thread for a few minutes (the fewer the better). Note that you must measure both the fault rate *and* the number of jobs actively running in the pool.

4. Once you have arrived at a value for the faults/thread/second, multiply the result by the number of active threads.

5. Multiply the number of threads by two.

6. Subtract the result in step 5 from the result in step 4. (Sounds like an income tax form!) This is your base faulting rate. If your jobs share a lot of objects, have very little job-unique data, and use much of the same data, you might have a negative result.

This process is not very easy, not very scientific, not very conclusive, and not a good exercise to try in most locations. Just use the default minimum paging values.

Next, focus on the faults that are occurring for each job (thread) in the pool. To derive a default value, the following rationale is used for interactive/server jobs:

1. Page faults are assumed to take 0.010 seconds of elapsed time (worst case).

2. Ten page faults for each transaction would result in 0.10 seconds of response. This is an acceptable paging overhead for these types of jobs.

3. Interactive and server jobs process a transaction every 20 seconds.

4. Ten faults in a 20-second period is 0.5 faults per second.

This rationale is used for batch jobs:

1. A single batch job running in a pool should be CPU-bound. That is, it should use approximately 88 percent of the CPU.

2. Since each page fault takes 0.010 seconds, or 1 percent of a second, 12 page faults for a batch job will result in 0.12 seconds, or 12 percent of a second.

3. The minimum page-fault rate in a batch pool is 10, so the faults per second per job (thread) is two. Note that the minimum page faults are counted for each of the batch jobs in the pool. That is, you do not need to add 10 faults to the minimum for each thread that is running.

These assumptions might not reflect the situation in your environment, but by modifying the values, you might be able to influence the tuning decisions made by the dynamic performance adjustment function.

Some goals, however, might not be achievable. For example, you could have an I/O-bound batch job that runs at 20 percent CPU utilization. Without rewriting the application and/or rearranging the data processed by the job, storage allocations alone will not produce a batch job that runs at 88 percent CPU utilization, regardless of the fault rates that we'd all like to see.

Finally, the third value represents the maximum number of page faults that you would like the pool to reach. The maximum value for the machine pool has been set equal to the minimum value. As you recall, the performance adjustment feature will try to deliver page faulting at less than 10 faults per second and has fixed maximum sizes to use (1.5 times the reserved size and four times the reserved size, respectively). So, the maximum page fault rate is not meaningful for this pool. To determine a value for the maximum number of page faults for the other pools, let's start with the total number of faults that a system can sustain. A very simple rule is to assume that each processor in your system can produce 100 page faults per second. Next, determine the percent of CPU that is used by jobs in each of the pools. You can obtain this information from the performance tools available with OS/400. Multiply the percent, expressed as a decimal (25% = 0.25), by the total number of faults to get the maximum page fault rates in each pool.

It's time for another example. Suppose you have a four-way processor that is running at 70 percent CPU busy. Using the performance tools, you can find the CPU use shown in Table 4.5. As a result of this calculation, you arrive at the maximum page faults in each of the pools.

	Table 4.5: Sample Calculation of Maximum Page-Fault Rate per Pool			
Pool	Measured CPU Percent of Jobs in the Pool	Percent of Total CPU Used by all Jobs (Measured Percent Divided by 70)	Decimal Equivalent of Column 3	Maximum Page Faults (Decimal Equivalent Times 400)
*BASE	14	20	0.2	80
*INTERACT	45.5	65	0.65	260
*SPOOL	3.5	5	0.05	20

WRKSHRPOOL *Customization*

The customization capability is designed to allow user input to the performance adjustment function. The first time you are presented with these capabilities, the task might seem daunting, and you'll be inclined to just accept the defaults. That's fine. The defaults are designed to deliver acceptable performance for a wide range of workloads. As a simple starting point for customization, use the values in Table 4.6.

	Table 4.6: Initial Customization Values for Tuning Shared Pools				
Pool	Minimum %	Maximum %	Minimum Faults	Faults per Job	Maximum Faults
*BASE	15	50	5	5	0.5 x 100 x Number of Processors
*INTERACT	50	80	15	0.5	0.7 x 100 x Number of Processors
*SPOOL	1	5	5	1	20

Further customization should be done only after you have noticed throughput variances that are introduced by overaggressive actions by the performance adjustment algorithms. Also, using the customization features is a better alternative than disabling the performance adjustment function. When you start to customize these values, make small adjustments, and measure the effects of each change. Do not be discouraged if the results that you want are not achieved on your first attempt. As the saying goes, "If at first you don't succeed, try and try again."

Getting Help from Main Storage Management

Once the shared pool tuning parameters have been customized, another modification can improve efficiency in shared pools: adjusting the algorithms that main storage management uses to transfer pages into your pools. The adjustments made to these algorithms are designed to reduce the number of I/O operations taking place in each of your pools. Changes to the algorithm are very simple to make, take place immediately, and usually provide benefit in both interactive and batch pools. As with the performance adjustment function, the changes to these algorithms can be activated only for shared pools. Let's start by returning to the WRKSHRPOOL display, shown in Figure 4.6.

```
                    Work with Shared Pools
                                              System:   TSCSAP01
Main storage size (M)  . :        4352.00

Type changes (if allowed), press Enter.

              Defined   Max   Allocated   Pool  -Paging Option-
Pool          Size (M)  Active Size (M)    ID   Defined  Current
*MACHINE       325.00   +++++     325.00    1   *FIXED   *FIXED
*BASE         1283.50       4    1283.50    2   *FIXED   *FIXED
*INTERACT     2700.00     197    2700.00    3   *FIXED   *FIXED
*SPOOL          43.50       1      43.50    4   *FIXED   *FIXED
*SHRPOOL1         .00       0                   *FIXED
*SHRPOOL2         .00       0                   *FIXED
*SHRPOOL3         .00       0                   *FIXED
*SHRPOOL4         .00       0                   *FIXED
*SHRPOOL5         .00       0                   *FIXED
*SHRPOOL6         .00       0                   *FIXED
                                                              More...
Command
===>
F3=Exit   F4=Prompt   F5=Refresh   F9=Retrieve   F11=Display tuning data
F12=Cancel
```

Figure 4.6: The Work with Shared Pools Display shows the paging option for all of the shared pools.

Look at the last two columns: defined and current paging options. The value specified for the paging option defines the algorithm to be used by main storage management.

Paging Option—*FIXED

The default value for the paging option is *FIXED. When this option is in effect, main storage management will use its traditional algorithms. It will retrieve pages only when they are requested, transfer small amounts of information from disk to main storage, and limit the amount of space used to cache database pages in memory. This algorithm works fine if there is a shortage of main storage in the pools running the jobs, that is, the page faults are fairly high. However, since the algorithm was developed when there was much less main storage, you might not be using your main storage effectively.

Paging Option—*CALC

Setting the paging option for a shared pool to *CALC allows main storage management to analyze references to objects in the pool. The analysis is done for each pool that has *CALC specified. As your jobs reference information, one of four reference patterns will be detected, and main storage management will use the reference pattern information to make adjustments:

1. References are completely random within the objects being used—no adjustments will be made to transfers from disk.

2. References are sequential within an object—larger blocks of information will be transferred from disk each time a request is made. In addition, more of the object will be cached in main storage.

3. Several references are made to a block of information that is read from disk—larger blocks of information will be transferred from disk for each request.

4. Continual references to a portion of an object cause the object to remain in main storage for a long period of time—future requests for information from this type of object will produce large transfers from disk. In addition, if the pages that are being used heavily are being

changed, they will be written to disk periodically in order to save their contents in the unlikely event of a system failure.

The entire time that main storage management is making adjustments to the transfers from disk, it continues to monitor the page faulting in the pool. If the page fault rate in the pool begins to get too high (determined by main storage management algorithms), the blocking factors will be reduced. The best part of using *CALC is that all of the analysis is done by the system without any work on your part (other than to change the paging option to *CALC). *CALC should be specified for all shared pools.

Paging Option—USRDFN

When you select USRDFN, you must use the QUSCHGPA and QWCCHGTN APIs to set the paging parameters that you would like main storage management to use when it retrieves information from disk. To use these APIs, you need to understand the fundamentals of main storage management. A discussion of these issues is beyond the scope of this book, and *USRDFN is not a recommended value for the paging option.

Paging Option—Defined and Current

Finally, notice that there are two columns under the paging option: Defined and Current. When you set the paging option for a shared pool, you are setting the *defined* value for this parameter. Typically, the current value will be the same as the defined value. However, if you have set the paging option to *USRDFN and are using the APIs to change the paging option from *FIXED to *CALC or vice versa, the defined value will be *USRDFN, and the current value will reflect the setting specified on your most recent use of the QUSCHGPA API.

In Review

You've reached the end of another information-heavy chapter. It might seem like a long time ago when you started the discussion of the WRKSYSSTS display. The following are some of the key points of this chapter:

1. A job's efficiency depends on the number of page faults that occur in the job's pool and the *MACHINE pool.

2. You can adjust the page faulting in a pool by reducing the number of jobs in a pool at the same time (using Max Active) or by increasing the amount of main storage in a pool.

3. Adjustments to pools can be done manually or automatically via the QPFRADJ system value.

4. The parameters used by QPFRADJ can be customized using the WRKSHRPOOL displays.

5. The main storage management algorithms can provide better paging characteristics in a pool by specifying *CALC for the paging option on all shared pools.

6. Once again, additional detail is provided in this chapter to help you better understand the processes used to manage the contents of and paging in a pool. With this information, you will be able to establish parameters that can be used by the system functions to manage the pool performance of your environment and free you from the drudgery of doing it yourself.

5

More About Starting, Stopping, and Managing Jobs

Chapter 2 covers the basic subsystem elements regarding the initiation of jobs. That chapter explains the defaults for the subsystems and the jobs, but nothing about what happens when a job ends. This chapter provides additional information about job initiation, completion, and management beyond the basic defaults provided by OS/400.

Job Initiation Revisited

The system defaults make it possible for you to run your environment without any knowledge of work management, but they aren't necessarily correct for all situations. In addition, the displays they present to the end user can be rather cold and, sometimes, ugly. This section describes ways to modify your sign-on screen, provid an initial menu, and make several other modifications to job initiation.

Requiring a Sign-on Password

As you might recall from earlier chapters, the job-initiation process finds work by adding job queue entries and workstation entries to your subsystems. These entries allow you to find sources of work and initiate jobs from these sources. In the case of interactive jobs, the workstation entry provides the name of the job description. The default is to use the job description specified by the user profile.

So far, so good. However, look at the USER parameter of the job description in Figure 5.1. Notice that you can either place a user profile name in this parameter or specify *RQD. If you specify a user name, anyone can walk up to a workstation with a sign-on screen displayed, press the Enter key, and have all the privileges of the person specified by the USER parameter! This could present serious security issues for you. Fortunately, it only works when the QSECURITY system value is set to 10 (no security). More fortunately, systems have been shipped with the system value set to 40 for a long time. Even more fortunately, you have not been able to change the system value to 10 for a long time. Therefore, the likelihood of ever seeing this situation is very, very small.

```
                       Create Job Description (CRTJOBD)


  Type choices, press Enter.

  Job description . . . . . . . JOBD        > NEWJOBD
    Library . . . . . . . . . .               *CURLIB
  Job queue . . . . . . . . . . JOBQ        QBATCH
    Library . . . . . . . . . .               *LIBL
  Job priority (on JOBQ) . . . . JOBPTY     5
  Output priority (on OUTQ) . . OUTPTY      5
  Print device . . . . . . . . . PRTDEV     *USRPRF
  Output queue . . . . . . . . . OUTQ       *USRPRF
    Library . . . . . . . . . .
  Text 'description' . . . . . . TEXT       *BLANK

                         Additional Parameters

  User . . . . . . . . . . . . . USER        *RQD
```

Figure 5.1: The USER parameter of a job description is used to require a user name and password to sign on to the system.

On the other hand, if you specify *RQD for the USER parameter of the job description, the user *must* enter a user name and password to access the system. That's a lot better. In addition, once you have required a user name and password, you can customize work management for any of your users.

Modifying the Sign-on Screen

When a subsystem finds a varied-on workstation matching one of its workstation entries, it sends the sign-on display to the workstation. The default sign-on display is QDSIGNON in library QSYS. It looks like Figure 5.2.

```
                        Sign On
                                        System  . . . . . :  TSCSAP02
                                        Subsystem . . . . :  QINTER
                                        Display . . . . . :  QPADEV0024

             User . . . . . . . . . . . . . .   _____
             Password . . . . . . . . . . .     _____
             Program/procedure . . . . . . .    _____
             Menu . . . . . . . . . . . . .     _____
             Current library . . . . . . . .    _____
```

Figure 5.2: This display shows the standard sign-on screen that is shipped with OS/400.

Wow! Just takes your breath away, doesn't it? Clearly not. You'd probably like something customized, maybe with your company name and a welcome message. Also, you don't need to burden your users with the PROGRAM/PROCEDURE, MENU, and CURRENT LIBRARY fields. Consider how you can customize the sign-on screen to be better looking and more friendly than the system default.

First, you need to locate the source for the display. As of Version 5, Release 1.0 of OS/400, there arc two different sign-on screens available—one for passwords that can be up to 10 characters long and the other for passwords that can be up to 128 characters long. Use the sign-on screen that supports only shorter passwords. It is found in member QDSIGNON in the file QAWTSSRC in library QSYS. (The 128-character password version, the source is located in QDSIGNON2 in the file QAWTSSRC in library QSYS.) If you are working on a system that does not have Version 5, Release 1.0 installed, only the 10-character password is supported, and the source is found in member QDSIGNON in the file QDDSSRC in library QGPL. Figure 5.3 shows the code for the 10-character password screen.

```
A* START OF SPECIFICATIONS    ***********************************
A*                                                              *
A* PHYSICAL FILE MEMBER NAME:  QDSIGNON                         *
A*                                                              *
A*  END OF SPECIFICATIONS    ***********************************
A****************************************************************
A*                                                              *
A* RECORD FORMAT - NAME: SIGNON                                 *
A*              FUNCTION: SIGN ON DISPLAY                       *
A*              INDICATORS USED: 01 02                          *
A*              FUNCTION KEYS USED: NONE                        *
A*              NUMBER OF I/O FIELDS:  11                       *
```

Figure 5.3: The source code shown produces the 10-character password sign-on screen that is shipped with OS/400. (Part 1 of 2)

```
A*                  KEYWORDS USED: DSPATR CHGINPDFT CLEAR       *
A*                                 CHECK                        *
A*                                                             *
A*************************************************************************
A*
A           R SIGNON
A                                             CLEAR
A                                             BLINK
A                                          1 23'             Sign On            '
A                                             DSPATR(HI)
A                                          2 48'System . . . . . . :'
A             SYSNAME        8A   O  2 70
A                                          3 48'Subsystem . . . . . :'
A             SBSNAME       10A   O  3 70
A                                          4 48'Display . . . . . . :'
A             DEVNAME       10A   O  4 70
A                                          6 17'User . . . . . . . . . . . . . '
A             USERID        10A   B  6 53
A   01                                     7 17'Password . . . . . . . . . . . '
A   01        PASSWRD       10A   I  7 53DSPATR(ND)
A                                          8 17'Program/procedure . . . . . . . '
A             PROGRAM       10A   B  8 53CHECK(LC)
A                                          9 17'Menu . . . . . . . . . . . . . '
A             MENU          10A   B  9 53CHECK(LC)
A                                         10 17'Current library . . . . . . . . '
A             CURLIB        10A   B 10 53CHECK(LC)
A   02        QSNERROR      80A   O 24  1DSPATR(HI)
A             COPYRIGHT     40A   O 24 40DSPATR(HI)
A             UBUFFER      128A   H
```

Figure 5.3: The source code shown produces the 10-character password sign-on screen that is shipped with OS/400. (Part 2 of 2)

The first thing to do when modifying the sign-on is to design the new display. Because you are dealing with non-intelligent stations (green screens), there is not too much that you can do, but at least you can hide some of the fields from the user and provide a greeting. Design a display screen that looks similar to the one in Figure 5.4. It's still not wonderful, but at least you've provided a friendly greeting and eliminated the unnecessary information.

```
                                      System  . . . . . :   TSCSAP02
                                      Subsystem . . . . :   QINTER
                                      Display . . . . . :   QPADEV0024

  W       W  EEEEE  L     CCC   000   M   M  EEEEE      TTTTT  000
  W       W  E      L    C     O   O  MM MM  E            T   0   0
  W   W   W  EEE    L    C     O   O  M M M  EEE          T   0   0
  W  W W  W  E      L    C     O   O  M   M  E            T   0   0
   W     W   EEEEE  LLLL  CCC   000   M   M  EEEEE        T      000

   TTTTT  H   H  EEEEE    H   H   000    M   M  EEEEE
     T    H   H  E        H   H  O   O   MM MM  E
     T    HHHHH  EEE      HHHHH  O   O   M M M  EEE
     T    H   H  E        H   H  O   O   M   M  E
     T    H   H  EEEEE    H   H   000    M   M  EEEEE

        Please Enter Your User Name and Password:
        User Name . . . . . . . . . . .   _____
        Password  . . . . . . . . . .
```

Figure 5.4: This is the sign-on screen your interactive users should see.

Once you have completed the design of the screen, you need to return to the QDSIGNON source and change it. Before you make any changes to the source, however, it is a good idea to copy it to another member and modify the copy. Copy the 10-character password source from its shipped location to member OURSIGNON in file QDDSSRC in library QGPL. Then, using your new sign-on display, modify the source in OURSIGNON as shown in Figure 5.5. It might not be a lot of fun, but your users will appreciate your efforts.

```
A*   START OF SPECIFICATIONS     *********************************
A*                                                               *
A* PHYSICAL FILE MEMBER NAME:   OURSIGNON                        *
A*                                                               *
A*   END OF SPECIFICATIONS     **********************************
A***************************************************************
A*   RECORD FORMAT - NAME: SIGNON                               *
A*               FUNCTION: SIGN ON DISPLAY                       *
A*               INDICATORS USED: 01 02                          *
A*               FUNCTION KEYS USED: NONE                        *
A*               NUMBER OF I/O FIELDS:  11                       *
A*               KEYWORDS USED: DSPATR CHGINPDFT CLEAR           *
A*                              CHECK                            *
A***************************************************************
A          R SIGNON
A                                        CLEAR
A                                        BLINK
A                                        DSPATR(HI)
A                                    1 48'System  . . . . . :'
```

Figure 5.5: Modify the source in OURSIGNON to create the screen in Figure 5.4. (Part 1 of 2)

```
A               SYSNAME     8A  O  1 70
A                                  2 48'Subsystem . . . . :'
A               SBSNAME    10A  O  2 70
A                                  3 48'Display . . . . . :'
A               DEVNAME    10A  O  3 70
A                                 19 17'User . . . . . . . . . . . . . .'
A               USERID     10A  B 19 53
A  01                             20 17'Password . . . . . . . . . . . .'
A  01           PASSWRD    10A  I 20 53DSPATR(ND)
A                                 21 17'Program/procedure . . . . . . . .'
A               PROGRAM    10A  H 21 53CHECK(LC)
A                          H  22 17'Menu . . . . . . . . . . . . . .'
A               MENU       10A  H 22 53CHECK(LC)
A                          H  23 17'Current library . . . . . . . . .'
A               CURLIB     10A  H 23 53CHECK(LC)
A  02           QSNERROR   80A  O 24  1DSPATR(HI)
A               COPYRIGHT  40A  O 24 40DSPATR(HI)
A               UBUFFER   128A  H
A                                  5  5'W        W  EEEEE L     CCC    000'
A                                  6  5'W        W  E     L    C      0   0'
A                                  7  5' W  W  W  EEE   L    C      0   0'
A                                  8  5' W W W W E     L    C      0   0'
A                                  9  5'  W    W  EEEEE LLLL  CCC    000'
A                                  5 40'M    M  EEEEE       TTTTT   000'
A                                  6 40'MM MM  E              T    0   0'
A                                  7 40'M M M  EEE            T    0   0'
A                                  8 40'M   M  E              T    0   0'
A                                  9 40'M   M  EEEEE          T      000'
A                                 11 13'TTTTT  H   H  EEEEE'
A                                 12 13'  T    H   H  E'
A                                 13 13'  T    HHHHH  EEE'
A                                 14 13'  T    H   H  E'
A                                 15 13'  T    H   H  EEEEE'
A                                 11 37'H   H   000  M   M  EEEEE'
A                                 12 37'H   H  0   0 MM MM  E'
A                                 13 37'HHHHH  0   0 M M M  EEE'
A                                 14 37'H   H  0   0 M   M  E'
A                                 15 37'H   H   000  M   M  EEEEE'
A                                 17 18'Please Enter Your User Name'
A                                 17 46'and Password'
```

Figure 5.5: Modify the source in OURSIGNON to create the screen in Figure 5.4. (Part 2 of 2)

Before you create the new sign-on display file, there are a couple of things to point out:

- Although you have removed unnecessary information from the display, the fields are still there; they're just described as hidden (H in column 38). The information retrieved from the sign-on display is placed in a buffer in the order defined in your display file. The system program that processes the sign-on information requires that these fields be included in the buffer. Therefore, you must still define them on your display.

- The fields in your source file, such as user name and password, must be described in the order shown. If you alter their position in the source file, the fields will appear in a different position in the buffer. The sign-on processing program will not like this, and the results of your sign-on will be unpredictable.

- While the fields must appear in the proper sequence in the display file, they may be placed on the screen in any order. For example, the menu field could be placed on line 1 and be hidden from the user. Just re-member, the order of the fields maps the buffer used by the sign-on program, while the location is used to position the fields on the display.

Now you're ready to create a new display file from the revised source. Don't re-place the system display file QDSIGNON in library QSYS, however. Instead, create a new sign-on display in a test library using the Create Display File command (CRTDSPF):

```
CRTDSPF FILE(TESTLIB/OURSIGNON) SRCFILE(QGPL/QDDSSRC) SRCMBR(OURSIGNON)
```

You need to test your new sign-on display to prevent problems for your users. To do this, create a test subsystem description with only your display in it. To set this subsystem up, run the following commands:

```
CRTSBSD SBSD(TEST) POOLS((1 *BASE)) SGNDSPF(TESTLIB/OURSIGNON)
ADDWSE  SBSD(TEST) WRKSTN(MYDISP)
ADDRTGE SBSD(TEST) SEQNBR(10) CMPVAL('QCMDI') CLS(*LIBL/QINTER)
```

Next, sign off your workstation, and find another workstation to sign on. When you have signed on, start the test subsystem with the Start Subsystem command (STRSBS):

```
STRSBS TEST
```

You should see a new sign-on display at your original workstation. Sign on to the system at your original workstation. Run a few tests to make sure it works.

After you are satisfied that your new sign-on display is working the way you want, you can replace the QDSIGNON display file in QSYS with your new display. Now, when a subsystem locates a workstation that is varied on and powered on, it will display the new sign-on screen. The user will only see fields that require input and not be confused by extraneous prompts.

Improving the Initial User Display

Now that you have improved the sign-on, consider the first default display that a user will see after sign-on, as shown in Figure 5.6. This display has two major problems:

- It does not provide any clear direction for the user. For example, how do you get to the order-entry program? What other applications are available? A user who moves from one job to another will need to learn new applications to access and the methods required to access them.

- It provides menu choices that are not needed by most users. For example, option 5, Programming, is used by programmers; an end user wouldn't want to access it, and shouldn't be able to. Allowing users access to some of these functions could compromise the security of your system.

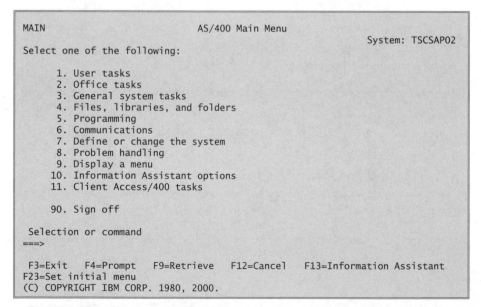

```
 MAIN                        AS/400 Main Menu
                                                        System: TSCSAP02
 Select one of the following:

         1. User tasks
         2. Office tasks
         3. General system tasks
         4. Files, libraries, and folders
         5. Programming
         6. Communications
         7. Define or change the system
         8. Problem handling
         9. Display a menu
        10. Information Assistant options
        11. Client Access/400 tasks

        90. Sign off

  Selection or command
  ===>

  F3=Exit   F4=Prompt   F9=Retrieve   F12=Cancel   F13=Information Assistant
  F23=Set initial menu
  (C) COPYRIGHT IBM CORP. 1980, 2000.
```

Figure 5.6: The main menu is the first display seen by the user after sign-on.

To display a more meaningful screen to your users, you need to be able to change the first program that is run when your job is initiated. Several methods can be used to provide this function. All of the methods require a modification to the default job description or the specification of a unique job description.

Modifying the Routing Entry Used by a Job

A simple method to change the initial program is to modify the routing entry used when the job is initiated by the subsystem. Take a look at the default routing entry for interactive jobs, shown in Figure 5.7.

```
                      Display Routing Entry Detail
                                                  System:    TSCSAP02
       Subsystem description:    QBASE         Status:    ACTIVE

   Routing entry sequence number . . . . . . . :    50
   Program . . . . . . . . . . . . . . . . . . :    QCMD
   Library . . . . . . . . . . . . . . . . . . :    QSYS
   Class . . . . . . . . . . . . . . . . . . . :    QINTER
   Library . . . . . . . . . . . . . . . . . . :    QGPL
   Maximum active routing steps  . . . . . . . :    *NOMAX
   Pool identifier . . . . . . . . . . . . . . :    2
   Compare value . . . . . . . . . . . . . . . :    'QCMDI'

   Compare start position  . . . . . . . . . . :    1
```

Figure 5.7: This is the detail information for the IBM-supplied interactive job routing entry in QBASE.

Notice that the initial program is specified as QCMD. To get a different program to run when the job is initiated, just change the routing entry. For example, if you want all of your users to see the main application menu for your location, you can run the following command:

```
CHGRTGE SBSD(QBASE) SEQNBR(50) PGM(MNUPGM)
```

Currently, any user who signs on to a workstation sees the same display. If you'd like different users to see different menus, using this method becomes more complex. For each of your different initial programs, you need to run the following commands:

```
ADDRTGE QBASE SEQNBR(xxx) CMPVAL('MNUnn') PGM(DSPMNUnn) POOLID(2)
        CRTJOBD JOBD(USERnn) USER(*RQD) RTGDTA('MNUnn')
```

Make the following modifications to these code lines:

- Replace SEQNBR(XXX) with a unique sequence number for each entry you add.

- Replace the *nn* suffix in CMPVAL and the PGM in the ADDRTGE command, as well as the JOBD and RTGDTA parameters in CRTJOBD, with the same two digits.

For example, to create three unique initial user programs, run these commands:

```
ADDRTGE QBASE SEQNBR(120) CMPVAL('MNU01') PGM(DSPMNU01) POOLID(2)
        CRTJOBD JOBD(USER01) USER(*RQD) RTGDTA('MNU01')
ADDRTGE QBASE SEQNBR(130) CMPVAL('MNU02') PGM(DSPMNU02) POOLID(2)
        CRTJOBD JOBD(USER02) USER(*RQD) RTGDTA('MNU02')
ADDRTGE QBASE SEQNBR(140) CMPVAL('MNU03') PGM(DSPMNU03) POOLID(2)
        CRTJOBD JOBD(USER03) USER(*RQD) RTGDTA('MNU03')
```

You need to make one final adjustment. In keeping with work management's flexibility theme, there are two ways to make it:

- Create user profiles for each user, and specify the appropriate job description for him or her.

- Create a workstation entry by name for each of the workstations that are to run a unique initial program.

After you've made the last adjustment, you have jobs that will have different initial programs.

Look at your job initialization diagram with your changes using both methods. First, consider the additional routing entries, job descriptions, and user profiles. Because you've already created the routing entries and job descriptions, all you need to do is create the user profiles for your three users, with the Create User Profile command (CRTUSRPRF):

```
CRTUSRPRF USER01 JOBD(USER01)
CRTUSRPRF USER02 JOBD(USER02)
CRTUSRPRF USER03 JOBD(USER03)
```

The result of running the commands is shown in Figure 5.8. In this case, when a user signs on to a workstation, the user profile is used to locate a job description, which specifies the routing data that is used to find the routing entry containing the initial program to be run.

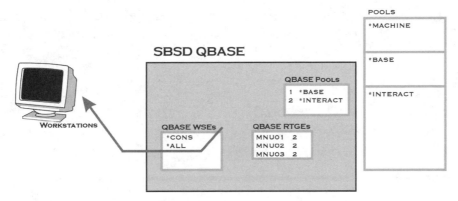

Figure 5.8: Three new routing entries in QBASE, each with a different initial program, are used to show different menus to users when they sign on to the system.

Before looking at the second method, review the structure of the subsystem. Remember, as a default, the only workstation entries are by type, as shown in Figure 5.9. However, the subsystem also lets you specify workstation entries by name. To create a workstation entry by name, run the following commands:

```
ADDWSE QBASE WRKSTN(USER01) JOBD(USER01)
ADDWSE QBASE WRKSTN(USER02) JOBD(USER02)
ADDWSE QBASE WRKSTN(USER03) JOBD(USER03)
```

Whenever a user signs on to one of the three workstations identified by the name entries, he or she will use the job description associated with the appropriate workstation name entry which will link them to the correct routing entry. The complete picture of the method is shown in Figure 5.10.

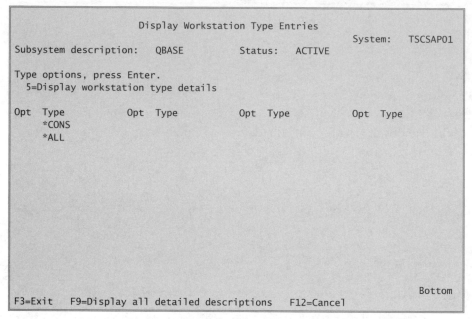

Figure 5.9: *This display shows the workstation type entries that are shipped with QBASE.*

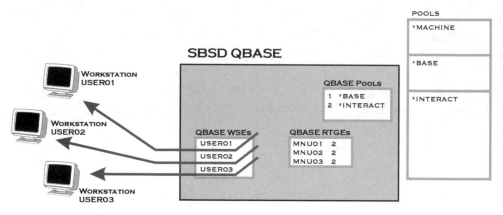

Figure 5.10: *QBASE has been modified to use three workstation name entries that specify different job descriptions, so that the correct routing entry is selected when a user signs on to the system.*

Now your subsystem recognizes each of the named workstations and sends a sign-on screen to the display. Any user who signs on to one of these workstations must supply a user ID and a password. When the sign-on is processed by the subsystem, it will use the workstation entry by name to find the job description, which will supply the routing data to locate the routing entry, which will, in turn, run the initial program. As you can see, the process of job initiation is like a treasure hunt—you are given an initial clue to a location, where you find another clue, until you finally find the treasure.

Neither of these two job-initiation methods is particular difficult, just time-consuming. There is, however, a subtle difference: the first method recognizes the user who is starting a job, while the second recognizes the workstation being used to start the job. Since users are not necessarily restricted to specific workstations, multiple users can use the same workstation, and you have probably created separate user profiles for security reasons, the first approach is usually the best way to complete this method of customization.

Specifying Unique Routing Data

Consider another method to customize the initial program for a job. In using this method, you will modify the job description's request data to call the initial program. Continuing the preceding example, assume that you'd like to have all users for job description USER01 have the DSPMNU01 program be the initial program, regardless of the program specified on the routing entry used to start the job. In this case, create the USER01 job description differently:

```
CRTJOBD JOBD(USER01) USER(*RQD) RQSDTA('CALL DSPMNU01') RTGDTA(QCMDI)
```

As in the preceding case, you need to provide unique user profiles or workstation entries to run different initial programs.

When the job is started, you will find the routing entry in the subsystem that matches QCMDI. Rather than run the initial program shown on the routing entry, however, the RQSDTA from the job description will be used to run DSPMNU01. The technique of specifying RQSDTA to indicate the initial program is used mostly to start batch jobs. This method is revisited in the next chapter, in the discussion on batch job initiation.

Specifying an Initial Program in a User Profile

It is a good idea to have individual user profiles on the system. While the primary reason is for security purposes, you have also seen that you can use these profiles to customize interaction with the iSeries400. In this and the next example of customization, you will take advantage of your user profiles. In the previous two examples, you might have needed to make numerous changes to your operating environment to customize your initiation process. There is a much easier way to specify a different initial program. Simply run the following command:

```
CHGUSRPRF USER01 INLPGM(DSPMNU01) INLMNU(*SIGNOFF)
```

In this case, none of the shipped defaults need to be changed. You need to create profiles only for each of your users, and specify an initial program for them.

There are a few things to be aware of when using this procedure:

- QSYS/QCMD should be specified as the initial program on the routing entry. When QSYS/QCMD is specified, the system will automatically detect the initial program in the user profile and call it. If a different initial program is specified in the routing entry, the system will only call the initial program in the routing entry. If you would like the routing entry program to call the initial program specified in the user profile, the routing entry program must retrieve the user profile information with the RTVUSRPRF command, determine if an initial program is specified, and call the program. It's a lot easier to just use QSYS/QCMD.

- Since *SIGNOFF is specified in the INLMNU parameter, when the initial program ends, the sign-on screen will be displayed.

- If the initial program does not end, it will remain active until the system ends or the job is ended.

As you can see, this is a simple but effective method of customizing the initial program that runs when a user signs on to a workstation.

Specifying an Initial Menu and an Initial Program

One final customization is to provide both an initial menu and an initial program in the user profile:

```
CHGUSRPRF USER01 INLPGM(DSPPGM01) INLMNU(DSPMNU01)
```

If QSYS/QCMD is specified as the initial program in the routing entry, the initial program, DSPPGM01, will be called, and the initial menu, DSPMNU01, will be automatically displayed by the system. As in the previous method, any other routing-entry initial program must retrieve the user profile information to call DSPPGM01 and display DSPMNU01. Also, the menu continues to be displayed until the user signs off. Just ending DSPPGM01 will not remove the DSPMNU01 display. Most programs that use this approach provide a sign-off option on the initial menu.

Job Initiation Customization Summary

Presenting a friendlier and less error-prone interface to your end users is very important. The system defaults do not provide either. Requiring a user name and password, creating individual user profiles, modifying the sign-on screen, and providing a customized initial menu/program can be used to accomplish these goals.

Methods for Ending Interactive Jobs

Once you have jobs started, you need to be able to end them whenever you have completed work for the day. There are many methods for ending interactive jobs, some good, some not so good. Simply stated, jobs either end normally (good) or abnormally (not so good). This section focuses primarily on jobs that end normally. First, however, take a look at jobs that end abnormally.

Abnormal Job End

As you might have guessed, jobs that end abnormally are usually the result of some type of error, such as the following:

- The program the user is running receives an exception and fails to handle it.

- The communication line or LAN used to connect the workstation to the system fails.

- The job is ended or cancelled from the WRKACTJOB display or by running a command.

- The workstation running the job becomes unplugged.

- The user, after waiting an extended period of time for a response, takes the typical action for any electronic device that appears to be inoperative: turn it off and on to "reset" it.

These are just some of the typical situations that result in the abnormal ending of a job. One thing all abnormal job ends have in common is extensive use of system resources to end the job. These resources are used to record the error, attempt to recover the device, write a JOBLOG, dump information that might be useful to analyze the problem, etc. It is a good idea to limit the number of jobs that end abnormally in order to avoid momentary performance situations in your environment.

Normal Job End

As with abnormal job ends, there are many ways to end a job normally, including these:

- A user signs off the workstation.
- The initial program ends and *SIGNON is specified as the initial menu.
- An End Connection command (ENDCNN) is run.

When a job ends normally, there is far less system overhead than for an abnormal end. In addition, once the sign-on screen is displayed at a workstation, turning the device off will not have an adverse affect on system resource usage.

Disconnecting a Job—Almost an End

If users running jobs are called away or leave for lunch, you might not want to end and restart all of their jobs because it uses a lot of system resources and takes a fair amount of time. Instead, you might want the user jobs to remain active, with the users disconnected from the jobs. When you disconnect a user from a job, the job remains active, but a sign-on screen appears on the user's workstation. When users return to their workstations and sign on, they are notified that they are disconnected from their active jobs and are given an opportunity to resume running the original jobs. If a different user returns to a workstation with a disconnected job, a new job will be started.

The easiest way to disconnect a job is to provide a menu option for users to select. Since most users would be unfamiliar with the meaning of "Disconnect Job," some other term should be used for the menu option. For example, the menu option might read, "Bye for Now, Returning Later." When a user selects this option, the Disconnect Job command (DSCJOB) is run. You can take the defaults for all of the parameters of the DSCJOB, so all you need to code is this:

```
DSCJOB
```

After the user has been disconnected from the job, the job will remain active until the user returns. While this presents no security risk unless multiple users have the same profile, it might lead to a large number of orphaned jobs in the system. To prevent this, the QDSCJOBITV system value ends disconnected jobs that are not reactivated. QDSCJOBITV specifies the amount of time in minutes that a disconnected job can be unused. When the time limit has been used, the job will end.

Rather than complicate users' lives with a choice of disconnecting or signing off, you can use QDSCJOBITV to simplify things. Provide only one menu option, "Sign Off." When the user selects this option, run the Disconnect Job command. When the QDSCJOBITV time is reached, the job will be ended. A user returning before the interval expires will be reconnected to the previous job. Thus, you get the benefits of reduced sign-off/sign-on activity and still have a secure operating environment.

Suppose, though, that a user leaves a workstation without disconnecting from the job for what is supposed to be a short break and doesn't return for an hour or more. The job will remain active, creating potential security exposure—any user could walk up to the workstation and begin exploring. Situations like this can be handled by the system values QINACTITV and QINACTMSGQ. QINACTITV specifies the length of time that a workstation can be inactive, that is, have no interaction between the workstation and the running job. QINACTMSGQ specifies the action to be taken if the inactive time limit is reached. Setting QINACTMSGQ to *DSCJOB causes an inactive user workstation to be disconnected from the job that it is running. Then, the job will remain active until the QDSCJOBITV value is reached. You can use a small value for QINACTITV to limit the amount of time that an active workstation can be left unattended, and a larger value for QDSCJOBITV to reduce the sign-off/sign-on overhead.

Reducing the Impact of Communication Line Failures

One of the situations that can cause a job to end abnormally is a communication line or LAN failure. Usually, this type of failure affects more than one job—

actually, it can affect a whole lot of jobs. When many jobs fail at the same time, the system usually goes into a tailspin trying to recover all the failed devices and trying to end all of the jobs at the same time. You must avoid these problems.

If you look at the attributes of your jobs, you will see a parameter in the job description called Device Recovery Action (DEVRCYACN). DEVRCYACN has several possible settings, listed in Table 5.1.

Table 5.1: DEVRCYACN Values	
Setting	**Meaning**
*SYSVAL	The action for the job is obtained from the system value QDEVRCYACN. This is the default for the DEVRCYACN attribute.
*MSG	An error message is sent to the application. It is up to the application to handle the message. This is the default for the QDEVRCYACN system value.
*DSCMSG	The failing workstation is disconnected from the job. When, the workstation is recovered, and the user signs on, the program will be sent a message. The program can reconnect to the previous job.
*DSCENDRQS	The failing workstation is disconnected. When the workstation is recovered and the user signs on, the job is reconnected, but the last request level is cancelled.
*ENDJOB	The job is ended and a job log is produced. In addition, a message is placed in the job log and in QHST, indicating that the job ended due to a device failure.
*ENDJOBNOLIST	The job is ended and a job log is not produced. A message is placed in QHST indicating that the job ended due to a device failure.

*SYSVAL and *MSG will not reduce the overhead at all, but any of the other four parameters can be used to reduce overhead. *ENDJOBNOLIST produces the least amount of overhead. Regardless of the DEVRCYACN value, the system tries to limit the impact of the ending jobs by

- Lowering the RUNPTY to allow jobs that are still running a better chance to use the CPU.

- Reducing the timeslice value to prevent failing jobs from using too much CPU when they do get a chance to run.

- Setting the purge attribute to *YES to allow a failing job's pages to be replaced more quickly. (This action is not meaningful after Version 4, Release 4 of OS/400.)

You do not need to take action to enable these functions.

Job Logs

When jobs are running on the system, information regarding each job's activities is being generated. This information is stored in the job log. The type of information placed in the job log includes the following:

- Messages.
- Commands run by the job.
- Commands run by a CL program in the job in either of the following cases:

    ➤ LOG(*YES) is specified when the Create CL Program command (CRTCLPGM) is run.

    ➤ LOG(*JOB) is specified when the CRTCLPGM command is run, and the Change Job command (CHGJOB) is run with the Log CL Program parameter (LOGCLPGM) set to *YES.

When the job ends, job logs may be produced. When job logs are produced, they are usually spooled to the joblog output queue. If you do not periodically remove old job logs, your system will become cluttered, you'll lose disk space, and you might have performance issues for certain system operations. The following sections describe some actions you can take to reduce the number and content of your job logs.

Reducing the Amount of Information in a Job Log

The more information is written into a job log, the longer the job takes, and the more space the log uses. Once again, look at your job descriptions. Notice that there is a parameter on the job description called LOG.

The LOG parameter describes to the system the level of information sent to the job log. LOG has three values that can be specified: message level, message severity, and message text. Let's take a look at these three values in more detail.

Message Level

The first part of the log parameter filters the type of information sent to the job log. There are five possible values for this parameter, listed in Table 5.2.

Table 5.2: Message Level Values	
Value	**Meaning**
0	No data is placed in the job log. A job log will not be produced by this job.
1	All messages sent to the job's external message queue will be placed in the job log if the message severity is equal to or greater than the value specified in the severity level portion of the log parameter.
2	The log contains all level 1 information plus the following: • Any requests or commands logged from a CL program that result in a message with a severity code equal to or greater than the severity level portion of the log parameter. • All messages generated by a logged request or command with a severity code equal to or greater than the severity portion of the log parameter.
3	The log contains all level 1 information plus the following: • All requests or commands logged from a CL program. • All messages generated by a logged request or command with a severity code equal to or greater than the severity portion of the log parameter.
4	All requests or commands being logged from a CL program and all messages with a severity code greater than or equal to the severity specified, including trace messages, will be logged. This is the default value.

The messages referred to in the table are those sent to the program message queue of the job running the commands. The relationship between the commands, messages, and what gets logged in the table might seem unclear. In particular, the bulleted points for value 2 seem to be saying the same thing. However, consider the sequence of events:

- The CL program runs a command or request that might generate a message.

- If no messages result from the command or request, the command or request will not be logged.

- If the command or request produces messages that are less than the severity specify in the second part of the log parameter, neither the command nor the messages will be logged.

- If the command or request produces messages that are greater than or equal to the severity specified in the second part of the log parameter, the command and any message that exceeds the severity will be logged.

In summary, the first bullet for value 2 refers to the command or request; the second value refers to the messages that caused the command to be logged.

Severity Level

The second of the three values of the LOG parameter specifies the minimum severity level that causes error messages to be logged. Messages have a range of severity from 00 to 99. The default for this value is 00. If you specify 00, any message will cause the command and messages to be logged. Specifying 99, on the other hand, will result in very little logging. Messages with a severity of 40 are usually serious enough to cause a program failure. Since jobs running normally usually do not generate messages of level 40 severity, 40 might be a good choice for this part of the LOG parameter.

Job Log Level

The third of the three values of the LOG parameter specifies the level of message text that is written in the job log. This part of the LOG parameter can have the following values:

- *NOLIST—No job log is produced for jobs that end normally. If the job ends abnormally, a job log is produced. The messages appearing in the job's log contain both message and help information. This is the default value.

- *MSG—Only message text is logged in the job's log.

- *SECLVL—Both the message and the on-line help information for the error message are logged in the job's log.

Since most jobs end normally, *NOLIST is a great choice for this parameter.

Choosing Different Logging Levels

The default log values are usually the best choice for interactive jobs. However, when you are testing a new application or new functions in an application, you might want more logging. Also, when you are running a batch job, a higher degree of logging will help you diagnose any errors that might have caused the job to fail.

You can change the logging level in two ways:

- Create a new job description that is used whenever higher logging levels are needed. For batch jobs, specify the new job description on any SBMJOB commands. In addition, you might create a user profile for testing new applications or application changes that specifies the new job description. Whenever you are testing new code, sign on using the test profile.

- Run the CHGJOB command. The logging level will be changed only for the job specified on the command.

For these types of situations, you may want to set the parameter as:

```
LOG(4 00 *SECLVL)
```

This will get the maximum amount of information logged for your job.

Making Sense(?) of MAXACT

Before finishing this discussion, there is one more value that you can specify: MAXACT. As you have seen in previous chapters, MAXACT appears in several different places. In some places it seems to mean the same thing, but in others it means something different. Also, with all these places for MAXACT, which one, if any, means the most?

To clear things up, start by reviewing the places where you can specify MAXACT:

- Subsystem—When the number of active jobs started by the subsystem equals the MAXACT value, the subsystem cannot start any new jobs.

- Routing entry—When the number of active jobs started via the routing entry equals the MAXACT value, no more jobs can be started with this routing entry.

120

- Workstation entry—When the number of workstation that have at least one active job equals the MAXACT value, no jobs trying to use this workstation entry will be started.

- Job queue entry—When the number of active jobs that have been started using this job queue entry equals the MAXACT value, no more jobs can be started from the job queue entry.

- Job queue—When the number of active jobs started from this job queue for this priority equals MAXPTYN, no additional jobs of this priority can be started.

Because there are fewer values for interactive jobs, take a look at them first. Figure 5.11 shows them in the form of a flow diagram.

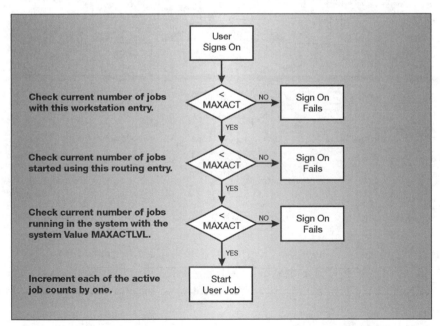

Figure 5.11: Two maximum activity level values are tested to determine if an interactive job can be started.

Consider how these different values are applied for batch jobs. Unlike interactive jobs where a user is attempting to sign on, the batch jobs are already on the queue waiting to be started. In this case, the flow diagram looks like Figure 5.12.

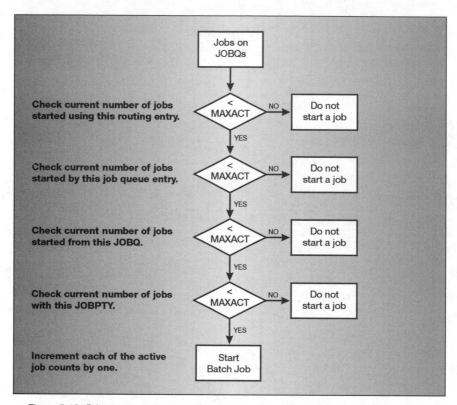

Figure 5.12: Prior to starting a batch job, three maximum activity level tests are performed.

These values are not intended to confuse you, but to provide you flexibility in balancing the type of work running on your system. For example, in the default environment with QBASE, you would have the MAXACT for QBASE set very large. Then, you'd use either the job queue entry MAXACT or the batch job routing entry MAXACT to limit the number of batch jobs that your subsystem would run.

In Review

This chapter covers some of the initial and final aspects of jobs in your system:

- Requiring an interactive user to supply a user name and password
- Modifying the sign-on display.
- Changing the initial program and menu.
- Normal and abnormal job end.
- Disconnecting users from jobs.
- Job logs and logging levels.
- The hierarchy of MAXACT values that exist in the system.

Having covered more of the basics regarding jobs and subsystems, it's time to look at moving from the default subsystem structure. The next two chapters examine ways to separate the different types of work you'll want to run on your system.

6

Beyond the Defaults:
Real Work Management

In all of the chapters so far, you have left the work management defaults for your subsystems and pools in place. These defaults will work well in a wide variety of workloads, but you can do better. This chapter focuses on the batch workload running at the same time as your interactive workload. This type of batch workload is often referred to as *concurrent batch*. The chapter begins with a quick reminder of the defaults and their potential impacts to batch processing. Then, you'll learn techniques for improving the throughput of concurrent batch.

Batch Job Defaults

Take another look at the way your batch jobs are initiated by the QBASE subsystem. Use Figure 6.1 to refresh your memory.

As you will recall, the QBATCH job queue entry in QBASE was used to locate the QBATCH job queue and initiate one job at a time in the *BASE pool. But what if your system has additional capacity? What if it can run more than one batch job at a time? If that's the case, how many batch jobs should it run?

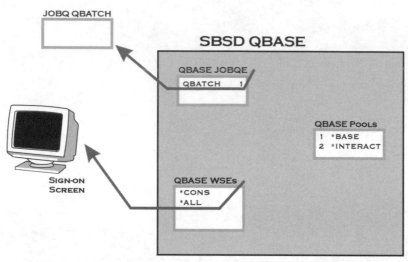

Figure 6.1:The default values for QBASE initiate one job at a time from the QBATCH job queue.

As long as your CPU utilization is less than 90 percent, you can probably initiate additional batch jobs. For example, suppose that while you are running your interactive jobs, your system can also run three batch jobs. You can tell QBASE to initiate the additional jobs simply by using the Change Job Queue Entry command (CHGJOBQE):

```
CHGJOBQE QBASE JOBQE(QBATCH) MAXACT(3)
```

That's all there is to it. As shown in Figure 6.2, QBASE will initiate three jobs from the QBATCH job queue.

If your CPU utilization is still less than 90 percent, you can add additional batch jobs to use more of the CPU. Assume, however, that you are now using 98 percent of the CPU. You are making full use of your CPU resource. Is this enough modification? Will the three jobs run efficiently in *BASE? The remainder of this chapter looks at further modifications to work management that will help your jobs run more efficiently.

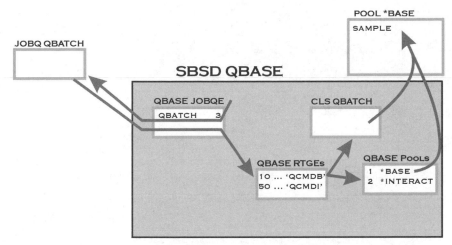

Figure 6.2: The QBATCH job queue entry in QBASE has been changed to initiate three jobs at the same time.

Start by looking at some of the other routing entries in QBASE, shown in Figure 6.3. This figure is a combination of multiple displays that illustrates all of the routing entries shipped with QBASE. (You will need to use the PageDown key to see all the entries.)

```
                        Display Routing Entries
                                                     System:TSCSAP02
    Subsystem description:    QBASE           Status:    INACTIVE

    Type options, press Enter.
      5=Display details

                                                              Start
    Opt    Seq Nbr    Program      Library      Compare Value    Pos

            10       QCMD         QSYS         'QCMDB'            1
            50       QCMD         QSYS         'QCMDI'            1
            70       *RTGDTA                   'QNMAPINGD'       37
            80       QNMAREXECD   QSYS         'AREXECD'         37
           100       QCMD         QSYS         'QS36EVOKE'        1
           150       QCMD         QSYS         'QS36MRT'          1
           200       QCMD         QSYS         'QIGC'             1
           260       *RTGDTA                   'QOCEVOKE'        37
           300       QARDRIVE     QSYS         '525XTEST'         1
           310       *RTGDTA                   'QZSCSRVR'        37
           320       *RTGDTA                   'QZRCSRVR'        37
           330       *RTGDTA                   'QZHQTRG'         37
```

Figure 6.3: This is a condensed view of all of the routing entries in QBASE. (Part 1 of 2)

127

350	*RTGDTA		'QVPPRINT'	37
360	*RTGDTA		'QNPSERVR'	37
400	*RTGDTA		'QTFDWNLD'	37
450	*RTGDTA		'QMFRCVR'	37
500	*RTGDTA		'QMFSNDR'	37
510	*RTGDTA		'QHQTRGT'	37
520	*RTGDTA		'QRQSRV'	37
540	*RTGDTA		'QLZPSERV'	37
550	*RTGDTA		'QCNPCSUP'	37
590	*RTGDTA		'QPCSUPP'	1
595	*RTGDTA		'QCASERVR'	1
599	*RTGDTA		'#INTER'	1
600	*RTGDTA		'PGMEVOKE'	29
650	QCL	QSYS	'QCMD38'	1
9999	QCMD	QSYS	*ANY	

Figure 6.3: This is a condensed view of all of the routing entries in QBASE. (Part 2 of 2)

There are a lot of routing entries in addition to the standard interactive and batch ones. Some of these routing entries are actually used to start jobs in most environments. If you take a closer look, you will find that sequence numbers 50, 100, 200 to 360, and 650 are used to route work to the *INTERACT pool. All of the other routing entries direct work to *BASE, where it will compete with your batch jobs.

Don't forget QTSEPOOL. As mentioned in chapter 5, you should set the QTSEPOOL system value to *BASE. When you do this, the interactive jobs that exceed time slice will have any pages read into main storage directed to *BASE, further affecting your batch jobs. To protect your batch jobs from these impacts, you should route them to a new pool.

A Pool to Call Their Own

To get batch jobs a pool of their own, the subsystem description needs to be changed to provide a pool and a routing entry to direct batch jobs to a pool other than *BASE. You will want to make the necessary modifications to the default environment without making too many changes at once.

First, you need another pool for your QBASE subsystem. This is easily done with the Change Subsystem Description command (CHGSBSD):

```
CHGSBSD QBASE POOLS((1 *BASE)(2 *INTERACT)(3 *SHRPOOL1))
```

By making this simple change, QBASE now knows that it has another pool to use for running jobs. However, it is not yet ready to start any jobs in *SHRPOOL1; a pool is of no value without a routing entry to start work in it.

Before providing a routing entry that will use the pool, wait for batch jobs that are currently running to end. In addition, you don't want any new batch jobs to start before you have a routing entry that will use the new pool. To prevent the subsystem from starting more batch jobs, run the Hold Job Queue command (HLDJOBQ):

```
HLDJOBQ QBATCH
```

Now you can run the Change Routing Entry command (CHGRTGE) to modify your batch routing entry to use the new pool:

```
CHGRTGE QBASE SEQNBR(10)POOLID(3)
```

You're almost there. The last step in the preparation for using the new pool is providing storage and tuning parameters for it. When you assign storage to a pool, the storage is reassigned from *BASE. Therefore, you must have enough storage in *BASE to reassign to the new pool. Also, the system value QBASPOOL must be set small enough to take storage from *BASE.

You have chosen a shared pool so that QPFRADJ can modify the pool's size if you have not assigned enough storage to it. Assume that you are running three concurrent batch jobs. Figure 6.4 shows your current WRKSHRPOOL display.

```
                      Work with Shared Pools
                                                    System:  TSCSAP01
Main storage size (M)  . :         4352.00

Type changes (if allowed), press Enter.

                Defined    Max   Allocated   Pool  -Paging Option-
Pool            Size (M)  Active  Size (M)    ID   Defined  Current
*MACHINE         325.00   +++++    325.00     1    *FIXED   *FIXED
*BASE            889.50       4    889.50     2    *CALC    *CALC
*INTERACT       3100.00     197   3100.00     3    *CALC    *CALC
*SPOOL            37.50       1     37.50     4    *CALC    *CALC
*SHRPOOL1           .00       0                    *FIXED
*SHRPOOL2           .00       0                    *FIXED
*SHRPOOL3           .00       0                    *FIXED
*SHRPOOL4           .00       0                    *FIXED
*SHRPOOL5           .00       0                    *FIXED
*SHRPOOL6           .00       0                    *FIXED
                                                              More...
Command
===>
F3=Exit   F4=Prompt   F5=Refresh   F9=Retrieve   F11=Display tuning data
```

Figure 6.4: This Work with Shared Pools display shows the current pool sizes, activity levels, and paging option values.

The batch jobs that were running in *BASE have finished. When you divide *BASE by the activity level, which represents your three batch jobs and one other job, you get a little more than 222 Mb. For your batch jobs, go to the next full megabyte, 223. This leaves 220.5 Mb for the other job running in *BASE. Be sure that the QBASPOOL system value is set no higher than 220.5 Mb:

```
CHGSYSVAL QBASPOOL 220500
```

The value used is 220500 because the QBASPOOL system value is specified in kilobytes, while your display shows megabytes. Also, QBASPOOL cannot be set to a value that is less than 5 percent of your main storage size. In this case, 220.5 Mb is slightly more than 5 percent of the main storage size.

Because you want to run the three batch jobs in *SHRPOOL1, use the WRKSHRPOOL display to change the size of *SHRPOOL1 to 669 Mb with a MAXACT value of three and a paging option of *CALC, as shown in Figure 6.5.

```
                        Work with Shared Pools
                                                    System:    TSCSAP01
Main storage size (M)   . :        4352.00

      Type changes (if allowed), press Enter.

            Defined   Max    Allocated   Pool  -Paging Option-
Pool        Size (M)  Active Size (M)     ID   Defined  Current
*MACHINE     325.00   +++++    325.00      1   *FIXED   *FIXED
*BASE        889.50       4    889.50      2   *CALC    *CALC
*INTERACT   3100.00     197   3100.00      3   *CALC    *CALC
*SPOOL        37.50       1     37.50      4   *CALC    *CALC
*SHRPOOL1    669         3                     *CALC
*SHRPOOL2     .00        0                     *FIXED
*SHRPOOL3     .00        0                     *FIXED
*SHRPOOL4     .00        0                     *FIXED
*SHRPOOL5     .00        0                     *FIXED
*SHRPOOL6     .00        0                     *FIXED
                                                        More...
    Command===>
    F3=Exit  F4=Prompt   F5=Refresh   F9=Retrieve   F11=Display tuning data
    F12=Cancel
```

*Figure 6.5: The pool definitions can be changed by entering information for *SHRPOOL1 on the Work with Shared Pools display.*

After you press the Enter key, the WRKSHRPOOL display shown in Figure 6.6 appears. Now you need to set the tuning parameters. Press F11 to display the screen in Figure 6.7.

```
                        Work with Shared Pools
                                                    System:    TSCSAP01
Main storage size (M)   . :        4352.00

      Type changes (if allowed), press Enter.

            Defined   Max    Allocated   Pool  -Paging Option-
Pool        Size (M)  Active Size (M)     ID   Defined  Current
*MACHINE     325.00   +++++    325.00      1   *FIXED   *FIXED
*BASE        220.50       4    220.50      2   *CALC    *CALC
*INTERACT   3100.00     197   3100.00      3   *CALC    *CALC
*SPOOL        37.50       1     37.50      4   *CALC    *CALC
*SHRPOOL1    669.00       3    669.00          *CALC    *CALC
*SHRPOOL2     .00        0                     *FIXED
*SHRPOOL3     .00        0                     *FIXED
*SHRPOOL4     .00        0                     *FIXED
*SHRPOOL5     .00        0                     *FIXED
*SHRPOOL6     .00        0                     *FIXED
                                                        More...
    Command===>
    F3=Exit  F4=Prompt   F5=Refresh   F9=Retrieve   F11=Display tuning data
    F12=Cancel
```

Figure 6.6: When the Enter key is pressed, changes to the Work with Shared Pools display take effect.

```
                     Work with Shared Pools
                                                     System:    TSCSAP01
 Main storage size (M)  . :          4352.00

   Type changes (if allowed), press Enter.

                      ---Size %---  ---Faults/Second---
 Pool           Priority  Minimum  Maximum  Minimum   Thread   Maximum
 *MACHINE          1        6.16     100      10.00     .00     10.00
 *BASE             2        4.99      20      10.00    2.00      100
 *INTERACT         1       40.00      70       5.00     .50      200
 *SPOOL            2        1.00      10       5.00    1.00      100
 *SHRPOOL1         2        1.00     100      10.00    2.00      100
 *SHRPOOL2         2        1.00     100      10.00    2.00      100
 *SHRPOOL3         2        1.00     100      10.00    2.00      100
 *SHRPOOL4         2        1.00     100      10.00    2.00      100
 *SHRPOOL5         2        1.00     100      10.00    2.00      100
 *SHRPOOL6         2        1.00     100      10.00    2.00      100
                                                              More...
 Command===>
  F3=Exit   F4=Prompt   F5=Refresh   F9=Retrieve    F11=Display text
  F12=Cancel
```

Figure 6.7: Press F11 on the first display of Work with Shared Pools to show the tuning information for the shared pools.

Provide the tuning information for *SHRPOOL1. Because you are running batch jobs, the pool priority should stay at two. The faults-per-second values are the recommended settings for batch jobs, so you don't need to change them, either. All you need to change are the minimum and maximum values for the size percent. Your initial pool size is about 15 percent of the machine size. Set the minimum to half that, or 7.5 percent, and the maximum to twice that, or 30 percent. This range of size will allow QPFRADJ enough flexibility to tune your environment to run efficiently. Once again, you can enter the changes on the display as shown in Figure 6.8.

```
                          Work with Shared Pools
                                                       System:   TSCSAP01
        Main storage size (M)  . :        4352.00

           Type changes (if allowed), press Enter.

                            ---Size %---   ---Faults/Second---
           Pool       Priority  Minimum  Maximum  Minimum  Thread  Maximum
           *MACHINE      1        6.16      100     10.00    .00     10.00
           *BASE         2        4.99      100     10.00    2.00     100
           *INTERACT     1       10.00      100      5.00    .50      200
           *SPOOL        2        1.00      100      5.00    1.00     100
           *SHRPOOL1     2        7.5        30     10.00    2.00     100
           *SHRPOOL2     2        1.00      100     10.00    2.00     100
           *SHRPOOL3     2        1.00      100     10.00    2.00     100
           *SHRPOOL4     2        1.00      100     10.00    2.00     100
           *SHRPOOL5     2        1.00      100     10.00    2.00     100
           *SHRPOOL6     2        1.00      100     10.00    2.00     100
                                                                  More...
        Command===>
           F3=Exit   F4=Prompt   F5=Refresh   F9=Retrieve   F11=Display text
           F12=Cancel
```

Figure 6.8: The second Work with Shared Pools display provides tuning parameters for the dynamic performance adjustment function.

Press the Enter key, and the display shown in Figure 6.9 appears.

```
                          Work with Shared Pools
                                                       System:   TSCSAP01
        Main storage size (M)  . :        4352.00

           Type changes (if allowed), press Enter.

                            ---Size %---   ---Faults/Second---
           Pool       Priority  Minimum  Maximum  Minimum  Thread  Maximum
           *MACHINE      1        6.16      100     10.00    .00     10.00
           *BASE         2        4.99      100     10.00    2.00     100
           *INTERACT     1       10.00      100      5.00    .50      200
           *SPOOL        2        1.00      100      5.00    1.00     100
           *SHRPOOL1     2        7.50       30     10.00    2.00     100
           *SHRPOOL2     2        1.00      100     10.00    2.00     100
           *SHRPOOL3     2        1.00      100     10.00    2.00     100
           *SHRPOOL4     2        1.00      100     10.00    2.00     100
           ^SHRPOOL5     2        1.00      100     10.00    2.00     100
           *SHRPOOL6     2        1.00      100     10.00    2.00     100
                                                                  More...
        Command===>
           F3=Exit   F4=Prompt   F5=Refresh   F9=Retrieve   F11=Display text
           F12=Cancel
```

Figure 6.9: The tuning parameters entered on the second Work with Shared Pools display take effect when the enter key is pressed.

Your pool and subsystem are ready to go. Release the jobs that are waiting to run with the Release Job Queue command (RLSJOBQ):

```
RLSJOBQ QBATCH
```

Take a look at the QBASE batch routing diagram shown in Figure 6.10. As you can see, the subsystem now has a third pool in its list, the batch routing entry (sequence 10) indicates that jobs are to use the third pool, and jobs are running in *SHRPOOL1. You did not need to change anything else. All of your job descriptions, user profiles, previously submitted jobs, etc. remain the same, but you now have batch jobs running in their own pool, where they will not be affected by any other jobs.

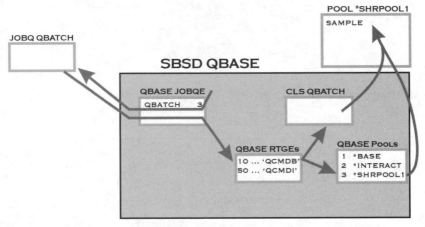

Figure 6.10: QBASE is modified to run three jobs in a shared pool (*SHRPOOL1).

More Than One Pool for Batch

Now that you have provided a pool for your batch jobs, take a closer look at what is happening in the batch pool:

1. You are running three different types of batch jobs, such as these:

   a. Production batch jobs submitted by the system operator.

   b. Short-running batch jobs submitted by interactive users.

   c. Development jobs (compiles, etc.) submitted by programmers.

2. Three jobs are competing for the same storage.

3. All jobs are submitted to and initiated from the same job queue.

When you have three different types of batch jobs to run, you'd like the subsystem to initiate one of each type of job. However, your current settings for QBASE will not produce the desired result. Actually, you are at the mercy of the order of the jobs on the job queue. Also, if the system operator has just submitted a large number of longer-running batch jobs, the jobs submitted by interactive users might not run for quite a while. Usually, they require faster turn-around time. Finally, when all three jobs are in the same pool, they will compete for the available main storage. This competition might slow turn-around time.

You need a way to introduce one of each class of batch job to its own pool. While there might be many ways to do this, three methods are used more often than any others:

1. One subsystem with three job queues.

2. Three subsystems with one job queue each.

3. One subsystem with one job queue using three different job priorities.

The following sections look at each of these three methods.

One Subsystem with Three Job Queues

Figure 6.11 shows the current QBASE. The first thing you need to do is define the two new job queues with the Create Job Queue command (CRTJOBQ). Assuming that you'll still use QBATCH for short-running batch jobs, that you'll add a job queue called PRODBAT for long-running production jobs, and that you'll use a job queue called PGMRBAT for development jobs, run the following commands:

```
CRTJOBQ PRODBAT
CRTJOBQ PGMRBAT
```

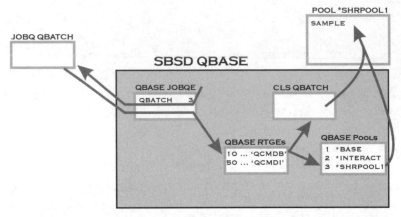

Figure 6.11: *The current QBASE environment initiates three jobs from QBATCH to run in *SHRPOOL1.*

You can take the defaults for all of the other parameters. You now have the environment shown in Figure 6.12.

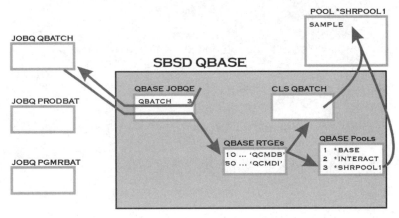

Figure 6.12: *Two additional job queues have been defined, but QBASE still initiates three jobs from the QBATCH job queue to run in *SHRPOOL1.*

Now you need to begin making changes to the QBASE subsystem. Start by adding the two new pools to the subsystem:

```
CHGSBSD QBASE POOLS((1 *BASE)(2 *INTERACT)(3 *SHRPOOL1)(4 *SHRPOOL2)
        (5 *SHRPOOL3))
```

Once again, you can take the default for all of the other parameters. Before adding storage and defining the tuning attributes for these pools, you'll need to find a way to get the job queues attached to QBASE. You'll also need to provide a way for jobs to be routed to the new pools.

Attaching the job queues to the subsystem is accomplished with the Add Job Queue Entry command (ADDJOBQE):

```
ADDJOBQE QBASE JOBQ(PRODBAT) MAXACT(1)
ADDJOBQE QBASE JOBQ(PGMRBAT) MAXACT(1)
```

Just in case some jobs accidentally get submitted to these job queues, hold the job queues so that the jobs will not be started:

```
HLDJOBQ PRODBAT
HLDJOBQ PGMRBAT
```

QBASE should now look like Figure 6.13. Because you didn't change any of your other defaults and haven't held your job queues, any jobs submitted to the new job queues would be started and placed in *SHRPOOL1. You could have as many as five jobs running in *SHRPOOL1! It's a good thing that you held them.

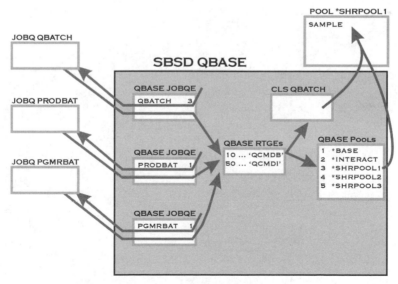

*Figure 6.13: QBASE has been modified to initiate work from three different job queues to run in *SHRPOOL1.*

As you might have guessed, the next thing you need to do is add some routing entries to QBASE. For the production batch jobs, use sequence number 11 in QBASE with a compare value of PROD starting in position 1. You'll still use QCMD as your initial program and use the QBATCH job class. Finally, you want these jobs to go to *SHRPOOL2, so you'll use the number 4 as the pool identifier. Run the following Add Routing Entry command (ADDRTGE):

```
ADDRTGE QBASE SEQNBR(11) CMPVAL(PROD 1) PGM(QCMD) CLS(QBATCH)
        POOLID(4)
```

For the development job, use sequence number 12, compare value PGMR in position 1, QCMD as the initial program, the QBATCH class, and pool identifier 5 (so the jobs run in *SHRPOOL3):

```
ADDRTGE QBASE SEQNBR(12) CMPVAL(PGMR 1) PGM(QCMD) CLS(QBATCH)
        POOLID(5)
```

Your subsystem should now look like Figure 6.14. Because you still don't have all the information you need, the routing entries are pointing to the correct pools, but the jobs are not supplying the correct routing information.

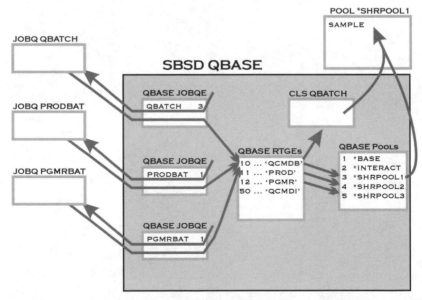

Figure 6.14: QBASE has been modified to provide routing entries to run batch jobs in three different shared pools: *SHRPOOL1, *SHRPOOL2, and *SHRPOOL3.

You can get jobs submitted to the correct queue with the correct routing information by specifying all the information you need on the Submit Job command (SBMJOB):

```
SBMJOB CMD(CALL PGM(PROD1)) JOB(PROD1) JOBQ(PRODBAT) RTGDTA(PROD)
SBMJOB CMD(CALL PGM(PGMR1)) JOB(PGMR1) JOBQ(PGMRBAT) RTGDTA(PGMR)
```

Your jobs are submitted to the correct job queue with the correct routing data.

Now that you're ready to submit work to your new queues and get it started correctly, change the QBATCH queue entry so that only one job at a time is initiated by QBASE:

```
CHGJOBQE QBASE QBATCH MAXACT(1)
```

You're getting close now. You've got:

- The queues.

- The job queue entries.

- All the job queue entries with a MAXACT of one.

- The routing entries.

- The pools identified.

- Jobs going to the right queues.

- Jobs with the correct routing data.

All you need is storage and tuning information for the new pools, and you'll be ready to release the job queues! So, bring up the Work with Shared Pools display (WRKSHRPOOL) shown in Figure 6.15 and finish your pool definitions.

```
                      Work with Shared Pools
                                               System:    TSCSAP01
 Main storage size (M)  . :          4352.00

     Type changes (if allowed), press Enter.

                 Defined   Max    Allocated  Pool  -Paging Option-
 Pool            Size (M) Active  Size (M)    ID   Defined  Current
 *MACHINE         325.00  +++++    325.00      1   *FIXED   *FIXED
 *BASE            220.50      4    220.50      2   *CALC    *CALC
 *INTERACT       3100.00    197   3100.00      3   *CALC    *CALC
 *SPOOL            37.50      1     37.50      4   *CALC    *CALC
 *SHRPOOL1        669.00      3    669.00      5   *CALC    *CALC
 *SHRPOOL2           .00      0                    *FIXED
 *SHRPOOL3           .00      0                    *FIXED
 *SHRPOOL4           .00      0                    *FIXED
 *SHRPOOL5           .00      0                    *FIXED
 *SHRPOOL6           .00      0                    *FIXED
                                                          More...
   Command===>
   F3=Exit   F4=Prompt   F5=Refresh   F9=Retrieve   F11=Display tuning data
   F12=Cancel
```

*Figure 6.15: The Work with Shared Pools display shows the current pool definitions. *SHRPOOL1 is used to run all of the batch jobs initiated by QBASE.*

You want to divide the storage in *SHRPOOL1 evenly among your three batch pools, with a MAXACT of one for each pool. So, make the changes shown in Figure 6.16.

```
                      Work with Shared Pools
                                               System:    TSCSAP01
 Main storage size (M)  . :          4352.00

     Type changes (if allowed), press Enter.

                 Defined   Max    Allocated  Pool  -Paging Option-
 Pool            Size (M) Active  Size (M)    ID   Defined  Current
 *MACHINE         325.00  +++++    325.00      1   *FIXED   *FIXED
 *BASE            220.50      4    220.50      2   *CALC    *CALC
 *INTERACT       3100.00    197   3100.00      3   *CALC    *CALC
 *SPOOL            37.50      1     37.50      4   *CALC    *CALC
 *SHRPOOL1        223         1    669.00      5   *CALC    *CALC
 *SHRPOOL2        223         1                    *CALC
 *SHRPOOL3        223         1                    *CALC
 *SHRPOOL4           .00      0                    *FIXED
 *SHRPOOL5           .00      0                    *FIXED
 *SHRPOOL6           .00      0                    *FIXED
                                                          More...
   Command===>
   F3=Exit   F4=Prompt   F5=Refresh   F9=Retrieve   F11=Display tuning data
   F12=Cancel
```

*Figure 6.16: The Work with Shared Pools display is used to provide storage for *SHRPOOL2 and *SHRPOOL3.*

When you press the Enter key, the display reflects your changes, as shown in Figure 6.17.

```
                        Work with Shared Pools
                                                    System:    TSCSAP01
Main storage size (M)  . :          4352.00

      Type changes (if allowed), press Enter.

                  Defined    Max    Allocated    Pool  -Paging Option-
Pool              Size (M)  Active  Size (M)     ID   Defined  Current
*MACHINE           325.00   +++++     325.00      1   *FIXED   *FIXED
*BASE              220.50      4      220.50      2   *CALC    *CALC
*INTERACT         3100.00    197     3100.00      3   *CALC    *CALC
*SPOOL              37.50      1       37.50      4   *CALC    *CALC
*SHRPOOL1          223.00      1      223.00      5   *CALC    *CALC
*SHRPOOL2          223.00      1      223.00      6   *CALC    *CALC
*SHRPOOL3          223.00      1      223.00      7   *CALC    *CALC
*SHRPOOL4             .00      0                      *FIXED
*SHRPOOL5             .00      0                      *FIXED
*SHRPOOL6             .00      0                      *FIXED
                                                             More...
  Command===>
  F3=Exit   F4=Prompt   F5=Refresh   F9=Retrieve   F11=Display tuning data
  F12=Cancel
```

Figure 6.17: The Work with Shared Pools display shows the new pool sizes when the Enter key is pressed.

Set the tuning parameters for your revised pool allocations by making the changes shown in Figure 6.18. After pressing the Enter key, you now have everything in place to separate the three types of batch jobs. All you need to do is the following:

```
RLSJOBQ PRODBAT
RLSJOBQ PGMRBAT
```

```
                         Work with Shared Pools
                                                        System: TSCSAP01
     Main storage size (M)  . :          4352.00

        Type changes (if allowed), press Enter.

                         ---Size %---   ---Faults/Second---
     Pool         Priority  Minimum  Maximum  Minimum  Thread  Maximum
     *MACHINE         1       6.16      100     10.00     .00    10.00
     *BASE            2       4.99      100     10.00    2.00     100
     *INTERACT        1      10.00      100      5.00     .50     200
     *SPOOL           2       1.00      100      5.00    1.00     100
     *SHRPOOL1        2       2.5        10     10.00    2.00     100
     *SHRPOOL2        2       2.5        10     10.00    2.00     100
     *SHRPOOL3        2       2.5        10     10.00    2.00     100
     *SHRPOOL4        2       1.00      100     10.00    2.00     100
     *SHRPOOL5        2       1.00      100     10.00    2.00     100
     *SHRPOOL6        2       1.00      100     10.00    2.00     100
                                                              More...
 Command===>
   F3=Exit   F4=Prompt   F5=Refresh   F9=Retrieve   F11=Display text
   F12=Cancel
```

*Figure 6.18: The second Work with Shared Pools display is used to set the tuning parameters for *SHRPOOL1, *SHRPOOL2, and *SHRPOOL3.*

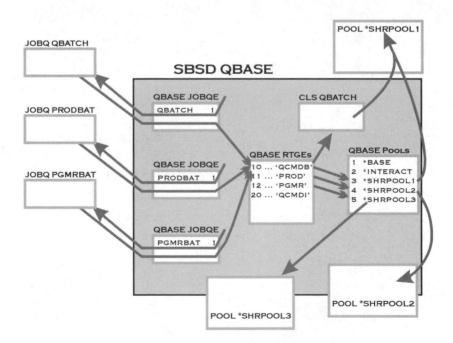

Figure 6.19: QBASE has been modified to initiate one job from each of three job queues to three different pools.

142

Now your batch jobs will not compete with each other for main storage. Your environment should look like Figure 6.19.

Before looking at the other two methods, notice the size of the batch pools. Although 2.5 percent of storage doesn't sound like much, it's 109 Mb! That's a lot more main storage than a batch job normally needs—10 Mb is usually more than enough. Therefore, you should probably set your pool sizes and tuning attributes as shown in Figures 6.20 and 21.

With these settings, the pool will range from approximately 4 Mb to 40 Mb, which should handle most batch jobs. Note that you assign the rest of the batch allocation to *INTERACT to support interactive users.

```
                        Work with Shared Pools
                                                    System:    TSCSAP01
    Main storage size (M)  . :          4352.00

        Type changes (if allowed), press Enter.

                   Defined    Max    Allocated    Pool -Paging Option-
    Pool           Size (M) Active  Size (M)    ID  Defined  Current
    *MACHINE        325.00   +++++    325.00     1  *FIXED   *FIXED
    *BASE           220.50       4    220.50     2  *CALC    *CALC
    *INTERACT      3739.00     197   3739.00     3  *CALC    *CALC
    *SPOOL           35.00       1     35.00     4  *CALC    *CALC
    *SHRPOOL1        10.00       1     10.00     5  *CALC    *CALC
    *SHRPOOL2        10.00       1     10.00     6  *CALC    *CALC
    *SHRPOOL3        10.00       1     10.00     7  *CALC    *CALC
    *SHRPOOL4          .00       0                  *FIXED
    *SHRPOOL5          .00       0                  *FIXED
    *SHRPOOL6          .00       0                  *FIXED
                                                                More...
    Command===>
     F3=Exit   F4=Prompt    F5=Refresh   F9=Retrieve   F11=Display tuning data
     F12=Cancel
```

*Figure 6.20: Pool sizes for batch jobs (*SHRPOOL1, *SHRPOOL2, and *SHRPOOL3) have been reduced to 10 Mb each. The storage removed from these pools has been added to *INTERACT to support interactive work.*

```
                    Work with Shared Pools
                                                System:    TSCSAP01
Main storage size (M)  . :        4352.00

   Type changes (if allowed), press Enter.

                      ---Size %---  ---Faults/Second---
Pool          Priority  Minimum  Maximum  Minimum  Thread  Maximum
*MACHINE         1        6.16      100     10.00     .00    10.00
*BASE            2        4.99      100     10.00    2.00     100
*INTERACT        1       10.00      100      5.00     .50     200
*SPOOL           2        1.00      100      5.00    1.00     100
*SHRPOOL1        2         .01        1     10.00    2.00     100
*SHRPOOL2        2         .01        1     10.00    2.00     100
*SHRPOOL3        2         .01        1     10.00    2.00     100
*SHRPOOL4        2        1.00      100     10.00    2.00     100
*SHRPOOL5        2        1.00      100     10.00    2.00     100
*SHRPOOL6        2        1.00      100     10.00    2.00     100
                                                         More...
Command===>
  F3=Exit   F4=Prompt   F5=Refresh   F9=Retrieve   F11=Display text
  F12=Cancel
```

*Figure 6.21: The tuning parameters for the minimum and maximum size percent have been changed for *SHRPOOL1, *SHRPOOL2, and *SHRPOOL3.*

Three Subsystems

In the next example of separating batch jobs into three different pools, you'll create two new subsystems to start work from two new job queues. Begin by going back to the environment of three batch jobs running in the same pool, as shown in Figure 6.22.

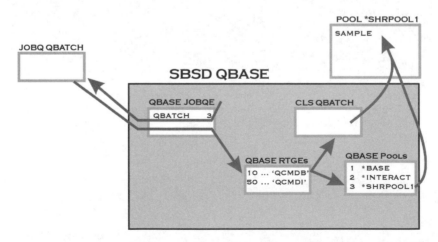

*Figure 6.22: QBASE has been modified to initiate three batch jobs from the QBATCH job queue to run in *SHRPOOL1.*

Create two new subsystems with the Create Subsystem Description command (CRTSBSD):

```
CRTSBSD  PRODBAT  POOLS((1  *SHRPOOL2)
CRTSBSD  PGMRBAT  POOLS((1  *SHRPOOL3)
```

As you have probably guessed, the subsystem PRODBAT will be used to run your production batch jobs in *SHRPOOL2, and PGMRBAT will run your development batch jobs in *SHRPOOL3. When you create the subsystem description, it is only necessary to specify the pools. You can use the defaults for the other parameters.

As before, you need to create new job queues:

```
CRTJOBQ  PRODBAT
CRTJOBQ  PGMRBAT
```

Add job queue entries to the new subsystems:

```
ADDJOBQE  PRODBAT  JOBQ(PRODBAT)  MAXACT(1)
ADDJOBQE  PGMRBAT  JOBQ(PGMRBAT)  MAXACT(1)
```

Add routing entries to the new subsystems:

```
ADDRTGE  PRODBAT  SEQNBR(10)  CMPVAL(QCMDB  1)  PGM(QCMD)  CLS(QBATCH)
         POOLID(1)
ADDRTGE  PGMRBAT  SEQNBR(10)  CMPVAL(QCMDB  1)  PGM(QCMD)  CLS(QBATCH)
         POOLID(1)
```

Take a minute to see where you are in this process. Look at your three subsystems, starting with QBASE, as shown in Figure 6.23.

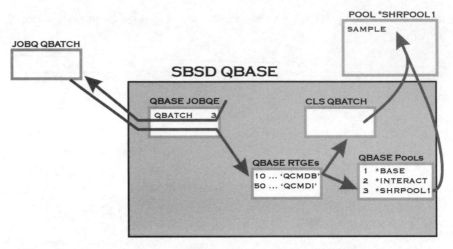

Figure 6.23: QBASE has been modified to initiate three batch jobs from the QBATCH job queue to run in *SHRPOOL1.

As you can see, you haven't changed anything in QBASE yet. Figure 6.24 shows the current state of PRODBAT, while Figure 6.25 shows PGMRBAT.

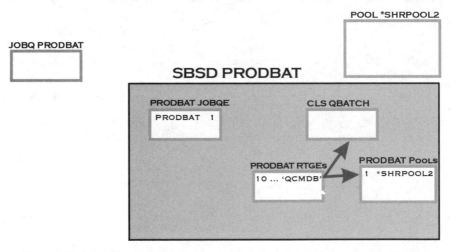

Figure 6.24: Subsystem PRODBAT has been defined to initiate jobs from the PRODBAT job queue to run in *SHRPOOL2.

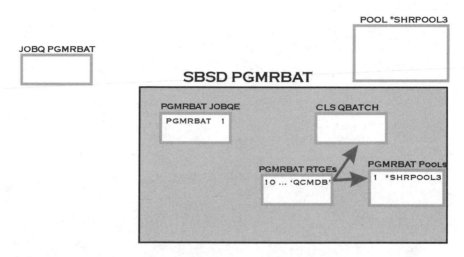

Figure 6.25: Subsystem PGMRBAT has been defined to initiate jobs from the PGMRBAT job queue to run in *SHRPOOL3.

All of the parts are there, but the mechanism to start jobs doesn't exist yet—you have not started the subsystem. Because you haven't allocated storage to either *SHRPOOL2 or *SHRPOOL3, it's not a good idea to start the subsystem yet.

Just as in the previous method, you need to ensure that your users get their work to the right job queue by specifying the correct routing data (RTGDTA) on the Submit Job (SBMJOB) command.

Finally, allocate storage and set the tuning parameters for *SHRPOOL1, *SHRPOOL2, and SHRPOOL3, as shown in Figures 6.26 and 6.27. Use the values suggested at the end of the last section.

```
                      Work with Shared Pools
                                                System:    TSCSAP01
Main storage size (M)  . :        4352.00

     Type changes (if allowed), press Enter.

                  Defined   Max   Allocated   Pool  -Paging Option-
Pool             Size (M)  Active  Size (M)    ID   Defined  Current
*MACHINE          325.00   +++++    325.00      1   *FIXED   *FIXED
*BASE             220.50      4     220.50      2   *CALC    *CALC
*INTERACT        3739.00    197    3739.00      3   *CALC    *CALC
*SPOOL             35.00      1      35.00      4   *CALC    *CALC
*SHRPOOL1          10.00      1      10.00      5   *CALC    *CALC
*SHRPOOL2          10.00      1      10.00      6   *CALC    *CALC
*SHRPOOL3          10.00      1      10.00      7   *CALC    *CALC
*SHRPOOL4            .00      0                     *FIXED
*SHRPOOL5            .00      0                     *FIXED
*SHRPOOL6            .00      0                     *FIXED
                                                              More...
   Command===>
   F3=Exit   F4=Prompt   F5=Refresh   F9=Retrieve   F11=Display tuning data
   F12=Cancel
```

Figure 6.26: The first Work with Shared Pools display is used to provide main storage allocations for *SHRPOOL1, *SHRPOOL2, and *SHRPOOL3. *INTERACT has been increased to support interactive work.

```
                      Work with Shared Pools
                                                System:    TSCSAP01
Main storage size (M)  . :        4352.00

     Type changes (if allowed), press Enter.

                        ---Size %---   ---Faults/Second---
Pool            Priority Minimum Maximum Minimum Thread Maximum
*MACHINE           1      6.16     100    10.00    .00    10.00
*BASE              2      4.99     100    10.00   2.00    100
*INTERACT          1     10.00     100     5.00    .50    200
*SPOOL             2      1.00     100     5.00   1.00    100
*SHRPOOL1          2       .01       1    10.00   2.00    100
*SHRPOOL2          2       .01       1    10.00   2.00    100
*SHRPOOL3          2       .01       1    10.00   2.00    100
*SHRPOOL4          2      1.00     100    10.00   2.00    100
*SHRPOOL5          2      1.00     100    10.00   2.00    100
*SHRPOOL6          2      1.00     100    10.00   2.00    100
                                                          More...
Command===>
   F3=Exit   F4=Prompt   F5=Refresh   F9=Retrieve   F11=Display text
   F12=Cancel
```

Figure 6.27: The second Work with Shared Pools display is used to provide the minimum and maximum size percent values for *SHRPOOL1, *SHRPOOL2, and *SHRPOOL3.

Now you're ready to use these new subsystems. Just run the following commands:

```
CHGJOBQE QBASE QBATCH MAXACT(1)
STRSBS   PRODBAT
STRSBS   PGMRBAT
```

One job at a time will be run from each of the job queues by a different subsystem. The operational characteristics of the subsystems are shown in Figures 6.28, 6.29, and 6.30.

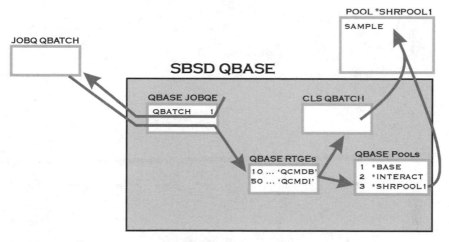

Figure 6.28: QBASE has been modified to initiate one job at a time from the QBATCH job queue to run in *SHRPOOL1.

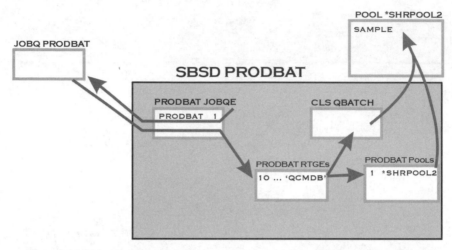

*Figure 6.29: Subsystem PRODBAT is created to run one job from the PRODBAT job queue in *SHRPOOL2.*

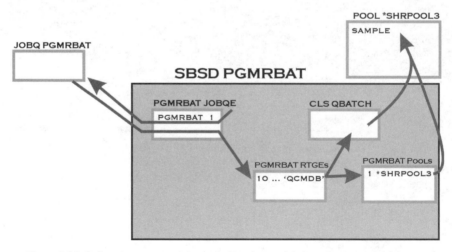

*Figure 6.30: Subsystem PGMRBAT is created to run one job from the PGMRBAT job queue in *SHRPOOL3.*

Before moving on to the third method, notice that the first two methods are the same. Both methods:

- Use *SHRPOOL1, *SHRPOOL2, and *SHRPOOL3, and set the pool sizes and tuning parameters the same.

- Create two new job queues, PRODBAT and PGMRBAT.

- Add routing entries to a subsystem to place work in *SHRPOOL2 and *SHRPOOL3.

- Create new job descriptions to use the new job queues and modify user profiles to use the correct job description.

Both methods also produce the same results. The only differences are operational and personal preferences.

One Subsystem, One Job Queue—Different Job Priorities

You've finished two of the three methods for running three different batch jobs at the same time. Like the first method, this last approach continues to use QBASE. However, instead of creating new job queues and job queue entries, it uses only the QBATCH job queue and the QBATCH job queue entry in QBASE.

Once again, return to your environment with three jobs running in *SHRPOOL1. Start with the environment of three batch jobs running in the same pool, as shown in Figure 6.31.

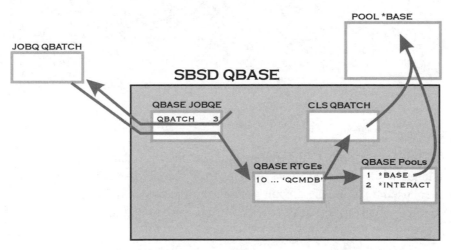

*Figure 6.31: QBASE has been modified to initiate three batch jobs from the QBATCH job queue to run in *SHRPOOL1.*

151

Add *SHRPOOL1 and *SHRPOOL2 to the pool list for QBASE:

```
CHGSBSD QBASE POOLS((1 *BASE)(2 *INTERACT)(3 *SHRPOOL1)
                    (4 *SHRPOOL2) (5 *SHRPOOL3))
```

Next, add routing entries to enable the subsystem to assign work to the new pools:

```
ADDRTGE QBASE SEQNBR(11) CMPVAL(PROD 1) PGM(QCMD) CLS(QBATCH)
        POOLID(4)
ADDRTGE QBASE SEQNBR(12) CMPVAL(PGMR 1) PGM(QCMD) CLS(QBATCH)
        POOLID(5)
```

QBASE now looks like Figure 6.32.

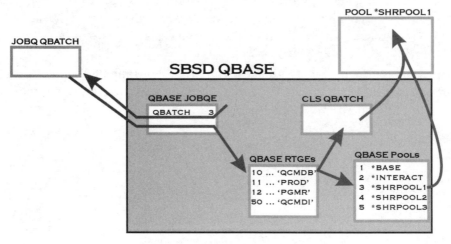

*Figure 6.32: QBASE has been modified with additional routing entries and pools, but all batch jobs run in *SHRPOOL1 only.*

So far, this looks a lot like the first method, but has only one job queue. You need to change the method used to choose jobs from the job queue. Looking at the parameters used to create the default job description, shown in Figure 6.33, you can see that the job priority (JOBPTY) used for jobs submitted to a job queue is five.

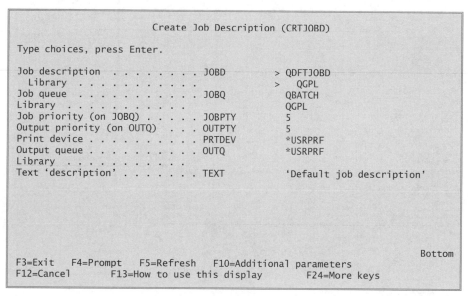

```
                    Create Job Description (CRTJOBD)

Type choices, press Enter.

Job description . . . . . . . . JOBD       > QDFTJOBD
  Library . . . . . . . . . . .            >   QGPL
Job queue . . . . . . . . . . JOBQ          QBATCH
Library . . . . . . . . .                   QGPL
Job priority (on JOBQ) . . . . . JOBPTY     5
Output priority (on OUTQ)  . . . OUTPTY     5
Print device . . . . . . . . . . PRTDEV     *USRPRF
Output queue . . . . . . . . . . OUTQ       *USRPRF
Library . . . . . . . . . .
Text 'description' . . . . . . . TEXT       'Default job description'




                                                              Bottom
F3=Exit   F4=Prompt   F5=Refresh   F10=Additional parameters
F12=Cancel        F13=How to use this display      F24=More keys
```

Figure 6.33: The default job description used to submit jobs specifies a JOBPTY value of five.

As you have done in the two previous methods, you need to submit jobs to the QBATCH job queue using the appropriate priority and routing data.

This isn't an easy concept to visualize; but try to think of each JOBPTY as representing a line of people waiting to get into a building (a subsystem). In the first method of introducing work, you had three different doors (job queue entries), each with one line (job queue) for the people (jobs) to enter. In the second method, there are three buildings (subsystems), each with one door (job queue entry) and one line (job queue) for the people (jobs). The third method has a single building (subsystem) and door (job queue entry), but with three lines (job priority on the job queue) for the people (jobs). The biggest difference between this method and the other two is that the job queue does not represent a single line of people.

Allocate main storage and set the tuning parameters for *SHRPOOL1, *SHRPOOL2, and *SHRPOOL3 as you did before. Figures 6.34 and 35 illustrate the process. All that remains is to restrict the number of jobs that have a priority of five, and to allow jobs that have a job priority of six and seven to run:

```
CHGJOBQE QBASE JOBQ(QBATCH) MAXACT(3) MAXPTY5(1) MAXPTY6(1)
          MAXPTY7(1)
```

```
                      Work with Shared Pools
                                                 System:   TSCSAP01
Main storage size (M)  . :         4352.00

     Type changes (if allowed), press Enter.

                  Defined   Max    Allocated   Pool  -Paging Option-
Pool              Size (M)  Active  Size (M)    ID   Defined   Current
*MACHINE          325.00    +++++   325.00      1    *FIXED    *FIXED
*BASE             220.50    4       220.50      2    *CALC     *CALC
*INTERACT         3739.00   197     3739.00     3    *CALC     *CALC
*SPOOL            37.50     1       37.50       4    *CALC     *CALC
*SHRPOOL1         10.00     1       10.00       5    *CALC     *CALC
*SHRPOOL2         10.00     1       10.00       6    *CALC     *CALC
*SHRPOOL3         10.00     1       10.00       7    *CALC     *CALC
*SHRPOOL4         .00       0                        *FIXED
*SHRPOOL5         .00       0                        *FIXED
*SHRPOOL6         .00       0                        *FIXED
                                                              More...

   Command===>
   F3=Exit   F4=Prompt   F5=Refresh   F9=Retrieve   F11=Display tuning data
   F12=Cancel
```

Figure 6.34: As with the previous methods, the first Work with Shared Pools display is used to provide main storage allocations for *SHRPOOL1, *SHRPOOL2, and *SHRPOOL3.

```
                      Work with Shared Pools
                                                 System:   TSCSAP01
Main storage size (M)  . :         4352.00

     Type changes (if allowed), press Enter.

                      ---Size %---   ---Faults/Second---
Pool          Priority  Minimum  Maximum  Minimum  Thread  Maximum
*MACHINE        1        6.16     100      10.00    .00     10.00
*BASE           2        4.99     100      10.00    2.00    100
*INTERACT       1        10.00    100      5.00     .50     200
*SPOOL          2        1.00     100      5.00     1.00    100
*SHRPOOL1       2        .01      1        10.00    2.00    100
*SHRPOOL2       2        .01      1        10.00    2.00    100
*SHRPOOL3       2        .01      1        10.00    2.00    100
*SHRPOOL4       2        1.00     100      10.00    2.00    100
*SHRPOOL5       2        1.00     100      10.00    2.00    100
*SHRPOOL6       2        1.00     100      10.00    2.00    100
                                                           More...

Command===>
   F3=Exit   F4=Prompt   F5=Refresh   F9=Retrieve   F11=Display text
   F12=Cancel
```

Figure 6.35: As with the previous methods, the second Work with Shared Pools display is used to provide the minimum and maximum Size % values for *SHRPOOL1, *SHRPOOL2, and *SHRPOOL3.

You now have your jobs submitted to the job queue with the correct job priority, and with one of each type of priority selected by QBASE, as shown in Figure 6.36.

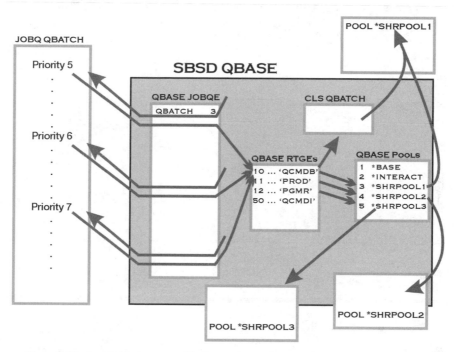

Figure 6.36: QBASE has been modified to start one job from each of three different priorities that will run in different pools.

That's it for the final method of introducing three different types of batch jobs in three different pools. This method required the least amount of change, but is usually more confusing to users. It is also a method commonly used in iSeries 400 environments that had been predominantly System/36 installations.

In Review

This chapter examines how running with the default environment might not always produce the best results. In particular, the focus is on the concurrent batch aspects of the default environment.

It's better to establish a separate area of main storage for batch jobs. Also, providing separate storage for different types of batch jobs is advisable. In addition, the flexibility of work management is displayed by three methods of providing separate storage for different types of batch jobs. While displaying the flexibility of work management, these different methods are also designed to prepare you to work in nearly every iSeries 400 environment that runs concurrent batch.

7

Further Beyond the Defaults: More Real Work Management

This chapter looks at making adjustments to the default work-management settings for interactive jobs. In many instances, there is a need to separate the different types of interactive jobs into separate pools. In addition to looking at two methods for separating work, you'll see how to adjust the runtime attributes of your jobs to benefit (or penalize) certain types of users.

Separating Incompatible Users

Maybe talking about "incompatible" users is a little harsh; I mean users who have few, if any, objects in common with most other users. For example, you might have programmers who are working on new applications or modifications to existing applications. These developers will not be using any of the same objects that your production users are using, and the programmers' objects will compete for storage with your production users—not a good idea. You might have other users who do nothing but complex queries that result in special database index builds and reading large amounts of data into main storage. Once again, these items are less likely to be used by production users and will increase the competition for main storage.

Once you have identified these users, you need to separate them from your more compatible users. There are two common methods for separating interactive users:

1. Use multiple subsystems with workstation entries that specify the names of workstations.

2. Use a single subsystem with multiple routing entries defined.

Multiple Subsystems

Take another look at the QBASE subsystem description. Figure 7.1 shows the Display Subsystem Description menu.

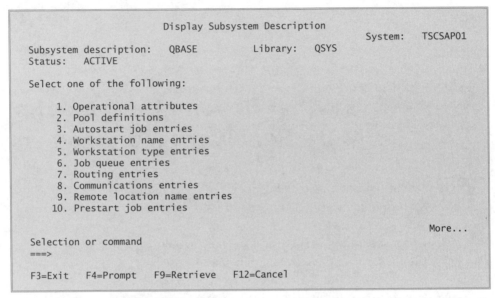

```
                      Display Subsystem Description
                                                    System:    TSCSAP01
        Subsystem description:   QBASE         Library:    QSYS
        Status:    ACTIVE

        Select one of the following:

             1. Operational attributes
             2. Pool definitions
             3. Autostart job entries
             4. Workstation name entries
             5. Workstation type entries
             6. Job queue entries
             7. Routing entries
             8. Communications entries
             9. Remote location name entries
            10. Prestart job entries

                                                              More...

        Selection or command
        ===>

        F3=Exit    F4=Prompt    F9=Retrieve    F12=Cancel
```

Figure 7.1: The Work with Subsystem Description command (WRKSBSD) displays a menu of subsystem attributes to select for viewing.

There are two menu items for workstation entries, one for name and the other for type. In the default subsystem description, there are no entries for workstation names. However, as you have seen, if more than one subsystem has the same workstation type entry, the subsystem that is actually used to initiate work from any workstation is unpredictable. If you are trying to separate users, you really need to know which subsystem will initiate them and the pool in which the jobs will run. This can be accomplished using the workstation name entries.

To create a workstation entry by name, use the Add Workstation Entry command (ADDWSE). The parameters for ADDWSE are listed in Table 7.1.

Table 7.1: ADDWSE Command Parameters

Keyword	Value	Result/Comments
WRKSTN	WSNAME	This parameter is used if the subsystem locates devices based on workstation names. In this example, you will specify the names of workstations that subsystems will own, from which they will initiate jobs. A generic name may be specified, reducing the number of times you need to enter the addwse command.
WRKSTNTYPE	N/A	This parameter is used if the subsystem locates workstations based on the type. Up to now, QBASE has only workstation type entries. These entries should be removed if your subsystems use workstation name entries to separate different types of users.
JOBD	*USRPRF	When the user of a workstation signs on, the subsystem will initiate a job. The operational attributes of the job are obtained from a job description. In this case, the job description is specified by the user profile of the person signing on.
MAXACT	*NOMAX	This parameter is used to control the number of jobs that can be initiated using this workstation entry. When *NOMAX is used, there is no limit to the number of jobs that can use this entry. Typically, *NOMAX is the correct value for this parameter. Otherwise, a sign-on screen will appear at the workstation, but an attempt to use the workstation might result in the error "Routing step terminated abnormally."
AT	*SIGNON	This value indicates that the subsystem can send a sign-on screen to any workstation meeting the criteria for this workstation entry. In this case, all varied-on and powered-on devices with a name that matches a workstation name entry will receive a sign-on screen from QBASE. This parameter has another value, *ENTER, which is discussed in a later chapter.

As you can see, there are parameters for both name and type, but only one can be specified for each workstation entry you add. It is possible for a subsystem to have both kinds of workstation entries, in which case name entries are processed first, then type.

This section's approach to separating users involves multiple subsystems. Therefore, start by creating a new subsystem that will introduce work in *SHRPOOL4.

(From the previous chapter, you already have batch running in *SHRPOOL1, *SHRPOOL2, and *SHRPOOL3):

```
CRTSBSD    PGMR   POOLS((1 *SHRPOOL4))
```

This example involves development users, but you could have picked any set of users who have different objects than most of your production users.

The subsystem needs a routing entry:

```
ADDRTGE    PGMR SEQNBR(20) CMPVAL(1 QCMDI) POOLID(1) CLS(QINTER)
```

This completes the first two steps of this method. So far, it isn't all that difficult. Your new subsystem is shown in Figure 7.2.

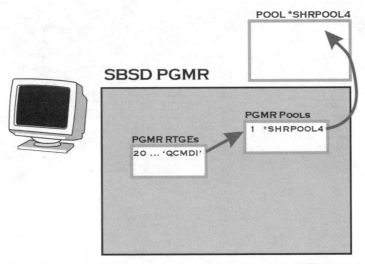

*Figure 7.2: The PGMR subsystem has been created to run jobs in *SHRPOOL4, but it does not have any workstation entries.*

It's time to add workstation entries by name to your new subsystem. Once you have located your users, note their workstation name. Then, use the Add Workstation Entry command (ADDWSE) to add them to your subsystem. For this example, assume that nine people in your development organizations use workstation

names WS004, WS005, WS010, WS021, WS042, WS060, WS82, WS103, and WS126.
Here are the commands:

```
ADDWSE  PGMR  WRKSTN(WS004)
ADDWSE  PGMR  WRKSTN(WS005)
ADDWSE  PGMR  WRKSTN(WS010)
ADDWSE  PGMR  WRKSTN(WS021)
ADDWSE  PGMR  WRKSTN(WS042)
ADDWSE  PGMR  WRKSTN(WS060)
ADDWSE  PGMR  WRKSTN(WS082)
ADDWSE  PGMR  WRKSTN(WS103)
ADDWSE  PGMR  WRKSTN(WS126)
```

Use the defaults for the rest of the parameters. The subsystem now looks like
Figure 7.3. All that is left to make this subsystem usable is to allocate storage to
*SHRPOOL4 and start the subsystem.

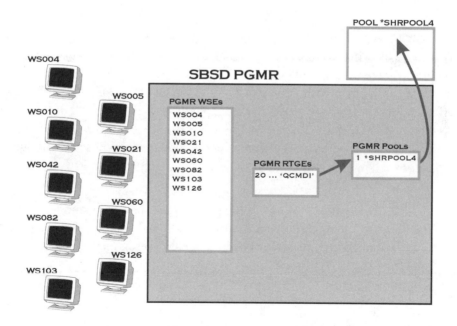

*Figure 7.3: The PGMR subsystem has nine workstations that can be used to run work
in *SHRPOOL4.*

But what about QBASE? Remember that QBASE has workstation type entries. In particular, it has a workstation type of *ALL. The workstations you named in PGMR are going to be sent a sign-on screen by QBASE. Any of your selected users who sign on before PGMR is started will be initiated by QBASE and placed in *INTERACT with all of your other users. Clearly, this is not what you want. To prevent this situation from occurring, you need to redefine your workstation entries in QBASE to be workstation name entries. Yikes! You've got over 300 workstations! Do you need to enter an ADDWSE command for each and every one?!

Given the remedial naming scheme, the answer is a resounding *yes*! However, if some foresight is shown in naming workstation devices, you can make your life a lot simpler. For example, by naming your development workstations PGMR01 through PGMR09, you could use one command to create workstation name entries for all nine workstations:

```
ADDWSE PGMR WRKSTN(PGMR*)
```

The ADDWSE command lets you use a generic name entry so all workstations that start with PGMR will have a workstation name entry in the PGMR subsystem. As an additional benefit, any new workstations that start with PGMR will be included in the PGMR subsystem without you needing to run an ADDWSE command. Any similar naming scheme will work. For example, you might name all of the order entry workstations OE001, OE002, etc. This will certainly cut down the number of ADDWSE commands needed to set up this environment, and will greatly reduce the maintenance of your workstation name entries in general.

Back to the job that you started to do: separating your users. Assuming you've bitten the bullet and done all of your ADDWSE commands for QBASE, you need to remove the workstation type *ALL workstation entry from QBASE:

```
RMVWSE QBASE WRKSTNTYPE(*ALL)
```

This should eliminate any conflicts that you might have had. Now you can move on to allocating storage and setting the tuning parameters for *SHRPOOL4.

Since you are using a shared pool, the system tuning adjustment function can re-allocate storage if you don't set it up quite right. Because this is an interactive pool, as an initial value for the pool size of *SHRPOOL4, start with 10 Mb and add 1.0 Mb for each potential user. In this example, that means an allocation of 19 Mb. For the activity level (MAXACT), assume that at most one-third of the workstations will have a transaction in process at the same time. Because this example involves nine workstations, MAXACT should be three.

Figure 7.4 shows the current pool definitions. Enter the new values for *SHRPOOL4 using the Work with Shared Pools command (WRKSHRPOOL), as shown in Figure 7.5. Notice that you are taking the storage for your new pool from *INTERACT. Because you're moving interactive users, this makes sense.

```
                    Work with Shared Pools
                                               System:   TSCSAP01
   Main storage size (M)  . :        4352.00

        Type changes (if allowed), press Enter.

                    Defined   Max   Allocated   Pool   -Paging Option-
   Pool             Size (M) Active  Size (M)    ID    Defined  Current
   *MACHINE          325.00  +++++     325.00    1     *FIXED   *FIXED
   *BASE             220.50      4     220.50    2     *CALC    *CALC
   *INTERACT        3739.00    197    3739.00    3     *CALC    *CALC
   *SPOOL             37.50      1      37.50    4     *CALC    *CALC
   *SHRPOOL1          10.00      1      10.00    5     *CALC    *CALC
   *SHRPOOL2          10.00      1      10.00    6     *CALC    *CALC
   *SHRPOOL3          10.00      1      10.00    7     *CALC    *CALC
   *SHRPOOL4            .00      0                     *FIXED
   *SHRPOOL5            .00      0                     *FIXED
   *SHRPOOL6            .00      0                     *FIXED
                                                                More...
     Command===>
     F3=Exit   F4=Prompt   F5=Refresh   F9=Retrieve   F11=Display tuning data
     F12=Cancel
```

Figure 7.4: The Work with Shared Pools command shows the current pool definitions.

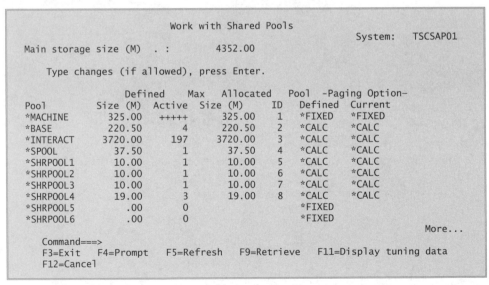

```
                        Work with Shared Pools
                                                  System:    TSCSAP01
        Main storage size (M)  . :        4352.00

        Type changes (if allowed), press Enter.

                   Defined    Max   Allocated    Pool  -Paging Option-
        Pool       Size (M)  Active  Size (M)    ID   Defined  Current
        *MACHINE     325.00   +++++    325.00     1   *FIXED   *FIXED
        *BASE        220.50      4     220.50     2   *CALC    *CALC
        *INTERACT   3720       197    3739.00     3   *CALC    *CALC
        *SPOOL        37.50      1      37.50     4   *CALC    *CALC
        *SHRPOOL1     10.00      1      10.00     5   *CALC    *CALC
        *SHRPOOL2     10.00      1      10.00     6   *CALC    *CALC
        *SHRPOOL3     10.00      1      10.00     7   *CALC    *CALC
        *SHRPOOL4     19          3                   *CALC
        *SHRPOOL5       .00       0                   *FIXED
        *SHRPOOL6       .00       0                   *FIXED
                                                                More...
        Command===>
        F3=Exit   F4=Prompt   F5=Refresh   F9=Retrieve   F11=Display tuning data
        F12=Cancel
```

Figure 7.5:The first display of Work with Shared Pools is used to define the pool size, activity level, and paging options of *SHRPOOL4. The size of *INTERACT is changed at the same time, to provide storage for *SHRPOOL4.

When you press the Enter key, the display will show the pool descriptions in Figure 7.6.

```
                        Work with Shared Pools
                                                  System:    TSCSAP01
        Main storage size (M)  . :        4352.00

        Type changes (if allowed), press Enter.

                   Defined    Max   Allocated    Pool  -Paging Option-
        Pool       Size (M)  Active  Size (M)    ID   Defined  Current
        *MACHINE     325.00   +++++    325.00     1   *FIXED   *FIXED
        *BASE        220.50      4     220.50     2   *CALC    *CALC
        *INTERACT   3720.00    197    3720.00     3   *CALC    *CALC
        *SPOOL        37.50      1      37.50     4   *CALC    *CALC
        *SHRPOOL1     10.00      1      10.00     5   *CALC    *CALC
        *SHRPOOL2     10.00      1      10.00     6   *CALC    *CALC
        *SHRPOOL3     10.00      1      10.00     7   *CALC    *CALC
        *SHRPOOL4     19.00      3      19.00     8   *CALC    *CALC
        *SHRPOOL5       .00       0                   *FIXED
        *SHRPOOL6       .00       0                   *FIXED
                                                                More...
        Command===>
        F3=Exit   F4=Prompt   F5=Refresh   F9=Retrieve   F11=Display tuning data
        F12=Cancel
```

Figure 7.6: After changes have been entered and the Enter key pressed, the first display of Work with Shared Pools shows the revised pool descriptions.

So far, so good. Now, you need to set the tuning parameters for *SHRPOOL4.
Your initial allocation for *SHRPOOL4 is 19 Mb, or approximately 0.05 percent
of all main storage in the system. Set the minimum size of your pool to 0.03
percent. For the maximum pool size of *SHRPOOL4, double the maximum allocation of your batch pools, and set this value to 2 percent. For the faults per
second, use the same values as *INTERACT. Finally, because in most people's
minds, development is less important than production users, leave the priority
value at two, which is low.

Press F11 to get the screen shown in Figure 7.7, then enter the values for
*SHRPOOL4, as shown in Figure 7.8.

```
Work with Shared Pools
                                                      System:   TSCSAP01

Main storage size (M)  . :        4352.00

   Type changes (if allowed), press Enter.

                       ---Size %---  ---Faults/Second---
Pool          Priority Minimum Maximum Minimum Thread Maximum
*MACHINE         1       6.16    100    10.00   .00    10.00
*BASE            2       4.99    100    10.00   2.00   100
*INTERACT        1      10.00    100     5.00   .50    200
*SPOOL           2       1.00    100     5.00   1.00   100
*SHRPOOL1        2        .01      1    10.00   2.00   100
*SHRPOOL2        2        .01      1    10.00   2.00   100
*SHRPOOL3        2        .01      1    10.00   2.00   100
*SHRPOOL4        2       1.00    100    10.00   2.00   100
*SHRPOOL5        2       1.00    100    10.00   2.00   100
*SHRPOOL6        2       1.00    100    10.00   2.00   100
                                                       More...
Command===>
  F3=Exit   F4=Prompt   F5=Refresh   F9=Retrieve   F11=Display text
  F12=Cancel
```

Figure 7.7: The second Work with Shared Pools display shows the current tuning parameters.

```
                        Work with Shared Pools
                                                   System:    TSCSAP01

Main storage size (M)   . :         4352.00

   Type changes (if allowed), press Enter.

                        ---Size %---  ---Faults/Second---
Pool         Priority  Minimum  Maximum  Minimum  Thread  Maximum
*MACHINE        1        6.16      100    10.00      .00    10.00
*BASE           2        4.99      100    10.00     2.00    100
*INTERACT       1       10.00      100     5.00      .50    200
*SPOOL          2        1.00      100     5.00     1.00    100
*SHRPOOL1       2         .01        1    10.00     2.00    100
*SHRPOOL2       2         .01        1    10.00     2.00    100
*SHRPOOL3       2         .01        1    10.00     2.00    100
*SHRPOOL4       2         .05        2    5         .50     200
*SHRPOOL5       2        1.00      100    10.00     2.00    100
*SHRPOOL6       2        1.00      100    10.00     2.00    100
                                                             More...
Command===>

   F3=Exit   F4=Prompt   F5=Refresh   F9=Retrieve   F11=Display text
   F12=Cancel
```

Figure 7.8: This display shows the tuning parameters entered for *SHRPOOL4.

When you press Enter, you can see the results of your changes, as shown in Figure 7.9.

```
                        Work with Shared Pools
                                                   System:    TSCSAP01
Main storage size (M)   . :         4352.00

   Type changes (if allowed), press Enter.

                        ---Size %---  ---Faults/Second---
Pool         Priority  Minimum  Maximum  Minimum  Thread  Maximum
*MACHINE        1        6.16      100    10.00      .00    10.00
*BASE           2        4.99      100    10.00     2.00    100
*INTERACT       1       10.00      100     5.00      .50    200
*SPOOL          2        1.00      100     5.00     1.00    100
*SHRPOOL1       2         .01        1    10.00     2.00    100
*SHRPOOL2       2         .01        1    10.00     2.00    100
*SHRPOOL3       2         .01        1    10.00     2.00    100
*SHRPOOL4       2         .05        2     5.00      .50    200
*SHRPOOL5       2        1.00      100    10.00     2.00    100
*SHRPOOL6       2        1.00      100    10.00     2.00    100
                                                             More...
Command===>

   F3=Exit   F4=Prompt   F5=Refresh   F9=Retrieve   F11=Display text
   F12=Cancel
```

Figure 7.9: The new values for *SHRPOOL4 are shown on the second display of Work with Shared Pools.

166

At last, you're ready to start the PGMR subsystem:

```
STRSBS  PGMR
```

Your two subsystems are shown in Figure 7.10. As you can see, QBASE is getting pretty complicated.

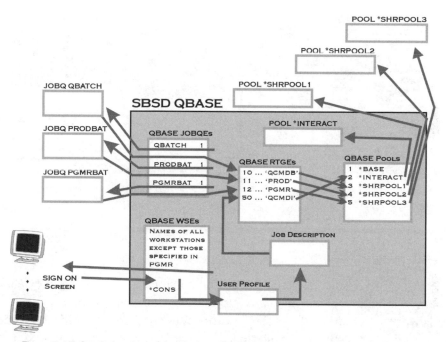

Figure 7.10: QBASE has been modified to send sign-on screens only to workstations with workstation name entries.

You are now starting one batch job from each of three queues in three different pools. You're also sending sign-on screens to all of your named workstations, and starting their jobs in *INTERACT. The PGMR subsystem is shown in Figure 7.11.

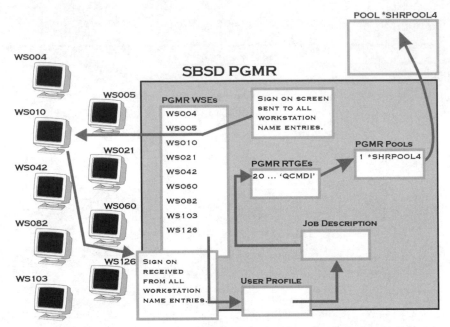

*Figure 7.11: The PGMR subsystem sends a sign-on screen to ten displays and initiates jobs in *SHRPOOL4.*

Your environment is now complete. However, it was a lot of work, and a few issues still remain:

- The work of maintaining the workstation name entries can be alleviated, but not eliminated, with a better naming convention. However, if a workstation moves from one department to another, it should be renamed. And what about a user who floats between departments? How do you describe that workstation? This can become a nightmare very quickly.

- You can't ensure that users always use the same workstation. What if a programmer uses a workstation that has a name other than the nine set aside for programmers? The programmer will be treated as a production user and placed in *INTERACT. You can prevent some of the problems caused by this action if you specify a job description on the workstation name entries. Thus, whenever a user signs on to any of your workstation name entries, he or she will be assigned the job description associated with the workstation. By tying the workstation name to a job description, and an initial program and/or menu to the job description, you can at least prevent the programmer from gaining access to the production users' main storage. However, you still have some of the same problems mentioned in the previous issue, namely, "floaters" and reassignments.

After all of the work you've done, you still might not have accomplished what you set out to do. That's why you're going to do it all again with a better approach!

Customizing QBASE to Separate Interactive Work

Interestingly, you nearly have everything in place with your default environment. Take another look at QBASE after you've addressed the batch jobs. Figure 7.12 shows where you are.

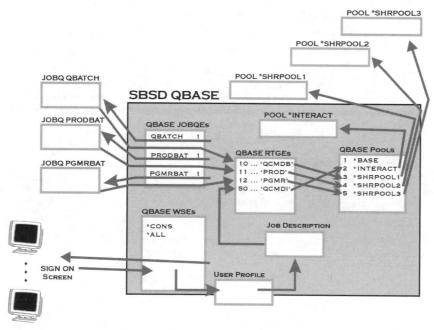

Figure 7.12: QBASE is modified to run three different types of batch jobs in three different pools, and all interactive users run in INTERACT.

Remember that when you set up the batch environment, you set up user profiles for all of your interactive users, to get the right job description for your users. Getting the right job description enables you to place jobs on the right job queue. You can do more with job descriptions, however. For example, you can use them to provide different routing data for the two types of interactive users (production and programming).

Begin by creating the new job description for your programmers:

```
CRTJOBD PGMR JOBQ(PGMR) RTGDTA(PGMRINT)
```

Take the defaults for all of the other parameters. You now have a job description for your programmers. Next, you need to change all of the programmers' user profiles to specify the new job description:

```
CHGUSRPRF xxxxxx JOBD(PGMR)
```

Replace the *xxxxxx* with the user profile name, and repeat this command for each programmer's user profile. You don't need to make any changes for your other users.

Now you need to add *SHRPOOL4 to the pools that QBASE can use to run jobs.

```
CHGSBSD QBASE POOLS((1 *BASE)(2 *BASE)(3 *SHRPOOL1)(4*SHRPOOL2) +
                    (5 *SHRPOOL3) (6 *SHRPOOL4))
```

Add a routing entry to use the new pool:

```
ADDRTGE QBASE SEQNBR(51) CMPVAL(1 PGMRINT) CLS(QINTER) POOLID(6)
```

Finally, set the size and tuning values for *SHRPOOL4 as you did in the previous example. Figures 7.13 and 7.14 show the results of the changes that you have made to the pools.

```
                      Work with Shared Pools
                                                  System:    TSCSAP01
Main storage size (M)  . :         4352.00

     Type changes (if allowed), press Enter.

                  Defined   Max   Allocated   Pool  -Paging Option-
  Pool            Size (M)  Active  Size (M)   ID   Defined   Current
  *MACHINE         325.00   +++++    325.00     1   *FIXED    *FIXED
  *BASE            220.50       4    220.50     2   *CALC     *CALC
  *INTERACT       3720.00     197   3720.00     3   *CALC     *CALC
  *SPOOL            37.50       1     37.50     4   *CALC     *CALC
  *SHRPOOL1         10.00       1     10.00     5   *CALC     *CALC
  *SHRPOOL2         10.00       1     10.00     6   *CALC     *CALC
  *SHRPOOL3         10.00       1     10.00     7   *CALC     *CALC
  *SHRPOOL4         19.00       3     19.00     8   *CALC     *CALC
  *SHRPOOL5           .00       0                   *FIXED
  *SHRPOOL6           .00       0                   *FIXED
                                                              More...
     Command===>
     F3=Exit   F4=Prompt   F5=Refresh   F9=Retrieve   F11=Display tuning data
     F12=Cancel
```

*Figure 7.13: After pressing Enter, the first display of Work with Shared Pools shows the pool sizes, activity levels, and paging options for the system after *SHRPOOL4 has been defined.*

```
                      Work with Shared Pools
                                                  System:    TSCSAP01
Main storage size (M)  . :         4352.00

     Type changes (if allowed), press Enter.

                       ---Size %---   ---Faults/Second---
  Pool           Priority Minimum Maximum Minimum Thread Maximum
  *MACHINE          1      6.16    100    10.00    .00   10.00
  *BASE             2      4.99    100    10.00   2.00   100
  *INTERACT         1     10.00    100     5.00    .50   200
  *SPOOL            2      1.00    100     5.00   1.00   100
  *SHRPOOL1         2       .01      1    10.00   2.00   100
  *SHRPOOL2         2       .01      1    10.00   2.00   100
  *SHRPOOL3         2       .01      1    10.00   2.00   100
  *SHRPOOL4         2       .05      2     5.00    .50   200
  *SHRPOOL5         2      1.00    100    10.00   2.00   100
  *SHRPOOL6         2      1.00    100    10.00   2.00   100
                                                              More...
  Command===>
     F3=Exit   F4=Prompt   F5=Refresh   F9=Retrieve   F11=Display text
     F12=Cancel
```

*Figure 7.14: The second display of Work with Shared Pools shows the pool-tuning parameters for the system after *SHRPOOL4 has been defined.*

That's it! The revised QBASE is shown in Figure 7.15. The diagram is complicated, but the operation is really quite simple. When QBASE finds any workstation, it will send a sign-on screen. When the user signs on, the user profile provides the job description, and the job description provides the routing data, which puts the job into the correct pool—either *SHRPOOL4 or *INTERACT.

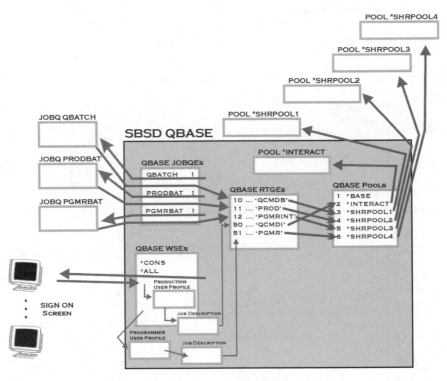

Figure 7.15: QBASE has been modified to introduce batch work in three different pools, and interactive work in two different pools.

With this method, not only is it easier to separate your programmers, but you have eliminated most of the problems of the first method:

- The issue of maintaining the workstation name entries doesn't exist because you didn't use workstation name entries.

- The issue of ensuring that users always use the same workstations is also nonexistent. The user profile information determines the routing action to be taken by the subsystem. Users can sign on to any workstation, as long as they always use the same profile.

When it comes to separating different types of interactive users, this method is a hands-down winner!

Providing Benefits to Special Users

So far in this chapter, you've seen how to separate interactive work that is potentially disruptive for most of the other interactive workers. However, in many environments, some users should receive preferential treatment. For example, if you're using your system to manage a hotel, your customers' first and last impressions of your business occur at the front desk when they check in and out. If the front desk workstations perform poorly, your customers might not have a favorable impression of your hotel, and they might not return. In this case, you want to provide separate storage for these users to ensure that the objects they are using are not replaced by other users like those in accounts payable or accounts receivable.

Providing a Separate Pool

You know the routine. Go back to QBASE to add another pool definition (*SHRPOOL5), add another routing entry, create a new job description, size the pool, set the tuning parameters, and adjust user profiles. Here are the commands to run:

```
CHGSBSD QBASE POOLS((1 *BASE)(2 *BASE)(3 *SHRPOOL1)(4*SHRPOOL2) +
                    (5 *SHRPOOL3) (6 *SHRPOOL4)(7 *SHRPOOL5))
ADDRTGE QBASE SEQNBR(52) CMPVAL(1 FRTDSK) CLS(QINTER) POOLID(7)
CRTJOBD FRTDSK JOBQ(QBATCH) RTGDTA(FRTDSK)
CHGUSRPRF xxxxxx JOBD(FRTDSK)
```

Even if you have fewer than 10 front-desk workstations (10 front-desk workstations is a very large hotel!), you want to ensure that these users have a large amount of main storage, since they are the most important users. So, reallocate 80 Mb of main storage from *INTERACT to *SHRPOOL5, and set MAXACT to five. Of course, you'll use *CALC for the PAGING option. After running WRKSHRPOOL, typing the changes on the display, and pressing Enter, you will see the main storage allocations shown in Figure 7.16.

Press F11 to change the tuning parameters for *SHRPOOL5. Set the priority to one (high), the minimum percent to two, and the maximum percent to four. Use the same values as *INTERACT for the faults per second. After typing in the changes and pressing Enter, you have the screen as shown in Figure 7.17.

The interactive aspects of the current QBASE definition are shown in Figure 7.18. Although the batch aspects of QBASE aren't shown on this diagram for the sake of simplicity, they are still there and are being used to route the batch jobs to *SHRPOOL1, *SHRPOOL2, and *SHRPOOL3.

```
                        Work with Shared Pools
                                              System:    TSCSAP01
     Main storage size (M)  . :         4352.00

         Type changes (if allowed), press Enter.

                   Defined    Max   Allocated    Pool -Paging Option-
     Pool          Size (M)  Active Size (M)    ID  Defined  Current
     *MACHINE       325.00   +++++    325.00     1  *FIXED   *FIXED
     *BASE          223.00      4     223.00     2  *CALC    *CALC
     *INTERACT     3640.00    197    3640.00     3  *CALC    *CALC
     *SPOOL          35.00      1      35.00     4  *CALC    *CALC
     *SHRPOOL1       10.00      1      10.00     5  *CALC    *CALC
     *SHRPOOL2       10.00      1      10.00     6  *CALC    *CALC
     *SHRPOOL3       10.00      1      10.00     7  *CALC    *CALC
     *SHRPOOL4       19.00      3      19.00     8  *CALC    *CALC
     *SHRPOOL5       80.00      5      80.00     9  *CALC    *CALC
     *SHRPOOL6         .00      0                   *FIXED
                                                              More...
       Command===>
       F3=Exit    F4=Prompt    F5=Refresh    F9=Retrieve    F11=Display tuning data
       F12=Cancel
```

Figure 7.16: The first display of Work with Shared Pools shows the initial pool size, activity level, and paging option for *SHRPOOL5, which has been created to run users deserving preferential treatment.

```
Work with Shared Pools

Main storage size (M)  . :        4352.00               System:   TSCSAP01

    Type changes (if allowed), press Enter.

                        ---Size %---   ---Faults/Second---
Pool         Priority  Minimum Maximum  Minimum Thread  Maximum
*MACHINE         1       6.16    100     10.00    .00    10.00
*BASE            2       4.99    100     10.00   2.00    100
*INTERACT        1      10.00    100      5.00    .50    200
*SPOOL           2       1.00    100      5.00   1.00    100
*SHRPOOL1        2        .01      1     10.00   2.00    100
*SHRPOOL2        2        .01      1     10.00   2.00    100
*SHRPOOL3        2        .01      1     10.00   2.00    100
*SHRPOOL4        2        .05      2      5.00    .50    200
*SHRPOOL5        1       2.00      4      5.00    .50    200
*SHRPOOL6        2       1.00    100     10.00   2.00    100
                                                          More...
Command===>
  F3=Exit   F4=Prompt   F5=Refresh   F9=Retrieve   F11=Display text
  F12=Cancel
```

*Figure 7.17: The second display of Work with Shared Pools shows the tuning parameters for *SHRPOOL5.*

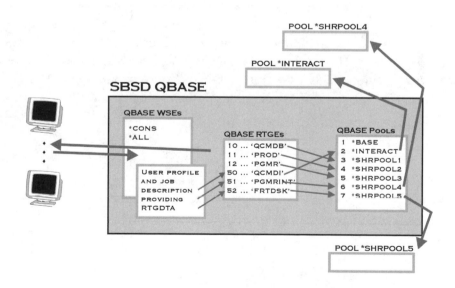

Figure 7.18: This diagram shows the modifications made to the interactive job aspects of QBASE.

As you can see, choosing the second method of routing interactive work to different pools can be easily adapted to separate many different user types. However, you shouldn't carry this process to the extremes. Rather, isolate one set of users at a time. You might find that you only needed to separate your front-desk users, and everything else will continue to run great. Why make more work for yourself?

Providing Special Runtime Attributes

Now that you have separated your important users, have you done enough? In many instances, yes. In others, no. While separating the jobs helps them keep their pages in main storage, they must still compete for disk and processor resources.

You can influence a job's ability to utilize these resources more efficiently with the runtime attributes you assign to a job when it is started by the subsystem. The three main runtime attributes are PURGE, TIMESLICE, and RUNPTY. To help with special jobs, you might need to adjust these values. But which attributes should you adjust, and what values should you use?

The PURGE runtime attribute instructed the system how to manage the pages in main storage that were unique to each job and were contained in the Process Access Group (PAG). If you were using PAG, you might be able to reduce the disk component of the front desk's response by altering PURGE. Unfortunately, with the demise of the PAG, modifying this attribute is of little use.

The TIMESLICE value limits the amount of CPU time that a job can use during any single transaction. Few, if any, front-desk transactions should use 2 seconds of CPU time (the default for TIMESLICE). Unless your most important jobs average more than 1 second of CPU time per transaction, changing this value will be of little benefit. In fact, most environments will see no improvement.

The RUNPTY value is used to establish the initial cost of a job whenever it enters a transaction to be processed. In addition, RUNPTY is used to determine which of the delay cost curves will be used to calculate the increase in cost as your jobs wait for resources. Changing this runtime value could, indeed, provide additional benefits to your interactive job, but you need more information to determine what the setting should be. Start by looking at the delay cost curves shown in Figure 7.19.

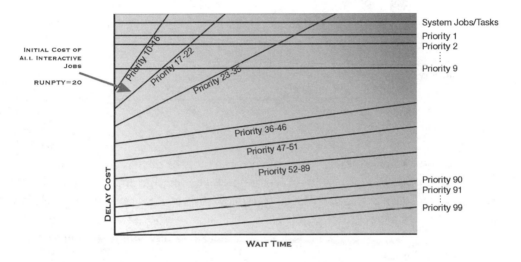

Figure 7.19: These delay cost curves are used to schedule and dispatch work in your system.

All interactive jobs are assigned the default RUNPTY of 20. This value is found in the class that is named in the routing entry used when the job is started. Because all of your interactive routing entries specify QINTER as the class (CLS), all the jobs are assigned the same runtime attributes. (Figuring out how all these work management pieces fit together is like attending a reunion of your in-laws. You know everyone is related, it's just figuring out how!)

Because all of your routing entries are using the QINTER class, you can't just change the class. Otherwise, everybody will pick up the same runtime attributes again. You need to create a new class with a different RUNPTY value from the one in the QINTER class (20). You also need to change the routing entry at SEQNBR(52) to use the new class. All you need to do is figure out the value of RUNPTY in your new class.

From the delay cost diagram in Figure 7.19, you can see that if you change RUNPTY for your valuable users to 19, 18, or 17, you'll still be on the same cost curve as all your other interactive jobs. That will help some, but notice what will happen if you change the RUNPTY to 16: you have placed your users on a different cost curve. The cost of waiting increases faster (the slope of the line is steeper) on the RUNPTY 16 curve, and there is no CPU usage penalty on this curve. That is, the important jobs will not be reassigned to a lower cost curve regardless of the amount of CPU they use. Sounds like you ought to set RUNPTY to 16, doesn't it?

Run these commands:

```
CRTCLS FRTDSK RUNPTY(16)
CHGRTGE QBASE SEQNBR(52) CLS(FRTDSK)
```

Take the default values for all of the other parameters of the Create Class command (CRTCLS), and you're done! Well, almost. The runtime attributes are assigned at the time a job is started. To have interactive jobs reassigned to different pools or given different runtime attributes, the users will need to sign off their workstations and sign on again. As long as it means preferential treatment, most users can deal with that.

In Review

This chapter explains the methods for separating interactive users and shows that using a single subsystem is the better of the two choices presented. Also covered is how to establish pool sizes and the tuning values for pools. Additionally, this chapter demonstrates that if a separate pool doesn't provide enough benefit, you can change the RUNPTY of a job to provide additional benefits.

At this point, you deserve a break! After covering most of the basic work-management functions you need to know, there is still a lot to learn. The remaining chapters discuss other types of jobs, methods for running more than one job at a workstation, threads, and much more. So rest up for a while, and come back refreshed and ready to go!

More About Jobs

The first seven chapters of this book cover a lot of the functions of work management. The material in these chapters is designed to show you how you can customize your job initiation and your subsystem environment. Now that you've seen the capabilities of additional pools and subsystems, it's time to consider some other things that can be done with the jobs in your environment.

Batch Jobs and Job Queues

Environments have many different users, who are submitting batch jobs to different queues. You'd like to have some type of operational control or management of these submitted jobs. Consider several of the operations management functions that are performed the most often.

Finding All of the Job Queues

In the examples in previous chapters, you have created three different job queues. These are not the job queues that have been created in your environment, however. Many others are shipped with OS/400.

To see all of the job queues in your environment, run the Work with Job Queues command:

```
WRKJOBQ
```

When you do not specify the name of a job queue on the WRKJOBQ command, you get a display like the ones in Figures 8.1a through 8.1d, showing all of the job queues in the system.

```
                         Work with All Job Queues

 Type options, press Enter.
   3=Hold    4=Delete    5=Work with     6=Release
   8=Work with job schedule entries      14=Clear

 Opt      Queue          Library         Jobs    Subsystem     Status
          CCJAVA1        CALCULATE         0                   RLS
          CCJAVA2        CALCULATE         0                   RLS
          CCJAVA1        CRGTEST           0                   RLS
          CCJAVA2        CRGTEST           0                   RLS
          RMTQ           OPC               0                   RLS
          NETBLDJQ       QBLDSYS           0                   RLS
          QCPRJOBQ       QBLDSYS           0                   RLS
          QD2BPTFQ       QBLDSYS           0                   RLS
          Q1ABRMNET      QBRM              0                   RLS
          QCTPLSJOBQ     QDEVELOP          0                   RLS
          QDMT           QDMT              0                   RLS
          QDNNOTIFY      QDMT              0                   RLS
                                                                 More...
 Command
 ===>
 F3=Exit    F4=Prompt    F5=Refresh    F12=Cancel    F24=More keys
```

Figure 8.1a: The Work with Job Queues command with no parameters will show all of the job queues in the system.

```
                         Work with All Job Queues

 Type options, press Enter.
   3=Hold    4=Delete    5=Work with     6=Release
   8=Work with job schedule entries      14=Clear

 Opt      Queue          Library         Jobs    Subsystem     Status
          QPGMR          QDMT              0                   RLS
          QEJBJOBQ       QEJB              0                   RLS
          PGMRBAT        QGPL              8      PGMRBAT       RLS
          PRODBAT        QGPL             22      PRODBAT       RLS
          QBASE          QGPL              0      QBASE         RLS
          QBATCH         QGPL             48      QBASE         RLS
          QFNC           QGPL              0      QBASE         RLS
          QINTER         QGPL              0      QBASE         RLS
          QPGMR          QGPL              0      QBASE         RLS
          QSNADS         QGPL              0      QBASE         RLS
          QSPL           QGPL              0      QSPL          RLS
          QS36EVOKE      QGPL              0      QBASE         RLS
                                                                 More...
 Command
 ===>
 F3=Exit    F4=Prompt    F5=Refresh    F12=Cancel    F24=More keys
```

Figure 8.1b: The Work with JOb Queues command with no parameters will show all of the job queues in the system..

```
                      Work with All Job Queues

Type options, press Enter.
   3=Hold    4=Delete    5=Work with    6=Release
   8=Work with job schedule entries    14=Clear

Opt    Queue        Library       Jobs   Subsystem    Status
       QS36MRT      QGPL             0    QBASE        RLS
       QTXTSRCH     QGPL             0    QBASE        RLS
       QZHBHTTP     QHTTPSVR         0    QHTTPSVR     RLS
       QIJSSCD      QIJS             0    QSYSWRK      RLS
       Q1PSCHQ      QMPGLIB          0    Q1PGSCH      RLS
       Q1PSCHQ2     QMPGLIB          0    Q1PGSCH      RLS
       Q1PSCHQ3     QMPGLIB          0    Q1PGSCH      RLS
       QSOC         QSOC             0    QSOC         RLS
       QCTL         QSYS             0    QBASE        RLS
       QESAUTON     QSYS             0    QSYSWRK      RLS
       QLPINSTALL   QSYS             0                 RLS
       QNMSVQ       QSYS             0    QSYSWRK      RLS
                                                      More...
Command
===>
F3=Exit    F4=Prompt    F5=Refresh    F12=Cancel    F24=More keys
```

Figure 8.1c: The Work with Job Queues command with no parameters will show all of the job queues in the system.

```
                      Work with All Job Queues

Type options, press Enter.
   3=Hold    4=Delete    5=Work with    6=Release
   8=Work with job schedule entries    14=Clear

Opt    Queue        Library       Jobs   Subsystem    Status
       QPDAUTOPAR   QSYS             0    QSYSWRK      RLS
       QPWFSERVER   QSYS             0    QSERVER      RLS
       QSYSNOMAX    QSYS             0    QSYSWRK      RLS
       QSYSSBSD     QSYS             0                 RLS
       QUSRNOMAX    QSYS             0    QUSRWRK      RLS
       QTCP         QTCP             0                 RLS




                                                      More...
Command
===>
F3=Exit    F4=Prompt    F5=Refresh    F12=Cancel    F24=More keys
```

Figure 8.1d: The Work with Job Queues command with no parameters will show all of the job queues in the system.

There are certainly a lot of job queues in your environment. Many of them are shipped with OS/400 or some other AS/400 licensed product. All of the IBM-supplied job queues start with the letter *Q* and are located in a library that starts with the letter *Q*. Because there are a large number of IBM-supplied job queues, you will get several pages of job queues. While this is not a serious problem, it makes locating a specific job queue more difficult.

Using these displays, you can find which job queues have been created, how many jobs are on each job queue, the subsystem that will initiate work from the queue, and the status of the queue. In this case, notice that two job queues are being managed by separate subsystems rather than QBASE. Table 8.1 provides additional information for each job queue.

Table 8.1: Columns on the Job Queue Display	
Heading	**Meaning**
Jobs	This value shows the number of jobs that have been submitted to each of the job queues in the system.
Subsystem	If a name appears in this column, a subsystem that has an entry for the job queue is active, and will initiate work from the queue. If there is no name, either the job queue does not have a job queue entry in any subsystem, or all subsystems with job queue entries for the queue are inactive.
Status	This is the current status of the job queue, as follows: • Rls—The job queue has been released. Jobs on the job queue may be started by the active subsystem. • Hld—The job queue has been held. None of the jobs on the job queue will be started.

Checking the Jobs on a Job Queue

Now that you have located your job queues and have determined that they have been released and that jobs are being initiated from them, look at the jobs on the PRODBAT job queue. To look at jobs on any particular job queue, run WRKJOBQ and specify a job queue name:

```
WRKJOBQ PRODBAT
```

Alternatively, use WRKJOBQ without a job queue name, and enter a five in front of the queue you are interested in, as shown in Figure 8.2. In either case, you will be shown a list of the jobs that are currently on the job queue, as in Figure 8.3. Details about Figure 8.3 are given in Table 8.2.

```
                        Work with All Job Queues

  Type options, press Enter.
    3=Hold    4=Delete    5=Work with    6=Release
    8=Work with job schedule entries    14=Clear

  Opt      Queue           Library         Jobs    Subsystem     Status
           QPGMR           QDMT               0                  RLS
           QEJBJOBQ        QEJB               0                  RLS
           PGMRBAT         QGPL               8    PGMRBAT       RLS
    5      PRODBAT         QGPL              22    PRODBAT       RLS
           QBASE           QGPL               0    QBASE         RLS
           QBATCH          QGPL              48    QBASE         RLS
           QFNC            QGPL               0    QBASE         RLS
           QINTER          QGPL               0    QBASE         RLS
           QPGMR           QGPL               0    QBASE         RLS
           QSNADS          QGPL               0    QBASE         RLS
           QSPL            QGPL               0    QSPL          RLS
           QS36EVOKE       QGPL               0    QBASE         RLS
                                                              More...
  Command
  ===>
  F3=Exit    F4=Prompt    F5=Refresh    F12=Cancel    F24=More keys
```

Figure 8.2: Enter a five in front of a job queue to see the jobs on the queue waiting to be started.

```
                         Work with Job Queue

  Queue:    PRODBAT        Library:   QGPL           Status:   RLS

  Type options, press Enter.
    2=Change    3=Hold    4=End    5=Work with    6=Release

  Opt      Job             User            Number    Priority    Status
           PRODBAT         PRODUS02        158870       5        RLS
           PRODBAT         PRODUS01        158871       5        RLS
           PRODBAT         PRODUS01        158872       5        RLS
           PRODBAT         PRODUS01        158873       5        RLS
           PRODBAT         PRODUS02        158902       5        RLS
           PRODBAT         PRODUS02        158915       5        RLS
           PRODBAT         PGMRUS06        158945       5        RLS
           PRODBAT         PRODUS01        158966       5        RLS
           PRODBAT         WILLIAMS        158984       5        RLS
           PRODBAT         PRODUS01        106869       5        HLD
                                                              More...
  Parameters for options 2, 3 or command
  ===>
  F3=Exit    F4=Prompt    F6=Submit job    F12=Cancel
  F22=Work with job schedule entries       F24=More keys
```

Figure 8.3: The jobs on the job queue appear in the order in which they will be started—held jobs (HLD) will follow all released jobs (HLS).

Notice that the jobs on this queue have the name as the job description specified (or taken as a default) on the Submit Job command (SBMJOB). In addition, you can see the user profile specified on the Submit Job command. The default for this value is the user profile of the user who submitted the job.

Table 8.2: Columns on the WRKJOBQ Screen	
Heading	**Meaning**
Number	Whenever a job exists in the iSeries 400, the name of the job consists of three parts: the job name, the user name, and the job number. The job number is assigned by OS/400.
Priority	The job priority (JOBPTY) of the job on the queue. This can be in the range of one to nine.
Status	Each job on the job queue can have a status of HLD (held), RLS (released), or SCD (scheduled).

With the information shown on this display, you can see which jobs have been accidentally submitted to the wrong queue, which users are submitting jobs, the order of jobs on the job queue, and whether a job is being held. In the example in Figure 8.3, two jobs have been submitted to the wrong queue, one submitted by PGMRUS06 and one by WILLIAMS. If throughput on the queue normally used by one of these users is faster than the PRODBAT queue, the user who submitted the job might call to ask why the job hasn't run yet. Now, you will be able to explain what has caused the delay.

Also notice that one of the jobs on the queue has been held. Perhaps this is a job that should have run the previous night, but was not able to for some reason. Rather than have the job plow ahead anyway and conflict with the interactive jobs, the job has been held and will run tonight.

Checking a Job on the Job Queue

If you are not certain about any of the jobs that are on the job queue, you can enter the Work with Job command (WRKJOB):

```
WRKJOB jobnumber/username/jobname
```

You might not know all of this information. Suppose, for example, you enter only the job name. You will get all of the jobs that have that name. Since the job name defaults to the job description, you could be presented with a long list, so you'll want to enter at least the job name and user name:

```
WRKJOB username/jobname
```

From the results, you can select the particular job(s) you are interested in. It's probably easier to work with a job once you've located it via WRKJOBQ, however. All you need to do is choose option 5 (Work with) and press Enter. For example, you might not be sure about the job that WILLIAMS submitted to PRODBAT. Place a five by that item, as shown in Figure 8.4, to get additional information.

```
                        Work with Job Queue

   Queue:     PRODBAT        Library:   QGPL          Status:    RLS

   Type options, press Enter.
     2=Change   3=Hold    4=End    5=Work with   6=Release

   Opt    Job           User          Number    Priority      Status
          PRODBAT       PRODUS02      158870        5          RLS
          PRODBAT       PRODUS01      158871        5          RLS
          PRODBAT       PRODUS01      158872        5          RLS
          PRODBAT       PRODUS01      158873        5          RLS
          PRODBAT       PRODUS02      158902        5          RLS
          PRODBAT       PRODUS02      158915        5          RLS
          PRODBAT       PGMRUS06      158945        5          RLS
          PRODBAT       PRODUS01      158966        5          RLS
     5    PRODBAT       WILLIAMS      158984        5          RLS
          PRODBAT       PRODUS01      106869        5          HLD

                                                           More...
   Parameters for options 2, 3 or command
   ===>
   F3=Exit    F4=Prompt   F6=Submit job    F12=Cancel
   F22=Work with job schedule entries      F24=More keys
```

Figure 8.4: Enter a five in front of a job on the job queue to see additional information about the job.

This will provide you with the menu shown in Figure 8.5, to let you look at more detailed information about the job that WILLIAMS submitted to the PRODBAT job queue. If you select option 2 and press Enter, you get the job information shown in Figures 8.6a through 8.6c.

```
                         Work with Job
                                             System:TSCSAP02
Job:   PRODBAT        User:   WILLIAMS      Number:   158984

Select one of the following:

      1. Display job status attributes
      2. Display job definition attributes
      3. Display job run attributes, if active
      4. Work with spooled files

     10. Display job log, if active or on job queue
     11. Display call stack, if active
     12. Work with locks, if active
     13. Display library list, if active
     14. Display open files, if active
     15. Display file overrides, if active
     16. Display commitment control status, if active
                                                        More...
Selection or command
===> 2

F3=Exit    F4=Prompt    F9=Retrieve    F12=Cancel
```

Figure 8.5: The Work with Job menu gives you several selections that will show additional information about the job.

```
                  Display Job Definition Attributes
                                             System:TSCSAP02
Job:   PRODBAT        User:   WILLIAMS      Number:   158984

Job description . . . . . . . . . . . . . . . . . :   PRODBAT
  Library . . . . . . . . . . . . . . . . . . . :     QGPL
Job queue . . . . . . . . . . . . . . . . . . . :   PRODBAT
  Library . . . . . . . . . . . . . . . . . . . :     QGPL
Job priority (on job queue) . . . . . . . . . . :   5
Output priority (on output queue) . . . . . . . :   5
End severity . . . . . . . . . . . . . . . . . :   30
Message logging:
  Level . . . . . . . . . . . . . . . . . . . . :   4
  Severity . . . . . . . . . . . . . . . . . . :   0
  Text . . . . . . . . . . . . . . . . . . . . :   *SECLVL
Log CL program commands . . . . . . . . . . . . :   *YES
Printer device . . . . . . . . . . . . . . . . :   PRT01
Default output queue . . . . . . . . . . . . . :   *DEV
  Library . . . . . . . . . . . . . . . . . . . :
                                                        More...
Press Enter to continue.

F3=Exit    F5=Refresh    F9=Change job    F12=Cancel    F16=Job menu
```

Figure 8.6a: The definition attributes of a job are shown when option 2 is selected from the Work with Job menu.

```
                    Display Job Definition Attributes
                                                    System:TSCSAP02
    Job:   PRODBAT        User:   WILLIAMS        Number:   158984

    Job date . . . . . . . . . . . . . . . . . . . :
    Date format . . . . . . . . . . . . . . . . . :    *MDY
    Date separator  . . . . . . . . . . . . . . . :    /
    Time separator . . . . . . . . . . . . . . . . :    :
    Decimal format . . . . . . . . . . . . . . . . :    *BLANK
    Job switches . . . . . . . . . . . . . . . . . :    00000000
    Inquiry message reply . . . . . . . . . . . . . :    *RQD
    Accounting code . . . . . . . . . . . . . . . . :
    Print text . . . . . . . . . . . . . . . . . . :    '
          '
    DDM conversation  . . . . . . . . . . . . . . . :    *KEEP
    Break message handling  . . . . . . . . . . . . :    *NORMAL
    Status message  . . . . . . . . . . . . . . . . :    *NORMAL
    Device recovery action  . . . . . . . . . . . . :    *MSG
    Time slice end pool . . . . . . . . . . . . . . :    *NONE
                                                                More...
    Press Enter to continue.

    F3=Exit    F5=Refresh    F9=Change job    F12=Cancel    F16=Job menu
```

Figure 8.6b: The definition attributes of a job are shown when option 2 is selected from the Work with Job menu.

```
                    Display Job Definition Attributes
                                                    System:TSCSAP02
    Job:   PRODBAT        User:   WILLIAMS        Number:   158984

    Print key format . . . . . . . . . . . . . . . :    *PRTHDR
    Sort sequence . . . . . . . . . . . . . . . . . :    *HEX
      Library . . . . . . . . . . . . . . . . . . . :
    Language identifier . . . . . . . . . . . . . . :    ENU
    Country identifier  . . . . . . . . . . . . . . :    US
    Coded character set identifier  . . . . . . . . :    65535
    Default coded character set identifier  . . . . :    0
    Character identifier control  . . . . . . . . . :    *DEVD
    Job message queue maximum size  . . . . . . . . :    16
    Job message queue full action . . . . . . . . . :    *WRAP
    Allow multiple threads  . . . . . . . . . . . . :    *NO




                                                                Bottom
    Press Enter to continue.

    F3=Exit    F5=Refresh    F9=Change job    F12=Cancel    F16=Job menu
```

Figure 8.6c: The definition attributes of a job are shown when option 2 is selected from the Work with Job menu.

While you get a lot of information about the job on the job queue, you still can't determine if it is on the right queue. Rather, the information gives you the job's characteristics once it begins running. For example, you can see the logging level that has been selected for the job, the name of the output queue that will contain any printed information produced by the job, and date and time formats. Also, notice that you cannot tell the routing data that the subsystem will use to route the job. So, although it appears that many of the jobs are submitted by the right user to the right queue, you can't be certain that the job will enter the system correctly. This uncertainty is one of the reasons for having multiple subsystems that have only one queue and one routing entry for batch job processing.

If you can't get the information you need to be certain that a job is on the right queue from the Work with Job Queue or Work with Job commands, how do you get it? That's a good question, but it doesn't have a particularly good answer. Mostly, knowing if a job belongs on a particular job queue is a matter of being familiar with your operating environment. As long as you know the PRODBAT job description is used to submit jobs to the PRODBAT job queue, you can be fairly certain that the two jobs submitted by other users are on the wrong queue. Now you need to know how to move them.

Moving a Job to a Different Job Queue

Actually, moving a job from one job queue to another is very simple, using the Change Job command (CHGJOB):

```
CHGJOB JOB(158984/WILLIAMS/PRODBAT) JOBQ(QBATCH)
CHGJOB JOB(158945/PGMRUS06/PRODBAT) JOBQ(PGMRBAT)
```

Once again, notice that you need to know the full name of the job to run this command. You could also have made the change right from your display by entering a two on the line in front of the job you wanted to change, and entering the parameter that you wanted to change at the bottom of the screen, as shown in Figure 8.7. After you have entered the information and pressed Enter, the WILLIAMS job no longer appears on your display, as you can see in Figure 8.8.

```
                        Work with Job Queue

Queue:    PRODBAT        Library:   QGPL          Status:    RLS

Type options, press Enter.
  2=Change    3=Hold    4=End    5=Work with    6=Release

Opt    Job            User         Number    Priority      Status
       PRODBAT        PRODUS02     158870       5           RLS
       PRODBAT        PRODUS01     158871       5           RLS
       PRODBAT        PRODUS01     158872       5           RLS
       PRODBAT        PRODUS01     158873       5           RLS
       PRODBAT        PRODUS02     158902       5           RLS
       PRODBAT        PRODUS02     158915       5           RLS
       PRODBAT        PGMRUS06     158945       5           RLS
       PRODBAT        PRODUS01     158966       5           RLS
2      PRODBAT        WILLIAMS     158984       5           RLS
       PRODBAT        PRODUS01     106869       5           RLS
                                                           More...
Parameters for options 2, 3 or command
===>JOBQ(QBATCH)
F3=Exit    F4=Prompt    F6=Submit job    F12=Cancel
F22=Work with job schedule entries      F24=More keys
```

Figure 8.7: A job on the job queue can be changed by placing a two in front of the job and typing in the parameter and new value on the input line.

```
                        Work with Job Queue

Queue:    PRODBAT        Library:   QGPL          Status:    RLS

Type options, press Enter.
  2=Change    3=Hold    4=End    5=Work with    6=Release

Opt    Job            User         Number    Priority      Status
       PRODBAT        PRODUS02     158870       5           RLS
       PRODBAT        PRODUS01     158871       5           RLS
       PRODBAT        PRODUS01     158872       5           RLS
       PRODBAT        PRODUS01     158873       5           RLS
       PRODBAT        PRODUS02     158902       5           RLS
       PRODBAT        PRODUS02     158915       5           RLS
       PRODBAT        PGMRUS06     158945       5           RLS
       PRODBAT        PRODUS01     158966       5           RLS
       PRODBAT        PRODUS01     106869       5           HLD
       PRODBAT        PRODUS01     109004       5           HLD
                                                           More...
Parameters for options 2, 3 or command
===>
F3=Exit    F4=Prompt    F6=Submit job    F12=Cancel
F22=Work with job schedule entries      F24=More keys
```

Figure 8.8: The job that was moved no longer appears in the incorrect queue.

189

Repeat the process to move the job submitted by PGMRUS06. The only modification you have to make is to specify PGMRBAT as the job queue name, instead of QBATCH. To move more than one job to the same queue, place a two in front of each of the jobs you want to move, and specify the JOBQ parameter only once.

Finding Jobs That You Have Submitted—The Easy Way

Often, when you are looking for batch jobs, you're looking only for the jobs that you have submitted. While the methods just reviewed could be used to find your jobs, there is a much easier way. All you need to do to see your submitted jobs is to run the Work with Submitted Jobs command:

```
WRKSBMJOB
```

The jobs shown will be on a job queue, running, or waiting for output to print. You can usually take the defaults for this command, but the SBMFRM parameter, discussed in Table 8.3, provides a few options for displaying the jobs. When you enter WRKSBMJOB, you are shown a list of jobs that match the choice you made for the first parameter, as shown in Figure 8.9.

Table 8.3: Values for the SBMFRM Parameter

SBMFRM	Submitted Jobs Displayed
*USER	Show all jobs submitted using the same user profile as the user running the command. If the user has been submitting jobs for several days, there might be a long list of submitted jobs, especially if you haven't printed the output files. This is the default value.
*JOB	Show only jobs that have been submitted by the job running the command. This is a good method for reducing the number of jobs that are displayed.
*WRKSTN	Show all jobs submitted from the workstation that is running the command, regardless of the user. If a user has been submitting jobs, but is unable to determine what has been happening to them, you can sign on to the user's workstation and run WRKSBMJOB(*WRKSTN) to find the jobs. This would be a faster method than trying to sift through all the jobs that are on job queues, running, or waiting for printout.

```
                        Work with Submitted Jobs              TSCSAP02
                                                    12/27/00  16:33:13
Submitted from . . . . . . . . :    *USER

Type options, press Enter.
  2=Change    3=Hold   4=End    5=Work with    6=Release    7=Display message
  8=Work with spooled files


Opt  Job          User         Type      ---Status---  Function
     PRODJOBD     PRODUS02     BATCH     OUTQ
     QDFTJOBD     PRODUS02     BATCH     JOBQ
     QDFTJOBD     PRODUS02     BATCH     JOBQ
     QDFTJOBD     PRODUS02     BATCH     JOBQ
     QDFTJOBD     PRODUS02     BATCH     JOBQ
     QDFTJOBD     PRODUS02     BATCH     JOBQ
     QDFTJOBD     PRODUS02     BATCH     JOBQ

                                                                   Bottom
Parameters or command
===>
F3=Exit       F4=Prompt    F5=Refresh   F9=Retrieve   F11=Display schedule data
F12=Cancel    F17=Top      F18=Bottom
```

Figure 8.9: Entering the WRKSBMJOB command results in a list of jobs matching the choice made for the first parameter.

This display shows all of the jobs that have been submitted by the person running the command—PRODUS02, in this case. Also, the display shows the status of each job. The status of the job has two parts. The first part of the status can have the following values:

- JOBQ—The submitted job is on a job queue waiting to be started. The job was either submitted directly to the job queue or moved to the queue with the CHGJOB command. If you want to locate the job queue for a job, just type a five in front of it and you will get the Work with Job displays discussed earlier in this chapter.

- OUTQ—The submitted job has finished running and has produced printed output that is on an output queue waiting to be printed. To examine the output files produced by a job, place an eight in front of the job.

- ACTIVE—The job is running. The Function column of this display gives you a general idea of what the job is doing.

- DSC—The job has been disconnected.

- TFRJOB—The job reached the job queue as a result of the TFRJOB command.

- TFRBCH—The job reached the job queue as result of the TFRBCH command.

- SYSREQ—The job has been suspended as a result of the system request key. This function is applicable to interactive jobs, and is discussed in the next chapter.

- FIN—The job has finished.

- END—The job is in the process of being ended by the ENDJOB or ENDSBS command.

- EOJ—The job is ending for some other reason than described in the end status.

- MSGW—The initial thread of a job is waiting for a message.

- SCD—The job is scheduled to be run at a specified time.

The second part of the status indicates if the job is being held. Held jobs have a status of HELD; otherwise, the second part of the status will be blank. Finally, the two parts of the status will show JOBLOG PENDING if the system failed while the job was active.

That certainly was an easier and more straightforward way to find submitted jobs than trying to work your way through the job queue sequence. In addition, you can still make any changes to the job from this display by simply typing a two in front of the job and entering the new parameters on the input line.

Printed Output

The first part of this chapter discusses the work management functions that enable you to view and manage batch jobs. This discussion includes the obvious fact that jobs produce printed output. What happens to the printed output? Where does it go before it gets printed? How does it get printed? After it's printed, how do you find it?

Tracking printed output in the iSeries 400 is simplified by certain commands. In addition, if you set up your environment carefully, you can eliminate much of the mystery that surrounds printed output.

QSPL—The Spool Subsystem

To this point, you have only dealt with the QBASE subsystem, batch jobs, and interactive jobs. However, after your controlling subsystem (QBASE) is activated, the system will automatically start the spool subsystem, QSPL. The QSPL subsystem is similar to all other subsystems in its structure; that is, it has pools, job queue entries, routing entries, etc. Since you've already been through the mechanics of a subsystem more than once, there is no need to do it again. The following sections take a brief look at some of the key elements of the QSPL subsystem.

Pool Definitions

First, look at the pool definitions for QSPL by selecting option 1 on the Display Subsystem Description menu which will bring up the screen shown in Figure 8.10.

```
                         Display Pool Definitions
                                                    System:    TSCSAP02
        Subsystem description:    QSPL          Status:    ACTIVE

        Pool            Storage      Activity
         ID             Size (K)      Level
          1              *BASE
          2              *SPOOL








                                                               Bottom
        Press Enter to continue.

        F3=Exit    F12-Cancel
```

*Figure 8.10: The IBM-supplied QSPL subsystem is shipped with two shared pools, *BASE and *SPOOL.*

There's not much exciting here. There are two pools that can be used by QSPL to start jobs: *BASE and *SPOOL. In the previous examples, you saw that *SPOOL has storage allocated to it, but not much detail was provided about the contents. While I won't go into excruciating detail regarding the content of the pool, you should at least know what goes on in *SPOOL.

Job Queue Entries

Jobs are initiated by QSPOOL via job queue entries. Figure 8.11 shows the job queue entry that is shipped with the QSPL subsystem.

```
                          Display Job Queue Entries
                                                     System:   TSCSAP02
       Subsystem description:   QSPL          Status:   ACTIVE

       Seq  Job                      Max    ------Max by Priority------
       Nbr  Queue     Library     Active   1   2   3   4   5   6   7   8   9
        10  QSPL      QGPL        *NOMAX   *   *   *   *   *   *   *   *   *














                                                                  Bottom
       Press Enter to continue.

       F3=Exit    F12=Cancel
```

Figure 8.11: All jobs that are initiated by the QSPL subsystem arrive from the QSPL job queue.

There's nothing here that you haven't seen before. There are two basic classes of spool jobs: *readers* and *writers*. Writers are jobs that convert spool files to printed output. They enter the system as jobs placed on a job queue allocated to QSPL. Readers are not used much anymore. Their primary purpose was to take batch-job command input from some media, like punched cards, and convert them to a job stream that was placed on a batch job queue. Since most people have never seen a punched card (until the 2000 presidential election, anyway), you can see how archaic spool readers have become.

Routing Entries

Now that you have pools and a source of work for QSPL, you need some routing
entries for the work. Figure 8.12 shows the QSPL routing entries.

```
                    Display Routing Entries
                                              System:    TSCSAP02
   Subsystem description:    QSPL         Status:   ACTIVE

   Type options, press Enter.
     5=Display details

                                                             Start
   Opt    Seq Nbr   Program      Library      Compare Value   Pos
          10        QCMD         QSYS         'QWTRPT'         1
          50        QCMD         QSYS         'QAFPWT'         1
          60        QCMD         QSYS         'QRMTWT'         1
          9999      QCMD         QSYS         *ANY




                                                            Bottom
   F3=Exit    F9=Display all detailed descriptions    F12=Cancel
```

Figure 8.12: Jobs initiated by QSPL will use one of the four entries shipped with the QSPL subsystem.

Again, there's nothing new here. The first three routing entries are all used for writers. The first entry will be used by most of the writers, while the other two are for
advanced function printers (sequence 50) and remote writers (sequence 60). The
last routing entry is used by readers. The routing entries divide the work from QSPL
into the two available pools. The first three entries will place the writers in *SPOOL,
while the last entry routes jobs to *BASE. It should be noted that writer jobs receive
a very high priority of 15. Don't worry, the print jobs do not use a lot of CPU, and
the high priority allows them quick access to the processors. As a result, high-speed
printers can be kept busy printing even when a lot of other jobs are running.

An overview of QSPL is shown in Figure 8.13.

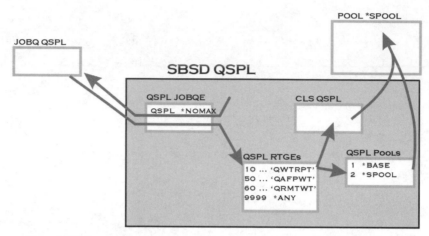

Figure 8.13: QSPL will locate work on its job queue and initiate a job using one of four routing entries.

Spool Writers

Since spool writing is the primary function of QSPL, and since you are looking for printed output, look only at the function of the spool writers. Whenever a job produces output, it can print directly to the printer, or it can send the output to a spool file.

Printing large amounts of information to a shared printer is not advised. First, your job will slow down dramatically while it waits for the output to be printed by the printer. Second, if it is a shared printer, only one job will be allowed access to the printer at a time. As a result, your job could wait for access to the printer for a long time, until the job currently using the printer releases. Then, you will be in a mad scramble with other users to try to get the lock. You're much better off producing a spool file.

Once a spool writer has been started, it looks like Figure 8.14. The spool writer job will be running in the *SPOOL pool.

Now you can see that QSPL is used to start your writers, and your writers allocate a device and an output queue. But how do you find out what's on the queue? How do you know what other queues are being processed by writers? And, most importantly, how do you find your output files?

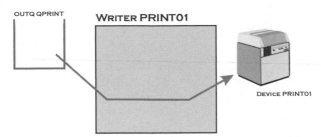

Figure 8.14: When a writer is started, a job is submitted to the QSPL job queue and is initiated by the QSPL subsystem. The job will indicate which printer device and output queue it will use.

Finding the Output Queues

Finding the output queues in the system is very similar to finding the job queues. You merely enter the Work with Output Queue command:

```
WRKOUTQ
```

Once again, by not specifying the name of an output queue, you are shown all of the output queues in the system, like the example in Figure 8.15.

```
                    Work with All Output Queues

 Type options, press Enter.
 2=Change    3=Hold      4=Delete    5=Work with   6=Release   8=Description
 9=Work with Writers    14=Clear

 Opt    Queue       Library       Files     Writer        Status
        OPCOUTQA    OPCLIBA           0                    RLS
        QDMT        QDMT              0                    RLS
        PGMROUTQ    QGPL             33                    RLS
        SYSADMOQ    QGPL              8                    RLS
        QDKT        QGPL              0                    RLS
        QPFROUTQ    QGPL             56                    RLS
        QPRINT      QGPL            199     PRINT01        RLS
        QPRINTS     QGPL              0                    RLS
        QPRINT2     QGPL              0                    RLS
        SAPR3       QGPL              0                    RLS
        QEZDEBUG    QUSRSYS           0                    RLS
        QEZJOBLOG   QUSRSYS        5403                    RLS
                                                              More...
 Command
 ===>

 F3=Exit    F4=Prompt    F5=Refresh    F12=Cancel    F24=More keys
```

Figure 8.15: The Work with Output Queue command with no parameters will show all of the output queues in the system.

In addition to showing all of the output queues in the system, this display shows how many files are waiting to be printed, the name of the print writer currently writing the files to a printer, and the status of the output queue (held or released).

When you look at your list of output queues, you see that QPRINT has quite a few files associated with it. In addition, a print writer is producing output on a printer. QPRINT is the default output queue for user jobs. You usually have a writer sending output to an extremely fast printer in order to get through your print files, especially the print files that are produced by your long-running batch jobs. There are usually a large number of rather lengthy print files produced by such jobs.

Before moving on, look at QEZJOBLOG. It looks like you are producing job logs for all of your jobs. In the discussion of logging levels earlier in the chapter, the conclusion was that it wasn't such a good idea, so you should examine the logging level specified for your job descriptions.

Checking the Files on an Output Queue

It shouldn't surprise you that you can look at the files on an output queue by specifying the name of the queue with the Work with Output Queue command (WRKOUTQ):

```
WRKOUTQ QEZJOBLOG
```

You can also select option 5 (Work with) from the display that has the name as your output queue, as shown in Figure 8.16. In either case, you are shown all the job logs waiting to be printed, as in Figure 8.17.

```
                    Work with All Output Queues

Type options, press Enter.
 2=Change   3=Hold     4=Delete    5=Work with   6=Release   8=Description
 9=Work with Writers   14=Clear

Opt    Queue        Library        Files      Writer        Status
       OPCOUTQA     OPCLIBA           0                      RLS
       QDMT         QDMT              0                      RLS
       PGMROUTQ     QGPL             33                      RLS
       SYSADMOQ     QGPL              8                      RLS
       QDKT         QGPL              0                      RLS
       QPFROUTQ     QGPL             56                      RLS
       QPRINT       QGPL            199      PRINT01         RLS
       QPRINTS      QGPL              0                      RLS
       QPRINT2      QGPL              0                      RLS
       SAPR3        QGPL              0                      RLS
       QEZDEBUG     QUSRSYS           0                      RLS
 5     QEZJOBLOG    QUSRSYS        5403                      RLS
                                                            More...
Command
 ===>
 F3=Exit   F4=Prompt   F5=Refresh   F12=Cancel   F24=More keys
```

Figure 8.16: Placing a five in front of an output queue on the Work with All Output Queues display will show the spool files on the selected queue.

```
                    Work with Output Queue

  Queue:  QEZJOBLOG    Library:  QUSRSYS      Status:  RLS

   Type options, press Enter.
    1=Send   2=Change   3=Hold   4=Delete   5=Display   6=Release   7=Messages
    8=Attributes        9=Work with printing status

Opt   File        User       User Data   Sts   Pages   Copies  Form Type  Pty
      QPJOBLOG    QPM400     Q1PDR       RDY     1       1      *STD        5
      QPJOBLOG    QUSER      QZLSFILE    RDY     1       1      *STD        5
      QPJOBLOG    QUSER      QZLSFILE    RDY     1       1      *STD        5
      QPJOBLOG    QUSER      QZLSFILE    RDY     1       1      *STD        5
      QPJOBLOG    QPM400     Q1PDAY      RDY     1       1      *STD        5
      QPJOBLOG    QUSER      QZLSFILE    RDY     1       1      *STD        5
      QPJOBLOG    QUSER      QZLSFILE    RDY     1       1      *STD        5
      QPJOBLOG    QUSER      QZLSFILE    RDY     1       1      *STD        5
      QPJOBLOG    QUSER      QZLSFILE    RDY     1       1      *STD        5
                                                              More...
 Parameters for options 1, 2, 3 or command
 ===>
 F3=Exit   F11=View 2   F12=Cancel   F20=Writers   F22=Printers
 F24=More keys
```

Figure 8.17: The Work with Output Queue display shows all the spool files on an output queue.

If you are looking for a failed job's log to find out what went wrong, you'll have your work cut out for you. You'll need to page through all of the uninteresting job logs to find the one that failed. Along the way, you might encounter jobs with the same user name, further complicating your search. This is another good reason to set your logging level to 4 0 *NOLIST.

Getting Rid of Unwanted Output Files

Once you have reached the list of files on the output queue, removing the files you don't want to print is a simple process of placing a four (the Delete option) in front of each file you no longer want. You can select as many files as necessary, including files on displays that follow the one you are viewing. While this provides some help, it will still take a long time if you have, say, more than 5,000 files to delete.

If you know that you are not interested in printing or viewing any of the files on an output queue, you can eliminate them all with the Clear Output Queue command (CLROUTQ):

```
CLROUTQ QEZJOBLOG
```

Fortunately, this command requires the name of an output queue and gives a confirmation screen. Otherwise, you could potentially wipe out all of your queues.

Another method for clearing the contents of an output queue is to use the Work with All Output Queues (WRKOUTQ with no parameters). When you are shown the output queues in the system, you can place a 14 (the Clear option) in front of each queue you wish to clear. To clear QEZJOBLOG, then, you would enter a 14 in front of it, as shown in Figure 8.18.

After pressing Enter or entering the CLROUTQ command, you are given a confirmation screen like the one shown in Figure 8.19. This is your last chance to change your mind. If any of the output queues shown should not be cleared, press F12 immediately! You will be returned to the Work with All Output Queues Display, and can correct your error.

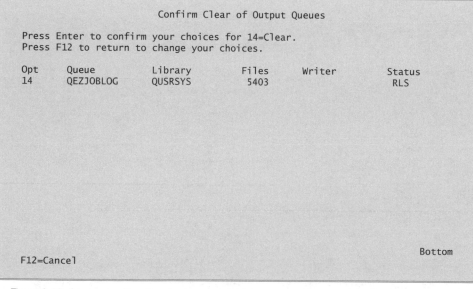

```
                    Work with All Output Queues

Type options, press Enter.
  2=Change   3=Hold      4=Delete    5=Work with   6=Release   8=Description
  9=Work with Writers   14=Clear

  Opt      Queue        Library       Files    Writer       Status
           OPCOUTQA     OPCLIBA          0                  RLS
           QDMT         QDMT             0                  RLS
           PGMROUTQ     QGPL            33                  RLS
           SYSADMOQ     QGPL             8                  RLS
           QDKT         QGPL             0                  RLS
           QPFROUTQ     QGPL            56                  RLS
           QPRINT       QGPL           199    PRINT01       RLS
           QPRINTS      QGPL             0                  RLS
           QPRINT2      QGPL             0                  RLS
           SAPR3        QGPL             0                  RLS
           QEZDEBUG     QUSRSYS          0                  RLS
  14       QEZJOBLOG    QUSRSYS       5403                  RLS
                                                              More...
  Command
  ===>
   F3=Exit    F4=Prompt    F5=Refresh    F12=Cancel    F24=More keys
```

Figure 8.18: Placing a 14 in front of a queue name on the Work with All Output Queues display will clear (remove all of the spool files from) an output queue.

```
                    Confirm Clear of Output Queues

  Press Enter to confirm your choices for 14=Clear.
  Press F12 to return to change your choices.

  Opt      Queue        Library       Files    Writer       Status
  14       QEZJOBLOG    QUSRSYS       5403                  RLS




                                                              Bottom
  F12=Cancel
```

Figure 8.19: A severe action, like clearing an output queue, requires a confirmation before the action is performed.

Finding Active Print Writers

When you run the Work with Output Queue command (WRKOUTQ), you will be shown all of the output queues and any writers that are assigned to them. Often, a large number of output queues exist, but the output sent to the output queues is not always printed. In some cases, the printed output is viewed online to save time and paper. As a result, you might page through several displays of output queues to find all of the active print writers. Or, you can take the easy way and enter the Work with Writers command:

```
WRKWTR
```

Since you did not specify the name of a print writer, you will be shown all of the active print writers in the system, as in Figure 8.20. To see the output queue for each writer, just place an eight (the Work with Output Queue option) in front of each active writer, as shown in Figure 8.21.

When you press Enter, you will see the queue that the writer is processing and any print files that are on the queue, as shown in Figure 8.22. From this display, you can hold print files, change their priority, delete them, etc.

```
                        Work with All Printers

     Type options, press Enter.
       1=Start    2=Change    3=Hold    4=End    5=Work with    6=Release
       7=Display messages    8=Work with output queue

     Opt  Device      Sts   Sep   Form Type    File         User        User Data
          LAB20       STR   *FILE  *ALL
          PRT4312     STR   *FILE  *ALL
          TSCPRT1     STR   *FILE  *ALL




                                                                          Bottom
     Parameters for options 1, 2, 3, 4, 6 or command
     ===>
     F3=Exit    F11=View 2    F12=Cancel    F17=Top    F18=Bottom    F24=More keys
```

Figure 8.20: Running the Work with Writers command with no parameters shows all of the active writers.

```
                        Work with All Printers

 Type options, press Enter.
   1=Start   2=Change    3=Hold    4=End   5=Work with    6=Release
   7=Display messages    8=Work with output queue

 Opt  Device       Sts   Sep   Form Type   File          User       User Data
 8    LAB20        STR   *FILE  *ALL
      PRT4312      STR   *FILE  *ALL
      TSCPRT1      STR   *FILE  *ALL




                                                                    Bottom
 Parameters for options 1, 2, 3, 4, 6 or command
 ===>
 F3=Exit   F11=View 2   F12=Cancel   F17=Top   F18=Bottom   F24=More keys
```

Figure 8.21: Placing an eight in front of a writer on the Work with All Printers display will show the contents of the output queue that the writer is sending to the print device.

```
                        Work with Output Queue

 Queue:   LAB20           Library:   QUSRSYS        Status:   RLS/WTR

 Type options, press Enter.
   1=Send   2=Change    3=Hold   4=Delete   5=Display   6=Release   7=Messages
   8=Attributes         9=Work with printing status

 Opt  File       User       User Data   Sts   Pages   Copies  Form Type  Pty

   (No spooled output files)




                                                                    Bottom
 Parameters for options 1, 2, 3 or command
 ===>
 F3=Exit   F11=View 2   F12=Cancel   F20=Writers   F22=Printers
 F24=More keys
```

Figure 8.22: The Work with Output Queue display lists spool files that are waiting to be printed.

Getting from Output Queue to Paper

When you have finished looking at all of your active writers, you might find that an output queue you would like to process does not have an active writer assigned to it. In this example, you want a writer to print output from output queue QPRINT to print device PRINT01. However, you currently do not have an active writer for the QPRINT output queue. You can fix that by running the Start Print Writer command (STRPRTWTR):

```
STRPRTWTR DEV(PRINT01) OUTQ(QGPL/QPRINT)
```

This command submits a job to the QSPL job queue, which will be processed by the QSPL subsystem, which will, in turn, start your writer in the *SPOOL pool. As a result, files on the QPRINT output queue will begin to be printed at the PRINT01 device.

Finding Output Files

Now that you have an understanding of the components of QSPL and the mechanics for printing output files, you need a way to find the printed files that you've created. While there are a lot of methods for finding printed files created by an interactive job or any job that you submitted, many of them are time-consuming and subject to error. The most direct approach is to simply enter the Work with Spool Files command:

```
WRKSPLF
```

The default values for WRKSPLF can be used. When the command is run, you will see a display of all of the spool files you have produced, as shown in Figure 8.23.

From this display, you can perform many management functions, as listed in Table 8.4.

```
                    Work with All Spooled Files

Type options, press Enter.
  1=Send    2=Change   3=Hold   4=Delete   5=Display   6=Release   7=Messages
  8=Attributes         9=Work with printing status


                             Device or                    Total   Cur
Opt   File        User        Queue       User Data   Sts  Pages   Page  Copy
      QPJOBLOG    PGMRUS06    QEZJOBLOG   QPADEV0026   RDY    2           1
      QPJOBLOG    PGMRUS06    QEZJOBLOG   QPADEV0026   RDY    2           1
      QPJOBLOG    PGMRUS06    QEZJOBLOG   QPADEV0026   RDY    2           1
      QPJOBLOG    PGMRUS06    QEZJOBLOG   QPADEV0026   RDY    2           1
      QPJOBLOG    PGMRUS06    QEZJOBLOG   QPADEV0026   RDY    2           1
      QPJOBLOG    PGMRUS06    QEZJOBLOG   QPADEV0026   RDY    2           1
      QPJOBLOG    PGMRUS06    QEZJOBLOG   QPADEV0026   RDY    2           1
      QPJOBLOG    PGMRUS06    QEZJOBLOG   QPADEV0026   RDY    2           1
      QPJOBLOG    PGMRUS06    QEZJOBLOG   QPADEV0026   RDY    2           1
                                                                More...
Parameters for options 1, 2, 3 or command
===>
F3=Exit   F10=View 4   F11=View 2   F12=Cancel   F22=Printers   F24=More keys
```

Figure 8.23: The Work with All Spooled Files display shows all the spool files produced by the job running WRKSPLF with the default values taken for all parameters.

Table 8.4: Spool File Options (1 of 2)

Option	Action
1—Send	This option lets you send the spool file to another system. You might use this option if a user on a remote system produced a print file on an output queue that is being printed to a local device. If you send the spool file to the originator's system, it can be printed at the user's location.
2—Change	This option can be used to change the attributes of the spool file. For example, you might wish to move the file to a different output queue.
3—Hold	Hold the file. If you have produced an extremely long file, printing it may affect the throughput of other user's files. You might wish to hold the file and print it later.
4—Delete	Delete the spool file. This is a good choice for any job logs you have produced. When you select this option, you will be given a confirmation screen.

Table 8.4: Spool File Options (2 of 2)	
Option	**Action**
5—Display	View the contents of the spool file online. This option can be used to look at results in a more timely fashion. For example, assume that the output file created when you ran the CRTDSPF file (to modify your sign-on) indicated errors in your file. Rather than wait for the file to get to the top of the queue, get printed, and delivered, you can just look at the output online find your errors, make the necessary corrections, and delete the file.
6—Release	Release a file so that it can be printed.
7—Messages	Display any messages associated with the file while it is printing. If your output is not appearing or appears to be stopped, it could be caused by the writer waiting for a message to be handled.
8—Attributes	Work with the attributes of the spool file. If you are uncertain of the attributes of the file, select this option. You will be shown the attributes, but you cannot make changes to any of them using this selection.
9—Work with Printing Status	This selection shows you the printing status of the file. You will be shown any writer associated with the file. If no writer is associated with the file, you will be shown a display from which you can assign the file to a print device.

Use the SELECT parameter of the WRKSPLF command to choose what spool files you'd like to see. The SELECT parameter has the choices shown in Table 8.5.

Table 8.5: Select Parameters for the WRKSPLF command	
Option	**Meaning/Values**
User	The User parameter has the following possible values: • *CURRENT—The files created by the user running this command are shown. This is the default value. • *ALL—Files created by all users are shown. it is a good idea to specify one of the other selection options if you choose this option. • *User name*—The files created by the specified user name are shown.
Print Device	The Print Device parameter has the following possible values: • *ALL—Files on all output queue are shown. This is the default value. • *OUTQ—The files on any user-created output queue are selected. A user-created output queue is any output queue that is not automatically created by a device. • *Device name*—The files on the device-created output queue for the device name specified are shown. (A *device-created output queue* is one that has the same name as a device and resides in the QUSRSYS library. Unless it already exists, it will automatically be created by the system when the device is created. A device-created output queue cannot be deleted.)
Form Type	The Form Type parameter has the following possible values: • *ALL—Files for all form types are shown. This is the default value. • *STD—The files that specify the standard form type are shown. • *Form type*—Only files that use the specified form type are shown.
User Data	The User Data parameter has the following possible values: • *ALL—Files with any user data tag specified are shown. This is the default value. • *User data*—Only files that have the specified user data tag are shown.
ASP	The Auxiliary Storage Pool (ASP) parameter has the following possible values: • *ALL—Files in all auxiliary storage pools are shown. This is the default value. • ASP number—Only files in the specified auxiliary storage pool are shown. Valid values are one to 32. Note: ASPs refers to disk drives that have been grouped together in order to direct objects to disk drives. This concept is beyond the scope of this book.

What happens if your output has already been printed? In that case, you can no longer locate it with any of the commands available to you. To find your printed output, you must make certain assumptions regarding the consistency of your environment. You must assume that your spool files are placed on the output queue associated with your job description. In the case of a batch job, assume that you used the job description associated with your user profile.

You now have an idea of the output queue that was used. Once you have the output queue identified, you can use WRKOUTQ to find the print writer and device currently associated with that queue. If your environment has remained consistent, you can assume that your print will be located on this device. Unfortunately, inconsistencies in your environment or overrides of default values (on the SBMJOB command, for example) might make it very difficult to locate your output. Any time a change is made to your defaults, you should record the change so that you can locate your printed output later.

Spool Summary

This section provides an overview of iSeries 400 spool support as it relates to work management. There is much more to spool processing, printing, and printer devices than is covered here. However, you should now be able to manage output queues, determine how output gets to an output queue, determine how output gets from the output queue to a printer, find output files, start writers, and work with spool files.

Moving Jobs

Once your jobs have been started, you might find that they have entered the system with the wrong routing information, or they might have even entered the wrong the subsystem. You could simply cancel these jobs and make the users start over, or you could try to correct the problem. If you are going to try to correct the problem, then the programs that your jobs are running will need to analyze the situation and take corrective action.

Finding Your Identity

As you have seen, subsystems route jobs based on routing data and routing entries. Once initiated, you can see the runtime attributes of a job by running the Work with Job command:

```
WRKJOB
```

You've seen the results of this command before, but Figure 8.24 shows it again, for your review.

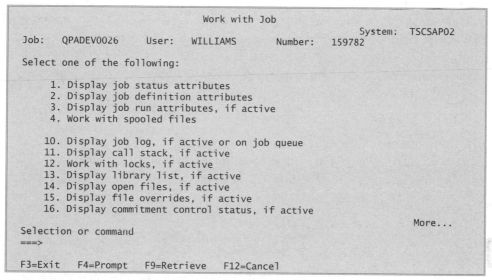

```
                      Work with Job
                                        System:  TSCSAP02
Job:  QPADEV0026    User:   WILLIAMS    Number:  159782

Select one of the following:

     1. Display job status attributes
     2. Display job definition attributes
     3. Display job run attributes, if active
     4. Work with spooled files

    10. Display job log, if active or on job queue
    11. Display call stack, if active
    12. Work with locks, if active
    13. Display library list, if active
    14. Display open files, if active
    15. Display file overrides, if active
    16. Display commitment control status, if active
                                                     More...
Selection or command
===>

F3=Exit   F4=Prompt   F9=Retrieve   F12=Cancel
```

Figure 8.24: When the Work with Job command is run, a menu to find additional information about the job is shown.

Since you are looking at an active job and want to make sure it is in the right place at the right time, select option 1 (Display Job Status Attributes). The screen in Figure 8.25 is displayed.

```
                Display Job Status Attributes
                                        System:  TSCSAP02
Job:  QPADEV0026    User:   WILLIAMS    Number:  159782

Status of job . . . . . . . . . . . . . :   ACTIVE
Current user profile  . . . . . . . . . :   JCSTUPCA
Job user identity . . . . . . . . . . . :   JCSTUPCA
  Set by  . . . . . . . . . . . . . . . :    *DEFAULT
Entered system:
  Date  . . . . . . . . . . . . . . . . :   01/04/01
  Time  . . . . . . . . . . . . . . . . :   09:15:56
Started:
  Date  . . . . . . . . . . . . . . . . :   01/04/01
  Time  . . . . . . . . . . . . . . . . :   09:15:56
Subsystem . . . . . . . . . . . . . . . :   QINTER
  Subsystem pool ID . . . . . . . . . . :    2
Type of job . . . . . . . . . . . . . . :   INTER
Special environment . . . . . . . . . . :   *NONE
Program return code . . . . . . . . . . :   0
                                                     More...
Press Enter to continue.

F3=Exit    F5=Refresh   F12=Cancel    F16=Job menu
```

Figure 8.25: Selecting option 1 on the Work with Job menu shows the job status attributes.

The information you want to see appears on this screen—namely, the subsystem that started the job and the pool that it is using. If you are interested in other runtime aspects of the job, press F12 to return to the Work with Job Display, then select option 3 to see the runtime attributes assigned to the job by the class specified on the routing entry, as shown in Figure 8.26.

The information in Figures 8.25 and 8.26 tells you if the job has been initiated correctly, but what do you do with this information? In other words, how do you use this information to fix a job that has been routed incorrectly?

```
                        Display Job Run Attributes
                                              System:  TSCSAP02
   Job:   QPADEV0026    User:   WILLIAMS    Number:   159782

   Run priority . . . . . . . . . . . . . . . . . . :   20
   Time slice in milliseconds . . . . . . . . . . :   2000
   Eligible for purge . . . . . . . . . . . . . . :   *YES
   Default wait time in seconds . . . . . . . . . :   30
   Maximum CPU time in milliseconds . . . . . . . :   *NOMAX
     CPU time used . . . . . . . . . . . . . . . :   294
   Maximum temporary storage in megabytes . . . . :   *NOMAX
     Temporary storage used . . . . . . . . . . . :   2
   Maximum threads . . . . . . . . . . . . . . . . :   *NOMAX
     Threads . . . . . . . . . . . . . . . . . . . :   1




   Press Enter to continue.

   F3=Exit    F5=Refresh    F9=Change job    F12=Cancel    F16=Job menu
```

Figure 8.26: These runtime attributes were assigned to the job by the class specified on the routing entry.

Incorrect Routing Within a Subsystem

The first type of problem that you want to examine is a job that has been routed incorrectly. Remember the example of multiple batch job types in chapter 6? In two of the methods, you needed to supply the correct routing data for your batch jobs so that the right routing entry would be selected and the job placed in the correct pool.

If you want to be absolutely certain that this works every time, you need to perform the RTVJOBA function in every batch job that you run. For example, if your analysis shows that a programmer's batch job is running in QBASE pool 3 rather than pool 5, you need to run the following RRTJOB command:

```
RRTJOB RTGDTA(PGMR)
```

That should do it, but it could be extremely difficult to do for all of your batch jobs. As discussed in chapters 6 and 7, a multiple subsystem approach would prevent such routing errors from occurring in the first place.

Jobs Started in the Wrong Subsystem

In both the batch and interactive subsystem examples in chapter 6 and 7, you used multiple subsystems to separate different types of jobs. What happens, however, if a batch job gets to the wrong queue, and you don't find out about it until the job starts? Or what about the case of workstations in a subsystem being used to run the wrong kind of work?

Once again, you can find these erroneous jobs with RTVJOBA. When you find them, you can transfer them to another system with the Transfer Batch Job command (TFRBCHJOB) or the Transfer Job command (TFRJOB). For example, in the case of the programmer's batch job running in QBASE instead of PGMRBAT, you would run the following:

```
TFRBCHJOB JOBQ(PGMRBAT) RTGDTA(PGMR)
```

For an interactive job that started in the wrong system, you need to run this:

```
TFRJOB JOBQ(PGMRINT) RTGDTA(QCMDI)
```

An interactive job going to a job queue?! Yes, as strange as it seems, interactive jobs are transferred to another subsystem via a job queue. Once the job is initiated, it appears as an interactive job. So, you need to add a job queue to your subsystem in order to transfer interactive jobs.

Providing the job queue is not enough to get the interactive job into the subsystem, however. In chapter 2's discussion of workstation entries, you learned that one of the parameters of the ADDWSE command is AT. You have two choices for this parameter:

- *SIGNON, the default, means that subsystems try to stake their claims on any workstation that is in or reaches the varied-on state.

- *ENTER means that a subsystem will not try to allocate the workstations.

To accept an interactive job via the TFRJOB command, you need to have a workstation entry with the AT parameter set to *ENTER.

If you go back to the multiple subsystem example, you could have one subsystem with workstation entries with the AT parameter set to *SIGNON, and the other subsystems with workstation entries set to *ENTER. In this case, only the first subsystem will send a sign-on screen. When the user signs on, the application will determine the correct subsystem to use and run the TFRJOB command.

Your first subsystem is like a card dealer. The dealer has all the cards (workstations) allocated. When a user signs on, the subsystem deals (transfers) the job to another player (active subsystem).

In Review

You now have much of the information you need to manage your environment. You can:

- Find job queues and manage the jobs on them.
- Easily locate submitted jobs and manage them.
- Find spooled output, print it, and find it after it has been printed.
- Correct routing and job initiation errors.

Now, not only are you familiar with most of the subsystem environments that are used, you are able to find and manage jobs, job queues, output queues, writers, and spool files.

9

The Schizoid Workstation

So far in this book, you've been looking at workstations as devices capable of running only one job. However, the workstation can have multiple personalities. This chapter looks at OS/400 support that allows a user to have more than one job per workstation.

System Request and the Second Job

All keyboards have a System Request key (SYSREQ), or a combination of keys mapped to the System Request key. (Subsequent references to the System Request key include both conditions.) When you press the System Request key, an input line at the bottom of the display (line 24) is enabled. If this is your first usage of the System Request key, you won't know what to put in the line; just press Enter to get the menu shown in Figure 9.1. Table 9.1 describes the menu options.

```
                         System Request
                                                System:  TSCSAP02
   Select one of the following:

        1. Display sign on for alternative job
        2. End previous request
        3. Display current job
        4. Display messages
        5. Send a message
        6. Display system operator messages
        7. Display work station user

       80. Disconnect job

       90. Sign off


                                                           Bottom
   Selection


   F3=Exit   F12=Cancel
   (C) COPYRIGHT IBM CORP. 1980, 2000.
```

Figure 9.1: The System Request menu is shown whenever the System Request key is pressed. It gives a workstation user several work management options.

Table 9.1: Options on the System Request Menu (1 of 2)

Option	Meaning/Action
1—Display sign on for alternative job	Selecting option 1 will present you with the sign-on display. When you sign on to the system from the display, your workstation will have a second job!
2—End previous request	Suppose the job you are running is testing a new version of your application, and, well, you have a little bit of a problem—the application is looping. When the job starts to loop, how do you stop it? You can wait for it to exceed the maximum amount of CPU that it is allowed to use, but the default is usually *NOMAX. You can have someone else use the Work with Active Jobs command (WRKACTJOB), locate your job, and select the option to end your job immediately.

The easiest method, however, is to select option 2 from the System Request menu. This will interrupt the function you were running, end it and return you to the previous program in the invocation stack—in most instances, the screen you were using when you entered the problem transaction will be redisplayed. When the action is complete, you will be returned to the job you were running. |

Table 9.1: Options on the System Request Menu (2 of 2)

Option	Meaning/Action
3—Display current job	When your job does not appear to be running correctly, but you're not quite sure whether to cancel it, select this option. The information about your job will be displayed. You will be able to see if you are using a lot of CPU and are in a loop. You'll also be able to see if your job is waiting for a message. Once you have examined the status of your job, you can return to this screen and select the appropriate action.
4—Display messages	This option will display your user-profile and workstation messages. If your job is not progressing because it is waiting for a response from one of these two message queues, you can enter your response. When you return to your job, you can see if the job is progressing as expected. If not, use the System Request function again.
5—Send a message	If you are having difficulty analyzing the problem that your job is having, you can send a message to another user to explain your predicament.
6—Display system operator messages	If your job is not waiting for a message on one of the user-profile or workstation queues, it might be waiting for a message sent to the system operator queue (QSYSOPR). This option displays QSYSOPR and allows you to respond to any messages that your job has sent.
7—Display work station user	If you walk up to a workstation and want to use it, but a user has entered a long-running function, you can use this option to find the identity of the user. Or, if you have two jobs running at your workstation and can't remember where you are, this option might help.
80—Disconnect job	It takes a large amount of overhead to initiate job. If you have a large number of users leaving at the same time, and returning at the same time (like for lunch), the sign-off/sign-on activity might cause performance problems. If you have failed to allow a "Disconnect Job" option on your menu, you can instruct your users to use System Request option 80. When they return to their workstations and sign on, they will be reconnected with their original jobs.
90—Sign off	This option ends the job that you were running when you activated the System Request function. If you have two active jobs at your workstation, you will be returned to the remaining active job.
F3—Exit	Use F3 to leave the System Request menu and return to the job that activated the function.
F12—Cancel	Use F12 to leave the System Request menu and return to the job that activated the function.

Take a closer look at option 1. If you select it, you will see the sign-on screen. When you sign on, you will get a second job at your workstation. Once you have the second job, you can repeat this action to toggle back and forth between your two jobs.

FUNCTION 1 STRUCTURE

Figure 9.2: To reach the program that will process the user input, the job must call a number of programs.

So what's the big deal with toggling between two jobs? Chapter 3 provides an example of an application where it comes in handy. An overview of this example is shown in Figure 9.2.

In this example, the user has navigated through several menus to reach the program that receives and processes the production input. If the application has more than one major function, the user will need to navigate another sequence of programs to reach the program that actually receives and processes the production input. Figure 9.3 shows this scenario.

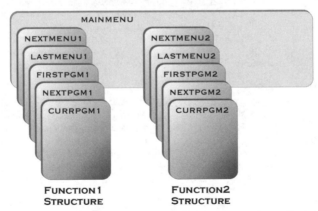

Figure 9.3: This application has more than one type of user input. Each type requires a different sequence of program calls to reach the program that will process the input.

With this application structure, the user would need to exit (back out of) five different programs to return to the main menu. Then, the user would need to start five new programs to finally reach the main input display for this function. If the user moves back and forth between these two functions regularly, frustration will set in very quickly. In addition, each time you leave and enter a program, you are burning up system resources for nonproductive work.

Imagine several hundred users going through this, and you can see the benefit of being able to toggle between the two jobs. When the first job is started, the user, will traverse the programs to set up the entry display for the first function. Once the first function is prepared, the user runs through the System Request function to start the second job and establish its data entry position. Switching between the two jobs only requires the user to choose option 1 from the System Request menu.

This procedure can be made even simpler. Remember that when the System Request key is pressed, the last line of the display becomes input-capable. Rather than displaying the System Request menu, educate your users to press the System Request key, simply enter a one on the last line of the display, and press Enter. The user will be switched to the other job without any intervening screens. How about that? You have made life much easier for your users and dramatically reduced system overhead caused by all the unnecessary interactions.

The Workstation Named Sybil—Group Jobs

If a workstation with two personalities provides that much additional benefit, think of what you could do with more—like 32. That's what the Group Job function of OS/400 allows you to do. No matter how complex the application, and no matter how many functions your users need to perform, you can eliminate large amounts of system overhead with Group Jobs.

The Attn Key

Getting more than two jobs at a workstation starts with the Attn key. All keyboards have an Attn key, or a combination of keys that map to the Attn key. (Subsequent references to the Attn key mean either the key or combination of keys.) When you press the Attn key, the Operational Assistant menu shown in Figure 9.4 is displayed.

As you can see, this menu can provide much of the operational support discussed in the previous chapter. It is an excellent display for your operations staff, but it is not what you would like your users to see when they press the Attn key. In any case, if users are running application programs (which they should be), the Attn key is disabled. You need to enable group jobs, activate the Attn key, and allow users to start more jobs.

```
ASSIST              AS/400 Operational Assistant (TM) Menu
                                                  System:  TSCSAP02
  To select one of the following, type its number below and press Enter:

        1. Work with printer output
        2. Work with jobs
        3. Work with messages
        4. Send messages
        5. Change your password

       10. Manage your system, users, and devices
       11. Customize your system, users, and devices

       75. Information and problem handling

       80. Temporary sign-off



  Type a menu option below


  F1=Help    F3=Exit    F9=Command line    F12=Cancel
```

Figure 9.4: The Operational Assistant menu, which appears whenever a system display is on the screen and the Attn key is pressed, provides a system operator, programmer, or administrator several management functions.

Enabling Group Jobs

Start by looking at the way a job becomes enabled for group jobs. In order for a job to support group jobs, set the group attributes of the job with the Change Group Attributes command (CHGGRPA). This command has only one required parameter, the name of the group job:

```
CHGGRPA GRPJOB(FUNCTION1)
```

When you run this command, the job becomes a member of a group job and is named FUNCTION1. Once you have established the group job, you navigate through the program sequence (just as you did before for a group job) to reach the data entry display for FUNCTION1.

The command used to create the group job needs to be included in the program that is run in the workstation job. It is a good idea to place this command in the initial user program that is run. In this simple example, you would include the CHGGRPA command in the program MAINMENU prior to displaying the menu.

While specifying a group job name before you know which of the two functions a user will choose seems to be out of order, you need to assume that one of the two functions will be selected from the menu. FUNCTION1 is as good a choice as any. Don't get too worried about this now; an example later in this chapter shows how to put all of the pieces together. The important thing to understand is that you have changed your single-user, single-function job to a group job.

Activating the Attn Key

Now that you have a group job, you can activate the Attn key in an application program with the SETATNPGM command. This command allows you to name a program that will be called whenever the Attn key is pressed. The command has two parameters, as shown in Table 9.2.

Table 9.2: Parameters for SETATNPGM	
Parameter	Meaning/Values
PGM	This parameter specifies the program that is to be called when the Attn key is pressed. It has the following possible values:
	• *Library/program*—The specified program will be called.
	• *CURRENT—The program that contains this SETATNPGM command will be called.
	• *PRVINVLVL—This parameter is used whenever more than one Attn key program has been specified. For example, you might have a generic Attn key program that will work for the main menu options. Suppose, however, that one of your main functions splits into subfunctions that traverse several layers of programs to reach data entry. In this case, the first program in this function may choose to use a different Attn key program. When you leave this function, you would reset the Attn key program to the generic program using this parameter. (You are not likely to use this value.)
	This is a required parameter; it has no default value.
SET	This parameter is used to activate or deactivate Attn key. It has the following possible values:
	• *ON—The Attn key is activated. This is the default value.
	• *OFF—The Attn key is deactivated.

In most instances, it is best to provide a program that is different from your main menu program as the Attn key program. It's not necessary, but, as you will see in the example, it makes the programs less complex.

Starting More Than One Job

The discussion of the System Request key indicates the procedure for starting a second job. What you didn't see was an underlying command that allowed the second job to be started. The same command is used to toggle between the two jobs. This command is the Transfer to Secondary Job command (TFRSECJOB). I won't go into the details of TFRSECJOB here, since the system handles the support for you. As you might have concluded, you need a command similar to TFRSECJOB to start more than one group job at a workstation. The command that provides this support is the Transfer to Group Job command (TFRGRPJOB). Its parameters are shown in Table 9.3.

Table 9.3: Parameters for TFRGRPJOB (1 of 2)	
Parameter	**Meaning/Values**
GRPJOB	This is the group job that is to be activated after the current job has been suspended. These are its possible values:
	• *PRV—Return to the group job that was suspended when you transferred to the current job. If the suspended job no longer exists, you will return to the most recently suspended group job that is still active. Work management maintains a log of suspended group jobs that is similar to the program invocation stack within a job. The *PRV value acts as a return to the last job in this "invocation stack." This value, which is valid only if there is suspended group job, is the default value.
	• *SELECT—Show the Group Job Selection display, which lists all of the currently active group jobs. When you choose a job from the list, you will be transferred to the last program that was run when you left the job. To start a new group job, press F6 on the display.
	• Group-job-name—Specify the name of the group job that you wish to transfer to. If the job is already started, you will be transferred to the last program run when you left the job. If the job does not exist, it will be started, and the program specified by the INLGRPPGM parameter will be called.

Table 9.3: Parameters for TFRGRPJOB (2 of 2)

Parameter	Meaning/Values
INLGRPPGM	This parameter specifies the name of the program to call when the job being transferred to is being created. If the job already exists, this parameter is ignored. The name of the program is specified in the form of *library/program*. This parameter is required; there is no default value.
SPCENV	If the job being transferred to is being created, this parameter describes the operating system environment that will be used to run the job. OS/400 has two environments that jobs can run in: AS/400 (iSeries) or S/36. If the initial program called when the job is created is QCMD, the operating system environment used will be taken from the value in the user profile, and this parameter will be used. If the initial program is something other than QCMD, the environment will be specified by one of the following values: • *DFT—The new group job will run in the same environment that is running this TFRGRPJOB command. This is the default value. • *INLGRPPGM—The new job will run in the same environment as the first job that was created. • *S36—The new job will start in the S/36 environment. • *NONE—The new job will start in the AS/400 (iSeries) environment. In most uses of the group job, all of the jobs will run in the same environment. However, as usual, work management provides the flexibility to run a group job in either environment.
RSTDSP	This parameter controls the handling of the display that is active (on the screen) when the Attn key is pressed. The possible values are as follows: • *NO—The display on the workstation when the Attn key is pressed is not saved. When you return to the job that had sent the display, the original display, without any of the in-process input, will be sent to the workstation. This is the default value. • *YES—The display on the workstation when the Attn key was pressed is saved. When you return to the job that sent the display, the job will retrieve the saved information and send the display, including the in-process input, to the workstation. For many applications, this is the appropriate setting.
TEXT	Up to 50 characters of text information, enclosed in quotes, can be used to help you identify the different group jobs. This parameter is optional and will default to blank. Also, this parameter is only checked when the group job is started.

You are now very close to having all the information needed to write your Attn-key handling program. But first, look at how you end a group job and how you determine the identity of your group jobs.

Ending a Group Job

Once you have activated a group job, it can be ended in a number of ways:

1. It can simply complete processing and end normally, that is, the user chooses a sign-off option from one of the menu programs.

2. It can encounter an error and end abnormally.

3. It can be ended by the ENDJOB command or by selecting the end job option on any of several displays.

4. It can be ended by the ENDGRPJOB command.

In the first three cases, ending the job will produce a result similar to the TFRGRPJOB command with the GRPJOB parameter set to *PRV. When the ENDGRPJOB command is used, you can control the group job that gains control. Table 9.4 lists the parameters of ENDGRPJOB.

Table 9.4: Parameters for ENDGRPJOB	
Parameter	**Values/Meaning**
GRPJOB	This is the group job that is to be ended. It has the following possible values:
	• *Asterisk* (*)—The job running the ENDGRPJOB command is ended. This is the default value.
	• *Jobname*—The specified group job is ended.
RSMGRPJOB	This parameter specifies the group job that is to gain control after the group job is ended. This value is used only when the GRPJOB parameter is set to * (asterisk). The values for this parameter are as follows:
	• *PRV—The most recently used group job (that is still active) gains control. This is the default value.
	• *Jobname*—The specified group job gains control.
JOBLOG	This parameter determines if a job log is produced for the job being ended. It has the following possible values are:
	• *NOLIST—No job log is produced. This is the default value.
	• *LIST—A job log is produced.

Who Am I?

If you have a job that can have "multiple personalities," you must determine which personality is active. To get this information, run the Retrieve Group Attributes command (RTVGRPA). This command allows you to specify the names of variables that will contain the information returned by the command. At least one of the parameters must have a variable name specified, but not all of the parameters need to be specified. The parameters that can be specified and the information returned are shown in Table 9.5.

Table 9.5: Parameters for RTVGRPA (1 of 2)	
Parameter	**Variable Size/Value Returned**
GRPJOB	This variable, the name of the group job active at the time the Attn key was pressed, must be a CHAR(10) field. If it is less than 10 characters, the group job name is padded on the right with blanks. Obtaining this value is important, since the user might choose to return to the job that was active when the Attn key was pressed. When this situation occurs, you do not want to run TFRGRPJOB; you only need to run the RETURN command.
GRPJOBL	This variable must be a CHAR(1056) field. The value returned is an array of the 16 possible active group job names. Each entry in the array consists of 66 characters of information. The first 10 characters are the name of the job (padded on the right if less than 10 characters). The next six characters are the group number. The final 50 characters are the text used to describe the job. If you use the *SELECT value for the GRPJOB parameter of TFRGRPJOB, use this variable to get the list of names that the user would use for the selection.
GRPJOBCNT	This variable, the number of active group jobs, must be a DEC(30) field. This value is useful in processing the list of jobs returned in the GRPJOBL variable.
MSGQ	This variable, the name of the message queue associated with the group jobs, must be a CHAR(10) field. A name that is less than 10 characters will be padded on the right with blanks. If there is no message queue, *NONE is placed in the variable.
MSGQLIB	This variable, the name of the library containing the message queue, is a CHAR(10) field. The name will be padded on the right with blanks if it is less than 10 characters long. If there is no message queue, blanks are returned.
PRVGRPJOB	When the Attn key is pressed, a job is running. If the job is running as a result of the TFRGRPJOB command, this value will contain the name of the job that ran TFRGRPJOB, to get to the job that is running RTVGRPA. The variable is a CHAR(16) field. The first 10 characters are the job name padded on the right with blanks; the remaining six are the job number.

Table 9.5: Parameters for RTVGRPA (2 of 2)	
Parameter	**Variable Size/Value Returned**
CTLCDE	This is the reason the active job gained control. The control code variable is a decimal field with a length of three and no decimal places. The possible values for CTLCDE are as follows: • 0—The job running RTVGRPA is the only active group job. • 10—The job obtained control from another group job via TFRGRPJOB. • 20—The group job that had been running ended normally, and the job gaining control was the most recently used group job that is still active. • 30—The group job that had been running was ended by ENDGRPJOB, and this job was specified in the RSMGRPJOB parameter. • 40—The group job that was active was ended with ENDGRPJOB specified and an inactive job in the RSMGRPJOB parameter. This job was the most recently used group job that is still active. • 50—The group job that was active was ended with ENDGRPJOB, with the RSMGRPJOB parameter set to *PRV. This job was the most recently used group job that is still active. • 60—The group job that had been running ended abnormally. This job was the most recently used group job that is still active. • 70—The group job that had been running was ended with ENDJOB. This job was the most recently used group job that is still active.

Finally, you have all the pieces needed to implement group jobs at your workstation.

A Group Job Example

This section looks at a simple example that puts together the pieces just covered to convert the single-job workstation into a group-job workstation. This example starts with the basic job structure shown earlier in this chapter. Assume that each user is assigned to perform three functions. The job structure, then, looks like Figure 9.5.

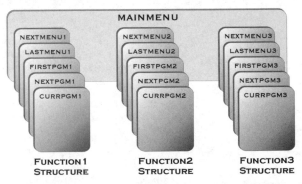

Figure 9.5: A user application performs three main functions, which require several program calls to reach the primary input screen.

Apart from the obviously lame naming convention, this structure represents an excellent candidate for group jobs. Moving from one input function to another requires many tedious, unnecessary, and frustrating transactions.

To start the implementation of group jobs, initiate your jobs with a routing entry that specifies QCMD as the initial program. All of the users of this application will have MAINMENU specified as the initial program in their user profiles. Now, you're ready to look at what is needed to set up your group jobs.

MAINMENU—The Initial Application Program

The program MAINMENU will be the initial program called when a user signs on to a workstation. As indicated in the discussion of the requirements for a group-job program, one of the first things that an application must do is run the CHGGRPA command to convert the single job to a group job. Then, you need to activate the Attn key with the SETATNPGM command. Both of these statements are included in the MAINMENU program shown in Figure 9.6. After enabling group jobs and activating the Attn key, your program will display the main menu at the workstation. When a user enters a menu choice, this program will process the input.

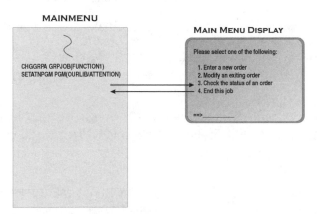

Figure 9.6: The initial program, MAINMENU, has enabled group jobs, activated the Attn key, sent a display containing four menu choices to a workstation, and read the input from the workstation.

Notice that MAINMENU made the assumption that the user would choose FUNCTION1. It doesn't make a difference which of the functions you choose for the GRPJOB parameter; just pick one. Although I haven't shown the CL statement that defines the input variable to hold the input from the menu display, when the input is returned to MAINMENU, it is placed in the variable &MMOPT. (Variables in OS/400 CL programs begin with an ampersand.) The processing of &MMOPT is added to the MAINMENU program in Figure 9.7.

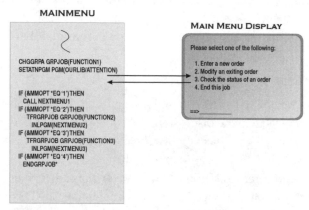

MAINMENU

```
CHGGRPA GRPJOB(FUNCTION1)
SETATNPGM PGM(OURLIB/ATTENTION)

IF (&MMOPT *EQ '1') THEN
   CALL NEXTMENU1
IF (&MMOPT *EQ '2') THEN
   TFRGRPJOB GRPJOB(FUNCTION2)
      INLPGM(NEXTMENU2)
IF (&MMOPT *EQ '3') THEN
   TFRGRPJOB GRPJOB(FUNCTION3)
      INLPGM(NEXTMENU3)
IF (&MMOPT *EQ '4') THEN
   ENDGRPJOB*
```

MAIN MENU DISPLAY

```
Please select one of the following:

1. Enter a new order
2. Modify an exiting order
3. Check the status of an order
4. End this job

==>_____
```

Figure 9.7: The input from the menu display is read and analyzed by the MAINMENU program to determine which application function the user wants.

You can see that things are starting to take shape. Take a look at what would happen for each of the menu options the user could choose, based on Figure 9.5:

- If the user selects option 1, the MAINMENU program will call the next program in the FUNCTION1 structure, which is NEXTMENU1.

- If the user selects option 2, MAINMENU will run the TFRGRPJOB command to create another group job named FUNCTION2, and will call the next program in the structure, NEXTMENU2.

- If the user selects option 3, MAINMENU will run TFRGRPJOB to create another group job named FUNCTION3, and will call the next program in the structure, NEXTMENU3.

- If the user selects option 4, MAINMENU will run the ENDGRPJOB command for the job that chose option 4 and return control to the most recently used group job that is still active (because the default for the RSMGRPJOB parameter on the ENDGRPJOB command is *PRV). In the current example, there is only one active group job, so this option will end it and display the sign-on screen at the workstation.

Assuming that the user chooses option 1 and navigates through the other programs of FUNCTION1, the environment looks like Figure 9.8.

This job structure looks a lot like the structure of the single job shown in Figure 9.2. The only difference is that, instead of the usual single-workstation job, you have created the group job FUNCTION1. The group job acts just like any other job:

GRPJOB(FUNCTION1)

- It has job-unique information that is not shared with other group jobs.

- It can produce a job log and other spool files that are unique to this job.

- It will open files and read records independent of other group jobs at the same workstation.

Since it acts like any other job, you shouldn't expect it to look different than a single-workstation job. You might need to provide information on the displays instructing the users to press the Attn key to access a different application function, but the rest of the application and displays remain the same.

Figure 9.8: The user of a group job application selects the menu option associated with the job chosen to be the first group job. One group job named FUNCTION1 is active.

Once you have one group job active, you will no longer need the MAINMENU program. Additional group jobs will be started by the Attn-key handling program, discussed next.

The Attn-Key Handling Program

Because you have the first group job running, it is now possible for the user to press the Attn key and start a second job. Remember that you ran the SETATNPGM command and called the program ATTENTION, so you need to figure what to put in the Attn-key handling program. One of the first things to do is to display the main menu so the user can select another function. This is the same code as in the MAINMENU program.

After the user has selected a function from the menu, you need to determine the job's identity by running the Retrieve Group Attributes command (RTVGRPA). For this simple example, retrieve only the name of the group job that was running when the Attn key was pressed. The information returned to your program will be placed in a 10-byte character field named &IDENT.

Once you have the identity, you are ready to process the user's selection. The ATTENTION program in Figure 9.9 includes the code used to coordinate the option selected with the identity of the job that is running ATTENTION. As you can see, if the user-selected menu option is the same as the function that was in use, you will stay in the same group job and return to the program that was interrupted with the Attn key. If the user selects a function other than the one that was running, you will run the Transfer Group Job command (TFRGRPJOB) to start or return to the selected function. This TFRGRPJOB command is identical to TFRGRPJOB in the MAINMENU program.

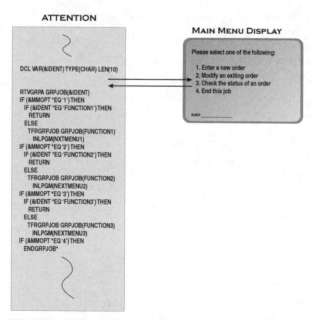

Figure 9.9: When the Attn key is pressed, the program ATTENTION is called. It will display an option menu, read the user's choice, and process the input.

When you are looking at this program, you might wonder, "Who would ever press the Attn key and then pick the same option?" Maybe the user originally pressed the Attn key by accident, and really didn't want to run a different function. Or, consider Ralph and Mary running group jobs at the workstations. Mary is entering a new order, and Ralph is checking the status of an order. Their manager enters the office and the following dialogue ensues:

> *Manager: "Mary, could you check on the status of an order for me?"*

> *Mary: "Sure. What's the customer number?" (Mary presses the Attn key while responding.)*

> *Ralph: "I'm in Inquiry. I can do it. What's the customer number?"*

> *Manager: "Thanks, Mary, but Ralph will get this one." (Mary returns to entering a new order.)*

There probably are many other instances that would result in a return to the same group job.

After the user has chosen all of the different functions the application can perform, the job structures will look like Figure 9.10. Notice that the structure of the initial job is the only one that includes the MAINMENU program.

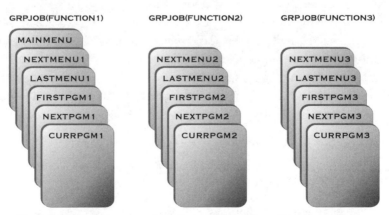

Figure 9.10: These programs have been called for three different group jobs running on a single station.

This is all you need to do to run group jobs! Once the users have navigated to the input screens for each function, they can quickly move among the input screens by pressing the Attn key and selecting the type of function they want to perform. Of course, much more code needs to be written for your CL programs (like message monitors), but writing the complete CL program is beyond the scope of this book.

Expanding the Number of Group Jobs

In this example, users had three different functions to choose from, and each job is capable of being divided into 16 different group jobs—a very complex application! To support the extra options, you need merely add additional CL statements to examine the option the user chooses and test the identity of the job that was active when the Attn key was pressed. No big deal.

At the start of this chapter, you read that a workstation could have 32 different identities (group jobs). How do you get from 16 to 32? Earlier, you learned how to use the System Request key to start an alternate job at a workstation.

To get to 32 jobs, you would press System Request to start the secondary job, then you would use the same techniques used in establishing 16 group jobs in the primary job to create 16 group jobs in the secondary job. But who has an application that complex?! How would users ever remain sane, trying to switch among 32 different group jobs using a combination of the System Request key and Attn key? However, should you ever need to support 32 personalities at a workstation, work management will gladly oblige.

Additional Attn-Key Program Issues

So far, you have completed the basic discussion of the Attn-key handling program. Prior to implementing group jobs, there are some things you should consider. In addition, after you have had a chance to experiment with the basics of group jobs, you might want to investigate some additional enhancements to your Attn-key handling program. This section covers these topics.

Attn- Key Handling Program Considerations

As with most other functions, you need to understand some operational consider-ations to avoid errors or unexpected results when implementing group jobs:

- Understand the situations that allow the Attn key to interrupt an in-process transaction.

- Be aware of the cases where the Attn key cannot be used to call your Attn-key handling program.

- Know coding tips and techniques for successful implementation of the Attn key.

- Understand the performance factors associated with group jobs.

Once you are aware of these considerations, you should have no trouble imple-menting group jobs successfully.

When the Attn Key Interrupts In-Process Transactions

In general, the Attn key will interrupt an in-process transaction whenever the keyboard is unlocked. So, just when is the keyboard unlocked? The keyboard will be unlocked when:

- An operation that reads input from the workstation is run. This includes any combined write-read operation.

- The unlock keyword is contained in the source statements for a dis-play being written to the workstation. If unlock is specified, the key-board will be unlocked before any read operation is performed.

- A get-no-wait operation is issued for a multiple device files. In these situations, an "Input Inhibited" condition may be shown on the device, but pressing the Attn key will interrupt any processing taking place. This could be dangerous. These types of files and operations are not very common, but they do exist. If you need to implement group jobs for this situation, you should disable the Attn key until after the operation is complete. When it is once again okay to press the Attn key, re-activate it. The application code looks something like this:

```
SETATNPGM PGM(*CURRENT) SET(*OFF)
Get-no-wait
More stuff
SETATNPGM PGM(*CURRENT) SET(*ON)
```

When Pressing the Attn Key Is Like Banging Your Head on the Wall

Obviously, if you've listed the only situations that the Attn key can be used to call your Attn-key handling program, it will not be active any other time. But that's too easy. If you press the Attn key under any of the following conditions, the Attn-key handling program will not be called:

- The keyboard is locked and a get-no-wait operation is not pending.

- The System Request menu is displayed, or one of the options from the System Request menu is being processed. If the user presses the Attn key under these conditions, the Operational Assistant menu will be shown, and the user will be lost and confused. There is no way to disable the Attn key in this situation. Users must be instructed to avoid using the Attn key under these conditions.

- The "Display Message" display is being shown. Again, in this case, the Operational Assistant menu will be shown.

- OS/400 is already processing the Attn key and is in the process of calling the Attn-key handling program. In most cases, the second use of the Attn key will be ignored. However, if one Attn-key handling program is used to activate a different Attn-key handling program, the second program will be called. (Multiple levels of Attn-key handling programs are discussed later in this chapter.)

- A BASIC program is running. The Attn key is a defined key that is handled by BASIC and passed to your application. Thus, although you may press the Attn key when a BASIC program is running, control is given to your BASIC program, not your Attn-key handling program.

That's better! You can now relate unusual Attn key results to one of these situations.

Tips for Writing Attn-Key Handling Programs

The most important thing to remember about the Attn-key handling program is that it runs in the same job that was active at the time the Attn key was pressed. It acts like another program in the invocation stack. If the program opens a file already in use by the job with the attribute of SHARE(*YES), and reads a record, the record that the Attn-key handling program read will be in the buffer when you return to the job. Figures 9.11 and 9.12 illustrate this condition.

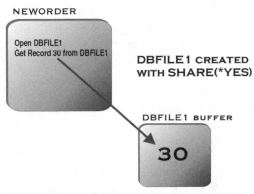

Figure 9.11: A single group job is running, using a file that has been opened with an attribute of SHARE(*YES). It has read record 30 into the file's buffer.

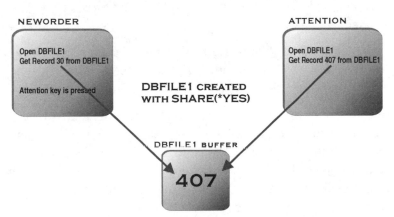

Figure 9.12: The Attn key program, running in the same job as NEWORDER, opens the same file as in Figure 9.11 with an attribute of SHARE(*YES), and reads record 407 into the same buffer.

As you can see, the NEWORDER program read record 30 into the buffer. Since the file is specified as SHARE(*YES), the job will only have one copy of the buffer. Therefore, when ATTENTION reads record 407, the contents of the DBFILE1 buffer is changed to 407. When NEWORDER is resumed, it will be working with record 407, not record 30.

That's one of the reasons for the following guidelines for Attn-key handling programs:

- Try not to place too much function in the Attn-key handling program. In the example, all you did with the Attn-key handling program was display a menu, analyze the user's selection, and transfer to the appropriate job. Most Attn-key handling programs should be kept as simple as that.

- It's a good idea to avoid using objects that any of the group jobs are using. This will greatly reduce the number of unexpected results from the implementation of group jobs.

- Avoid calling nonrecursive functions. It is impossible to call a nonrecursive function that has been interrupted. That is, if a nonrecursive function is in process (called by the Attn-key handling program), and the Attn key is pressed, the Attn-key handling program will fail. Many high-level languages (such as RPG IV and COBOL), functions, and iSeries utilities (such as DFU and SEU) are nonrecursive functions.

- Do not allow the user to inadvertently access the command entry display. In addition to being confusing, it is dangerous. Clearly, this should not be an option on the menu that you provide your users.

- Any authorities that have been adopted by the program in process when the Attn key is pressed are unavailable to the Attn-key handling program. If the Attn-key handling program tries to access objects that use the adopted authority of the interrupted job, the access will fail. (Understanding adopted authorities requires more details of OS/400 security than are covered in this book.)

- Like the buffers of files that are SHARE(*YES), any changes made to the local data area (*LDA) by the Attn-key handling program will change the *LDA of the interrupted job. Remember, the Attn-key handling program is running in the interrupted job.

While these tips are not intended to be complete, they will help you avoid most of the problems encountered the first time most programmers implement group jobs.

Performance and Group Jobs

When you consider that the main reason to implement group jobs is to make life easier for the end user who needs to perform multiple tasks, you might be surprised to learn that there are some performance benefits derived from implementing group jobs:

- By having multiple jobs running, the user avoids backing out of one function and starting another. Without group jobs, these nuisance transactions require the job to enter the system, do some processing, and leave the system repeatedly. If the user is at the end of a slow connection, this can be rather time-consuming. In addition, any files used by programs in the function will be repetitively opened and closed as the user moves back and forth between functions. With group jobs, once the files are opened and the data entry programs are running, the overhead for the user and the system is reduced to the effort to switch between jobs.

- Even if each job has many group jobs, the overhead for the jobs that are suspended is of no concern.

- When TFRGRPJOB causes a new group job to start, the system overhead is similar to the initial sign-on at the workstation. If TFRGRPJOB transfers to an established group job, the overhead is the same as transferring between jobs with the System Request key, regardless of the number of group jobs that exist. So, you pay the initialization price once, and reap the benefits of group jobs every time you switch between functions.

- Although each group job is treated as an individual job, the methods to limit the number of jobs in the system (such as the MAXJOBS parameter used on the CRTSBSD command) do not need to be changed. Only the initial job enters the system via a workstation entry. Only the initial job is routed to the system using all of the subsystem constructs. Group jobs are clones of existing jobs, and do not need to enter the system via the traditional methods described earlier.

With all these benefits, you still need to be concerned about getting carried away with group jobs. The system can only support about 160,000 jobs. A system with a large number of users, each having several jobs, might approach this serious system limitation. In addition, your job as a system administrator might be more difficult when there are more jobs to deal with on the system.

Providing a Group Job Dynamic Menu

The previous example uses an approach that is referred to as a *fixed menu*. In a fixed-menu implementation of group jobs, a user is presented a menu that includes all of the possible functions that the user might need to use. The user might not remember which functions have active group jobs and which functions do not, but it doesn't matter. The Attn-key handling program takes care of that.

If you wish to provide group jobs for your programmers, the fixed-menu approach will not be usable. There are far too many functions that programmers can perform. Instead of using the standard Attn-key handling program, you need something different. Your new program should use a *dynamic menu*. The following pages explain how this works.

The Initial Program

As you recall, when production users sign on to the system, they can specify an initial program to run. The initial program enables group jobs and activates the Attn key with the Set Attention Key Program command (SETATNPGM). For your programmers, you already have provided different user profiles and job descriptions that allow you to specify a different initial program. The initial program will still enable group jobs and run SETATNPGM. As you've probably figured out, however, your SETATNPGM command will use a different program.

The Attn-Key Handling Program

Once you have established a different initial program and Attn-key handling program, you can provide the flexibility programmers need with the Transfer to Group Job command (TFRGRPJOB). The GRPJOB parameter for this command includes a *SELECT option. When the GRPJOB parameter is *SELECT, the programmer will be shown a list of jobs that are currently active, and the job that was active at the time the Attn key was pressed.

From the *SELECT display, the programmer can transfer to any currently active job. To create a new group job, the programmer needs to press F6 and enter the command that is to be run when the new job starts. Consider how you might use this capability.

Dynamic Menu Example

If you looked at the tasks that a programmer performs when modifying an application, you might see the following:

- Change the source of a display file.
- Create the modified display file.
- Change the source of a CL program.
- Create the modified program.
- Change the source of an RPG IV program.
- Create the RPG program.
- Test the program.
- If the program fails, analyze the reason for the failure.

If the programmer needs to repetitively run these commands to successfully modify the application, it will be just as time-consuming and frustrating as it is for other users to switch jobs.

Assume that the initial program for your programmers, called PGMRMENU, establishes the group job environment, runs the SETATNPGM command, and displays the programmer menu. You've seen the code to do this in the MAINMENU program in Figure 9.7. Once you have completed your initial program functions, you call the program that displays the programmer menu. Once the menu has been displayed, you can begin to build your programmer's group job structure. Here are the steps to construct a dynamic-group job menu:

1. After the programmer has signed on and the programmer menu is sent to the workstation, the initial group job is in place. You will use this job to create any programs or files you are testing. The programmer menu is shown in Figure 9.13.

```
                        Programmer Menu
                                                System:  TSCSAP02
Select one of the following:
     1. Start AS/400 Data File Utility
     2. Work with AS/400 Query
     3. Create an object from a source file    object name, type, pgm for CMD
     4. Call a program                         program name
     5. Run a command                          command
     6. Submit a job                           (job name), , ,(command)
     7. Go to a menu                            menu name
     8. Edit a source file member              (srcmbr), (type)
     9. Design display format using SDA        (srcmbr), ,(mode)
    90. Sign off                               (*nolist, *list)

  Selection . . . . .            Parm . . . .
  Type  . . . . . . .            Parm 2 . . .
  Command . . . . . .

  Source file . . . .   QDDSSRC  Source library . . . . . . .    *LIBL
  Object library  . .            Job description  . . . . . .    *USRPRF

  F3=Exit       F4=Prompt          F6=Display messages   F10=Command entry
  F12=Cancel    F14=Work with submitted jobs             F18=Work with output
```

Figure 9.13: The initial group job for a programmer will use the Programmer menu to create programs and files.

2. Press the Attn key to start a job that will be used to edit your display file. When the Attn key is pressed, the Attn-key handling program will be called, and will run this command:

```
TFRGRPJOB GRPJOB(*SELECT)
```

When this command is run, you will see the display in Figure 9.14.

3. Since you only have one group job available, you are not given any group jobs to choose. To return to the previous job, press F3 or F12. To start a new job, press F6, which will prompt you for the parameters for the TFRGRPJOB command. Enter the information shown in Figure 9.15.

```
                         Transfer to Group Job
                                                  System:   TSCSAP02
      Active group job . . . . . : PGMRMENU

      Text . . . . . . . . . . : Create and test objects

      Type option, press Enter.
        1 = Transfer group job


          ----------Suspended Group Jobs------------------
      Opt   Group Job     Text




                                                         Bottom
      F3=Exit    F5=Refresh    F6=Start a new group job  F12=Cancel
```

Figure 9.14: When GRPJOB(*SELECT) is specified, the TFRGRPJOB command will not show any jobs if only one group job is active.

```
   Transfer to Group Job (TFRGRPJOB)

     Type choices, press Enter.

     Group job . . . . . . . . . . .   DSPEDIT      Name, *PRV, *SELECT
     Initial group program . . . . .   QPGMMNU      Name
       Library . . . . . . . . . . .     *LIBL      Name, *LIBL, *CURLIB
     Special environment . . . . . .   *DFT         *DFT, *INLGRPPGM, *S36, *NONE
     Restore display . . . . . . . .   *NO          *YES, *NO
     Text 'description' . . . . . . .  Display file edit







                                                         Bottom
     F3=Exit   F4=Prompt   F5=Refresh   F12=Cancel   F13=How to use this display
     F24=More keys
```

Figure 9.15: The Transfer Group Job command will be shown when F6 is pressed on the Group Job menu displayed when the GRPJOB(*SELECT) parameter is specified.

4. After you press the Enter key, the programmer menu will be displayed again. Enter your choice of display file to edit, and make your changes. You are now running a second job that will only be used to edit displays.

5. Assume that you need to check our CL program to ensure that it can handle the new display. You can quit the edit function, choose the CL program source to display, make our changes, quit the CL edit, and go back to the display file. This makes it impossible for you to look at both source files at the same time, so you can now start another group job to show any CL programs that are using the display. Once again, press the Attn key to see the display in Figure 9.16. There is now a group job that you can choose, but it's not the job you want. It is the job you are using to create programs and files.

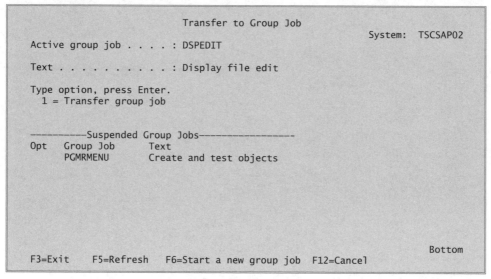

```
                        Transfer to Group Job
                                                  System:   TSCSAP02
     Active group job . . . . : DSPEDIT

     Text . . . . . . . . . . : Display file edit

     Type option, press Enter.
       1 = Transfer group job


     ----------Suspended Group Jobs-------------------
     Opt    Group Job     Text
            PGMRMENU      Create and test objects




                                                            Bottom
     F3=Exit    F5=Refresh    F6=Start a new group job  F12=Cancel
```

Figure 9.16: When two group jobs are active, the GRPJOB(*SELECT) parameter on the TFRGRPJOB command will display one job to choose.

6. To start the group job used to edit CL programs, press F6 and enter the information shown in Figure 9.17.

```
                    Transfer to Group Job (TFRGRPJOB)

Type choices, press Enter.

Group job . . . . . . . . . .    CLEDIT        Name, *PRV, *SELECT
Initial group program . . . . .  QPGMMNU       Name
  Library . . . . . . . . . .        *LIBL     Name, *LIBL, *CURLIB
Special environment . . . . . .  *DFT          *DFT, *INLGRPPGM, *S36, *NONE
Restore display . . . . . . . .  *NO           *YES, *NO
Text 'description' . . . . . .   CL program source file edit




                                                                   Bottom
F3=Exit   F4=Prompt   F5=Refresh   F12=Cancel   F13=How to use this display
F24=More keys
```

Figure 9.17. When you press F6 from the selection menu, a third group job starts.

Now you can proceed as you did with the job to display the file to edit. Remember to look at and edit your RPG source file. Press the Attn key once more to see the display as shown in Figure 9.18.

```
                        Transfer to Group Job
                                                  System:   SCSAP02
   Active group job . . . . : CLEDIT

   Text . . . . . . . . . . : CL program source file edit

   Type option, press Enter.
     1 = Transfer group job


         ----------Suspended Group Jobs----------------
   Opt    Group Job     Text
          PGMRMENU      Create and test objects
          DSPEDIT       Display file edit




                                                                   Bottom
   F3=Exit    F5=Refresh   F6=Start a new group job  F12=Cancel
```

Figure 9.18: Two group jobs are shown on the menu when three group jobs are active.

7. Use F6 and the information in Figure 9.19 to create a group job that
   you can use to edit your RPG program source.

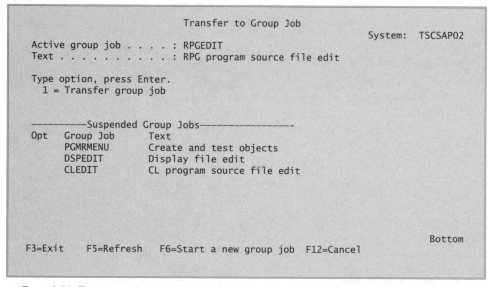

```
                      Transfer to Group Job (TFRGRPJOB)

 Type choices, press Enter.

 Group job . . . . . . . . . . .   RPGEDIT      Name, *PRV, *SELECT
 Initial group program . . . . .   QPGMMENU     Name
   Library . . . . . . . . . . .     *LIBL      Name, *LIBL, *CURLIB
 Special environment . . . . . .   *DFT         *DFT, *INLGRPPGM, *S36, *NONE
 Restore display . . . . . . . .   *NO          *YES, *NO
 Text 'description' . . . . . . .  RPG program source file edit




                                                                    Bottom
 F3=Exit    F4=Prompt    F5=Refresh    F12=Cancel   F13=How to use this display
 F24=More keys
```

Figure 9.19: *A fourth group job is created to edit RPG programs.*

8. Press the Attn key to get the display shown in Figure 9.20.

```
                     Transfer to Group Job
                                                  System:  TSCSAP02
 Active group job . . . . :  RPGEDIT
 Text . . . . . . . . . . :  RPG program source file edit

 Type option, press Enter.
   1 = Transfer group job


     ----------Suspended Group Jobs----------------
 Opt   Group Job     Text
       PGMRMENU      Create and test objects
       DSPEDIT       Display file edit
       CLEDIT        CL program source file edit




                                                                    Bottom
 F3=Exit    F5=Refresh   F6=Start a new group job  F12=Cancel
```

Figure 9.20: *The group jobs are shown on the menu when the Attn key is pressed.*

You now have the four primary activities that your programmer will set up as group jobs to provide an easy way to switch among tasks. The nice thing about this type of group job implementation is that you do not need to predict what functions the programmer will use when you establish the group job environment.

Multiple Attn-Key Handling Programs

As you progress through the various menu options in an application, you might want to provide Attn-key handling programs for each menu level, to reduce the users' choices while in a certain function. For most applications, this method is not a very good alternative, but you might encounter certain situations where multiple Attn-key handling programs are in use, so the concept is worth a look.

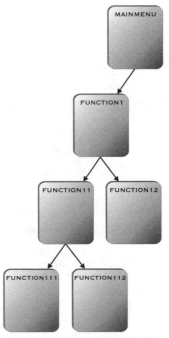

Going back to the simple application example, note that MAINMENU includes access to three functions: FUNCTION1, FUNCTION2, and FUNCTION3. Each of these functions may have two functions. The FUNCTION1 menu, for example, lets the user choose FUNCTION11 or FUNCTION12. Again, each of these functions has two choices; FUNCTION11 has choices for FUNCTIO111 and FUNCTIO112. Figure 9.21 shows the application structure.

Figure 9.21: The job structure for an application allows two options for each menu displayed.

The MAINMENU Attn-Key Handling Program

Earlier in this chapter, you saw how to create an Attn-key handling program that let users switch among three functions using the MAINMENU program. As a result of user selections, you create up to three group jobs. However, any user who wishes to switch between FUNCTIO111 and FUNCTIO112 must go back through several programs to make the switch. The same problem exists if the user wants to switch between FUNCTION11 and FUNCTION12. Your group jobs aren't as helpful as you would like.

The FUNCTION1 Attn-Key Handling Program

To make it possible for a user to switch between FUNCTION11 and FUNCTION12 more easily, add a SETATNPGM command to the program that displays the FUNCTION1 selection display. The command looks like this:

```
SETATNPGM PGM(FUN1MENU)
```

If the user is running FUNCTION11 or FUNCTION12 and the Attn key is pressed, the FUN1MENU program will be called. This program will let the user choose either FUNCTION11 or FUNCTION12.

The FUNCTION11 Attn-Key Handling Program

When you reach the FUNCTION11 program, run the SETATNPGM command again to establish an Attn-key handling program that will let the user easily switch between FUNCTIO111 and FUNCTIO112. The SETATNPGM command will be as follows:

```
SETATNPGM PGM(FUN11MNU)
```

If the user is running FUNCTIO111 and presses the Attn key, the FUN11MNU program will be called. It will present a display that will let the user choose between FUNCTIO111 and FUNCTIO112.

When Attn Is Pressed, Who Gets Called?

You have to be careful when implementing multiple levels of Attn-key handling programs. In these cases, pressing the Attn key is a lot like hitting the "redial" button on your telephone—you're going to call someone, but you aren't sure whose number it is. For example, say that you choose FUNCTION1, then FUNCTION11, then FUNCTIO111. When you return from FUNCTIO111, the FUNCTION11 program will display your choices for FUNCTIO111 and FUNCTIO112. If you press the Attn key at this point, who are you going to call? The answer is the FUN11MNU program, which will display the same menu. So, to switch from the FUNCTION11 program to the FUNCTION12 program, you need to go back one more level. This can be very confusing, provides minimal additional benefit, might produce unexpected results, and could frustrate both you and your users. In short, you will be unlikely to implement Attn-key handling programs in this manner.

In Review

This chapter exposes you to the world of multiple jobs on a single workstation through the use of secondary jobs and group jobs. These techniques can provide significant improvements in system performance and user satisfaction. However, remember to keep your implementation simple and limit the number of group jobs that you allow at a single workstation.

10

Additional Ways to Get Work Initiated

Up to this point, this book has dealt only with interactive, batch, and spool jobs. It's time to cover some of the additional kinds of jobs you are likely to see running on an iSeries system:

- Autostart jobs.
- Communications jobs.
- Prestart jobs.
- Threads.

Upon completing this chapter, you will have examined all the different types of iSeries user jobs.

Autostart Jobs

Autostart jobs run whenever a subsystem is started. They start before the subsystem initiates any other types of jobs. Typically, they help set up the runtime environment for your installation. For example, when discussing methods to separate different types of work, I suggested that the best approach might be separate subsystems. To automate the process of starting the additional subsystems in your environment, you could have an autostart job in QBASE. Sounds good, doesn't it?

By now, you know that the subsystem needs a method for defining the autostart jobs to be run whenever the subsystem is started. You've also, no doubt, figured out that the method for doing this is an entry similar to the workstation entries and job queue entries used by QBASE. And, of course, you're right. In this case, use an autostart job entry in the subsystem. To show how these entries are used, the following sections discuss the defaults that are shipped with QBASE, and then the commands that are used to implement the autostart job function.

Autostart Jobs Shipped with QBASE

It has been a long time since you looked at QBASE, so go back to the Display Subsystem Description display that you originally saw in chapter 2:

```
DSPSBSD QBASE
```

The Display Subsystem Description menu is shown in Figure 10.1. You don't need to look very far to see that the third option on the menu will display the autostart job entries shipped with QBASE. So, type a three and press Enter to display the screen shown in Figure 10.2.

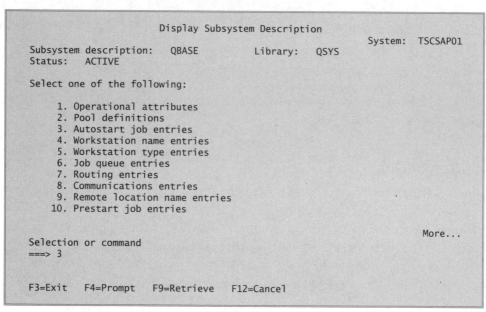

```
                    Display Subsystem Description
                                                    System:   TSCSAP01
    Subsystem description:    QBASE        Library:    QSYS
    Status:    ACTIVE

    Select one of the following:

         1. Operational attributes
         2. Pool definitions
         3. Autostart job entries
         4. Workstation name entries
         5. Workstation type entries
         6. Job queue entries
         7. Routing entries
         8. Communications entries
         9. Remote location name entries
        10. Prestart job entries

                                                          More...
    Selection or command
    ===> 3


    F3=Exit   F4=Prompt   F9=Retrieve   F12=Cancel
```

Figure 10.1: The Display Subsystem Description menu provides options that can be used to look at different parts of a subsystem.

```
                    Display Autostart Job Entries
                                                   System:   TSCSAP02
    Subsystem description:    QBASE          Status:    ACTIVE

    Job              Job Description    Library
    QPFRCOL          QPFRCOL            QGPL
    QSTRUPJD         QSTRUPJD           QSYS




                                                              Bottom
    Press Enter to continue.

    F3=Exit    F12=Cancel
```

Figure 10.2: Choosing option 3 on the Display Subsystem Description menu shows the autostart jobs that are shipped with QBASE.

There are two different autostart job entries that will cause a job to run when QBASE is started. The first, QPFRCOL, collects performance data used by PM/400 to help you analyze your environment's growth and prevent you from running short of resources like disk storage, CPU, and main storage. The second, QSTRUPJD, starts other functions for your environment. Among other things, it starts the QSPL subsystem. To see how these jobs are set up to run these programs, look at their job descriptions:

```
DSPJOBD JOBD(QGPL/QPFRCOL)
```

You get the information shown in Figures 10.3a through 10.3c.

```
                            Display Job Description
                                                    System:  TSCSAP02
        Job description:   QPFRCOL         Library:    QGPL

        User profile . . . . . . . . . . . . . . . . . :   QPGMR
        CL syntax check  . . . . . . . . . . . . . . . :   *NOCHK
        Hold on job queue  . . . . . . . . . . . . . . :   *NO
        End severity . . . . . . . . . . . . . . . . . :   30
        Job date . . . . . . . . . . . . . . . . . . . :   *SYSVAL
        Job switches . . . . . . . . . . . . . . . . . :   00000000
        Inquiry message reply  . . . . . . . . . . . . :   *RQD
        Job priority (on job queue) . . . . . . . . . . :   5
        Job queue  . . . . . . . . . . . . . . . . . . :   QCTL
          Library  . . . . . . . . . . . . . . . . . . :     QSYS
        Output priority (on output queue) . . . . . . . :   5
        Printer device . . . . . . . . . . . . . . . . :   *USRPRF
        Output queue . . . . . . . . . . . . . . . . . :   *USRPRF
          Library  . . . . . . . . . . . . . . . . . . :

                                                           More...

        Press Enter to continue.

        F3=Exit    F12=Cancel
```

Figure 10.3a: The autostart job QPFRCOL uses the QPFRCOL job description that is shipped with OS/400.

```
                            Display Job Description

                                                    System:  TSCSAP02
        Job description:   QPFRCOL         Library:    QGPL

        Message logging:
          Level  . . . . . . . . . . . . . . . . . . . :   4
          Severity . . . . . . . . . . . . . . . . . . :   0
          Text . . . . . . . . . . . . . . . . . . . . :   *SECLVL
        Log CL program commands  . . . . . . . . . . . :   *NO
        Accounting code  . . . . . . . . . . . . . . . :   *USRPRF
        Print text . . . . . . . . . . . . . . . . . . :   *SYSVAL

        Routing data . . . . . . . . . . . . . . . . . :   QCMDI

        Request data . . . . . . . . . . . . . . . . . :   CALL QSYS/QPMLWAIT


        Device recovery action . . . . . . . . . . . . :   *SYSVAL
                                                           More...
        Press Enter to continue.

        F3=Exit    F12=Cancel
```

Figure 10.3b: The autostart job QPFRCOL uses the QPFRCOL job description that is shipped with OS/400.

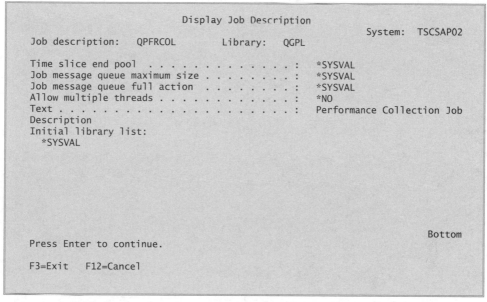

```
                          Display Job Description
                                                     System:   TSCSAP02
      Job description:   QPFRCOL          Library:   QGPL

      Time slice end pool  . . . . . . . . . . . . :   *SYSVAL
      Job message queue maximum size . . . . . . . :   *SYSVAL
      Job message queue full action  . . . . . . . :   *SYSVAL
      Allow multiple threads . . . . . . . . . . . :   *NO
      Text . . . . . . . . . . . . . . . . . . . . :   Performance Collection Job
      Description
      Initial library list:
        *SYSVAL




                                                                       Bottom
      Press Enter to continue.

      F3=Exit    F12=Cancel
```

Figure 10.3c: The autostart job QPFRCOL uses the QPFRCOL job description that is shipped with OS/400.

You now have everything you need to know about this autostart job. Sure, but what are you trying to find? The first of the three displays tells you about the operational aspects of the job, but it doesn't help you understand what program the job will run. The second display tells you about the routing data and program for this autostart job. For QPFRCOL, the routing data is QCMDI. Take another look at the routing entries and see what this means by running the DSPSBSD command again and selecting option 7 to display the routing entries shown in Figure 10.4.

Note that the QPFRCOL autostart job will match the routing entry with sequence number 50. Select option 5 to check the details of the routing entry, as shown in Figure 10.5.

You can see that the job will run in the second pool of QBASE, which means it will run in the *INTERACT pool. In addition, the job will have the runtime attributes specified in the QINTER class, so it will have a run priority (RUNPTY) value of 20. If you are running a large number of jobs on your iSeries machine, the performance-collection job might affect your response time. You'll see how to change this later, but you need to get through the rest of the defaults first.

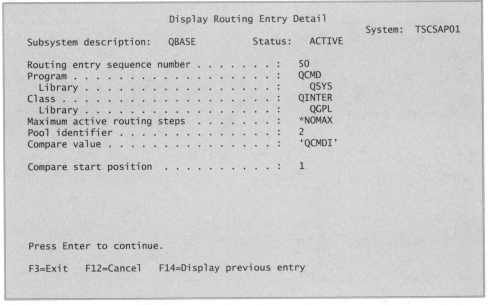

```
                      Display Routing Entries
                                               System:   TSCSAP01
    Subsystem description:   QBASE          Status:   ACTIVE

       Type options, press Enter.
       5=Display details

                                                               Start
    Opt    Seq Nbr    Program      Library     Compare Value    Pos
           10         QCMD         QSYS        'QCMDB'            1
     5     50         QCMD         QSYS        'QCMDI'            1
           70         *RTGDTA                  'QNMAPINGD'       37
           80         QNMAREXECD   QSYS        'AREXECD'         37
           100        QCMD         QSYS        'QS36EVOKE'        1
           150        QCMD         QSYS        'QS36MRT'          1
           260        *RTGDTA                  'QOCEVOKE'        37
           300        QARDRIVE     QSYS        '525XTEST'         1
           310        *RTGDTA                  'QZSCSRVR'        37
           320        *RTGDTA                  'QZRCSRVR'        37
           330        *RTGDTA                  'QZHQTRG'         37
           350        *RTGDTA                  'QVPPRINT'        37
                                                             More...

    F3=Exit    F9=Display all detailed descriptions    F12=Cancel
```

Figure 10.4: Selecting option 7 on the Display Subsystem Description menu shows the routing entries that are shipped with QBASE.

```
                      Display Routing Entry Detail
                                               System:   TSCSAP01
    Subsystem description:   QBASE          Status:   ACTIVE

    Routing entry sequence number . . . . . . . :   50
    Program . . . . . . . . . . . . . . . . . . :   QCMD
      Library . . . . . . . . . . . . . . . . . :     QSYS
    Class . . . . . . . . . . . . . . . . . . . :   QINTER
      Library . . . . . . . . . . . . . . . . . :     QGPL
    Maximum active routing steps  . . . . . . . :   *NOMAX
    Pool identifier . . . . . . . . . . . . . . :   2
    Compare value . . . . . . . . . . . . . . . :   'QCMDI'

    Compare start position  . . . . . . . . . . :   1




    Press Enter to continue.

    F3=Exit    F12=Cancel    F14=Display previous entry
```

Figure 10.5: The details of the routing entry used for the QPFRCOL autostart job show that it will be treated the same as interactive jobs.

Notice the request data parameter (RQSDTA) in Figure 10.3b. This parameter specifies a call to the program you'd like to run. So, when QBASE starts, it sees the autostart job entry for QPFRCOL, finds the routing data, initiates the job in *IN-TERACT with a run priority of 20, and calls the program that will collect performance data for PM/400. This is not much different from all of the other jobs you've looked at so far. Graphically, it looks like Figure 10.6.

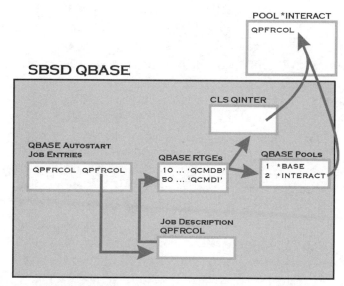

Figure 10.6: The QPFRCOL autostart job will be started by QBASE using the same runtime attributes as interactive jobs. It will run in the *INTERACT pool.

If you look at the job description for the QSTRUPJD autostart job entry, you will find that its job description is nearly the same as for QPFRCOL. In fact, the only difference is the request data (RQSDTA) because QSTRUPJD will run a different program when the job is started. That's not surprising. You will, however, use the same routing entry, the same class, and the same pool. Since this job starts immediately, does a little work, and then ends, it will not interfere with any of your interactive work. The defaults do not need to be changed for this autostart job.

You have seen how to get the routing entries, job descriptions, classes, and pools coordinated. The only thing new to discuss is the QBASE autostart job entries. You simply add these to the subsystem with the Add Autostart Job Entry command (ADDAJE):

```
ADDAJE SBSD(QBASE) JOB(QPFRCOL) JOBD(QPFRCOL)
ADDAJE SBSD(QBASE) JOB(QSTRUPJD) JOBD(QSTRUPJD)
```

Creating Autostart Job Entries

To add any additional autostart job entries, run the ADDAJE command and specify the subsystem, job name, and job description for your autostart job. For example, if you wanted to have an autostart job that would start the PRODBAT and PGMRBAT subsystems, you would create a program that would start the subsystems and add an autostart job entry in QBASE that would cause the program to be called. Assume that your program is called STRADLSBS. Here are the commands you would use to have the STRADLSBS program run as an autostart job:

```
CRTJOBD STRTSBS RTGDTA(1 QCMDI) RQSDTA(CALL STRADLSBS)
ADDAJE  QBASE   JOB(STRTSBS) JOBD(STRTSBS)
```

How simple is that? However, for the job to run as an autostart job, you need to end the subsystem and start it again. For the controlling subsystem (QBASE), this means either shutting the machine off and restarting it with the Power Down System command (PWRDWNSYS) or ending all of the active subsystems. Of course, you need to be careful when you perform these operations. Also, as long as the additional subsystems that you need have been started, there really is no need to power down and restart the system. You can just leave your autostart job entries in the subsystem, ready to use the next time you start the machine.

Changing Autostart Job Entries

In the discussion of QPFRCOL earlier in this chapter, I mentioned that I would rather have the job running *BASE with a run priority of 25 than in *INTERACT with a run priority of 20. You make that change using the Change Autostart Job Entry command (CHGAJE) and other commands that you already know:

```
CRTCLS     QGPL/PFRCOL RUNPTY(25)
ADDRTGE    QBASE SEQNBR(51) CMPVAL(1 PFRCOL) POOLID(1) CLS(PFRCOL)
CRTDUPOBJ  OBJ(QPFRCOL) FROMLIB(QGPL) OBJTYP(*JOBD) NEWOBJ(QPFRCOL2)
CHGJOBD    QGPL/PFRCOL2 RTGDTA(PFRCOL)
CHGAJE     QBASE JOB(QPFRCOL) JOBD(PFRCOL2)
```

With these commands, you have created a new class, PFRCOL, which will assign a run priority of 25 to any job that uses it. Then, you added a new routing entry that will look for a compare value of PFRCOL starting in position 1. Any job that uses this routing entry will be assigned to pool 1 (*BASE) and will use the PFRCOL class. You next made a duplicate of the PFRCOL job description, named QPFRCOL2, and changed the routing data for the QPFRCOL job from QCMDI to PFRCOL. When you want to create a new object that is nearly identical to an existing object, creating a duplicate is the easiest method. Finally, you changed your autostart job entry to use the new job description, so that the job will route correctly.

Of course, the current QPFRCOL job will not be ended, nor will the new job be started. To use your modified autostart job entry, you must end and restart the subsystem. As before, since QBASE is your controlling subsystem, you will need to run PWRDWNSYS or end all of the active subsystems. When the system or subsystems are restarted, the CHGAJE command will take effect, and QPFRCOL will run in *BASE with a RUNPTY of 25.

Getting Rid of Autostart Job Entries

If you are doing your own analysis of resource usage and the growth of your environment, you don't need the QPFRCOL job to do the work for you, so you will probably want to get rid of the QPFRCOL autostart job entry. This is very simple; just run the Remove Autostart Job Entry command (RMVAJE):

```
RMVAJE QBASE JOB(QPFRCOL)
```

As with all of the other autostart job-entry commands that modify the default environment, RMVAJE will not take affect until the subsystem is ended and restarted.

Communications Jobs

Communications jobs are another type of job that you find quite often in iSeries environments. These jobs are the result of work that is initiated on one system (the source), but run on another system (the target). In most instances, you will use these types implicitly, through the use of other OS/400 functions or commands. Here are some functions and commands that result in communications jobs on a target system:

- Accessing data on a target machine with the use of the Distributed Data Management (DDM) file protocol. When you open a DDM file and begin to use it, your file definition identifies the target system for your database requests.

- Running the Start Pass Through command (STRPASTHR). When you run STRPASTHR, you specify a target. The communications links between the system will be used to initiate a communications job that will cause a sign-on screen from the target system to be displayed at your workstation.

- Using the iSeries products that connect PCs (clients) to an iSeries machine (server). These client/server products allow the client to be the source of a communication request and the server to be the target. When the client contacts the server, it will cause the sign on display from the server to be shown as a window on the client.

This section doesn't discuss the communication configuration that you need to establish linkage between source and target systems. It also does not intend to show all of the different functions that use communications entries to initiate work, nor explain all of the routing entries that are used by communications jobs. So, you're done with this topic then, right? Well, not exactly. You still need to look at the communications entries and routing entries that are shipped with QBASE. You also need to look at the commands you can use to add, change, or remove communications entries.

QBASE and Communications Jobs

As with the other types of jobs in an iSeries environment, QBASE can initiate communications jobs. And, like all other kinds of work, QBASE needs a way to find sources for these jobs. It finds these sources through communications entries. Start the investigation into these types of jobs by running the command to display the QBASE subsystem description:

```
DSPSBSD QBASE
```

Once again, you get the subsystem description menu, as shown in Figure 10.7. This time, select option 8 to display the communications entries. You will be shown the display in Figure 10.8. It's pretty hard to understand what these entries are trying to tell you. Taking a look at the communication entry information in more detail, using Table 10.1, should help.

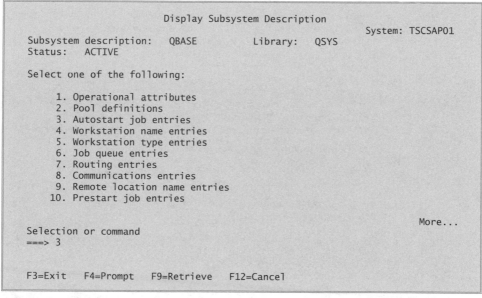

```
                     Display Subsystem Description
                                                    System: TSCSAP01
 Subsystem description:   QBASE          Library:   QSYS
 Status:   ACTIVE

 Select one of the following:

        1. Operational attributes
        2. Pool definitions
        3. Autostart job entries
        4. Workstation name entries
        5. Workstation type entries
        6. Job queue entries
        7. Routing entries
        8. Communications entries
        9. Remote location name entries
       10. Prestart job entries

                                                           More...
 Selection or command
 ===> 3


 F3=Exit   F4=Prompt   F9=Retrieve   F12=Cancel
```

Figure 10.7: The Display Subsystem Description command displays a menu of options that can be used to look at different parts of a subsystem.

```
                     Display Communications Entries
                                                    System:  TSCSAP02
 Subsystem description:   QBASE          Status:   ACTIVE

                            Job                    Default       Max
 Device      Mode          Description   Library   User          Active
 *ALL        *ANY          *USRPRF                 *SYS          *NOMAX
 *ALL        QCASERVR      *USRPRF                 *NONE         *NOMAX
 *ALL        QPCSUPP       *USRPRF                 *SYS          *NOMAX




                                                           Bottom
 Press Enter to continue.

 F3=Exit   F12=Cancel
```

Figure 10.8: Select option 8 on the Display Subsystem Description menu to see the communications entries that are shipped with QBASE.

Table 10.1: Display Communications Entries	
Value	**Setting/Meaning**
Device	This value shows the type of device that can use this communication entry. The types of devices, but for all of these communication entries, *ALL has been chosen, meaning any device can use these communication entries. The different types of devices are examined later in this chapter, in the discussion of the Add Communications Entry command.
Mode	This value gives the mode that the job will use to communicate with the target system. As with the device type, many different modes can be used. The three supplied entries have the following settings for the mode:
	• *ANY—The communication entry will support all modes.
	• QCASERVR—The communications entry is used by PCs running the IBM iSeries Client Server product.
	• QPCSUPP—The communications entry is used by PCs running the IBM iSeries PC Support product.
	Other choices are discussed later in this chapter, in the section on the Add Communications Entry command.
Job Description	This is the job description used by the job being initiated. All of the communications entries have *USRPRF specified. The job description is obtained from the user profile.
Library	This is the name of the library that contains the job description.
Default User	The user name for the job that is started via a communications entry is usually supplied by the request to run work on the target system. If no user name is supplied, the default user name will be used. For the three communications entries, the following default user settings are used:
	• *SYS—The system will supply a user name.
	• *NONE—The request must include a user name. For better security, it is a good idea to require a user name with the request for work.
Max Active	Here's that Max Active thing again! As before, this value refers to the maximum number of jobs that can use a communications entry. All of these entries specify *NOMAX.

Your target system now has more places to search for work to be initiated. Now look at some of the routing entries that QBASE would use to initiate jobs that arrive by way of one of the communications entries, shown in Figures 10.9a through 10.9c.

```
                        Display Routing Entries
                                                    System:  TSCSAP01
      Subsystem description:    QBASE          Status:   ACTIVE

         Type options, press Enter.
         5=Display details

                                                                    Start
      Opt    Seq Nbr    Program      Library      Compare Value      Pos
               10       QCMD         QSYS         'QCMDB'             1
               50       QCMD         QSYS         'QCMDI'             1
               70       *RTGDTA                   'QNMAPINGD'         37
               80       QNMAREXECD   QSYS         'AREXECD'           37
              100       QCMD         QSYS         'QS36EVOKE'         1
              150       QCMD         QSYS         'QS36MRT'           1
              260       *RTGDTA                   'QOCEVOKE'          37
              300       QARDRIVE     QSYS         '525XTEST'          1
              310       *RTGDTA                   'QZSCSRVR'          37
              320       *RTGDTA                   'QZRCSRVR'          37
              330       *RTGDTA                   'QZHQTRG'           37
              350       *RTGDTA                   'QVPPRI             37
                                                                    More...
      F3=Exit    F9=Display all detailed descriptions    F12=Cancel
```

Figure 10.9a: Select option 7 on the Display Subsystem Description menu to see the routing entries that are shipped with QBASE.

```
                        Display Routing Entries
                                                    System:  TSCSAP02
      Subsystem description:    QBASE          Status:   ACTIVE

      Type options, press Enter.
        5=Display details

                                                                    Start
      Opt    Seq Nbr    Program      Library      Compare Value      Pos
              350       *RTGDTA                   'QVPPRINT'          37
              360       *RTGDTA                   'QNPSERVR'          37
              400       *RTGDTA                   'QTFDWNLD'          37
              450       *RTGDTA                   'QMFRCVR'           37
              500       *RTGDTA                   'QMFSNDR'           37
              510       *RTGDTA                   'QHQTRGT'           37
              520       *RTGDTA                   'QRQSRV'            37
              540       *RTGDTA                   'QLZPSERV'          37
              550       *RTGDTA                   'QCNPCSUP'          37
              590       *RTGDTA                   'QPCSUPP'           1
       5      595       *RTGDTA                   'QCASERVR'          1
              599       *RTGDTA                   '#INTER'            1
                                                                    More...
      F3=Exit    F9=Display all detailed descriptions    F12=Cancel
```

Figure 10.9b: Select option 7 on the Display Subsystem Description menu to see the routing entries that are shipped with QBASE.

```
                         Display Routing Entries
                                                      System:   TSCSAP02
        Subsystem description:    QBASE          Status:    ACTIVE

        Type options, press Enter.
          5=Display details

                                                                    Start
        Opt    Seq Nbr    Program     Library      Compare Value     Pos
               600        *RTGDTA                  'PGMEVOKE'         29
               650        QCL         QSYS         'QCMD38'           1
               9999       QCMD        QSYS         *ANY

                                                               Bottom
          F3=Exit    F9=Display all detailed descriptions    F12=Cancel
```

Figure 10.9c: Select option 7 on the Display Subsystem Description menu to see the routing entries that are shipped with QBASE.

Nearly all of these routing entries are used by communications jobs. Also, many of them start the compare value in position 37 of the routing information. Position 29 of the routing data will always contain 'PGMEVOKE'. If you look at the routing entry with sequence number 600, you'll see that the compare value is 'PGMEVOKE' with a start position of 29. This is similar to the *ANY routing entry used for batch or interactive jobs that fail to match any of the other routing entries.

Notice that many of the routing entries specify *RTGDTA for the initial program. When a request for work arrives at the target system, the source system will provide a program name and library name in the routing data. The routing data will be located in position 37 of the information supplied by the source system. Thus, when the position-37 information fails to match any of the compare values for the routing entries that have a lower sequence than 595, sequence 595 is chosen, and the named program located in the supplied library name will be called when the job is started.

For routing entries that have routing data beginning in position 37, the routing data and the program that is called when the job is started are the same. This makes it easy for the system functions to supply what is needed to run the communications job. Now, look more closely at the routing entry for a Client Access job. Client Access jobs use the routing entry with sequence number 595. Go to that routing entry and place a five in the Option field. The details for the Client Access routing entry are shown in Figure 10.10.

```
                        Display Routing Entry Detail
                                                    System:   TSCSAP02
        Subsystem description:   QBASE          Status:    ACTIVE

        Routing entry sequence number . . . . . . . :   595
        Program . . . . . . . . . . . . . . . . . . :   *RTGDTA
          Library . . . . . . . . . . . . . . . . . :
        Class . . . . . . . . . . . . . . . . . . . :   QCASERVR
          Library . . . . . . . . . . . . . . . . . :    QGPL
        Maximum active routing steps  . . . . . . . :   *NOMAX
        Pool identifier . . . . . . . . . . . . . . :   1
        Compare value . . . . . . . . . . . . . . . :   'QCASERVR'


        Compare start position  . . . . . . . . . . :   1




        Press Enter to continue.

        F3=Exit   F12=Cancel   F14=Display previous entry
```

Figure 10.10: Type a five in front of the routing entry with sequence number 595 to see the details of the routing entry used by Client Access.

By selecting this routing entry, you see that the Client Access jobs start a server job that will run requests from a client. The server job will run in pool 1 (*BASE) of the QBASE subsystem. You also see that it assigns runtime attributes to the server job from the QCASERVR class. Take a closer look at the class by entering the following to get the display shown in Figure 10.11:

```
DSPCLS QCASERVR
```

Now you have all the information you need about the jobs that are started using a PC (client) as a workstation. Once the client has been contacted, it will be given a device name starting with the characters QPADEV, followed by four digits. This device is recognized as a workstation and is sent a sign-on screen using a workstation entry in QBASE. When you enter the information on the sign-on screen, your client enters the system as an interactive job, using the routing entries created earlier.

```
                       Display Class Information
                                              System:   TSCSAP02
  Class . . . . . . . . . . . . . . . . . . . . . :   QCASERVR
    Library . . . . . . . . . . . . . . . . . . :     QGPL
  Run priority  . . . . . . . . . . . . . . . . :   20
  Time slice in milliseconds  . . . . . . . . . :   500
  Eligible for purge  . . . . . . . . . . . . . :   *YES
  Default wait time in seconds  . . . . . . . . :   30
  Maximum CPU time in milliseconds  . . . . . . :   *NOMAX
  Maximum temporary storage in megabytes  . . . :   *NOMAX
  Maximum threads . . . . . . . . . . . . . . . :   *NOMAX
  Text  . . . . . . . . . . . . . . . . . . . . :   Client Access Class




  Press Enter to continue.
```

Figure 10.11: The QCASERVR class is used to assign runtime attributes to Client Access server jobs.

The nice thing about this scheme is that you don't need to modify any of the default information shipped with the system. All you need to do is load the Client Access code on your PC, start the Client Access code, and perform your sign-on, just like you were a green-screen workstation.

Commands to Create and Manage Communications Entries

As you might have guessed, the commands for managing the communications entries are the same as those used to manage the other types of entries in the subsystem—Add Communications Entry (ADDCMNE), Change Communications Entry (CHGCMNE), and Remove Communications Entry (RMVCMNE).

Adding Communications Entries to a Subsystem

To see what it takes to add a communications entry to the subsystem, begin with the Add Communications Entry (ADDCMNE) command. You will see that the command has the parameters shown in Figure 10.12. Table 10.2 describes each of these parameters in detail.

```
                        Add Communications Entry (ADDCMNE)

      Type choices, press Enter.

      Subsystem description  . . . . .   SBSD
        Library  . . . . . . . . . .                     *LIBL
      Device . . . . . . . . . . . .    DEV
      Remote location  . . . . . . .    RMTLOCNAME
      Job description  . . . . . . .    JOBD             *USRPRF
        Library  . . . . . . . . . .
      Default user profile . . . . .    DFTUSR           *NONE
      Mode . . . . . . . . . . . . .    MODE             *ANY
      Maximum active jobs  . . . . .    MAXACT           *NOMAX




                                                                    Bottom
      F3=Exit   F4=Prompt   F5=Refresh   F12=Cancel   F13=How to use this display
      F24=More keys
```

Figure 10.12: The Add Communication Entry command (ADDCMNE) is used to add additional communication entries to a subsystem.

Table 10.2: Parameters for ADDCMNE (1 of 2)

Parameter	Value/Meaning
Subsystem Name, Library Name	This is the name of the subsystem that will contain the new communications entry.
Device	This is the name of the device or the type of devices that will use the communications entry. Either this parameter or the Remote Location Name parameter must be supplied; you cannot specify both. Some of the values for this parameter require specific values for the mode. The possible values and associated devices are as follows: • *Device-name*—Only the device description named will use the entry. • *Generic*-device-name*—Devices that start with the characters preceding the asterisk will use the entry. • *ALL—All communications device types or names will use the entry. • *APPC—Only advanced program-to-program communications devices will use the entry. • *ASYNC—Only asynchronous communications will use the entry. This value is valid only when *ANY is specified as the mode. • *BSCEL—Only bisynchronous equivalency link communications devices will use the entry. This value is valid only when *ANY is specified as the mode. • *FINANCE—Only finance communications devices will use the entry. This value is valid only when *ANY is specified as the mode. • *RETAIL—Only retail communications devices will use the entry. This value is valid only when *ANY is specified as the mode. • *SNUF—Only SNA upline facility communications devices will use the entry. This value is valid only when *ANY is specified as the mode. It is not the intent of this book to describe all of these device types. Please see the iSeries (or AS/400) Data Communications Programmers' Guide for additional information.
Remote Location Name	This is the remote location name specified in the associated Create Device Description command. No validity checking is done on the remote location name.

Table 10.2: Parameters for ADDCMNE (2 of 2)	
Parameter	**Value/Meaning**
Job Description Name Library Name	This is the name of the job description that will be used for jobs that use the communication entry. The possible values for this parameter are as follows: • *USRPRF—The job description will be specified in the user profile of the user that submitted the request. This is the default value. • *SBSD—The job description with the same name as the subsystem used to run the job will be used. • *Job description name*—The specified job description will be used.
Default User Profile	This is the name of the user profile to run the job if none is supplied with the request. The possible values are as follows: • *NONE—A user name must be supplied. This is the default value. • *SYS—User-submitted requests must supply a user profile name. A user profile assigned to system functions will be used if the request is made by one of these functions. • *User profile name*—All jobs will run using the user profile name associated with this entry. The requestor does not need to supply a user profile name. For security reasons, providing a default user profile is not recommended.
Mode	This parameter provides the name of the communications mode to be used by any request that uses this communication entry. Many functions that use a communication entry use a mode to determine the type of communication being done. (Think of it as the "language" spoken between the device or remote location name and the program that is run as a result of the request.) The possible values are as follows: • *ANY—Any mode that is in use by the device or remote location is valid. This is the default value. • *Mode name*—The device or remote location name must be using the specified mode in order to use this entry.
Maximum Active Jobs	The maximum number of jobs that can use this entry at the same time is as follows: • *A number from one through 1,000*—Only the number of jobs specified may be active at the same time. • *NOMAX—There is no limit to the number of jobs. This is the default value.

This command is difficult to understand mostly because it involves more than work management; it also requires an understanding of communications and the system and user functions that can be performed. However, the OS/400-supplied communications entries can accommodate most communications devices and requests without any modifications or additions by you.

Changing Communications Entries

Once you have a communication entry in a subsystem, it can be changed with the Change Communications Entry command (CHGCMNE). Other than changing the first three letters to CHG, the syntax of this command is identical to ADDCMNE. It uses the same set of parameters with the same possible values. Any changes made to a communications entry can be made while the subsystem is active, and the changes are made immediately, with the following caveats:

- If the job description or default user profile is changed, jobs that are already running are not changed.

- If the maximum active value is reduced to a number less than the number of jobs that are running via the communications entry, jobs that have already started continue to run, but no new jobs will be started until the number of running jobs becomes less than the new value.

- If jobs are running via this entry, you cannot change the value of the mode.

Getting Rid of a Communications Entry

To eliminate a communications entry, run the Remove Communication Entry command (RMVCMNE). The RMVCMNE command has fewer parameters than ADDCMNE or CHGCMNE, but the meaning and possible values are the same. The format of RMVCMNE is shown in Figure 10.13. If any jobs initiated using the communications entry are still running, the communications entry cannot be removed.

```
Subsystem description  . . . . . SBSD
   Library . . . . . . . . . . .              *LIBL
Device . . . . . . . . . . . . . DEV
Remote location  . . . . . . . . RMTLOCNAME
Mode . . . . . . . . . . . . . . MODE         *ANY
```

Figure 10.13: The Remove Communication Entry command (RMVCMNE) is used to remove a communication entry from a subsystem.

Running Interactive Jobs on More than One System

Consider a commonly used system function that uses a communication entry. In many instances, a user, especially a system administrator or a programmer, will be attached to an iSeries machine, but will need to perform work on a different machine. This function is called *workstation pass-through*.

Starting Jobs on a Second System

To run work on a second system, the Start Pass Through command (STRPASTHR) is run. Looking at STRPASTHR (in Figures 10.14a and 10.14b), you can see that you can provide a lot of information when you make contact with the second system. There are quite a few parameters on STRPASTHR. Table 10.3 gives their meanings and values.

```
                    Start Pass-Through (STRPASTHR)

 Type choices, press Enter.

 Remote location  . . . . . . . RMTLOCNAME    >
 Virtual controller . . . . . . VRTCTL        *NONE
 Virtual display device . . . . VRTDEV        *NONE
                       + for more values
 Mode . . . . . . . . . . . . . MODE          *NETATR
 Local location . . . . . . . . LCLLOCNAME    *LOC
 Remote network identifier  . . RMTNETID      *LOC
 System request program . . . . SRQ10PGM      *SRQMNU
   Library  . . . . . . . . . .


                     Additional Parameters

 User profile . . . . . . . . . RMTUSER       *NONE
 User password  . . . . . . . . RMTPWD        *NONE
 Initial program to call  . . . RMTINLPGM     *RMTUSRPRF
 Initial menu . . . . . . . . . RMTINLMNU     *RMTUSRPRF
                                                        More...
 F3=Exit   F4=Prompt   F5=Refresh   F12=Cancel   F13=How to use this display
 F24=More keys
```

Figure 10.14a: The Start Pass-Through command (STRPASTHR) can be used to start an interactive job on a remote system.

```
                        Start Pass-Through (STRPASTHR)

 Type choices, press Enter.

 Current library  . . . . . . . .   RMTCURLIB       *RMTUSRPRF
 Display option . . . . . . . . .   PASTHRSCN       *YES




                                                                    Bottom
   F3=Exit   F4=Prompt   F5=Refresh   F12=Cancel   F13=How to use this display
   F24=More keys
```

Figure 10.14b: The Start Pass-Through command (STRPASTHR) can be used to start an interactive job on a remote system.

Table 10.3: STRPASTHR Parameters (1 of 4)

Parameter	Value/Meaning
Remote Location	This is the name of the remote system that will run your remote job. The name may specify an intermediate system that will pass your request on to the actual target. This required parameter is used together with the APPC Device parameter to determine the meaning of the remote location name. The possible values are as follows: • *Remote location name*—This is the name of the remote system. If the value of the APPC Device parameter is *LOC, the name of the remote system is the target system that will run the job. If the APPC Device parameter contains the names of devices, Remote Location is an intermediate system that will pass the request to the actual target system. • *CNNDEV—The name of the system will be obtained from the APPC device parameter.
APPC Device	This parameter is used together with Remote Location to reach the target system. The possible values for this parameter are as follows: • *LOC—The Remote Location parameter is the name of the target system, and there are no intermediate systems. This is the default value.

Table 10.3: STRPASTHR Parameters (2 of 4)

Parameter	Value/Meaning
APPC Device *continued*	• *Device name(s)*—This holds the names of device descriptions that are used to reach the target system. The location of the first device description in the list is determined by the value in the Remote Location parameter. If Remote Location contains a system name, the device description is on the system that is named. If Remote Location is *CNNDEV, the device description is located on the source machine (the machine running the job that issued the STRPASTHR command). If only one device description is specified, there are no intermediate nodes. If there are intermediate nodes between the system the job is using and the target system, multiple device names must be specified. The device names need to appear in the order that they are used to reach the target system; the last device in the list will reach the target. Up to 16 device names may be specified.
Virtual Controller	This is the name of the virtual controller on the target system that is used for the pass-through job. This parameter is not required, but if it is specified, the Virtual Device parameter can not be specified. The possible values are as follows: • *NONE—The pass-through job does not require a specific controller. If the Virtual Device parameter is *NONE, the target system will automatically assign a virtual controller and device to the pass-through job. This is the default value. • *Virtual controller name*—This is the name of the virtual controller that you wish to use. If the virtual controller does not exist on the target system or is unavailable, the pass-through request will fail.
Virtual Display Device	This names the virtual devices that will be used by the job that will run on the target system. Although the devices are attached to a virtual controller on the target system, you cannot specify a name for the Virtual Controller parameter if you specify a value for this parameter. The possible values are as follows: • *NONE—The pass-through job does not require a specific device. If the Virtual Device parameter is *NONE, the target system will automatically assign a virtual controller and device to the pass-through job. This is the default value. • *Virtual device name(s)*—One or more of the named virtual devices on the target system can be used to run the job. If more than one device is specified, the target system will try to match the user's device to the attributes of the device in use on the target system.

Table 10.3: STRPASTHR Parameters (3 of 4)

Parameter	Value/Meaning
Mode	This parameter specifies the mode that is used to communicate with the target system. The possible values for this parameter are as follows: • *NETATR—The mode that is specified in the network attribute is used. The default mode for the system's network attributes is blank—any mode can be used between the source and target systems. This is the default value. • *Mode name*—Only the mode specified can be used between the source and target systems.
Local Location	This is the local location name used for the source system, with the following possible values: • *LOC—The source system will choose (assign) a local location name. This is the default. • *NETATR—The local name is obtained form the source system network attributes. • *APPN location name*—The name specified will be used as the local location name.
Remote Network Identifier	This parameter identifies the remote network of the system specified in the Remote Location parameter. The possible values are as follows: • *LOC—Any network ID on the system is valid. This is the default value. • *NETATR—The local network ID found in the network attributes of the source system is used as the network ID of the remote location. • *NONE—The remote location does not support network IDs. • *APPN network identifier*—The specified name identifies the remote location network.
System Request Program Name and Library Name	When you are running a pass-through job, pressing the System Request key and selecting option 1 will let you start another job (or toggle to a secondary job) on your target system. However, you also have the ability to move back and forth between jobs on the source and target systems. When you press the System Request key and a pass-through job is active, the System Request menu will have additional selections: options 10, 11, 13, 14, and 15. This parameter identifies the program that will be run on the source system whenever option 10 or option 13 is selected. Its possible values are as follows: • *SRQMNU—The system-supplied System Request program will be called. This is the default value. • *System request program name and library name*—The name of a user-written program will be run on the source system. The usage of options 10, 11, 13, 14, and 15 is described in the following pages.

Table 10.3: STRPASTHR Parameters (4 of 4)

Parameter	Value/Meaning
User Profile	This and the next four parameters represent the information you can supply when you sign on to a workstation. If you supply information in these parameters, the user will automatically be signed on to the target system, and the first program will be called. This parameter provides the user profile to use when signing on to the target system. The only possible value is the user profile name to use on the target system.
User Password	This is the password to be used on the target system. Any password that is specified will be encrypted before it is transmitted to the target system. The possible values are as follows: • *NONE—The user is required to enter a password. If a user profile name is specified, and the target system has password security, you cannot specify *NONE for this parameter. This is the default value. • *Password*—This is the user password that will be used on the remote sign-on
Initial Program to Call	This is the name of the program to be called on the target system after sign-on is complete. The possible values are as follows: • *RMTUSRPRF—The initial program specified in the user profile on the target system will be called. This is the default value. • *NONE—No program will be called prior to displaying the initial menu. • *Program name*—The specified program will be called.
Initial Menu	This is the name of the menu to be displayed after the initial program is done. The possible values are as follows: • *RMTUSRPRF—The menu is obtained form the target system user profile. This is the default value. • *SIGNOFF—No initial menu is displayed. When the initial program ends, the user is signed off, and the pass-through session ends. • *Menu name*—This is the name of the menu to be displayed.
Current Library	This value specifies the library that becomes the current library (*CURLIB) after sign-on: • *RMTUSRPRF—The current library is obtained from the target system user profile. This is the default value *Library name*—The specified name becomes the current library.
Display Option	Messages are generated while the STRPASTHR command is being processed. This parameter indicates how you wish to handle the messages. The possible values are as follows: • *YES—Display the messages. This is the default. • *NO—Do not display the messages.

At long last, you've made it through all of the parameters of the STRPASTHR command. Is it really that complicated? Not really. Remember, only the first parameter must be specified, and the defaults can be taken for the rest. Most of the work to prepare for pass-through jobs has been done when you established your network of systems. Once again, this book doesn't address communications topics. More information can be obtained from IBM's *AS/400 Advanced Series Remote Workstation Support*, SC21-5402.

Using the System Request Key with Pass-Through Jobs

As mentioned in the discussion of STRPASTHR, additional options are available on the System Request menu. As described in SC21-5402, here they are:

- Option 10 (Start System Request at Previous System) takes you from an intermediate or end system to the previous system. The previous system is the source system. The program specified by the system request program parameter (SRQ10PGM) on the STRPASTHR command entered at the previous system will be running.

- Option 11 (Transfer to Previous System) takes you from an intermediate or end system to the alternate job on the previous system. The previous system is the source system.

- Option 13 (Start System Request at Home System) takes you from an intermediate or end system to the home system. The program specified by the system request program parameter (SRQ10PGM) on the STRPASTHR command entered at the home system will be running.

- Option 14 (Transfer to Home System) takes you from an intermediate or end system to the home system. Control is given to the alternate job at the home system.

- Option 15 (Transfer to End System) takes you from an intermediate or home system back to the system you came from. The system you came from is the system where you used System Request option 10, 11, 13, or 14 to get to the intermediate or home system. Using option 15, whatever job and program were interrupted when you left the end system resume control when you return to the end system.

Got that? Clearly, they are trying to tell you something, but it's hard to figure out just what. Consider some simple examples to illustrate the options on the System Request menu. In the first example, shown in Figure 10.15, there are no intermediate systems between the source and target. Neither the job running on the source machine nor the target machine has an alternate job. Figure 10.15 shows the actions taken by the system when the various options are selected from the System Request menu.

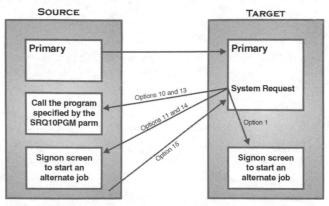

Figure 10.15: When the System Request key is pressed in a pass-through job, it provides five options that result in the actions illustrated here.

Now you can see how these options actually work. Option 1 allows you to start a secondary job on the target system. Options 10 and 13 call the program specified on the STRPASTHR command. The default program will present the System Request menu. Because no alternate job currently exists on the source system, options 11 and 14 present the sign-on screen on the source system that allows you to start an alternate job. Finally, if option 15 is selected after option 10, 11, 13, or 14, the user is returned to the system that handled the System Request key. This is similar to pressing F3 or F12 on the System Request Menu.

Now, expand the example to include an alternate job on the source system. Once again, press the System Request key while you are running the job on the target system. The diagram in Figure 10.16 shows the results of selecting the various options from the System Request menu. As you can see, the only difference from the previous example is the action that is taken whenever option 11 or option 14 is selected. In this example, control is returned to the alternate job.

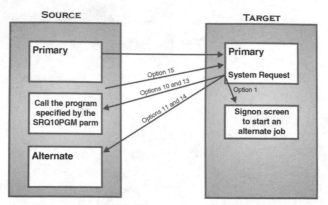

Figure 10.16: *When a secondary job exists for the source job of a pass-through job, the actions taken for the System Request options are illustrated here.*

Now, add another wrinkle. In the next example, the alternate job ALTRNAT runs the STRPASTHRU command and starts another job on the target system. Figure 10.17 shows what happens when the System Request key is pressed in either of the two target system jobs.

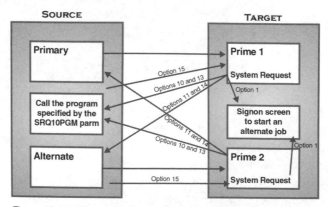

Figure 10.17: *When both the source job and its secondary job have a pass-through job started on another system, the options shown here are taken on the System Request menu in either of the pass-through jobs.*

Well, nobody said that keeping all of this straight was going to be easy! Notice that, whenever you make a selection from the System Request menu on the target system, the following occur:

- Options 10 and 13 will always call the program specified by the SRQ10PGM parameter of the STRPASTHR command.

- Options 11 and 14 will always return to the job that did not initiate the pass-through request. In other words, if options 11 and 14 are selected from the menu presented by the pass-through job started by primary, control is passed to ALTRNAT. Similarly, if options 11 and 14 are selected from the menu presented by the pass-through job started by ALTRNAT, control is passed to primary.

- Option 15 will return to the target system job that was active when control was returned to one of the jobs on the source system. This is one of the reasons why it pays to keep things simple when you are using features like pass-through—it's not long before you're so confused that you can't figure out where you are, where you're going, and where you'll be when you come back. Not only that, you need to find some way to make this easy for your users to understand!

That said, take a look at an example with an intermediate system in the pass-through environment. This time, you have a primary and alternate job on the source and intermediate system, and only a primary job on the target system. When you press System Request and make a menu selection, the actions taken are represented by Figure 10.18.

In this environment, the intermediate system will receive control for options 10 and 11, and the source system will retrieve control for options 13 and 14. No matter where option 15 is selected, control will be returned to the target system job. These examples should cover nearly every

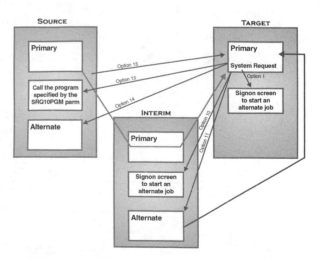

Figure 10.18: When an intermediate system exists between the source job and a pass-through job, these are the options from the System Request menu on the pass-through

use of STRPASTHR that you will be likely to encounter. Of course, there are bound to be some environments that will be far more complex than those illustrated here, but you can always break them down to these simple cases.

Prestart Jobs

The subsystems have still one more source of work: prestart jobs. These jobs are used by communications requests to provide a faster linkage between the requesting and serving systems. Many of the communication jobs are short-running, and the overhead of initiating a job each time a request is sent to the server is prohibitive. You can greatly reduce the overhead simply by having prestart jobs in your environment.

Setting up Prestart Jobs

As with all of the other sources of work in OS/400, the prestart jobs require an entry in the subsystem. Go back to the display you get when you run the Display Subsystem Description command (DSPSBSD) for QBASE, shown in Figure 10.19. This time, select option 10 to look at the prestart entries. After you press Enter, you get the screen shown in Figure 10.20.

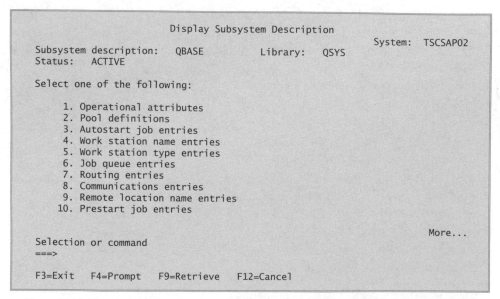

```
                    Display Subsystem Description
                                                   System:  TSCSAP02
        Subsystem description:   QBASE        Library:   QSYS
        Status:   ACTIVE

        Select one of the following:

             1. Operational attributes
             2. Pool definitions
             3. Autostart job entries
             4. Work station name entries
             5. Work station type entries
             6. Job queue entries
             7. Routing entries
             8. Communications entries
             9. Remote location name entries
            10. Prestart job entries

                                                            More...
        Selection or command
        ===>

        F3=Exit   F4=Prompt   F9=Retrieve   F12=Cancel
```

Figure 10.19: The Display Subsystem Description menu provides options that can be used to look at different parts of a subsystem.

```
                         Display Prestart Job Entries
                                                        System:   TSCSAP02
      Subsystem description:   QBASE           Status:    ACTIVE

      Type options, press Enter.
        5=Display details

      Opt      Program      Library        User Profile
               QACSOTP      QSYS           QUSER
               QLZPSERV     QIWS           QUSER
               QNMAPINGD    QSYS           QUSER
               QNMAREXECD   QSYS           QUSER
               QNPSERVR     QIWS           QUSER
               QOQSESRV     QSYS           QUSER
               QZRCSRVR     QIWS           QUSER
               QZSCSRVR     QIWS           QUSER




                                                                  Bottom
      F3=Exit    F9=Display all detailed descriptions    F12=Cancel
```

Figure 10.20: Option 10 from the Display Subsystem Description menu shows the prestart job entries that are shipped with QBASE.

When QBASE starts, at least eight jobs will be started as a result of the prestart job entries that are shown. As usual, you have the same types of commands to manage these entries in your subsystem:

- Add Prestart Job Entry (ADDPJE).
- Change Prestart Job Entry (CHGPJE).
- Remove Prestart Job Entry (RMVPJE).

Take a closer look at one of the prestart job entries by placing a five in front of one of the entries and pressing Enter. You will see the information in Figures 10.21a and 10.21b. The values shown represent the information specified on the Add Prestart Job Entry command. Now, look at ADDPJE in Figures 10.22a and 10.22b. Table 10.4 lists the parameters of the ADDPJE command.

```
                  Display Prestart Job Entry Detail
                                              System:   TSCSAP02
   Subsystem description:    QBASE         Status:   ACTIVE

   Program  . . . . . . . . . . . . . . . . . . . . . :   QZSCSRVR
     Library  . . . . . . . . . . . . . . . . . . . :     QIWS
   User profile . . . . . . . . . . . . . . . . . . :   QUSER
   Job  . . . . . . . . . . . . . . . . . . . . . . :   QZSCSRVR
   Job description  . . . . . . . . . . . . . . . . :   *USRPRF
     Library  . . . . . . . . . . . . . . . . . . . :
   Start jobs . . . . . . . . . . . . . . . . . . . :   *YES
   Initial number of jobs . . . . . . . . . . . . . :   1
   Threshold  . . . . . . . . . . . . . . . . . . . :   1
   Additional number of jobs  . . . . . . . . . . . :   3
   Maximum number of jobs . . . . . . . . . . . . . :   *NOMAX
   Maximum number of uses . . . . . . . . . . . . . :   200
   Wait for job . . . . . . . . . . . . . . . . . . :   *YES
   Pool identifier  . . . . . . . . . . . . . . . . :   2

                                                         More...

   Press Enter to continue.

   F3=Exit    F12=Cancel    F14=Display previous entry
```

Figure 10.21a: Placing a five in front of a prestart job entry shows the details of the selected entry.

```
                  Display Prestart Job Entry Detail
                                              System:   TSCSAP02
   Subsystem description:    QBASE         Status:   ACTIVE

   Class  . . . . . . . . . . . . . . . . . . . . . :   QCASERVR
     Library  . . . . . . . . . . . . . . . . . . . :     QGPL
     Number of jobs to use class  . . . . . . . . . :     *CALC
   Class  . . . . . . . . . . . . . . . . . . . . . :   *NONE
     Library  . . . . . . . . . . . . . . . . . . . :
     Number of jobs to use class  . . . . . . . . . :     *CALC

                                                         Bottom

   Press Enter to continue.

   F3=Exit    F12=Cancel    F14=Display previous entry
```

Figure 10.21b: Placing a five in front of a prestart job entry shows the details of the selected entry.

```
                    Add  Prestart  Job  Entry  (ADDPJE)

Type choices, press Enter.

Subsystem description . . . . .  SBSD        >
  Library . . . . . . . . . . .              *LIBL
Program . . . . . . . . . . .  PGM         >
  Library . . . . . . . . . . .              *LIBL
User profile . . . . . . . . .  USER        QUSER
Start jobs . . . . . . . . . .  STRJOBS     *YES
Initial number of jobs . . . .  INLJOBS     3
Threshold . . . . . . . . . .  THRESHOLD   2
Additional number of jobs  . . .  ADLJOBS     2
Maximum number of jobs . . . . .  MAXJOBS     *NOMAX

                    Additional Parameters

Job name . . . . . . . . . . .  JOB         *PGM
Job description . . . . . . .  JOBD        *USRPRF
  Library . . . . . . . . . .
                                                            More...
F3=Exit   F4=Prompt   F5=Refresh   F12=Cancel   F13=How to use this display
F24=More keys
```

Figure 10.22a: The Add Prestart Job Entry command (ADDPJE) is used to add prestart job entries to a subsystem.

```
                    Add  Prestart  Job  Entry  (ADDPJE)

Type choices, press Enter.

Maximum number of uses . . . . .  MAXUSE      200
Wait for job . . . . . . . . .  WAIT        *YES
Pool identifier . . . . . . . .  POOLID      1
Class:                           CLS
  Class . . . . . . . . . . .                *SBSD
    Library . . . . . . . . .
  Number of jobs to use class .              *CALC
  Class . . . . . . . . . . .                *NONE
    Library . . . . . . . . .
  Number of jobs to use class .              *CALC




                                                            Bottom
F3=Exit   F4=Prompt   F5=Refresh   F12=Cancel   F13=How to use this display
F24=More keys
```

Figure 10.22b: The Add Prestart Job Entry command (ADDPJE) is used to add prestart job entries to a subsystem.

Table 10.4: ADDPJE Parameters (1 of 3)

Parameter	Value/Meaning
Subsystem Name and Library Name	This is a required parameter. It provides the name of the subsystem that will contain the prestart job entry.
Program Name and Library Name	This required parameter is the name of the program that is to be run when the prestart job is started.
User Profile	This is the name of the user profile used to start the job. When a request from a remote location is assigned to the job, the job will be switched to the user profile of the requestor. Any routing and initial program information in the requestor's profile will be ignored.
Start Jobs	When the subsystem is started, this parameter will determine if the prestart jobs start. The possible values for this parameter are as follows: • *YES—The jobs defined by the prestart job entry are started automatically when the subsystem starts. • *NO—The jobs are not started automatically. To start a prestart job that has *NO specified, you need to run the Start Prestart Jobs command (STRPJ).
Initial Number of Jobs	When the prestarted jobs are started, you may start more than one. This parameter is a numeric value from one through 9,999. The larger the number, the longer it takes. The default value for this parameter is three.
Threshold	The prestarted jobs will be waiting for a request to use the program running in the prestart job. When a request for the prestart job is received, one of the prestart jobs will be put to use. When the number of prestart jobs waiting for a request falls below the value specified in Threshold, additional prestart jobs will be started. A numeric value from one through 9,999 is allowed for this parameter, but the threshold value must be less than or equal to the initial number of jobs. The default value for this parameter is two.
Additional Number of Jobs	When the threshold value is reached, the subsystem will automatically start additional jobs. The number of additional jobs to start is specified by this parameter. A numeric value from one through 999 is allowed for this parameter. The default value is two.
Maximum Number of Jobs	This parameter controls the maximum number of prestart jobs that can be active or waiting for a request at any time. You may specify any number from one through 9,999, but the value should be at least as large as the Initial Number of Jobs value. The default is *NOMAX.

Table 10.4: ADDPJE Parameters (2 of 3)

Parameter	Value/Meaning
Maximum Number of Uses	This value specifies the maximum number of times that a prestarted job can be put to use by requesters. When the number of requesters that have used this job reaches this value, the job will be ended following the last use. If ending the job reduces the number of active jobs to a number less than the initial number of jobs, a new job will be started to take its place. The possible values are as follows: • *Numeric value*—A number from one through 1,000 may be specified. • *NOMAX—The job can be used any number of times without being ended. The default value is 200. Occasionally, ending a job helps free up disk or main storage resources that are in use by the prestart job, so the default value represents a reasonable limit for the number of uses of a prestart job.
Wait for Job	When a request to use the prestart job is received, all of the available jobs may be in use. This parameters indicates whether the requester should wait for a job to become available. The possible values are as follows: • *YES—The requester will wait for a prestarted job to become available. If the number of prestart jobs is less than the maximum number of jobs, the requester will wait for the prestart job to be started. If no jobs are available and the maximum number of jobs have been started, the request will be rejected, and the requester will need to re-try the operation. This is the default. • *NO—The requester will not wait for a prestart job. If *NO is specified, the request will be rejected, and the requester will need to retry.
Pool Identifier	Identifies the pool where the prestart job will be assigned to run. You may specify a numeric value from one through 10. If the pool identifier is not available when the job starts, the routing will fail. To get the job(s) to start, the pools for the subsystem must be corrected, and the STRPJ command must be run. The default value is one.
Class	You may specify up to two classes that are used to obtain the runtime attributed for the prestarted jobs. In addition, you may specify the maximum number of prestart jobs that will use each class. As the prestart jobs are started, the first class will be used until the number of jobs value is reached, and then the second class will be used. The possible values for the first class are as follows: • *Class*—This is the name of the class used to obtain the runtime attributes. • *SBSD—The class has the same name as the subsystem that contains the prestart job entry. This is the default. • *Class name*—The name of the class is to be used. If the class does not exist at the time the prestart job entry is added, the library name must be specified.

Table 10.4: ADDPJE Parameters (3 of 3)	
Parameter	**Value/Meaning**
Class continued	• *Number of jobs to use class*—This is the maximum number of jobs that can use this class at one time.
	• *Numeric value*—You may specify any number from zero through 32,766. If the number exceeds the value of the maximum number of jobs parameter, only this class will be used.
	• *CALC—The subsystem calculates the number of jobs for this class. The calculated value will be derived from the value specified in the Maximum Number of Jobs parameter. If the maximum number of jobs is *NOMAX, all jobs will use this class. Otherwise, the calculated value will be half of the value specified in Maximum Number of Jobs. The result will be rounded up to the next whole number. This is the default value.
	• *MAXJOBS—All of the jobs will use this class.
	The values for the second class used to obtain runtime attributes are as follows.
	• *Class*—This is the name of the class used to obtain the runtime attributes.
	• *NONE –There is only one class. This is the default value.
	• *SBSD—The class has the same name as the subsystem that contains the prestart job entry.
	• *Class name*—This is the name of the class to be used. If the class does not exist at the time the prestart job entry is added, the library name must be specified.
	• *Number of jobs to use class*—This is the maximum number of jobs that can use this class at one time

One of the nice things about prestart jobs is that you specify all of the routing and runtime attribute information on the prestart job entry itself. Look at the parameters again, and notice that the pool, class, and initial program are all specified in the entry. If you create the entry correctly, your jobs can't go wrong.

Using Prestart Jobs

The diagrams in Figures 10.23 and 10.24 show how the communications entry and prestart jobs work together to improve the performance of requests from the remote system. Figure 10.23 shows the action taken by the subsystem to start the prestart job named CMNSVR. The CMNSVR job is running the CMNSVR program.

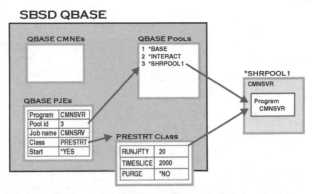

Figure 10.23: Prestart Job Entries will cause jobs to be started in *SHRPOOL1, which will wait for a communication job request.

As you can see, the prestart job entry specified a start value of *YES. Therefore, when the subsystem started, it started a job named CMNSVR, which called the CMNSVR program. The runtime attributes for the job were obtained from the class named PRESTRT. The pool chosen to run the job is *SHRPOOL1 because it is defined as pool ID 3.

Now that your prestart job is running, all you need to do is wait for a communication request that wants to run the CMNSVR program to arrive. Figure 10.24 shows the actions that the subsystem takes when one of these communications requests arrives.

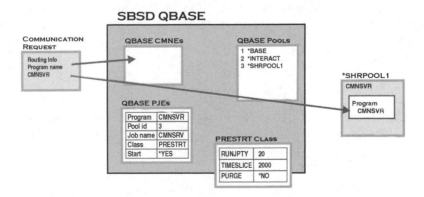

Figure 10.24: A communications job with routing information that has the program name CMNSVR is connected to a prestart job in *SHRPOOL1.

When the communications request arrives at the subsystem, it is checked to see if it matches one of the communications entries. If it does, the subsystem checks the requested program to see if a prestarted job using the program is available. In this case, a job is available, and the request is send to the active job to be processed. This procedure short-circuits much of the job initiation time. As a result, communications requests that do not last a long time (which accounts for most of them) produce much better response time and throughput.

Some Additional Prestart Job Issues

If you have set the number of prestart jobs for any entry to accommodate a peak period, you might have an abundance of prestart jobs available. The subsystem will monitor the usage of the prestart jobs. If it detects several jobs that are not being used, it will gradually end them. The subsystem will never reduce the number of prestart jobs to a value below the number specified as the initial number of jobs.

The prestart job should perform as much job initialization as possible so that, when the communications request attaches to the job, it can begin processing sooner. Remember that the primary reason for prestart jobs is to process communication requests as quickly as possible. For example, you may open all of the files that are common to requests that are handled by the initial program.

When you complete a request, leave objects used by the program attached to the job. Files that you have open should be left open. However, if you choose this action, your requests should not be dependent on the contents of the file buffers. There will be no guarantee that an intervening request did not change the contents of the program's file buffers.

Objects placed in the QTEMP library should be deleted when the request is completed. Only one copy of QTEMP exists for the duration of the job. As more and more requests are processed, there could be conflicting definitions and uses of object in QTEMP, making it rather large and unmanageable.

If you need to communicate information between requests, you can use the local data *LDA of the prestart job. As with QTEMP, there is only one copy of *LDA, so caution should be exercised when you use it to pass information from one request to another. There is no guarantee that the data in *LDA is unchanged.

Just as with other job types, you can change the attributes of a prestart job. Simply run the Change Prestart Job command (CHGPJ). Although the name is similar to the Change Prestart Job Entry command (CHGPJE), CHGPJ changes the attributes of an active prestart job, while CHGPJE changes the definition of any new prestart jobs that are started.

Finally, as you might have guessed, the prestart job entry and the communication entry that uses the prestart job must be defined in the same subsystem. It is not possible to connect a communications request from one subsystem to a prestart job running in another subsystem.

Really Fast Initiation—Threads

Many new applications use threads to assist in the processing of work that a job needs to do. Threads allow the job to start an asynchronous function that will be working on one thing, while the main part of the application works on another. It is possible to have multiple threads running in one job at the same time.

Threads are not initiated by work management in the traditional fashion, that is, there is no thread entry defined in the subsystem. Rather, threads are the result of a programming construct, which creates a thread that is tied closely to the job running the program. In fact, the thread derives most of its job attributes from the job that starts the thread.

As with your communication jobs, threads usually are started, run for a very short time, and ended. And, as with your communications jobs, threads cannot tolerate the full job-initiation ritual, so work management has built-in capabilities to make starting and stopping threads efficient.

A thread is not a job! It is a subset of a job. However, since it is running asynchronous to the job that started it and other threads, it is treated as a job whenever scheduling and dispatching decisions are made. That is, threads receive run priorities, pool assignments, and time slice values like other jobs running on the system.

It is not the intent of this book to teach thread techniques and concepts. They are merely mentioned here because, in a modern programming environment, you are likely to encounter them. Just remember that when you are trying to allocate main storage and determine an acceptable faulting rate in a pool, you should base your decisions not on the number of jobs that are running, but on the number of threads. For more information about multi-threaded applications, see *Programming Multithreaded Applications* in the iSeries documentation library.

In Review

You've now completed another step in your efforts to understand all of the different types of jobs running on your system. Congratulations! You'll be happy to know that there are no other job types. You should now be able to understand and construct subsystems that run any of the OS/400 types of jobs.

11

Picking Up the Pieces

On your way through work management so far, a few things have been left behind that you now need to pick up. For example, you have been working exclusively with QBASE as your controlling subsystem, but it doesn't have to be that way. This chapter covers the following topics:

- Using QCTL as the controlling subsystem.
- Multiple interactive subsystems.
- Other IBM-supplied subsystems.
- Running in restricted state.
- Using the OS/400 job scheduler function.
- System values that relate to work management.

Upon completing this chapter, you will have covered all the parts of work management that you can see and control.

Using QCTL as the Controlling Subsystem

OS/400 is shipped to run with QBASE as the controlling subsystem. The controlling subsystem is the first subsystem that is started when the system is IPLed (booted). However, as you have seen from customizations of QBASE, it can get pretty messy and difficult to manage. To simplify things a bit, OS/400 is shipped with a second controlling subsystem, QCTL.

To use QCTL as the controlling subsystem, you need to change the system value QCTLSBSD from QBASE to QCTL. You change the system value with the Change System Value command (CHGSYSVAL):

```
CHGSYSVAL QCTLSBSD QCTL
```

That's the easy part. Just as changing a routing entry or a class has no effect on jobs that are already running, changing the system value does not automatically cause the controlling subsystem to be switched from QBASE to QCTL. To complete the change from QBASE to QCTL, you need to power down and restart your system:

```
PWRDWNSYS RESTART(*YES)
```

When the system is restarted, QCTL will be the controlling subsystem.

However, QCTL is not used in the same way as QBASE. QCTL is designed to be a controlling subsystem only; it is not intended to initiate and terminate batch jobs, or interactive jobs, or communications requests. Typically, the job running at the system console is the only job in QCTL. So, how do you get the rest of your work initiated?

When QCTL is started, it runs an autostart job that starts subsystems QBATCH, QINTER, QCMN, QSERVER, QUSRWRK, and QSPL. As you might have guessed, QBATCH initiates batch jobs; QINTER, interactive jobs; QCMN, communications jobs; and QSPL, spool writers. (The functions that QUSRWRK and QSERVER provide are discussed later in this chapter.) Therefore, after the system is done booting, all of the sources of work you had before are available.

Before going farther, you need to address any modifications you might have made to QBASE. If you added job queue entries, workstation entries, communications entries, prestart job entries, autostart job entries, pools, or routing entries, you will need to add them all over again using the new subsystem structure. If you added pools, job queue entries, and routing entries to separate batch jobs, you'll need to make the same changes in QBATCH. Similarly, if you added pools and routing entries for interactive jobs, you'll need to make the same

modifications to QINTER, and any communications changes you've made will
have to be repeated in QCMN.

Take a look at some of the key features of each of the IBM-supplied subsystems,
starting with QCTL. As always, start with the Display Subsystem Description
command (DSPSBSD):

```
DSPSBSD QCTL
```

As usual, you get the menu shown in Figure 11.1.

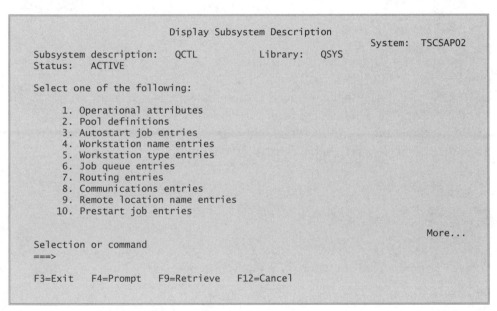

```
                     Display Subsystem Description
                                                    System:   TSCSAP02
    Subsystem description:   QCTL         Library:   QSYS
    Status:    ACTIVE

    Select one of the following:

         1. Operational attributes
         2. Pool definitions
         3. Autostart job entries
         4. Workstation name entries
         5. Workstation type entries
         6. Job queue entries
         7. Routing entries
         8. Communications entries
         9. Remote location name entries
        10. Prestart job entries

                                                            More...
    Selection or command
    ===>

    F3=Exit    F4=Prompt    F9=Retrieve    F12=Cancel
```

*Figure 11.1: The Display Subsystem Description menu provides several options that are used to
show the different parts of the subsystem.*

Take a look at the pools, autostart job entries, job queue entries, workstation entries, communications entries, prestart job entries, and routing entries. Start by
looking at the pool definitions for QCTL, as shown in Figure 11.2, by choosing
option 2 from the menu.

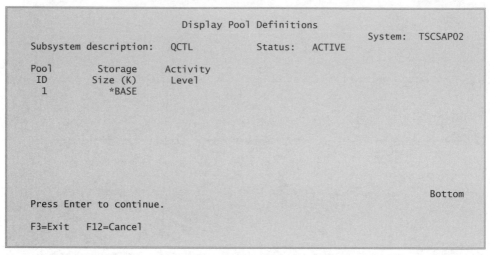

```
                           Display Pool Definitions
                                                       System:   TSCSAP02
        Subsystem description:   QCTL            Status:   ACTIVE

        Pool        Storage     Activity
         ID        Size (K)     Level
          1          *BASE



                                                              Bottom
        Press Enter to continue.

        F3=Exit   F12=Cancel
```

Figure 11.2: The only pool that is defined for QCTL is *BASE; all work initiated by QCTL will run in *BASE.

Note that the only pool defined for QCTL is *BASE. If you compare the pool definitions to those of QBASE, you'll notice that QCTL does not include the *INTERACT pool. This means that either QCTL will initiate interactive work in QBASE, or another subsystem will initiate interactive work. Fortunately, it is the latter. As mentioned, the subsystem QINTER will be started automatically and will be used to initiate interactive jobs into the *INTERACT pool.

Return to the Display Subsystem Description menu and select option 3 to look at the autostart job entries, shown in Figure 11.3.

The autostart job entries in QCTL are the same as those in QBASE. The same two jobs will be run, but there will be two minor differences:

- The performance collection job QPFRCOL will run in *BASE when started from QCTL, instead of *INTERACT when started from QBASE.

- The QSTRUPJD job will start QBATCH, QINTER, QCMN, QSERVER, QUSRWRK, and QSPL when started from QCTL. When QSTRUPJD is started from QCTL, only QSERVER, QUSRWRK, and QSPL are started.

Return to the Display Subsystem Description menu again and select option 5 to see the work station type entries in QCTL, shown in Figure 11.4.

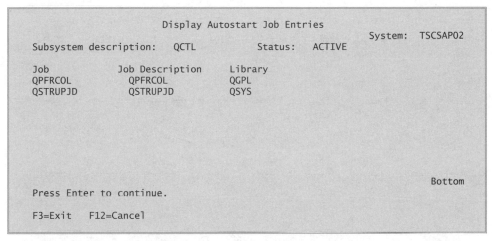

```
                      Display Autostart Job Entries
                                                     System:   TSCSAP02
       Subsystem description:   QCTL          Status:   ACTIVE

       Job              Job Description    Library
       QPFRCOL          QPFRCOL            QGPL
       QSTRUPJD         QSTRUPJD           QSYS




                                                              Bottom
       Press Enter to continue.

       F3=Exit    F12=Cancel
```

Figure 11.3: QCTL has two autostart job entries, which are the same as those in QBASE.

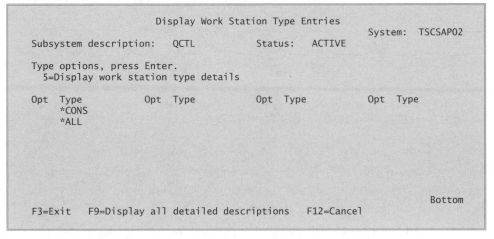

```
                      Display Work Station Type Entries
                                                     System:   TSCSAP02
       Subsystem description:   QCTL          Status:   ACTIVE

       Type options, press Enter.
         5=Display work station type details

       Opt  Type            Opt  Type           Opt  Type          Opt  Type
            *CONS
            *ALL




                                                              Bottom
       F3=Exit    F9=Display all detailed descriptions    F12=Cancel
```

Figure 11.4: The work station type entries in QCTL are the same as in QBASE.

The two entries are the same as those in QBASE, which indicates that QCTL has the potential to initiate interactive work. However, since QINTER is started by the QSTRUPJD autostart job, QINTER is usually started and has taken ownership of all the devices attached to the system other than the console. The console sign-on occurs before QINTER is started. As a result, the console job will be initiated by QCTL and will run in *BASE. When the QINTER subsystem is discussed in detail later in this chapter, you'll learn more about interactive job initiation.

After viewing the workstation type entries, go back to the Display Subsystem Description menu and select option 6 to look at the job queue entries that are shipped with QCTL, shown in Figure 11.5.

```
                        Display Job Queue Entries
                                                       System:   TSCSAP02
        Subsystem description:     QCTL            Status:    ACTIVE

        Seq  Job                      Max    -----Max by Priority-----
        Nbr  Queue        Library    Active   1   2   3   4   5   6   7   8   9
         10  QCTL         QSYS       *NOMAX   *   *   *   *   *   *   *   *   *




                                                                   Bottom
        Press Enter to continue.

        F3=Exit    F12=Cancel
```

Figure 11.5: *The job queue entries show that QCTL will only introduce batch work from the QCTL job queue.*

QCTL has only one job-queue QCTL. You haven't seen this before. In addition, you don't see the QBATCH job queue. Since most of the system defaults place most submitted jobs on the QBATCH job queue, QCTL will introduce very little batch work. In addition, another subsystem had better introduce batch work from the QBATCH job queue, or there will be little batch work done in your system. As you've probably figured out, the QBATCH subsystem that is started by QSTRUPJD will have a job queue entry for QBATCH, and will introduce the jobs that have been submitted to the QBATCH job queue.

Once again, return to the Display Subsystem Description menu. This time, select option 7 to look at the routing entries in QCTL, shown in Figure 11.6. As you can see, there are only three routing entries in QCTL. If you go back to QBASE, you will find that there are three *pages* of routing entries.

```
                       Display Routing Entries
                                                System:   TSCSAP02
    Subsystem description:   QCTL            Status:   ACTIVE

    Type options, press Enter.
      5=Display details

                                                           Start
    Opt    Seq Nbr    Program      Library      Compare Value    Pos
           10         QARDRIVE     QSYS         '525XTEST'        1
           700        QCL          QSYS         'QCMD38'          1
    5      9999       QCMD         QSYS         *ANY




                                                           Bottom
    F3=Exit    F9=Display all detailed descriptions    F12=Cancel
```

Figure 11.6: Since there are only three routing entries in QCTL, and the first two are very specialized, most jobs started in QCTL will use sequence 9999 to obtain runtime attributes and pool assignments.

So, what happens to the jobs that are initiated by QCTL? The first two routing entries are very specialized and are not used by many jobs. Most jobs initiated by QCTL will use the last routing entry, sequence number 9999. To see what that means, take a look at the routing entry detail by placing a five in front of the last routing entry. When you press Enter, you will see the routing entry detail shown in Figure 11.7.

```
                     Display Routing Entry Detail
                                                System:   TSCSAP02

    Subsystem description:   QCTL            Status:   ACTIVE

    Routing entry sequence number . . . . . . . :   9999
    Program . . . . . . . . . . . . . . . . . . :   QCMD
      Library . . . . . . . . . . . . . . . . . :     QSYS
    Class . . . . . . . . . . . . . . . . . . . :   QCTL
      Library . . . . . . . . . . . . . . . . . :     QSYS
    Maximum active routing steps  . . . . . . . :   *NOMAX
    Pool identifier . . . . . . . . . . . . . . :   1
    Compare value . . . . . . . . . . . . . . . :   *ANY

    Compare start position  . . . . . . . . . . :

    Press Enter to continue.

    F3=Exit    F12=Cancel    F14=Display previous entry
```

*Figure 11.7: The routing entry detail for most jobs started by QCTL shows that the class used for the runtime attributes is QCTL, and the jobs will be run in the first pool of QCTL—*BASE.*

293

The routing entry is used to identify the pool where jobs will run and to provide the name of the class used to assign runtime attributes to the jobs. QCTL only has one pool, *BASE, so the pool identifier must be one. The runtime attributes are obtained from the QCTL class. Because you haven't seen this class yet, take a look at it by running the Display Class command (DSPCLS):

```
DSPCLS QCTL
```

When you run the command, you see the class information shown in Figure 11.8. This class has many of the same attributes as the interactive class mentioned in chapter 2. Actually, the only attribute that is different is the RUNPTY, which is 10. Your other interactive class had a RUNPTY of 20. This is another reason that it is important to start the other subsystems in the QSTRUPJD autostart job. Otherwise, all of the jobs in your system would be running in *BASE with a priority of 10. Your performance would not be very good. Because all of the other subsystems are started before QCTL introduces any work other than the console job, you can avoid this problem.

Also, because the console job will be initiated by QCTL, it will have a RUNPTY of 10.This allows you to have one job that has a higher cost than all of the other jobs in most environments. Thus, if your system has a performance problem, like a looping interactive job, you can use the console to gain access to the processor and end the job.

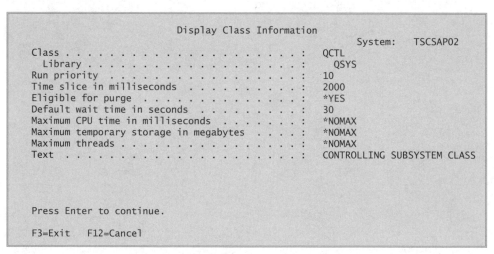

```
                      Display Class Information
                                              System:    TSCSAP02
  Class . . . . . . . . . . . . . . . . . . . :   QCTL
    Library . . . . . . . . . . . . . . . . :     QSYS
  Run priority . . . . . . . . . . . . . . . :   10
  Time slice in milliseconds  . . . . . . . . :   2000
  Eligible for purge  . . . . . . . . . . . . :   *YES
  Default wait time in seconds  . . . . . . . :   30
  Maximum CPU time in milliseconds  . . . . . . :   *NOMAX
  Maximum temporary storage in megabytes  . . . . :   *NOMAX
  Maximum threads . . . . . . . . . . . . . . :   *NOMAX
  Text  . . . . . . . . . . . . . . . . . . . :   CONTROLLING SUBSYSTEM CLASS




  Press Enter to continue.

  F3=Exit    F12=Cancel
```

Figure 11.8: The QCTL class assigns runtime attributes to jobs initiated by the QCTL subsystem.

It's time to go back to the Display Subsystem Description menu and select option 8 to look at the communication entries in QCTL, shown in Figure 11.9.

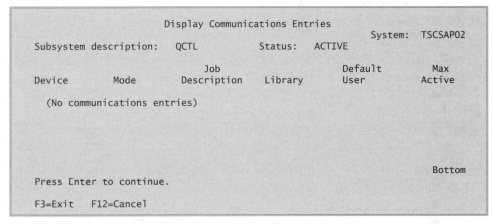

```
                      Display Communications Entries
                                                    System:   TSCSAP02
     Subsystem description:   QCTL          Status:   ACTIVE

                            Job                     Default      Max
     Device      Mode       Description  Library    User         Active

        (No communications entries)




                                                              Bottom
     Press Enter to continue.

     F3=Exit    F12=Cancel
```

Figure 11.9: The QCTL subsystem is shipped with no communications entries.

Here is another difference that is really easy to spot: QCTL has no communications entries, while QBASE has several. So, how do you get communications related work to run? Once again, look at the subsystems started by QSTRUPJD. One of these subsystems is QCMN. All of the communications entries that are in QBASE are also in QCMN. You'll validate their existence later.

Return to the Display Subsystem Description menu one last time and select option 10 to look at the prestart job entries in QCTL, shown in Figure 11.10.

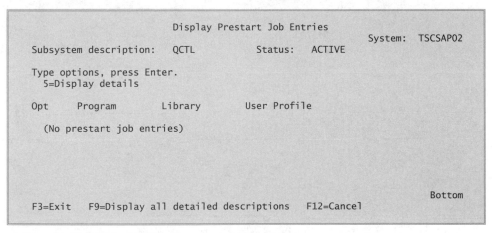

```
                      Display Prestart Job Entries
                                                    System:   TSCSAP02
     Subsystem description:   QCTL          Status:   ACTIVE

     Type options, press Enter.
       5=Display details

     Opt     Program      Library      User Profile

        (No prestart job entries)




                                                              Bottom
     F3=Exit    F9=Display all detailed descriptions    F12=Cancel
```

Figure 11.10: QCTL is shipped with no prestart job entries.

As you can see, there are no prestart job entries in QCTL. So, how do you get a fast connection for communications requests? I'm sure you've figured out the answer: the prestart job entries will appear in one of the subsystems started by QSTRUPJD. Actually, they are also included in QCMN.

As you can see, QCTL is intended to be purely a controlling subsystem, and run only the console job. Just to be sure that everything will still work the same as it does when QBASE is the controlling subsystem, look at QBATCH, QINTER, and QCTL to prove that the runtime environment composed of QCTL, QBATCH, QINTER, and QCMN is identical to the runtime environment of QBASE.

Start by looking at the key elements in QBATCH from the Display Subsystem Description menu:

```
DSPSBSD QBATCH
```

From the display in Figure 11.11, look at the pools defined for QBATCH by selecting option 2. These pools are shown in Figure 11.12.

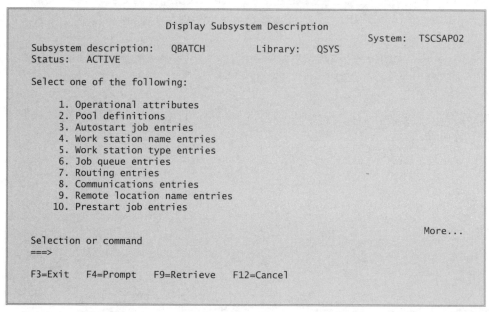

```
                       Display Subsystem Description
                                                     System:   TSCSAP02
     Subsystem description:    QBATCH        Library:   QSYS
     Status:    ACTIVE

     Select one of the following:

          1. Operational attributes
          2. Pool definitions
          3. Autostart job entries
          4. Work station name entries
          5. Work station type entries
          6. Job queue entries
          7. Routing entries
          8. Communications entries
          9. Remote location name entries
         10. Prestart job entries

                                                               More...
     Selection or command
     ===>

     F3=Exit   F4=Prompt   F9=Retrieve   F12=Cancel
```

Figure 11.11: This Display Subsystem Description menu provides options for viewing the different parts of the QBATCH subsystem.

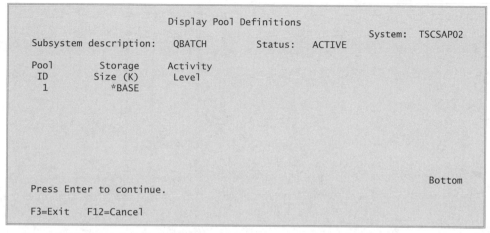

```
                          Display Pool Definitions
                                                        System:   TSCSAP02
           Subsystem description:    QBATCH          Status:   ACTIVE

           Pool          Storage      Activity
            ID           Size (K)     Level
             1             *BASE




                                                                     Bottom
           Press Enter to continue.

           F3=Exit    F12=Cancel
```

*Figure 11.12: Jobs initiated by the IBM-supplied subsystem QBATCH will run in *BASE.*

In the default QBASE subsystem, all batch work was initialized to run in *BASE. The QBATCH subsystem started when QCTL is the controlling subsystem is also set up to run batch work in *BASE. The combination of QCTL and QBATCH provide the same pool assignments for batch jobs.

Go back to the Display Subsystem Description menu and select option 6 to look at the job queue entries shipped with QBATCH. These entries are shown in Figure 11.13. As you can see, the job queue entries include QBATCH, so you have a subsystem that will start jobs from the QBATCH job queue that will run in *BASE.

```
                          Display Job Queue Entries
                                                        System:   TSCSAP02
           Subsystem description:    QBATCH          Status:   ACTIVE

           Seq   Job                    Max    -----Max by Priority-----
           Nbr   Queue     Library    Active   1   2   3   4   5   6   7   8   9
            10   QBATCH    QGPL       *NOMAX   *   *   *   *   *   *   *   *   *
            20   QS36EVOKE QGPL       *NOMAX   *   *   *   *   *   *   *   *   *
            50   QTXTSRCH  QGPL       *NOMAX   *   *   *   *   *   *   *   *   *




                                                                     Bottom
           Press Enter to continue.

           F3=Exit    F12=Cancel
```

Figure 11.13: These job queue entries are shipped with the QBATCH subsystem.

All that's left is to check the routing entries to see that you are ready for the jobs, so it's back to the Display Subsystem Description menu. Select option 7 to display the QBATCH routing entries shown in Figure 11.14.

```
                          Display Routing Entries
                                                      System:   TSCSAP02
      Subsystem description:    QBATCH         Status:    ACTIVE

      Type options, press Enter.
        5=Display details

                                                                   Start
      Opt    Seq Nbr    Program      Library    Compare Value       Pos
             300        QCMD         QSYS       'QS36EVOKE'           1
             700        QCL          QSYS       'QCMD38'              1
             9999       QCMD         QSYS       *ANY


                                                                  Bottom
      F3=Exit    F9=Display all detailed descriptions    F12=Cancel
```

Figure 11.14: Three routing entries in QBATCH are used to start batch jobs, but most jobs started by QBATCH will use the last entry, 9999.

Wait a minute! Something seems to be missing from the routing entries in QBATCH. If you go back to the examples of QBASE in chapter 2, you see a routing entry in QBASE with a compare value QCMDB. There is no routing with the QCMDB compare value in QBATCH, so how does the batch get routed? Because QCMDB fails to match any of the routing entries in QBATCH, the last routing entry that accepts any compare value will be used. If you look at the details of this routing entry, you will find that the jobs will run in *BASE and will receive their runtime attributes from the QBATCH class. As a result, the default values for QBATCH produce the same batch runtime environment as the QBASE defaults.

Chapter 6 describes changing the batch aspects of QBASE. For one thing, *SHRPOOL1 is used to run batch jobs. When you make this change, you have to add a pool definition to QBASE and modify routing entries to use the new pool.

To modify QBATCH to run jobs in *SHRPOOL1, you need to run the following command:

```
CHGSBSD QBATCH POOLS((1 *SHRPOOL1)
```

Your routing entries are all set up to use only one pool, so you don't need to change anything else. However, if you decide to use multiple job queues and pools to run different types of batch jobs (as with QBASE in chapter 6), you will need to make the same modifications to QBATCH that you made to QBASE.

Now that you have seen that batch jobs will run the same as they did when QBASE was the controlling subsystem, see if QINTER provides the same kind of environment for interactive jobs as QBASE. Once again, start with the Display Subsystem Description display to get the screen shown in Figure 11.15:

```
DSPSBSD QINTER
```

```
                        Display Subsystem Description

                                                     System:   TSCSAP02
      Subsystem description:   QINTER       Library:   QSYS
      Status:   ACTIVE

      Select one of the following:

           1. Operational attributes
           2. Pool definitions
           3. Autostart job entries
           4. Work station name entries
           5. Work station type entries
           6. Job queue entries
           7. Routing entries
           8. Communications entries
           9. Remote location name entries
          10. Prestart job entries

                                                             More...
      Selection or command
      ===>

      F3=Exit    F4=Prompt    F9=Retrieve    F12=Cancel
```

Figure 11.15: This Display Subsystem Description menu provides options for viewing the different parts of the QINTER subsystem.

Once again, start by selecting option 2 to see the pool definitions for QINTER, shown in Figure 11.16. It's reassuring to see that the *INTERACT pool is one of the two pools that is defined for QINTER. The QINTER subsystem will indeed start interactive jobs in *INTERACT, but go through the other parts of the subsystem description just to be sure.

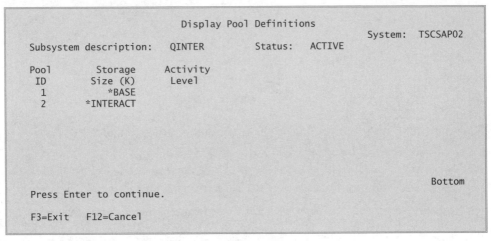

Figure 11.16: QINTER is shipped with two pool definitions.

QBASE found interactive work by using workstation type entries. Go back to the Display Subsystem Description menu and select option 5 to look at QINTER's workstation type entries, shown in Figure 11.17. They are the same as those for QBASE and QCTL.

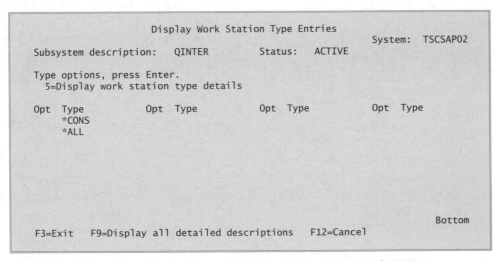

Figure 11.17: QINTER contains the same workstation type entries as QCTL and QBASE.

You now know that QINTER has the same capability to introduce interactive work as QBASE. Since QBASE is not active in this environment, that poses no problem. But QCTL *is* active. Is that a problem? How do you get the console in QCTL running in *BASE with a RUNPTY of 10, and everything else in QINTER running in *INTERACT with a RUNPTY of 20?

The discussion in chapter 3 regarding workstation ownership uses the analogy of prospectors and claims. A prospector (subsystem) can stake a claim (send a sign-on screen to a workstation) and begin to mine it (be signed on). However, if the prospector does not work the claim, another prospector (subsystem) can take over ownership of the claim (send a sign-on screen). It's all a matter of timing. In the case of QCTL and QINTER, the timing goes like this:

1. QCTL is started and sends a sign-on screen to all workstations that are varied on and powered on, including the console device.

2. A user signs on to the console device, and the job is initiated by QCTL.

3. Subsystem QINTER is started and sends a sign-on to all workstations that are varied on and powered on, but are not in use—the console does not get a sign-on.

4. Users sign on to other workstations, and the jobs are initiated by QINTER.

While it is possible for a user to sign on before QINTER "claim jumps" QCTL, it is highly unlikely.

Now that you're satisfied that workstation ownership isn't an issue, press on and look at the QINTER routing entries. Return to the Display Subsystem Description menu and choose option 7 to display the routing entries shown in Figure 11.18.

```
                      Display Routing Entries
                                              System:   TSCSAP02
   Subsystem description:   QINTER          Status:    ACTIVE

   Type options, press Enter.
     5=Display details

                                                              Start
   Opt    Seq Nbr    Program     Library    Compare Value      Pos
          10         QCMD        QSYS       'QCMDI'              1
          20         QCMD        QSYS       'QS36MRT'            1
          40         QARDRIVE    QSYS       '525XTEST'           1
          700        QCL         QSYS       'QCMD38'             1
          9999       QCMD        QSYS       *ANY

                                                             Bottom
   F3=Exit    F9=Display all detailed descriptions    F12=Cancel
```

Figure 11.18: QINTER is shipped with five routing entries that are used to initiate interactive jobs.

Notice that the routing entry at sequence number 10 contains the compare value of QCMDI, just like QBASE. In the routing entry detail shown in Figure 11.19, you can see that the pool identifier indicates that jobs using QCMDI as a compare value will be run in the *INTERACT pool.

The defaults for QINTER, therefore, match the interactive defaults for QBASE. Chapter 7 includes some extensive changes to QBASE to handle your interactive needs by separating programmers, production users, and critical users. To make those changes, you added pools and routing entries to the QBASE subsystem. Repeat those modifications in QINTER to produce the same environment.

Look at the defaults for QCMN. One last time, start with the Display Subsystem Description command to produce the screen in Figure 11.20:

```
DSPSBSD QCMN
```

As you have for all of the other subsystems, select option 2 to look at the pool definitions for QCMN, shown in Figure 11.21. Once again, the pool definitions look pretty much like you'd expect: one pool, *BASE, handles all of the jobs initiated by QCMN. This is the same as QBASE, which started all of the communication jobs in *BASE.

```
                    Display Routing Entry Detail
                                                  System:   TSCSAP02
    Subsystem description:   QINTER        Status:   ACTIVE

    Routing entry sequence number . . . . . . . :   10
    Program . . . . . . . . . . . . . . . . . :   QCMD
      Library . . . . . . . . . . . . . . . . :     QSYS
    Class . . . . . . . . . . . . . . . . . . :   QINTER
      Library . . . . . . . . . . . . . . . . :     QGPL
    Maximum active routing steps  . . . . . . :   *NOMAX
    Pool identifier . . . . . . . . . . . . . :   2
    Compare value . . . . . . . . . . . . . . :   'QCMDI'

    Compare start position  . . . . . . . . . :   1




    Press Enter to continue.

    F3=Exit    F12=Cancel    F14=Display previous entry
```

Figure 11.19: The QINTER routing entry with a compare value of QCMDI is the same as the routing entry with a compare value of QCMDI in QBASE.

```
                    Display Subsystem Description
                                                  System:   TSCSAP02
    Subsystem description:   QCMN        Library:   QSYS
    Status:   ACTIVE

    Select one of the following:

         1. Operational attributes
         2. Pool definitions
         3. Autostart job entries
         4. Work station name entries
         5. Work station type entries
         6. Job queue entries
         7. Routing entries
         8. Communications entries
         9. Remote location name entries
        10. Prestart job entries

                                                          More...
    Selection or command
    ===>

    F3=Exit    F4=Prompt    F9=Retrieve    F12=Cancel
```

Figure 11.20: This Display Subsystem Description menu provides options for viewing the different parts of the QCMN subsystem.

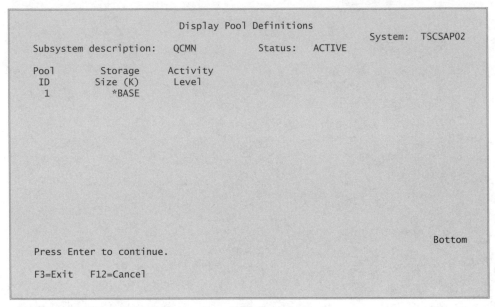

```
                      Display Pool Definitions
                                                  System:   TSCSAP02
      Subsystem description:   QCMN           Status:   ACTIVE

      Pool          Storage     Activity
       ID           Size (K)    Level
        1            *BASE




                                                               Bottom
      Press Enter to continue.

      F3=Exit    F12=Cancel
```

Figure 11.21: QCMN is shipped with one pool definition.

Go back to the Display Subsystem Description menu and select option 8 to look at the QCMN communication entries, shown in Figure 11.22. Once again, the communication entries in QCMN are the same as the communications entries in QBASE. You shouldn't have any trouble handling the same communication requests that you handled in QBASE.

Use option 7 on the Display Subsystems Description menu to look at the routing entries in QCMN, shown in Figures 11.23a and 11.23b. The QCMN communication routing entries are the same as in QBASE.

```
                     Display Communications Entries
                                                      System:  TSCSAP02
     Subsystem description:   QCMN         Status:   ACTIVE

                               Job                    Default        Max
     Device        Mode        Description   Library  User           Active
     *ALL          *ANY        *USRPRF                *SYS           *NOMAX
     *ALL          QBRM        *USRPRF                QBRMS          *NOMAX
     *ALL          QCASERVR    *USRPRF                *NONE          *NOMAX
     *ALL          QIJS        *USRPRF                QIJS           *NOMAX
     *ALL          QPCSUPP     *USRPRF                *SYS           *NOMAX
     *APPC         QSOCCT      *USRPRF                QUSER          *NOMAX




                                                                Bottom
     Press Enter to continue.

     F3=Exit    F12=Cancel
```

Figure 11.22: QCMN is shipped with the same communications entries as QBASE.

```
                        Display Routing Entries
                                                      System:  TSCSAP02
     Subsystem description:   QCMN         Status:   ACTIVE

     Type options, press Enter.
       5=Display details

                                                                     Start
     Opt   Seq Nbr   Program      Library    Compare Value           Pos
            10       *RTGDTA                  'QZSCSRVR'              37
            20       *RTGDTA                  'QZRCSRVR'              37
            30       *RTGDTA                  'QZHQTRG'               37
            50       *RTGDTA                  'QVPPRINT'              37
            60       *RTGDTA                  'QNPSERVR'              37
            70       *RTGDTA                  'QNMAPINGD'             37
            80       QNMAREXECD   QSYS        'AREXECD'               37
           100       *RTGDTA                  'QTFDWNLD'              37
           150       *RTGDTA                  'QMFRCVR'               37
           200       *RTGDTA                  'QMFSNDR'               37
           210       *RTGDTA                  'QHQTRGT'               37
           220       *RTGDTA                  'QRQSRV'                37
                                                                   More...
     F3=Exit    F9=Display all detailed descriptions    F12=Cancel
```

Figure 11.23a: The routing entries shipped with QCMN are the same as those shipped with QBASE.

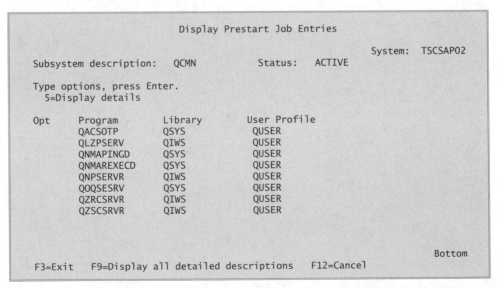

```
                        Display Routing Entries
                                                   System:   TSCSAP02
     Subsystem description:     QCMN           Status:    ACTIVE

     Type options, press Enter.
       5=Display details

                                                                   Start
     Opt    Seq Nbr    Program    Library     Compare Value        Pos
            240        *RTGDTA                 'QLZPSERV'           37
            250        *RTGDTA                 'QCNPCSUP'           37
            260        *RTGDTA                 'QOCEVOKE'           37
            290        *RTGDTA                 'QPCSUPP'            1
            295        *RTGDTA                 'QCASERVR'           1
            299        *RTGDTA                 '#INTER'             1
            300        *RTGDTA                 'PGMEVOKE'           29




                                                                   Bottom
     F3=Exit   F9=Display all detailed descriptions   F12=Cancel
```

Figure 11.23b: The routing entries shipped with QCMN are the same as those shipped with QBASE.

You are almost done validating that the communications aspects of QCMN are the same as QBATCH. All that remains is to determine if the prestart jobs that enable a faster job initiation are present in QCMN. So, select option 10 to look at the prestart job entries of QCMN, shown in Figure 11.24.

```
                        Display Prestart Job Entries
                                                   System:   TSCSAP02
     Subsystem description:     QCMN           Status:    ACTIVE

     Type options, press Enter.
       5=Display details

     Opt    Program      Library      User Profile
            QACSOTP      QSYS         QUSER
            QLZPSERV     QIWS         QUSER
            QNMAPINGD    QSYS         QUSER
            QNMAREXECD   QSYS         QUSER
            QNPSERVR     QIWS         QUSER
            QOQSESRV     QSYS         QUSER
            QZRCSRVR     QIWS         QUSER
            QZSCSRVR     QIWS         QUSER



                                                                   Bottom
     F3=Exit   F9=Display all detailed descriptions   F12=Cancel
```

Figure 11.24: The prestart job entries shipped in QCMN are the same as those shipped in QBASE.

And, as the final step in the comparison process, you see that QCMN contains the same prestart job entries as QBASE, so QCMN will provide the same support for communications jobs as in QBASE.

There you have it! After all of these displays, you have shown that the runtime environment established with QBASE is the same as the runtime environment established by QCTL, QBATCH, QINTER, and QCMN. So, why bother to change? There are several reasons for changing your controlling subsystem from QBASE to QCTL:

- The QCTL environment is more flexible. You can make changes to a subsystem, end it, and start it independent of the other subsystems. Only jobs initiated by the subsystem you working with are affected. All of the other jobs continue to process normally.

- The QCTL environment is a lot less cluttered. As you have seen by looking at the defaults, each subsystem is focused on one type of work, so there are fewer sources of work, fewer routing entries, etc. In addition, when you begin to customize the runtime environment, the customization is limited to a single subsystem, and the result is less complicated to understand.

- Once in a great while, a subsystem will get confused and will need to be stopped and started to clear it. Since all of the work is not running in a single subsystem, the problem can be isolated to the work running in the subsystem that has become confused.

I cannot emphasize enough that if you made any changes to QBASE before you switched to QCTL, you will need to make the same changes to QBATCH, QINTER, and/or QCMN. The following pages look at what you need to do to modify QINTER to match the environment in QBASE at the end of chapter 7.

Figure 11.25 shows the way QBASE looked when you had made all of your interactive changes. As a quick review, two additional pools for interactive jobs were added—pool ID 6 using *SHRPOOL4 and pool ID 7 using *SHRPOOL5. Two routing entries were added to direct work to the new pools. From each user's profile information, you got the correct job description that provided routing data. This routing data was matched against the compare value in the routing entry to get the job to the correct pool.

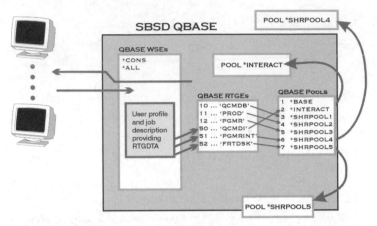

Figure 11.25: *QBASE has been modified to run three different types of users in three different pools.*

Take a few minutes to review this. When you feel comfortable that you remember how and why you did these things, go on to the same example using QINTER, shown in Figures 11.26 and 11.27. Start by looking at the default QINTER environment (Figure 11.26), which shows only the routing entry that used QCMDI as a compare value. (The other routing entries are not relevant to the example.)

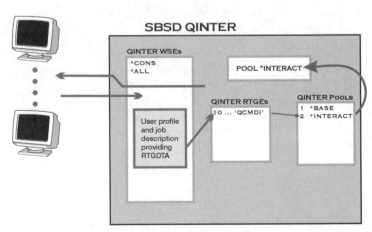

Figure 11.26: *The default environment of QINTER will run all interactive jobs in *INTERACT.*

This maps to the default interactive environment of QBASE before any modifications, but you *did* modify QBASE, and you want the same environment with QINTER. Start the QINTER modification by adding two pools and two routing entries to QINTER:

```
CHGSBSD QINTER POOLS((1 *BASE)(2 *INTERACT)(3 *SHRPOOL4)(4 *SHRPOOL5))
ADDRTGE QINTER SEQNBR(11) CMPVAL('PGMR' 1) POOLID(3)
ADDRTGE QINTER SEQNBR(12) CMPVAL('FRTDSK' 1) POOLID(4)
```

When your user profiles provide the correct job description, which gives you the appropriate routing data, the QINTER subsystem initiates work as shown in Figure 11.27.

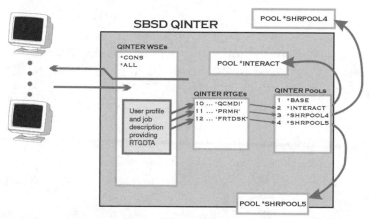

Figure 11.27: QINTER has been modified to run three different types of interactive users in three different pools.

And there you have the same setup you had with QBASE. If it seems easier now, it must be because you're learning work management!

Multiple Interactive Subsystems

Since I've been advocating the use of a single subsystem to introduce interactive work, you might be wondering why I would suddenly suggest multiple interactive subsystems. Ahem…, well, you see, ahem…. Actually, I have been advocating a single subsystem because of its simplicity. However, you are now so well versed in work management that you can see how easy it is to provide the same type of separation of interactive work with multiple subsystems.

The idea for the previous example is to separate interactive users into different pools. Chapter 7 discusses the multiple subsystem approach from the perspective of assigning workstations of different users to different subsystems. After concluding that assigning workstations to a subsystem isn't practical, it was decided to go with the single subsystem approach. Now you're going to see how easy it is to accomplish the same result with multiple subsystems.

In many instances, QINTER is all you will need. However, if you have several hundred workstations in your environment, starting your subsystem might take a long time. Remember that when a subsystem claims ownership of a workstation that is varied on and powered on, it will send a sign-on screen to each workstation. The sign-on screen is not broadcast to each of the workstations; it is sent to each workstation one at a time, serially and synchronously. While it is sending sign-on screens, the subsystem will accept no input—including any attempts to sign on. In addition, if QINTER gets confused, all of your interactive users need to stop working so that you can reset it. Neither of these situations is desirable, so a good rule of thumb is to have no more than 200 workstations in each interactive subsystem.

You've reached the point where you can see how easily this can be done. Actually, when you set up the user profiles and job descriptions, you did most of the hard work; the rest is mechanical. Use the now-famous naming scheme for your workstations—each workstation name will begin with the characters *WS* and be followed by a four-character number from 0001 through 9999—and you're ready to start the exercise of creating multiple interactive subsystems.

First, create the additional interactive subsystems with the same four pools that you used for QINTER. (That's the beauty of a shared pool—any number of systems can initiate work into the pool, making this whole procedure possible.) Then, add the same three routing entries you saw in QINTER. If you have 500 workstations in your environment, you will need two additional subsystems, QINTER2 and QINTER3. Here are the commands so far:

```
CRTSBSD QINTER2 POOLS((1*BASE)(2 *INTERACT)(3 *SHRPOOL4)(4 *SHRPOOL5))
CRTSBSD QINTER3 POOLS((1*BASE)(2 *INTERACT)(3 *SHRPOOL4)(4 *SHRPOOL5))
ADDRTGE QINTER2 SEQNBR(10) CMPVAL('QCMDI' 1) POOLID(2)
ADDRTGE QINTER2 SEQNBR(11) CMPVAL('PGMR' 1) POOLID(3)
ADDRTGE QINTER2 SEQNBR(12) CMPVAL('FRTDSK' 1) POOLID(4)
ADDRTGE QINTER3 SEQNBR(10) CMPVAL('QCMDI' 1) POOLID(2)
ADDRTGE QINTER3 SEQNBR(11) CMPVAL('PGMR' 1) POOLID(3)
ADDRTGE QINTER3 SEQNBR(12) CMPVAL('FRTDSK' 1) POOLID(4)
```

All you have left to do is to set up your workstation entries. Start by removing the workstation type entries from QINTER, then run the following commands to add workstation name entries to the three subsystems:

```
ADDWSE QINTER WRKSTN(WS00*)
ADDWSE QINTER WRKSTN(WS01*)
ADDWSE QINTER2 WRKSTN(WS02*)
ADDWSE QINTER2 WRKSTN(WS03*)
ADDWSE QINTER3 WRKSTN(WS04*)
```

After you have run these commands, QINTER will be assigned workstations WS0001 through WS0199. QINTER2 will be assigned workstations WS0200 through WS0399, and QINTER3 will be assigned WS0400 through WS0499. As you add additional workstations, assign them to QINTER3 using the generic name "QWS05*." PC devices and pass-through devices enter the system via the QCMN subsystem and are transferred to QINTER by default.

That's it! Figure 11.28 shows how it works.

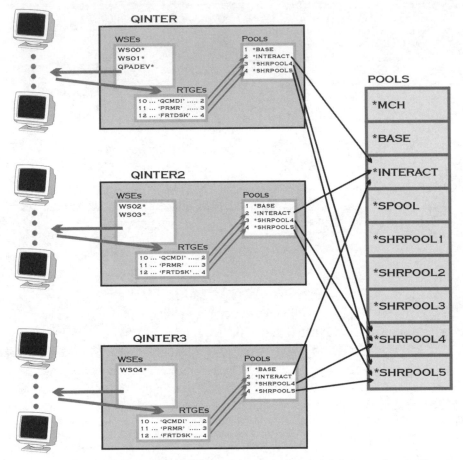

Figure 11.28: Three subsystems that initiate work from selected workstations can be used to run three different types of users in three different pools.

"Holy Moley, Rocky! There's a lot of lines on that picture!" There are, indeed, but notice the following:

- Each subsystem sends a sign-on screen to each of the displays allocated to it.

- When the user signs on, initiation of the workstation job is done by the subsystem that owns the workstation.

- The user profiles are used to get the routing data. The user profile information is invariant. That is, it doesn't matter which workstation the user signs on to; the user profile is used to retrieve the routing information.

- All three subsystems have the same three routing entries.

- All of the routing entries point to the same pool definition.

- All of the pool definitions use the same system pools.

You are applying the same principle used when you only had one subsystem: the user profile is the driving force for routing jobs. It does not matter that more than one subsystem is involved! You have the flexibility and performance you need from multiple subsystems, along with the consistent job routing you thought possible only with a single subsystem—and it was a pretty simple operation, right?

Other IBM-Supplied Subsystems

You've now learned how to work with all of the IBM subsystems that you will normally see in use. However, there are some other IBM-supplied subsystems that are shipped with the OS/400. This section tells you the function that each of these subsystems provides. Because it is unlikely that you will ever modify these subsystems, their attributes (pools, job queues, etc) aren't covered here.

QDSNX

The QDSNX subsystem supports the Distributed System Node Executive (DSNX), providing communications access to S/390 (now called zSeries) machines. This subsystem provides an autostart job that enables the DSNX support.

QFNC

The QFNC subsystem is used for finance devices and their associated jobs. The primary purpose of this subsystem is to provide compatibility with earlier versions of finance support. The QFNC subsystem was developed to make finance devices easily accessible to an S/38 (the predecessor to the AS/400, which is the predecessor to the iSeries). Any user wishing to implement finance on an S/38 would find the task far less daunting when most of what they needed was in the QFNC subsystem. Today, this work management support is available in QBASE and QCMN.

QLPINSTALL

When you receive OS/400, you will receive several IBM Licensed Products (LPs). If you have ordered an LP and have a licensed key for it, you can install the LP and use it. If you have not ordered an LP or do not have a key, many LPs can be installed and used for a trial period. The QLPINSTALL subsystem is used to run jobs that install the LPs. This subsystem is not used in a production environment.

QPGMR

By default, all interactive users are initiated by the same subsystem with the same runtime attributes. When you customized interactive subsystems, one type of interactive user to separate is the development programmer. In one of the examples in chapter 7, for example, you created a subsystem that identified programmer workstations via workstation name entries.

Instead of creating your own subsystem, you could have used QPGMR. Any user signing on to a workstation owned by QPGMR is assumed to be a programmer and is initiated with a run priority of 30. However, since workstations are assigned to QPGMR via workstation name entries, the use of QPGMR is not very common.

QSERVER

It is often necessary to transfer files from one system to another using a function known as *file transfer protocol* (*FTP*). This subsystem provides the server jobs that are used to process file transfers. The QSERVER subsystem will automatically start when the system is IPLed.

QSNADS

Systems Network Architecture Distribution Services (SNADS) provides support to distribute documents that conformed to Document Interchange Architecture (DIA) between systems. In other words, SNADS supported products like OV/400 and its predecessors. While support and enhancement of these products no longer exists, these products still exist and use SNADS to distribute information. Therefore this subsystem is still shipped with OS/400. You will have little, if any, occasion to ever modify a QSNADS subsystem.

QSYSSBSD

While you will not use QSYSSBSD or make changes to it, its existence can be important. In the unlikely event that your controlling subsystem cannot be started when the system is IPLed, OS/400 will attempt to start QSYSSBSD as the controlling subsystem. QSYSSBSD will only run a job from the console device, but at least it will allow you to sign on to the system and investigate what happened to your controlling subsystem. In addition, you will be able to change the QCTLSBSD system value to use QCTL or QBASE—the opposite of the controlling subsystem that failed to start.

QSYSWRK

QSYSWRK is another subsystem that is important to a smooth-running iSeries system. As more and more system functions require more and more support from the controlling subsystem, the controlling subsystem could become over-whelmed. The system functions use the controlling subsystem because they can rely on its existence and depend on it being active (started).

Rather than have each function create more subsystems, QSYSWRK was created to off-load work from the controlling subsystem, while still providing the exis-tence and availability characteristics required by OS/400. QSYSWRK is started when the system is IPLed and usually remains active until the system is powered down. You will rarely make changes to QSYSWRK.

QUSRWRK

QUSRWRK provides support similar to QSYSWRK, and is used to reduce the work being done by QSYSWRK. Instead of starting a single server job that can be re-used, some server functions are designed to start and end a job for each user be-ing served. When there are a lot of users, there are a lot of jobs, and QSYSWRK could be overwhelmed. In addition, it becomes difficult to determine which jobs support a single user and which jobs support multiple users. As a result, QUSRWRK was created to run all of the server jobs that support only one user. QUSRWRK is started automatically when the system is IPLed.

Licensed Product Subsystems

In addition to the subsystems that are shipped with OS/400, several IBM-licensed products are shipped with a subsystem definition that is customized to support the functions performed by the LP. The documentation for each product contains the description and uses of the subsystems provided with the LP.

Restricted State

When you are running OS/400, one or more subsystems are active that allow you to introduce work to the system. While the jobs that have been introduced are running, certain system functions, like Reclaim Storage (RCLSTG) and SAVSYS, are not allowed. In order to run these functions, all of the subsystems must be ended.

Wait a minute! Doesn't that sound like Power Down System? After all, how else do you end the controlling subsystem? While it sounds like it is impossible to end all of the subsystems and still run a command, that is the environment that exists when all of the subsystems are ended. The only job that is still running after all of the subsystems have been ended is the console job. When your system reaches the this point, it is said to be in *restricted state*. Before you learn how to get your machine to restricted state, you should realize that this is not an action to perform in the middle of a production workload. You should schedule a time that will not affect your company's business operation. Once you have the event scheduled, notify all users involved, so that nobody is running critical work when you put the machine in restricted state. Once you have your schedule in place, you can get to restricted state in one of three ways:

1. End each subsystem one by one with the End Subsystem command (ENDSBS). For example, if you were using QCTL as your controlling subsystem and had started the PGMRBAT and PRODBAT subsystems, you would run these commands:

```
ENDSBS PGMRBAT *IMMED
ENDSBS PRODBAT *IMMED
ENDSBS QINTER  *IMMED
ENDSBS QBATCH  *IMMED
ENDSBS QSPL    *IMMED
ENDSBS QCMN    *IMMED
ENDSBS QSERVER *IMMED
ENDSBS QSYSWRK *IMMED
ENDSBS QUSRWRK *IMMED
ENDSBS QCTL    *IMMED
```

The *IMMED parameter specifies that the subsystem is to be ended immediately. It will not wait for any job that is currently running to get "just one more thing" done. When all of the subsystems have ended, only the console job will be running.

2. End all of the subsystems at the same time with the following command:

```
ENDSBS *ALL  *IMMED
```

This command will produce the same results as the ten commands used in the first method.

3. Run the End System command (ENDSYS):

```
ENDSYS   *IMMED
```

Once again, the result is the same as the other two methods.
You can now use the console to run the functions that require the restricted state.

Scheduling Jobs

OS/400 is shipped with a function that allows you to schedule the days and times when you would like certain jobs to run. This section provides an example of using this job scheduler function to assist with one of the daily management tasks you are asked to do.

> **Note:** It is not my intent to discuss job scheduling in any great detail here, nor is it my intention to discuss either the IBM Job Scheduler LP or any vendor's job scheduler. I only want to show you some of the capabilities of the OS/400 job scheduler.

Many jobs are run on a regular basis, such as once a week, every week of the year. Rather than have someone run these jobs each week, you can use the OS/400 job scheduler to run them for you. That way, you won't forget to run them, and they will be run at the same time on the same day of the week, all year long. For this example, you might run a job that processes your payroll every Thursday night at 8:00.

Job Scheduling Basics

There are two basics uses for the job scheduler:

- Schedule a job that is to run only once.
- Schedule a job that is to run at a regular frequency and time.

To schedule a job that is to be run only once, you can use the Submit Job command (SBMJOB). If the job is to be run more than once, such as the payroll example, you should use the Add Job Schedule Entry command (ADDJOBSCDE).

Before looking into the ADDJOBSCDE command, look at the mechanics of the job scheduler and job schedule entries. By default, job schedule entries are held in an object named QDFTJOBSCD in library QUSRSYS. Each job schedule entry starts a timer that counts down to the time that the job is to be run. Once the timer counts down to zero, the job scheduler function, a job named QJOBSCD, will process the entry, which will run a Submit Job command (SBMJOB) to submit the scheduled job to a job queue. Figure 11.29 illustrates this process.

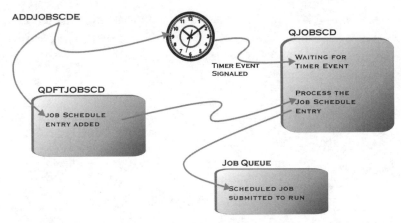

Figure 11.29: The OS/400 job scheduler can be used to submit a job to a job queue at a specified time and day.

Although there can be any number of job schedule entries in QDFTJOBSCD, there will be just one timer event for the earliest job schedule entry. When the timer event is signaled, the job schedule entry is processed, and another timer event is set for the next job schedule entry.

Using the ADDJOBSCDE Command

Before you use the ADDJOBSCE command to schedule the payroll job, take a look at the parameters for the command in Table 11.1.

	Table 11.1: Parameters for ADDJOBSCDE (1 of 5)

Parameter	Meaning/Values
Job Name	This parameter specifies the name that the job will have when it is run. The job name is also used to identify the job schedule entry. The name does not need to be unique. When an entry is placed in QDFTJOBSCD, it is assigned an entry number by the system. If another entry with the same job name already exists, the entry being added will be assigned a number that is one higher. This is a required parameter. Its possible values are as follows: • *Job name*—The name specified in the parameter will be the name of the job. • *JOBD—The job name will have the same name as the job description used to run the job.
Command to Run	When the job is started, the command specified in this parameter will be run. This is a required parameter, which may be any valid OS/400 command.
Frequency	This required parameter lets you specify how often you would like to run the job. It is used with the Scheduled Date parameter to schedule the day and time when the job is scheduled to run. The possible values are as follows: • *ONCE—The job will be run only once. The day and time when it is to be run are obtained from the Scheduled Date and Scheduled Time parameters. • *WEEKLY—The job is to be run once each week. If you choose this value, the Schedule Day parameter specifies the day of the week. • *MONTHLY—The job is to be run once each month. If you choose this value, you can specify the day of the month via the Scheduled Date parameter.
Scheduled Date	This parameter will be used with the Scheduled Time parameter to indicate the date on which the job is to be run. Either this parameter or the Schedule Day parameter must be specified, but both parameters cannot be specified. The possible values are as follows: • *CURRENT—The job is run on the day the job schedule entry is added. This is the default value. • *MONTHSTR—The job is run on the first day of the month. If you run the command on the first of the month, and you specify a value in Scheduled Time that is later than the time you are running the command, the job will be run on the same day you run the command. Otherwise, it will not be run until the first day of the next month. • *MONTHEND—The job is run on the last day of the month. If you run this command on the last day of the month, and the value you specify for Scheduled Time is earlier than the time you are running the command, the job will run on the last day of the next month. Otherwise, it will run on the last day of the current month.

Table 11.1: Parameters for ADDJOBSCDE (2 of 5)	
Parameter	**Meaning/Values**
Scheduled Date *continued*	• *NONE—There is no scheduled date. If *NONE is specified, the value for Schedule Day cannot be *NONE. • *Date*—The day of the month that the job is to be run. If you specify *MONTHLY for the frequency parameter, and specify a date that does not appear in a month, the job will not run during that month. For example, if you specify 31 for this parameter, the job will not run in February, April, June, September, or November. Also, if you are running this command on the date that you specify, and the value in Scheduled Time is earlier than the time you are running the command, the job will not run until the next time the scheduling criteria are met. If these conditions exist, and you have specified *ONCE for frequency, the job schedule entry will not be added.
Schedule Day	This parameter is used with the Scheduled Time parameter to specify the day of the week when the job will be run. Either this parameter or the Scheduled Date parameter must be specified, but both cannot be specified. The possible values are as follows: • *NONE—This is the default. If *NONE is specified, the value for Scheduled Date cannot be *NONE. • *ALL—The job is run every day. If the value specified for Scheduled Time is earlier than the time you are running the command, the job will not run until the next day. • *MON, *TUE..., *SUN—The job is run the day(s) of the week specified. This value is not valid if you are using something other than a Gregorian calendar on your system. Up to seven values may be specified. For example, to have a job run on Monday, Wednesday, and Friday, specify the values *MON, *WED, and *FRI. If you are running this command on one of the days that you specify for this parameter, and the schedule time is earlier than the time you are running the command, the job will not run on that day. If this condition exists, and *ONCE is specified for the frequency parameter, the entry will not be added.
Relative Day of the Month	This parameter is valid only if the value for the Frequency parameter is *MONTHLY and the parameter SCDDAY is specified. It is used to select the relative day of the month when the job is to be submitted. For example, you can use this parameter to schedule a job to be submitted on the first Monday of the month. If you are using the PROMPT function for this command, this parameter will be shown only when the frequency is *MONTHLY and a value is specified for the Schedule Day parameter. The possible values for this parameter are as follows: • 1—The job is submitted the first time the day specified in Schedule Day occurs in the month. For example, if the Schedule Day parameter is *WED and 1 is specified for this parameter, the job will be submitted on the first Wednesday of the month.

Table 11.1: Parameters for ADDJOBSCDE (3 of 5)

Parameter	Meaning/Values
Relative Day of the Month *continued*	• 2—The job is submitted the second time the day appears in the month. • 3—The job is submitted the third time the day appears in the month. • 4—The job is submitted the fourth time the day appears in the month. • 5—The job is submitted the fifth time the day appears in the month. If you choose this value, the job will not be submitted every month. • *LAST—The job is submitted the last time the day occurs in a month. This is a much better choice than 5. More than one value may be specified for this parameter. For example, you may specify RELDAYMON(1 3) to have the job run on the first and third occurrences of the day in each month.
Scheduled Time	The value in this parameter specifies the time when the job is to be submitted. It is used with the Frequency and Schedule Date or Schedule Day parameters. Although the time may be specified to the second, the likelihood of actually submitting the job at the specified second cannot be guaranteed. The possible values are as follows: • *CURRENT—The job is to be run at the same time as the ADDJOBSCDE command is run. This is the default value. It is also the least likely value to be used. • *Time*—This is the time of day when the job is to be submitted. You can use one of two formats for this parameter: A four- or six-character numeric value of the format HHMM or HHMMSS, where HH is the hour, MM the minute, and SS is the second the job is to be submitted. The time is specified in 24-hour format, so 1:00 pm is 13. The value for HH must be 00 through 23, and MM and SS must be 00 through 59. A five- or eight-character numeric value that specifies the time using the date separator used by the system. For example, if the separator is the period (.), you would specify 130828 as 13.08.28. The time is specified in 24-hour format and the same ranges of value for HH, MM, and SS are enforced as for the previous format.
Omit Date	Use this parameter to prevent the scheduled job from being submitted on specific dates. The possible values for this parameter are as follows: • *NONE—No days should be omitted from the schedule. This is the default value. • *Date*—On up to 20 specific dates, the job should not be submitted. For example, you might have a job that is run Monday through Friday at the same time, but you do not need to run it on a holiday. So, if you wanted to omit Christmas Day from the schedule, you would specify December 25th as an omit date. Clearly, this value only works for fixed holidays; you cannot use it for floating holidays like Memorial Day, Labor Day, and Hanukah.

Table 11.1: Parameters for ADDJOBSCDE (4 of 5)

Parameter	Meaning/Values
Recovery Action	If the system is not active at the time a scheduled job is to be submitted, this parameter tells how the entries that were not processed should be handled. The possible values are as follows: • *SBMRLS—Submit the job represented by the job schedule entry. The job may be initiated by the subsystem that is processing the job queue. This is the default value. • *SBMHLD—Submit the job represented by the job schedule entry. The job is held on the job queue pending action from an administrator to either release or delete the job. • *NOSBM—The job represented by the job schedule entry is not submitted. A few additional notes about this parameter: • Job schedule entries are not processed when the system is in restricted state. • If multiple occurrences of a schedule job entry have been missed, the job will only be submitted once. The use of *NOSBM only applies to missed job submissions. If the job schedule entry indicates that it should be submitted at a future day/date, the job will be submitted when the schedule event is reached.
Save	If you have specified *ONCE for the Frequency parameter, this parameter tells the system what to do with the entry after it has processed it and submitted a job. If you are using the prompt feature for the ADDJOBSCDE command, this parameter will appear only if you have specified *ONCE for the frequency. The possible values are as follows: • *YES—After the entry has been processed, it remains in QDFTJOBSCD. • *NO—After the entry has been processed, it is removed from QDFTJOBSCD. This is the default.
Job Description and Library	This is the name of the job description that is used to run the job submitted as a result of the job schedule entry. The possible values for this parameter are as follows: • *USRPRF—The name of the job description is obtained from the user profile that the submitted job runs uses. This is the default value. • *Job description and library*—Specify the name of the job description and library used to run the submitted job.

Table 11.1: Parameters for ADDJOBSCDE (5 of 5)	
Parameter	Meaning/Values
Job Queue and Library	When the job is submitted by the QJOBSCD job, it will be placed on the job queue specified by this parameter. The possible values are as follows: • *JOBD—The name of the job queue is obtained from the job description specified in the job description parameter. This is the default. • *Job description name*—The name of the job queue will be used on the submit job command.
User	This is the name of the user associated with the submitted job. As you recall, the full job name includes 10 characters of job name, 10 characters of user name and a six-character job number. The possible values for this parameter are as follows: • *CURRENT—The name of the user running the ADDJOBSCDE command will be used as the user name of the submitted job. This is the default. • *JOBD—The user name is taken from the job description specified in the JOBD parameter. • *User name*—The user name is the the user associated with the job. The name must correspond to a valid user profile name.
Message Queue and Library	The "job submitted" and "job completed" messages of the submitted job will be sent to the message queue specified by this parameter. The possible values are as follows: • *USRPRF—The message queue specified in the user profile is used to run the submitted job. • *Message queue name*—This names the message queue and library that will receive messages sent by the submitted job.
Text	Up to 50 characters of text that identify the job and the job schedule entry.

Hooray! You made it through the parameters of the command! To provide the scheduling flexibility required in most user environments, the job scheduler function needs a large number of parameters. You'll see some simple example of job scheduling options later in this chapter. For now, press on with the other commands you can use with the job scheduling function.

Other Job-Schedule Entry Commands

In the unlikely event that you made an error when you added your job schedule entry, you can correct it with the Change Job Schedule Entry command (CHGJOBSCDE). This command has parameters that allow you to change any of the values specified on the Add Job Schedule Entry command. You can also make changes to a job schedule entry from the display that appears when you run the Work with Job Schedule Entries command (WRKJOBSCDE).

To remove a job schedule entry, you run the Remove Job Schedule Entry command (RMVJOBSCDE). In addition, job schedule entries can be held and released with the Hold Job Schedule Entry command (HLDJOBSCDE) and Release Job Schedule Entry command (RLSJOBSCDE), respectively.

When you run the change, hold, release, and remove commands, you must have the special authority *JOBCTL to manipulate any entry. Otherwise, you will be able to use these commands only for entries that you added. In addition, if the same name has been used for more than one entry, you will be shown only the first entry. To see duplicate entries, specify *ALL for the entry number parameter on the command that you are running.

Job Scheduling Examples

"Enough already with the command stuff! Show me how I can use this function!" All right, all right. This section provides several examples of rather simple job scheduling functions:

- A job every Thursday (the weekly payroll example).
- A job on the second and fourth Thursdays (a biweekly payroll).
- A job on the last day of the month (month-end processing).
- A job every day of the week (timecard processing).
- Two jobs every weekday (one to set up a daytime interactive environment, and one to set up a nighttime environment).

That should give you enough examples to see how flexible the job scheduling function can be.

The Weekly Payroll

You would like to process payroll every Thursday night, so that payments can be distributed on Friday. Your frequency is weekly, the scheduled day is Thursday, and the scheduled time to submit the job is 10:00 P.M. Create this entry by running the following command:

```
ADDJOBSCDE JOB(PAYROLL) CMD('CALL PAYROLL') FRQ(*WEEKLY)
           SCDDAY(*THU) SCDTIME(2200)
```

You now have a job that will be submitted by the QJOBSCD job every Thursday. However, if Friday is a holiday and you want to move the submission from Thursday to Wednesday, it's not very easy to do.

The Biweekly Payroll

Suppose your payroll application changes to a biweekly job. You still want to submit the job on Thursday at 10:00 P.M. To schedule this biweekly payroll, run the following command:

```
ADDJOBSCDE PAYROLL CMD('CALL PAYROLL) FRQ(*MONTHLY) SCDDAY(*THU)
           RELDAYMON(1 3) SCDTIME(2200)
```

Your job now runs on the first and third Thursdays of each month. As with the previous job, it is not easy to provide for an exception to the scheduling rule.

Month-End Processing

So far, so good. Month-end processing is another easy example. If you want your month-end job submitted on the last day of every month at 4:00 P.M, here's the command you would use:

```
ADDJOBSCDE JOB(MNTHEND) CMD('CALL MNTHEND') FRQ(*MONTHLY) +
           SCDDATE(*MONTHEND) SCDTIME(1600)
```

Now for a little twist: say that your month-end processing is included in your quarter-end and year-end processing, so it does not need to be run on March 31, June 30, September 30, or December 31. No problem. Just eliminate those dates from the schedule for the next three years by modifying the command as follows:

```
ADDJOBSCDE JOB(MNTHEND) CMD('CALL MNTHEND') FRQ(*MONTHLY) +
           SCDDATE(*MONTHEND) SCDTIME(1600) OMITDATE('3/31/01' +
           '6/30/01' '9/30/01' '12/31/01' '3/31/02' '6/30/02' +
           '9/30/02' '12/31/02' '3/31/03' '6/30/03' 9/30/03' +
           '12/31/03')
```

Because you have used only 12 of the allowed 20 omit dates, you could set the job scheduler entry for up to five years! Because you are omitting this job from your schedule, you will need to add a new job schedule entry for quarter-end processing and another for year-end processing. The jobs that are run at the ends of quarters and years will either need to call the MNTHEND program or provide the same processing that was done by the MNTHEND program.

Daily Jobs

If you would like to process timecards (does anybody still use these?) every day at 2:00 A.M., here is the command:

```
ADDJOBSCDE JOB(TIMECARD) CMD('CALL TIMECARD') FRQ(*WEEKLY)
           SCDDAY(*ALL) SCDTIME(0200)
```

Simple enough.

Weekday Jobs

In most iSeries environments, you are likely to see at least two unique workloads every day: heavy-interactive/light-batch during the day, and heavy-batch/light-interactive at night. When these workloads run, the pool allocations are likely to be dramatically different. Although the performance adjustment feature discussed in chapter 4 will eventually allocate the storage efficiently for each workload, it might take a while before you get there. You can help things along by running a job that will set up an environment designed for each of the different workloads. In addition, you might want to activate additional batch subsystems at night and deactivate them in the morning.

To set up the different environments, you need to run two different jobs every weekday. Run the setup job for the daytime environment at 6:00 A.M, and the job for the nighttime environment at 5:30 P.M. Here are the two commands you need:

```
ADDJOBSCDE JOB(DAYTIME) CMD('CALL DAYTIME') FRQ(*WEEKLY)
           SCDDAY(*MON *TUE *WED *THU *FRI) SCDTIME(0600)
```

```
ADDJOBSCDE JOB(NITETIME) CMD('CALL NITETIME') FRQ(*WEEKLY)
           SCDDAY(*MON *TUE *WED *THU *FRI) SCDTIME(1730)
```

That's it! These jobs will now run every weekday and establish runtime environments for the different workloads that you have.

Defaults Supplied for You

When looking at the Submit Job command in chapter 2, you saw that many of its parameters had default values. However, when QJOBSCD submits jobs, several parameters on the Submit Job command will not use their usual default values. These values are supplied by the QJOBSCD command:

- Print device: *JOBD.
- Output queue: *JOBD.
- Print text: *JOBD.
- Routing entry: *JOBD.
- Initial library list: *JOBD.
- System library list: *SYSVAL.
- Current library: *USRPRF.
- Coded character set ID: *USRPRF.
- Language ID: *USRPRF.
- Country ID: *USRPRF.
- Sort Sequence: *USRPRF.

These default values cannot be changed or overridden.

Work Management System Values

The final topic of this chapter is system values. As there are about a bazillion of these (plus or minus a couple), this book only addresses the system values related to work management. The next chapter includes a discussion of system values related to the IPL process. The system values are presented here in alphabetical order.

QATNPGM

In the discussion of group jobs in chapter 9, you learned that if you pressed the Attn key, you would get the Operational Assistant menu. The QATNPGM system value is a 20-character field that specifies the program name and library to be called when the Attn key is pressed. The possible values are as follows:

- *ASSIST—The Operational Assistant program, QEZMAIN in library QSYS, will be called. This is the default value.

- *NONE—No program will be called.

- 'PGM LIB'—The name of the program and library specify the program to be called. Each name may be up to 10 characters long. If the program name is less than 10 characters, only one blank between the program name and library name is needed, that is, 'ATTKEY SMITH' will cause the program ATTKEY in library SMITH to be called. If the program name is 10 characters, there can be no blanks between the program name and library name; 'HANDLEATTNSMITH' will cause the program HANDLEATTN in library SMITH to be called.

QAUTOCFG

This system value provides automatic configuration of new devices that are locally attached to the system. It is a one-character field used with the QDEVNAMING system value to provide device names. The possible values are as follows:

- 0—Newly attached local devices are not automatically configured. If you want to use the new device, you must provide the configuration information manually.

- 1—Newly attached local devices are automatically configured, and a message is sent to the system operator regarding the change to the system's configuration. This is the default value.

QAUTORMT

This system value performs the same function for remote devices that QAUTOCFG performed for local devices. The possible values and default value are the same as for QAUTOCFG.

QAUTOVRT

This is another system value that deals with the automatic creation of devices, in this case, virtual devices that are used for functions like display station pass-through. This system value is a five-digit decimal number with no decimal places, for example, DEC(50). The possible values are as follows:

- 0—Do not automatically create virtual devices. This is the default value.

- 1 through 32500—Automatically create the specified number of virtual devices. If you specify a number for this system value that is lower than the current value, existing devices will not be deleted. For example, if the system value had been 1000, and you changed it to 500, there will still be a thousand virtual devices in your system.

- *NOMAX—There will be 32,767 virtual devices created.

The default value of zero will make your job harder. Replace this value with a number that represents the maximum number of pass-through sessions active at any time (remember to include PCs as pass-through devices).

It may be validly argued that the system values that control automatic device configuration are not related to work management. However, since device names are used to assign devices to different interactive subsystems, it can also be argued that they *are* related to work management.

QBASACTLVL

This system value provides the maximum number of jobs that can run in *BASE at the same time. As you recall from chapter 4, the maximum activity level value limits the number of jobs competing for main storage. This system value provides the initial value for Max Active in *BASE. When you change the Max Active value for *BASE from the Work with System Status command (WRKSYSSTS) or the Work with Shared Pools command (WRKSHRPOOL), you are actually changing this system value.

This system value is a five-digit decimal number with no decimal places. It cannot be zero. The default value for QBASACTLVL is based on the system size, model, configuration, etc. To determine how to set this value for your system, refer to chapters 4 and 5.

QBASPOOL

This system value is used to set the minimum size for the *BASE pool. It is a 10-decimal digit field with no decimal places. The default value, representing the size in kilobytes, is 2000. You cannot set this value lower than 256, and you cannot set the size of *BASE lower than this value. If you wish to make *BASE smaller, you must first make this value smaller.

The size of *BASE may be larger than the value specified in QBASPOOL. If you use WRKSYSSTS or WRKSHRPOOL to adjust pool sizes, you cannot increase the size of *BASE directly. *BASE is made larger by reducing the size of one or more other pools. In other words, you do not allocate space to *BASE. Rather, you allocate space to all of the other pools, and *BASE gets the leftovers.

QCMNARB

Many systems have large numbers of remote devices and/or communications jobs actives. These types of configurations usually have many activities to be processed. This large number of these activities, added to an already large number, is handled by the system arbiter job (QSYSARB) discussed in chapter 1. The system arbiter could fall behind in its attempts to handle such a large number of events. As a result, the communications events were off-loaded from the system arbiter and handled by communication arbiters.

QCMNARB is a ten-character field that controls the number of communications arbiters that will run on your system. The possible values are as follows:

- 0—All of the communications activities will be handled by the system arbiter and the system job QLUS.

- 1 through 999—Obviously, 10 characters allows you to specify a very large number. In fact, the number will be far larger than the maximum number of jobs that can exist on the system. If you are going to specify a number, pick something like six. You shouldn't need to set this to more than 10.

- *CALC—The system will determine the workload that the communications arbiters are experiencing. This is the default value. Leave it alone; it is a good choice.

QCONSOLE

This system value specifies the name of the console device. It is set to QCONSOLE and cannot be changed.

QCTLSBSD

As mentioned earlier in this chapter, QCTLSBSD indicates which subsystem is to be the controlling subsystem, which starts first and is not ended until the system is powered off. If you issue the End Subsystem command (ENDSBS) for this subsystem, the console device will remain active until the system is powered off. Once the system is running, you cannot delete or rename the controlling subsystem description. If the system is unable to use the subsystem that is named, one attempt will be made to start QSYSSBSD. If QSYSSBSD fails to start, the system will not start successfully. If this situation occurs, you can change the subsystem by performing an attended IPL and changing the name of the subsystem description during the IPL This procedure is described in the next chapter.

This system value is a 20-character field that allows for a subsystem description name of up to 10 characters and a library name of up to 10 characters. If the subsystem description name is less than 10 characters, only one blank between the program name and library name is needed. For example, 'QBASE QSYS' will cause the subsystem description QBASE in library QSYS to be the controlling subsystem called. If the subsystem description name is 10 characters, there can be no blanks between the program name and library name. For example, 'CONTROLSBSSMITH' will cause the subsystem description CONTROLSBS in library SMITH to be the controlling subsystem. The default for this system value is 'QBASE QSYS'.

QDEVNAMING

When you choose to have new devices automatically configured, they will be assigned a name by the system. QDEVNAMING describes the naming convention to be used. You cannot specify your own naming convention with this system value, but must use one of the default conventions:

- *NORMAL—iSeries naming conventions will be used. Under this convention, displays will start with *DSP*, printers with *PRT*, tape drives with *TAP*, and diskette drives (if anyone still has these) with *DKT*. This is the default value.

- *S36—The System/36 naming standards will be used.

- *DEVADDR—The device address will be used to generate the device name.

If you change this system value, devices that have already been named will not be changed.

QDEVRCYACN

In discussing the usage of the Device Recovery Action parameter in chapter 5, I mentioned the overhead associated when jobs are running and either the device or communications with the device fails. This system value provides the method for all jobs running in the system to deal with this situation. Here are the possible values:

- *MSG—An error message is sent to the application. It is up to the application to handle the message.

- *DSCMSG—The failing workstation is disconnected from the job. When the workstation is recovered and the user signs on, the program will be sent a message and can reconnect to the previous job. This is the default value.

- *DSCENDRQS—The failing workstation is disconnected. When the workstation is recovered and the user signs on, the job is reconnected, but the last request level is cancelled.

- *ENDJOB—The job is ended and a job log is produced. In addition, a message is placed in the job log and in QHST, indicating that the job ended due to a device failure.

- *ENDJOBNOLIST—The job is ended and a job log is not produced. A message is placed in QHST indicating that the job ended due to a device failure.

This is another instance of a reasonably good choice for a default value that should be acceptable in almost all environments.

QDSCJOBITV

When a workstation has been disconnected from a job (either by failure or user decision), the job remains active (but dormant) in the system. This system value, a 10-digit decimal number with no decimal places, indicates the amount of time a disconnected job can remain dormant before it ends. The possible values are as follows:

- 5 through 1440—The job will remain disconnected for the specified number of minutes before it ends.

- *NONE—The disconnected job will remain active for an unlimited amount of time.

The default value is 240.

QDYNPTYADJ

In describing dynamic-priority scheduling in chapter 4, I said that jobs that exceeded resource usage limits would be penalized when dynamic-priority scheduling was used. Jobs on the second and third cost curves would be penalized by being lowered one cost curve. Figure 11.30 explains the penalty.

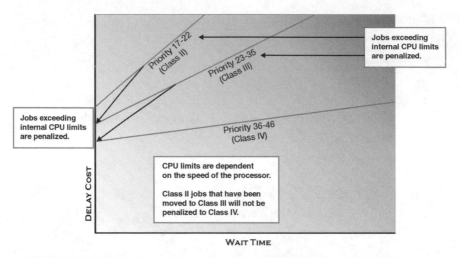

Figure 11.30: The default dynamic-priority scheduling scheme will penalize jobs that over-use CPU resources if the jobs are on either the Class II or Class III cost curves. The jobs will be penalized only to the cost curve immediately below.

However, some iSeries systems are shipped with two different processing ratings. One processor rating refers to the total capacity of the machine, the other refers to only the interactive capacity of the machine. On models with a lower interactive capacity than the total machine capacity, special system controls are put in place.

Whenever the CPU used by interactive jobs exceeds the interactive capacity, bad things happen. If the system is not an 8XX or a 270, internal tasks in the system will run. These tasks may use most of your CPU resources in an attempt to prevent interactive jobs from running. Unfortunately, batch jobs will not run under these conditions either.

Most of this problem is caused by the fact that interactive jobs run at a higher priority than batch jobs. Attempts to reduce the amount of CPU resource consumed by interactive jobs via the penalties are inadequate because the costs of interactive jobs are still higher and accelerate faster than batch. In an attempt to further reduce the interactive impact of interactive jobs, QDYNPTYADJ was introduced. When the function controlled by this system value is activated, the penalties to jobs running on any cost curve other than the first are modified so penalized jobs can be lowered more than one cost curve.

This penalty scheme is represented in Figure 11.31.

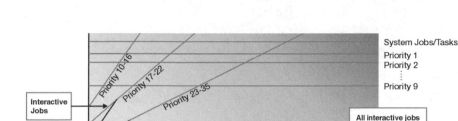

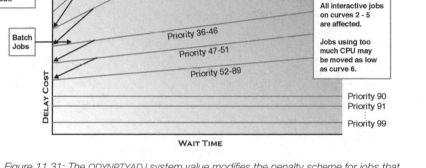

Figure 11.31: The QDYNPTYADJ system value modifies the penalty scheme for jobs that
overuse processor resources. Offending jobs may be lowered from the second curve to
the sixth curve, one curve at a time.

As you can see, this allows the system to lower the cost of interactive jobs to a
point below batch jobs. In addition, interactive jobs that are penalized below
batch jobs will accelerate in cost slightly slower than batch. Also, as you might
have noticed, the run priority (RUNPTY) for the batch jobs has changed from 50
to 40. While it is not necessary to change the batch job RUNPTY, it will help prevent interactive jobs from running as often.

QDYNPTYADJ is a one-digit decimal field with no decimal positions. The possible values are as follows:

- 0—Do not activate the additional interactive job penalties.

- 1—Activate the additional interactive job penalties. This is the default
  value.

This system value will only take effect if dynamic-priority scheduling, as described
in the next system value, has been activated. The default value should be used.

QDYNPTYSCD

This system value is used to select dynamic-priority or fixed-priority scheduling. Both of these types of scheduling are discussed in detail in chapter 4. QDYNPTYSCD is a one-digit decimal field with no decimal places. The possible values are as follows:

- 0—Use fixed-priority scheduling.
- 1—Use dynamic-priority scheduling. This is the default and should be used.

QINACTITV

This system value is primarily a security feature. It indicates how long an interactive job can remain active without doing any work. If an interactive job has not run for a long time, it usually means that the user has left and forgotten to sign off. This system value is included in this book because it provides another method for ending jobs.

QINACTITV is a 10-digit decimal field with no decimal places. Its possible values are as follows:

- *NONE–There is no inactivity time limit. This is the default value.
- 5 through 300—Specifies the number of minutes that a job may be inactive. When the specified inactive time is reached, the action indicated by the system value QINACTMSQ will be performed.

QINACTMSGQ

This system value is used with QINACTITV to handle interactive jobs that are inactive. The system value is 20 characters and has the following possible values:

- *DSCJOB—The job and any secondary or group jobs are disconnected.

- *ENDJOB—The job and any secondary or group jobs are ended. This is the default value.

- *Message queue name and library name*—A message queue name of up to 10 characters, followed by a library name of up to 10 characters, may be specified. The rules for supplying the message queue and library name are the same as the rules for specifying names for the

QATNPGM and QCTLSBSD system values. When an inactive job is detected, it will not be ended, but a message will be sent to the specified message queue in the specified library. If the message queue is not accessible, QSYSOPR will be used. Using this value, you can monitor users who might be violating your security practices.

QMAXACTLVL

This system value represents the maximum number of threads that can be in an activity level, anywhere in the system, at one time. If the sum of the activity levels in all the pools is greater than this value, a job that apparently should be granted access to a pool might be prevented from entering the system. This situation should not occur.

QMAXACTLVL should always be set higher than the sum of the activity levels in all of the pools. Better yet, set it to *NOMAX. This system value is a five-digit decimal field with no decimal places and the following possible values:

- 2 through 32767—Specifies the maximum number of threads that can occupy an activity level in the system.

- *NOMAX—Actually, there is a maximum, and it is the same as setting the value to 32767. This is the default and should be used. Controlling the number of jobs in the system should be done using the activity levels on the pools used to run jobs.

QMCHPOOL

As discussed in chapter 4, the size of the machine pool is set by this system value. When you change the size of the machine pool on the WRKSYSSTS or WRKSHRPOOL command, you are changing this system value.

QMCHPOOL is a 10-digit decimal field with no decimal positions. Each system has a minimum machine pool size that is derived from the system model, size, and configuration. If you attempt to set the machine pool size lower than the minimum size, the command will fail. In addition, the default size for each system is calculated using the system model size and configuration. Refer to chapter 4 in this book to determine the size for the machine pool—or better yet, let the system performance adjustment feature do the work for you.

QPASTHRSVR

This system value determines the number of server jobs that are available to handle pass-through requests generated by a job on another system, a PC running the Work Station Facility (WSF) function of Client Access, or a PC running some other form of 52520 emulation. Since each server job can process any number of pass-through requests, the number of pass-through server jobs is not the same as the number of pass-through jobs. In fact, it should be much lower. This system value is a ten-character field with the following possible values:

- *CALC—The system will calculate the number of pass-through server jobs and create them as needed. This is the default value and should be used.

- 5 through 100—The specified number of pass-through server jobs will be created.

QPFRADJ

The discussion of pools in chapters 4 and 6 covers the performance adjustment feature and its algorithms in great detail. QPFRADJ is used to activate the performance adjustment feature (which will only be used for shared pools). It is a one-character field with these possible values:

- 0—The system will not be used to dynamically adjust pool sizes and activity levels. In addition, there will be no pool size settings chosen when an IPL occurs. If you want to perform your own system setup and make your own adjustments, use this value.

- 1—The system will assign initial sizes to the machine pool, *BASE, *INTERACT, and *SPOOL, but will not make any adjustments to the pool sizes while the system is running. If you want the system to establish the initial settings on every IPL, but you want to adjust the pool sizes yourself, use this value. This is probably the least useful setting because all of your adjustments will be lost every time you IPL.

- 2—The system will assign initial sizes to the machine pool, *BASE, *INTERACT, and *spool, and will make adjustments to the pool sizes while the system is running. This is the default value. It is more useful than the previous value, but once again, all of the adjustments will be lost whenever you IPL.

- ■ 3—The system will not assign initial sizes to the machine pool, *BASE, *INTERACT, and *SPOOL, but will make adjustments to the pool sizes while the system is running. If you do not want the system to estimate the initial sizes of pools, but you want it to make adjustments while it is active, use this value.

A typical method of using this system value is to IPL the system using the default value of two only the first time you IPL the machine or make significant hardware changes (to main storage and/or the processor). Then set the system value to zero (do-it-yourself) or three (let the system do it).

QPRCMLTTSK

This system value is used to improve the CPU efficiency of 7XX and 8XX models. Each of these machines provides an L1 and L2 cache to make information available to processors faster. The L1 cache is faster and located closer to the processor. It provides the best assistance to your processor. However, it is the smallest. The L2 cache is a little slower (but still fast), a little further away from the processor, and larger than the L1 cache. It provides the next level of assistance. Finally, main storage, which acts like a cache in an iSeries, is used to make the processors run efficiently.

Try as they might, processors are unable to consistently run using the information in the L1 cache. When a processor fails to find what it needs in the L1 cache, a *cache miss* occurs, and the processor becomes idle until the L1 cache is filled with the requested information. As a result, the processor is less efficient. Studies conducted by the development team in Rochester found that splitting the L1 cache between two processes that were ready to use the processor improved the efficiency of the processor. Now, when a processor takes a cache miss on one of the processes it is serving, it does not need to wait for the information to be delivered to the L1 cache. Instead, it merely switches to the other half of the cache and begins serving the other process. Figure 11.32 is a rough depiction of this principle.

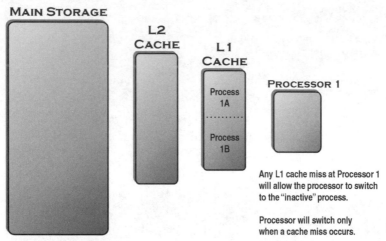

Figure 11.32: The QPRCMLTTSK system value is used to divide the L1 cache to support two different jobs at the same processor.

This system value is a one-character field with the following possible values:

- 0—Do not activate the multitasking feature.
- 1—Activate the multitasking feature. This is the default and should be used. If your system does not support multitasking, the system will reset this value to zero. It should be noted that a model 720 eight-way and a model 730 12-way processor do not support this feature.

QSTRPRTWTR

This system value is used to activate print writers after the system is IPLed and the subsystem QSPL has been started. The system-supplied startup program will use this system value to determine if print writers are to be started. QSTRPRTWTR is a one-character field that has the following possible values:

- 0—Do not start the print writers.
- 1—Start the print writers. This is the default value and should be used.

QSTRUPPGM

This system value is used to specify the startup program called from an autostart job in QCTL or QBASE. This system value is a 20-character field with these possible values:

- *NONE—The autostart job ends without calling a startup program.

- 'PGM LIB'—The name of the program and library specify the program to be called. Each name may be up to 10 characters long. If the program name is less than 10 characters, only one blank between the program name and library name is needed. For example, 'QSTRUP QSYS' will cause program QSTRUP in library QSYS to be called. If the program name is 10 characters, there can be no blanks between the program name and library name. For example, 'STARTINGUPSYSTEM' will cause program STARTINGUP in library SYSTEM to be called.

QTSEPOOL

This system value is used to activate the redirection of CPU-intensive interactive jobs from their assigned pool to *BASE. QTSEPOOL is a 10-character field with the following possible values:

- *NONE—The CPU-intensive interactive jobs are not redirected to *BASE. This is the default value.
- *BASE—The CPU-intensive jobs will be redirected to *BASE.

It is a good idea to try changing this system value to *BASE. Your performance might not improve, but it is unlikely to degrade, assuming the pool sizes and activity level of *BASE are set correctly. When you change this system value, only jobs started after you have made the change will be affected. Jobs that are already running will continue to run the value that was assigned to them when they were initiated.

In Review

Well, you've certainly picked up a lot of pieces. This chapter tries to anticipate all of the work management conditions you are likely to use. However, work management is a big world, and there could be some rare instances when you will need to use some functions that aren't covered here. When you encounter those conditions, refer to the IBM reference manuals for assistance.

12

IPL: The Land Before Time

For iSeries users, there will come a time when you will need to shut your system off. You might shut it off to prepare for a new release, add hardware, apply Program Temporary Fixes (PTFs), or just to give it a rest. Whatever the reason, when you are ready to use your system again, you will need to perform an Initial Program Load (IPL). In other words, you will boot your system.

During this time, the iSeries will be working very hard to deliver your system to you in working order. Depending on the size, speed, and configuration of your system, the IPL process might take anywhere from a few minutes to a lot of minutes. Predicting the time it takes to IPL is like predicting the weather. On occasion, all of the factors are known and behave predictably, and your projection is accurate. Other times (most of the time?), well, at least it provides something to talk about. This chapter examines the following topics:

- IPL modes.
- IPL types.
- Normal and abnormal IPLs.
- Phases of an IPL.
- Work-management-related OS/400 IPL functions.
- Changing the attributes of an IPL,
- Work management, system values, and IPL.
- The reasons to IPL a system.

For many people, IPL is a process that is to be endured rather than learned. It's like starting your car. You probably start your car several times a day. (At least an iSeries IPL is very infrequent.) Do you crave a status report from each electromechanical part in your vehicle prior to its starting? The answer is probably no—it either starts (it's working) or it doesn't (it's broken). However, if you learn some of the background of IPL, you can better understand some of the fundamental strengths of the iSeries system. In other words, when an iSeries starts, you know all of the parts are working to specification. Can you say the same after your car has started?

IPL Modes

There are two basic modes of an iSeries IPL: *unattended* and *attended*. That seems simple enough—unattended means that you start an IPL and walk away, while in attended IPL, you start it, hold the system's hand, and talk to it during its recovery. Most of the time, an iSeries IPL is unattended.

Unattended IPLs

According to the definition of an unattended IPL in IBM' *iSeries Diagnostic Aids Manual*, "An unattended IPL occurs when Normal mode is selected on the control, the system value QIPLTYPE is zero, and the Power On switch or the POWER ON CL command is used. After power is turned on from an auto restart, remote IPL, timed IPL, or pressing Power On, the system starts an IPL." Well that certainly explains it! Any questions—other than "Come again?"

Try to break down this statement into its different parts, starting with the Mode switch. On the operations panel of an iSeries, there are two switches. One tells you the mode you are using for the IPL. This switch has several settings, such as Manual, Normal, and Secure. The first step in achieving an unattended IPL, then, is to have the switch set to Normal.

Next, look at the QIPLTYPE system value. When the value of QIPLTYPE is zero, no displays will be shown during the IPL. In other words, if QIPLTYPE is zero, the IPL will be unattended. The QIPLTYPE system value is discussed in more detail later in this chapter.

Now, about starting power to the system. You can turn on the system using the Power On switch, or you can run the POWER ON CL command. Turning the switch is easy enough, but how do you run the POWER ON "CL command" when the system is powered off? Not only that, if you look at the commands shipped with OS/400, there is no such thing as a POWER ON command. In fact, the "command" that the document is referring to is actually a Power On function embedded in the Licensed Internal Code of the system. How do you run a Power On function when the system is powered off?

When you run the PWRDWNSYS command, you can specify RESTART(*YES). This is referred to as an *auto restart*. You can also have another machine dial into the machine that is powered off and power it on. This is referred to as a *remote IPL*. Finally, you can set a timer in your machine that will IPL the system at the specified time. This is referred to as a *timed IPL*. When these functions are performed, the Power On internal function is run.

After all of that, the system IPLs and delivers the sign-on screen to the system console. There is no other interaction between human and machine during the unattended IPL. An unattended IPL is the fastest form of IPL.

Attended IPLs

Unlike an unattended IPL, an attended IPL causes additional interactions between you and the machine. At each interaction, you can influence the outcome of the IPL. For example, you could choose to change IPL options that clean up objects on the system (although this might produce a longer IPL), or you could assign resources to logical partitions through the Dedicated Service Tool (DST). Attended IPLs are rare. They are usually only done after new hardware is installed, or disk units are moved between logical partitions, or other major system configuration changes are made.

You get an attended IPL when the iSeries Mode switch on the operations panel is set to Manual and either of the following is true:

- The front function panel switch is set to three.

- The QIPLTYPE system value is set to one or two. If QIPLTYPE is two, the operating system is IPLed in debug mode. This is a very slow operating system! Only set QIPLTYPE to two when requested by IBM Service.

You activate an attended IPL in the same way as an unattended IPL.

IPL Type

The source of the code used for an IPL is controlled by another switch on the operations panel of the iSeries, called the IPL Type switch. This switch can be set in any of four positions: A, B, C, or D. Each setting causes a different set of Licensed Internal Code (LIC) to run your system after the IPL is complete:

- Type A—Whenever you install an iSeries release, LIC is loaded on the system in an area referred to as the "A-side." The A-side is also referred to as the *permanent version* of LIC. After it is loaded on the system, it will not be changed until you permanently apply LIC PTFs. Type-A IPLs are usually done only when a release is installed. However, when you temporarily apply LIC PTFs, the system will internally perform an abbreviated type-A IPL.

- Type B—Whenever temporary PTFs have been applied to LIC, the modified LIC is stored in an area called the "B-side." Since you have applied the PTFs to make your system run better, you will almost always use a type-B IPL in order to use the better code.

- Type C—You will probably never use a type-C IPL, since it should be done only if requested by the iSeries development team in Rochester. Do not let anybody who is not a member of the iSeries development team use or tell you to use this type of IPL! If not used correctly, this type of IPL can wipe out a lot of your data. In other words, it could get real ugly, real fast!

- Type D—When you select a type-D IPL, you are installing a new version of LIC from the media that was shipped to you. Once your new LIC is installed, you should never need to perform this type of IPL.

Normal versus Abnormal IPL

So far, you've seen the different IPL modes and types. Next, you'll get a quick overview of the amount of internal validation that takes place when an iSeries system IPL takes place. Basically, there are two levels of validation: normal IPL processing and abnormal IPL processing. Each produces similar results at the end of the IPL. The only differences are the amount of work and length of time each method takes.

Normal IPL

A normal IPL takes place after the system has shut down normally. Over 95 percent of iSeries IPL operations are normal. As a result, many recovery steps will be bypassed or short-circuited because the objects that the steps are responsible for validating are in good shape.

With normal validation, the IPL can move quickly from phase to phase and function to function to produce the fastest possible start-up. While it is fast, the time it takes to perform a normal IPL will vary from system to system, but it should be fairly constant for an individual system.

Abnormal IPL

If you guessed that an abnormal IPL is caused by a shutdown because of an error, you have provided a very good generalization. There may be many underlying scenarios that end up causing an abnormal IPL, but all of them involve some sort of error that prevented the system from shutting down in an orderly fashion.

When an abnormal IPL is performed, the recovery steps are far more thorough in the validating the functions and objects that they are responsible for using. In some instances, this might mean reassembling pieces and making them complete. As a result, an abnormal IPL might take much longer than a normal IPL. On the other hand, most objects and structures could be perfect, in which case the recovery step merely checks them and moves on. In these instances, an abnormal IPL might take about the same amount of time as a normal IPL. For example, if you run the ENDJOBABN command to kill a job that was looping, your next IPL will be abnormal. While one single job didn't end normally, everything else did, and the time for the abnormal IPL will be about the same as a normal IPL. As a result of these conditions, not only are you unable to predict the length of time an abnormal IPL will take on different systems, you are unable to predict the length of time an abnormal IPL will take on an individual system (just like predicting the weather).

Phases of IPL

There are three phases to every IPL:

- Hardware and Hypervisor Licensed Internal Code (HLIC and PLIC).
- Supervisor Licensed Internal Code (SLIC).
- OS/400.

During each phase, a code will be displayed on the operations panel of the system. These codes can be translated to the function that is being performed. In addition, a range of codes is assigned to each phase of the IPL. These codes are generally of the form *Cp00 nnnn*, where *p* is a digit that represents the phase of the IPL and *nnnn* represents the function within the phase. HLIC and PLIC phases of the IPL have a value of one through five for *p*, SLIC has *p* equal to six, and OS/400 has *p* equal to nine.

Occasionally, codes for phases C1 and C3 will be followed by something other than *00*. When this occurs, the system is performing a specialized form of IPL. The type of IPL being performed is identified by the first character following the *C1* or *C3*, and will be one of the following:

- B—A continuously powered main (CPM) storage-recovery IPL is being performed. The steps are appearing before a main storage dump has been taken. A main storage dump is taken whenever a system failure has occurred and the iSeries development personnel need to analyze the cause of the failure. A main storage dump IPL is activated by setting the function switch on the operations panel of the system to 22.

- C—A continuously powered main (CPM) storage-recovery IPL is being performed. The steps are appearing after a main store dump has been completed. These steps are a continuation of those in the phases designated by B.

- D—A main storage dump is in progress.

- F—The Multi-Function Input/Output Processor (MFIOP) is being reset or reloaded. This situation does not occur very often.

As is indicated by the four digits used to identify the function, each of the phases performs many functions during an IPL. It is not my intent to cover all of the functions of all of the phases here. Because you are dealing with work management, an OS/400 function that uses LIC to complete its work, this chapter looks only at functions of the OS/400 phase of IPL related to work management. That doesn't mean the others aren't important, just that they are not applicable to work management. If you are interested in the gory details of IPL, please refer to the iSeries (AS/400) *Diagnostic Aids Reference*.

Work-Management-Related OS/400 IPL Functions

You can't put it off any longer. It's time to look at the various OS/400 function codes related to work management that are displayed on the operations panel of the system during an IPL—either normal or abnormal.

C900 2810 Reclaim Machine Context

You might be wondering what type of object a "context" is. You might also be wondering how you create and manage contexts. You don't deal with contexts directly; a context is an internal representation of the contents of a library. Thus, when you create a library, a context is created for you. When you create an object in a library, the context is updated for you.

The "machine context" is, if you will, a library of the libraries on the system. It contains the names and definitions of the libraries. In addition, the machine context contains other important system information that is used to IPL and run your iSeries. Some of these objects appear in QSYS. There really is no definitive list of these internal objects; you just need to trust that it's important stuff that only the system needs to know.

In this step of the IPL, OS/400 is locating the machine context to obtain the vital information it needs to IPL and run the system. Once the context is resolved, its contents are verified. It is particularly important to locate the libraries QSYS and QGPL.

C900 2820 Resolve System Objects

The system spends a long time preparing to run its first job. This is one of the early steps along the road. In the previous step, you were able to locate the machine context. Once you have the machine context, you need to find a set of internal system objects that will enable you to eventually start your first job, Start Control Program Facility (SCPF). The operating system on the System/38 was called the Control Program Facility (CPF), so SCPF is the job that starts the operating system.

C900 2825 Convert Work Control Block Table

Work management and other components of OS/400 use an internal object called the *Work Control Block Table* (WCBT) to keep information about jobs in the system. A job is considered to be in the system if any of the following conditions exist:

- The job is on a job queue waiting to be started.
- The job is running.
- The job has ended, but it has spool files (including its job log) on one or more output queues.

Prior to Version 4 Release 1 of OS/400, the maximum number of jobs in the system was 32,767. Many large environments were approaching, and exceeding, this number. To accommodate these large environments, the Work Control Block Table was restructured and reformatted to allow for more than 485,000 jobs in Version 5 Release 1. Prior to this release, the Work Control Block Table could contain a maximum of 160,000 entries. When the new format was implemented in Version 3 Release 1, it was designed to be easily expanded without requiring a reformat operation.

The first time you install a release that is Version 3 Release 1 or later, the WCBT is converted from the old format to the new format. Any entries for jobs in the system are reformatted and placed in the new WCBT. When the conversion takes place, this step might take a little time. Once converted, the format is merely checked, and IPL rolls on to the next step. Since Version 3 Release 1 was shipped before any of the current hardware models, there should not be any systems remaining in the world with an old format of the WCBT.

C900 2830 System Value Object

As mentioned in the preceding chapter, several system values are used by work management to run the system. In addition, several system values affect the IPL functions. So, you had better find the system values. This step locates the system value object and validates that it is usable. If the system value is not usable, it is reconstructed using the default values shipped with OS/400. Every time the system value is changed, it is written to disk. It is very, very seldom that the system value object is not usable.

C900 28C0 Prepare SCPF Job

Prior to starting the SCPF job, you need to check a few things associated with the WCBT. This will not be the last time you check the WCBT. Each entry in the

WCBT has, among other information, a pointer to the following objects associated with each job in it:

- The job message queue that receives messages sent to the job.

- A spool control block that is used to locate spool files produced by the job.

- A local data area that can be used to pass information between programs or group jobs.

This step will check for damage to the WCBT object. Objects do not become damaged very often on an iSeries, but you need to check to see if the WCBT is damaged and inaccessible. If there is no damage (almost all of the time), the existence of the message queue and spool control block for the SCPF job is ensured. SCPF does not have a local data area.

If the WCBT is damaged, it is rebuilt. During the rebuild process, all of the existing job message queues, spool control blocks, and local data areas are marked for deletion in a later step. At the end of the rebuild, there is only one entry in the WCBT—the SCPF job entry.

C900 2940 Console Configuration

At this point, no subsystems are active. However, if you are performing an attended IPL, you need to send a display to the console device to interact with someone. So, you will create the QCTL controller and QCONSOLE device, if they do not already exist. For an attended IPL, you will vary on both the controller and the device, so that the IPL can communicate with the outside world.

C900 2960 Sign-on Processing for Attended IPL

Well, it didn't take very long to put the console device to use. At this point, IPL has sent the standard sign-on display to the console device. The IPL will not continue until a valid sign-on has been completed.

C900 2967 PTF Apply During an Attended IPL

After the sign-on is complete, IPL will send a display of pending Program Temporary Fixes (PTFs) to the console device. At this point, you can choose PTFs that you would like to have applied to or removed from the system. You can also choose to have the PTFs applied temporarily (on the B-side code) or permanently (on the A-side code).

C900 2968 IPL Options During an Attended IPL

Finally, the last of three displays sent to the console during an attended IPL allows you to select options that you would like to apply during this IPL. You will see a display like the one in Figure 12.1.

```
                        IPL Options

Type choices, press enter

        System data . . . . . . . . . . . . . . : XX/XX.XX    MM/DD/YY
        System time . . . . . . . . . . . . . . : XX:XX:XX    HH:MM:SS
        Clear job queues  . . . . . . . . . . . : N           Y=Yes, N=No
        Clear output queues . . . . . . . . . . : N           Y=Yes, N=No
        Clear incomplete job logs . . . . . . . : N           Y=Yes, N=No
        Start print writers . . . . . . . . . . : Y           Y=Yes, N=No
        Start the system to restricted state  . : N           Y=Yes, N=No
        Run #STRTUP1 procedure. . . . . . . . . : Y           Y=Yes, N=No
        Run #STRTUP2 procedure. . . . . . . . . : Y           Y=Yes, N=No
        Set major system options. . . . . . . . : N           Y=Yes, N=No
        Define or change system at IPL. . . . . : N           Y=Yes, N=No



Last power-down operation was XXXXXXXX
```

Figure 12.1: The IPL Options display is shown during an attended IPL. It lets you modify IPL functions.

The following options are available to you:

- System date—The date is retrieved and displayed at the console in the format you have chosen. If the date is incorrect, you can change it. During Y2K testing, it was common to test the system by modifying this value from a date in 1999 to a date in 2000.

- System time—The time is retrieved and displayed at the console in the format you have chosen. If the time is incorrect, you can change it. Often, tests will be run to determine what happens to a job that is running at midnight. Is it like Cinderella—perfect until midnight, and a total mess afterwards? Changing this value can iron out problems of this type. Of course, changing the date and time to test applications should not be done on a production system.

- Clear job queues—The default for this option is N (do not clear job queues). If you choose to clear job queues, change the value to Y. The contents of all job queues will be cleared. Usually, clearing all job queues is not a good idea. It is better to use the Clear Job Queue command (CLRJOBQ) to clear specific queues.

- Clear output queues—The default for this option is N (do not clear output queues). If you change the value to Y, the contents of all output queues will be cleared. Again, it is a better idea to clear specific output queues with the Clear Output Queue command (CLROUTQ).

- Clear incomplete job log—If the system ended abnormally, jobs active at the time the system ended have incomplete job logs. The default value for this option is N (keep the incomplete job logs). If you had several hundred active jobs on the system that were running normally, it is often not necessary to see the job logs for these jobs—especially if they all tell you the same thing. Setting this option to Y will throw away the logs of incomplete jobs and delete their WCBT entries.

- Start print writers—This is the value of QSTRPRTWTR, discussed in the preceding chapter. You can only change this value on this screen or with the Change IPL Attributes command (CHGIPLA) discussed later in this chapter. The default value is Y (QSTRPRTWTR is one), and print writers will be started by the startup program that is run after the IPL is complete. If you change the value to N (QSTRPRTWTR is zero), no print writers will be started automatically. You will need to start print writers using the Start Print Writer command (STRPRTWTR).

- Start the system in restricted state—The previous chapter explains that only the console is active when the system is in restricted state. The default for this option is N (the system is to be made fully operational). If you change the value to Y, only the console will be available; no autostart or prestart jobs will run, and no print writers will be started.

- Run #STRTUP1 procedure—This will appear only if your system is using the System/36 environment (as indicated in the user profile used to sign on) and the procedure #STRTUP1 is found in #LIBRARY. The default for this option, Y, will cause the #STRTUP1 procedure to run at the completion of the IPL. If the IPL is unattended, or you change this value to N, #STRTUP1 will not run.

- Run #STRTUP2 procedure—This will appear only if your system is using the System/36 environment (as indicated in the user profile used to sign on) and the procedure #STRTUP2 is found in #LIBRARY. The default for this option, Y, will cause the #STRTUP2 procedure to run at the completion of the IPL. If the IPL is unattended, or you change this value to N, #STRTUP2 will not run.

- Set major system options—This will cause the Set Major Systems Options display in Figure 12.2 to be shown at the console when you have completed setting the IPL options and pressed Enter.

```
                    Set Major System Options

Type choices, press enter

     Enable automatic configuration . . . . . . . :    Y          Y=Yes, N=No
     Device configuration naming  . . . . . . . . :    *NORMAL    *NORMAL, *S36
                                                                  *DEVADR
     Default special environment  . . . . . . . . :    *NONE, *S36
```

Figure 12.2: The Set Major System Options display will appear if you choose Y for the last option on the Set Options display during an attended IPL.

This display allows you to manipulate the QAUTOCFG, QDEVNAMING, and QSPCENV system values discussed in chapter 11. This option is set to Y during the initial install of the system, and the Set Major Options display will be shown. After the initial install, the option is set to N, and the display will not be shown.

- Define or change system at IPL—This option will cause the Define or Change System at IPL menu in Figure 12.3 to be shown at the console. If the value for Set Major System Options is N, the display will be shown after you have completed setting the IPL options and have pressed Enter.

If the value for Set Major Systems Options is Y, the display will be shown after you have processed the Set Major Systems Options display.

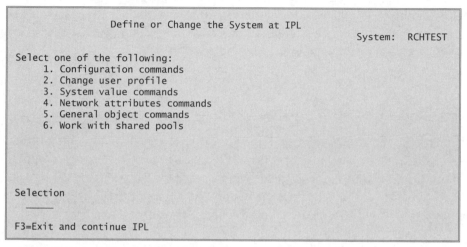

```
                 Define or Change the System at IPL
                                                    System:   RCHTEST

Select one of the following:
      1. Configuration commands
      2. Change user profile
      3. System value commands
      4. Network attributes commands
      5. General object commands
      6. Work with shared pools




Selection
_____

F3=Exit and continue IPL
```

Figure 12.3: The Define or Change the System at IPL display will appear during an attended IPL. It allows you to make changes to your system's operating environment.

This display allows you access to several OS/400 commands. You can make any adjustments to. your system at this point. It is not usually necessary to adjust your system during IPL, however. You should make these changes using the OS/400 commands while the system is active.

C900 2980 Storage Requirements

At this point, the IPL thinks it would be a good idea to see if your system will be able to complete the IPL. So, this step validates that your system's main storage and disk capacity meets the minimum system hardware requirements to run. Guaranteeing that your system will IPL is no guarantee of its runtime performance. It is up to you to ensure that your system has adequate main storage, processor capacity, and disk arms to provide good service to your users.

C900 29A0 System Control Block

If you look in the *Diagnostic Aids Manual* for a clarification of this step in the IPL process, you will see a big blank space. Therefore, the title of this step must say everything that needs to be said. Well, not exactly. When the system is running, OS/400 uses this object to maintain information used by the portion of work management that controls the runtime environment. Included in this block is information regarding the storage allocation and mapping of main storage pools to subsystems, status information regarding the runtime environment, and other values used in the work control functions of work management. This step in the IPL locates and initializes the System Control Block.

C900 29C0 Work Control Block Table

In looking at the WCBT, you determined if it was accessible and usable. At that time, you might have rebuilt the WCBT. If the WCBT was rebuilt, only a spool control block and job message queue were created for the SCPF job, so you need to create these structures for jobs that will be active after the IPL is complete. If this is an abnormal IPL, creating the structures is postponed to a later step.

Begin by examining the QTOTJOB system value. QTOTJOB is an estimate of the total number of jobs that you will have on your system (jobs on job queues, active jobs, and completed jobs with spool files). You do not need to be accurate with the number. If you underestimate, additional structures will be created based on the setting of the QADLTOTJ system value. If you overestimate, you have a small amount of wasted disk spaces (job structures that will never be used).

Once the system value has been retrieved, the system will begin to create additional job message queues, spool control block, and local data areas. But what if you set QTOTJOB to a really big number, like 30,000? Wouldn't creating 90,000 objects make for a really long IPL? Yes, it would. However, to provide some consistency in IPL time, only 100 of each object are created at this point. The rest are created by tasks that run in parallel with the remainder of the IPL steps. These tasks may continue run after the rest of the IPL is complete.

C900 2A90 Starting System Jobs

Now you are getting someplace; you're starting jobs. In this step, you start all of the system jobs described in chapter 1, except the system arbiter. For a complete list of the jobs that are started and there functions, refer to chapter 2.

C900 29C0 Abnormal Work Control Block Table Cleanup

I told you that you would see the WCBT appear in a number of IPL steps, and here it is again! This step reorganizes the WCBT during an abnormal IPL. Once again, start by determining if the WCBT was rebuilt.

If the WCBT was not rebuilt, perform the following:

1. Process each entry in the WCBT.

2. Verify the existence of the three permanent objects associated with each entry.

3. If the job was active at the time the system failed, close all related spool files. If the IPL options specify that incomplete job logs are to be cleared, clear the job log.

If the WCBT was rebuilt, perform these steps:

1. Delete all permanent objects that existed at the time the WCBT was rebuilt.

2. Create permanent objects using the setting of the QTOTJOB system value.

C900 2AC0 DLO Recovery

What does DLO recovery have to do with work management? Nothing. So, why is it here? While you really don't need to be interested in DLO recovery with respect to work management, this is the SRC that appears when you start the system arbiter. It is a "substep" within the SRC, so you don't see the step that is being run when the arbiter is being started.

While the system arbiter is actually five different jobs, only the first job, QSYSARB, is started during this step of the IPL. QSYSARB performs the synchronous tasks required to get the system running. These tasks are described in chapter 1.

C900 2B10 Establish Event Monitors

The system arbiter waits for events in the system to occur and be signaled. This step establishes the specific event monitors required by the arbiter jobs. In addition, the event monitors will be associated with the system arbiter jobs that handle and process the events.

C900 2B30 QLUS Job

This step starts the QLUS job, which performs Logical Unit Services (LUS) for the system. Specifically, QLUS supports peer devices in a Systems Network Architecture (SNA) environment and handles SNA alerts.

C900 2B40 Device Configuration

If you are performing an unattended IPL, the QCTL controller and QCONSOLE device will be varied on. In addition, all devices on the system that are specified as ONLINE(*YES) will be varied on.

C900 2C10 After System Arbiter

At this point, the system arbiter QSYSARB has completed the synchronous functions required to get the system running. As mentioned, the system arbiter is actually five jobs, and you have so far only started one of them. The remaining four jobs are discussed in the chapter 1.

Final Steps of the IPL Process

Now that you have made it through the internal wranglings of OS/400, you are reaching the final steps of the IPL. Once all of your arbiter and other system jobs are running and ready to support work on the system, the subsystem value for the controlling subsystem is retrieved, and the controlling subsystem is started. As you have seen, the controlling subsystem will have an autostart job to start other IBM-supplied subsystems. And your system is ready for use!

Changing the Attributes of an IPL

You have seen that you can change IPL attributes during an attended IPL at the IPL Options display. You can also change many of these options, as well as others, with the Change IPL Attributes command (CHGIPLA). Figure 12.4 shows the IPL attributes you can manage.

```
                    Change IPL Attributes (CHGIPLA)

 Type choices, press Enter.

 Restart type . . . . . . . . .   RESTART        *SYS
 Keylock position . . . . . . .   KEYLCKPOS      *NORMAL
 Hardware diagnostics . . . . .   HDWDIAG        *MIN
 Compress job tables  . . . . .   CPRJOBTBL      *NONE
 Check job tables . . . . . . .   CHKJOBTBL      *ABNORMAL
 Rebuild product directory  . . . RBDPRDDIR      *NONE
 Mail Server Framework recovery   MSFRCY         *NONE
 Display status . . . . . . . .   DSPSTS         *ALL
 Clear job queues . . . . . . .   CLRJOBQ        *NO
 Clear output queues  . . . . .   CLROUTQ        *NO
 Clear incomplete joblogs . . .   CLRINCJOB      *NO
 Start print writers  . . . . .   STRPRTWTR      *YES
 Start to restricted state  . .   STRRSTD        *NO




                                                                 Bottom
 F3=Exit    F4=Prompt    F5=Refresh    F12=Cancel   F13=How to use this display
 F24=More keys
```

Figure 12.4: The Change IPL Attributes command allows you to change the functions that will be performed during the next IPL.

As you can see, you have control over quite a few attributes. The last five attributes are the same as those shown on the IPL Options display that appears during an attended IPL. See the section on C900 2968 earlier in this chapter for a discussion of these five attributes; the remaining eight attributes are covered in the following pages.

Because this is an OS/400 "change" command, all of the attributes can have *SAME specified. If *SAME is specified, the current setting for the attribute will not be changed. Since the meaning of *SAME is consistent for all attributes, it is not included as a possible value in Table 12.1.

Table 12.1: Change IPL Attributes (1 of 3)

Attribute	Meaning/Values
Restart Type	This option is used to reduce the amount of time it takes to power down and restart the system. The possible values are as follows: • *SYS—The hardware will not be powered down and restarted. If a PTF that affects hardware is being applied, *SYS will be ignored, and the value will be "forced" to *FULL. This is the default value. • *FULL—The hardware is powered down and restarted. The value of this attribute can be overridden by the restart parameter of the Power Down System command (PWRDWNSYS). This value should be set to *SYS.
Keylock Position	This attribute can be used to modify the keylock position on the operations panel of the system. However, there are several restrictions regarding changes to this attribute: • You cannot change the keylock position to Manual. This is a security measure designed to prevent access to the attended IPL Options display. • Similarly, if the key position of the system is Secure, the attribute will not change the key position. • Regardless of the key position, if the system has a keylock and the key is removed, the attribute will not change the key position. You would typically use this attribute if you were performing a remote IPL. This attribute can have the following values: • *NORMAL—The keylock position is changed to Normal. • *AUTO—The keylock position is changed to Auto. • *SECURE—The keylock position is changed to Secure.
Hardware Diagnostics	This value is used to control the amount of hardware diagnostics that are done during the hardware phase of the IPL. The possible values are as follows: • *MIN—The hardware will perform minimal diagnostics. This is the default value. • *FULL—Full hardware diagnostics are performed. *FULL should only be used if new hardware has been installed or an IBM service representative has advised you to run full hardware diagnostics. If you change this attribute to *FULL, reset it to *MIN immediately following the full hardware diagnostic IPL. The function code on the operations panel of the system can be used to override this attribute. If you this attribute is *MIN, set the function code to two, and IPL, you will get a full IPL. If the attribute is *FULL and the function code is two, a minimal IPL will be performed.

Table 12.1: Change IPL Attributes (2 of 3)	
Attribute	**Meaning/Values**
Compress Job Tables	This attribute refers to the entries in the Work Control Block Table (WCBT). As entries come and go from the WCBT, spaces may occur. When the WCBT is processed from front to back, skipping over these spaces will reduce the efficiency of the operation. This attribute is used to eliminate the spaces in the WCBT. The possible values are as follows: • *NONE—Blank entries are not removed during any IPL operation. • *NORMAL—Blank entries are removed only during a normal IPL. • *ABNORMAL—Blank entries are removed only during abnormal IPL operations. This is the default value. Since the most thorough WCBT checking is done during an abnormal IPL, you might as well get rid of the blank entries at the same time. • *ALL—All the blank entries are removed on every IPL. Recent changes to the methods used to process the WCBT have nearly eliminated the need to compress it, so the default of *ABNORMAL should be used.
Check Job Tables	As in the discussion of the IPL steps, it is possible for an object to be damaged in the system. This attribute is used to determine when the WCBT is checked for damage. The possible values are as follows: • *ABNORMAL—The WCBT is checked for damage only during an abnormal IPL. This is the default value and should be used. • *ALL—The WCBT is checked for damage on every IPL. • *SYNC—The WCBT is synchronously checked for damage. No other steps of the IPL will start until the entire WCBT has been checked.
Rebuild Product Directory	The product directory ID used to catalog the Licensed Products (LPs) installed on your system. Your first IPL operation after installing a new release will ignore the value of this attribute, and the product directory will be rebuilt. Otherwise, this value will be used to rebuild the product directory. The following values are valid: • *NONE—The product directory is not rebuilt during any IPL. This is the default value and should be used. • *NORMAL—The product directory is rebuilt during each normal IPL. • *ABNORMAL—The product directory is rebuilt during each abnormal IPL. • *ALL—The product directory is rebuilt every IPL.
Mail Server Framework Recovery	During an abnormal IPL, recovering the Mail Server Framework might take quite a bit of time. It is usually postponed until the Mail Server Framework is started. However, users will be prevented from accessing this function before recovery is complete, possibly causing frustration among users. In order to avoid this, you can use this attribute to make the

Table 12.1: Change IPL Attributes (3 of 3)	
Attribute	**Meaning/Values**
Mail Server Framework Recovery *continued*	recovery of this function occur during the IPL. Thus, when a user signs on to the system and access the function, it will be available. However, IPL time will be extended. The possible values are as follows: • *NONE—Recovery is postponed until the Mail Server Framework is started. This is the default value. • *ABNORMAL—Recovery is done during the IPL for all abnormal IPL operations.
Display Status	Once the console has been powered on, you can observe the IPL status at the console rather than looking at the operations panel. If you are not physically located near the system, this is the only way you can track the progress of the IPL. No status will be displayed at the console during an installation IPL. The possible values are as follows: • *SYS—The status is displayed during attended and abnormal IPLs only. • *NONE—The status is not displayed during any IPL. • *ATTEND—The status is displayed only during attended IPLs. • *ABNORMAL—The status is displayed only during abnormal IPLs. • *ALL—The status is displayed during all IPLs other than an install IPL. This is the default value.

The defaults specified for the IPL attributes are designed to provide the fastest IPL time for normal IPL operations, which comprise more than 90 percent of iSeries IPL operations. In addition, the thoroughness required during abnormal IPL operations will still be retained using the default values for these attributes.

Work Management, System Values, and IPL

The following additional system values are related to the internals of work management or are only relevant during an IPL. There are not very many of them, but they cannot be ignored.

QABNORMSW

This system value indicates the IPL that was last done, normal or abnormal. You cannot change this system value; it is set internally by the system. QABNORMSW is a character field with a length of one and the following possible values:

- 0—The last IPL was normal. Since most system IPLs follow a PWRDWNSYS operation, QABNORMSW is usually zero.

- 1—The last IPL was abnormal. Certain system errors will cause an abnormal IPL, but the system will continue to run normally. If the value of QABNORMSW is one, you should check the system history log, qhst, to determine the reason why the last IPL was abnormal. When you look in QHST, look for messages with IDs of CPI091D and CPI0990.

QACTJOB

As discussed earlier, this system value determines the initial number of temporary job structures to create during an IPL (a response queue and the QTEMP library). These temporary structures are only used by jobs that are actively running on the system. Jobs on job queues, or completed jobs with spool files on an output queue, do not use these structures.

Both user and system jobs make use of these objects. If you have more active jobs than the number of structures you have created, additional structures will be created using the QADLACTJ system value, discussed next. If you change this system value, the change will be activated the next time the system is IPLed.

QACTJOB is a five-digit decimal number with no decimal places, DEC(50). Its default is 20, but this number is far too small for most iSeries environments. It should be set to a number that represents the maximum number of active jobs in your system. To estimate this number, run the Work with Active Jobs command (WRKACTJOB) during a peak workload. The active jobs will be shown. Count (or approximate) the active jobs, and use this number for QACTJOB.

QADLACTJ

Whenever you have more active jobs than the number specified for the system value QACTJOB, additional temporary structures that are used by jobs will be created. The number of additional structures to be created is obtained from this system value.

QADLACTJ is a five-digit decimal field with no decimal places. The default value is 10. While this might appear to be too small, especially after you have increased the value of QACTJOB, it is recommended that you use the default value. If you set the value lower, excessive overhead will occur. If you set this value too high, the job initiation might be delayed while additional structures are being created.

QADLTOTJ

Every job in the system—active, on a job queue, or completed with output on a print queue—uses three permanent structures: a job message queue, a spool control block, and a local data area. When the initial allocation of these structures, as determined by the system value QTOTJOB (discussed later), is in use, additional structures will be created based on QADLTOTJ. This system value is a five-digit decimal field with no decimal places. The default value is 10. The default value is recommended for the same reasons as QADLACTJ.

QIPLDATTIM

This system value is used to automatically IPL the system at a specified time. For example, if you have the luxury of powering your system down on weekends, you could set this system value to start an IPL on Monday morning at 5:30 A.M. That way, the system will be up and running when you arrive, and you can get some extra sleep. This system value provides a one-time occurrence of a timed IPL. That is, you cannot set it to IPL *every* Monday at 5:30 A.M.—you must reset it to a new date and time.

QIPLDATTIM is 20 characters long, and can have the following values:

- *NONE—A timed IPL will not take place. This is the default value.

- 'DATE TIME'—The system is to be IPLed on a particular date and time. The date is six characters using the system format with no separators, such as *mmddyy*. The time is six characters with no separators, such as *hhmmss*. Setting this value has the following restrictions:

➤ The time is specified in 24-hour format.

➤ The time must be at least five minutes later than the time when you ran the Change System Value command (CHGSYSVAL).

➤ The seconds portion (*ss*) must be specified, but is ignored.

➤ The date cannot be more than 11 months from the day you ran CHGSYSVAL.

Here are a couple of examples:

➤ You want the system to IPL at 5:30 A.M. on Monday, October 29, 2001. The system date format is *mmddyy*. You run the following command:

```
CHGSYSVAL IPLDATTIM VALUE('102901 053000')
```

➤ You want the system to IPL at 9:30 P.M. on Sunday, December 9, 2001. The system date format is *ddmmyy*. You run the following command:

```
CHGSYSVAL IPLDATTIM VALUE('091201 213000')
```

If the system is active or incapable of performing an IPL when IPLDATTIM is reached (because, for example, it's unplugged), the timed IPL will not be done. After a timed IPL is done, this system value is set to *NONE.

QIPLSTS

As you have seen, there are many ways to start an IPL. This system value shows the method used to initiate the last IPL. This value is set by the system and cannot be changed. QIPLSTS is a one-character field with the following values:

▪ 0—The IPL was started from the operations panel of the system.

▪ 1—The IPL was started automatically when power was restored to the system. This type of IPL is activated by the system value QPWRRSTIPL, discussed later in this chapter.

- 2—The IPL was started by the restart parameter on the Power Down System command (PWRDWNSYS):

```
PWRDWNSYS RESTART(*YES)
```

- 3—The IPL was started when the date and time in the IPLDATTIM system value was reached.

- 4—The IPL was started by a remote IPL request. Remote IPLs are enabled by the QRMTIPL system value, discussed later in this chapter.

QIPLTYPE

When the key location on the operations panel is set to Normal, and the system is powered on manually, this system value is used to determine the type of IPL to perform. QIPLTYPE is a one-character field with the following values:

- 0—The IPL is unattended. There will be no displays shown until the system is ready to use. This is the default value.

- 1—The IPL is attended, and all dedicated service tools (DSTs) are available. The IPL will present additional displays during the IPL.

- 2—The IPL is attended, and the console is in debug mode. You should only use this value when advised by an IBM service representative.

QPWRDWNLMT

When the Power Down System command (PWRDWNSYS) is run, you can specify a value for the OPTION parameter that is:

- *IMMED - all active jobs are ended abruptly, and system shutdown will start.

- *CNTRLD - the system will wait for a specified time (the delay parameter on the PWRDWNSYS command) before ending the active jobs. This allows users an opportunity to end their current work-in-progress. If jobs are still active at the end of the wait time, they will be ended abruptly and system shutdown will start.

QPWRDWNLMT specifies the amount of time (in seconds) allowed for system shutdown (for *CNTRLD this value is added to the time allowed for users to end their jobs). If the system has not finished shutting down when the time limit is reached, the system will be ended abnormally. The system value is a five digit numeric field with no decimal places. The default value is 600.

Other considerations:

- This system value is not applicable if the PWRDWNSYS command is run after a power failure and the system is running on backup power (power warning feature).
- If this value is set to 0, running the following command will immediately end the system abnormally:

```
PWRDWNSYS OPTION(*IMMED)
```

Not a good idea!

If you specify TIMOUTOPT(*MSD) on the PWRDWNSYS command, a main storage dump will be taken before the system ends.

QPWRRSTIPL

The QPWRRSTIPL system value can be used to have your system automatically IPL when power is restored. This can be useful if power should fail when you are unavailable. This system value is a one-character field with the following values:

- 0—Automatic IPL after power is restored is not allowed. Security practices might require you to use this value, which is the default.
- 1—Automatic IPL after power is restored is allowed.

QRMTIPL

When you are not located in the vicinity of the system to be IPLed, you can dial into the system and initiate an IPL if QRMTIPL is set to allow a remote IPL. This system value is a one-character field with the following values:

- 0—Remote power-on and IPL are not allowed. This is the default value.
- 1—Remote power-on and IPL are allowed.

QTOTJOB

This system value determines the initial number of permanent job structures to create during an IPL (job message queues, spool control blocks, and local data areas). These permanent structures are used by jobs actively running on the system, jobs on job queues, or completed jobs with spool files on an output queue. Both user and system jobs make use of these objects. If you have more jobs in the system than the number of structures you have created, additional structures will be created using the QADLTOTJ system value (described earlier). If you change this system value, the change will be activated the next time the system is IPLed.

QTOTJOB is a five-digit decimal number with no decimal places, DEC(50). Its default is 30, but this number is far too small for most iSeries environments. It should be set to a number that is 20 percent larger than the value used for the QACTJOB system value.

Reasons to IPL an iSeries System

After all of this discussion, do you really want to IPL? Maybe you think you should IPL more often. Since the iSeries machine is very stable, and OS/400 and LIC scale to large workloads without requiring an IPL to restructure the system, an iSeries system does not need to be IPLed very often. In general, you should IPL your machine only in the following situations:

- The system is running out of addresses. You can see how many addresses your system has used by running the Work with Systems Status command (WRKSYSSTS). When you run this command, you get the display shown in Figure 12.5.

  In the upper left corner of this display, you will see two items, "% perm addresses" and "% temp addresses." These values tell you the percentage of available addresses that have been used. When either of these values reaches 95 percent, it is time to IPL. Since the iSeries address space is humungous, as long as you are running a production environment, you should never need to IPL because you are running out of addresses. Never!

```
                      Work with System Status                    TSCSAP02
                                                       02/14/01  16:02:53
  % CPU used . . . . . . . :        73.7   Auxiliary storage:
  % DB capability . . . . :         34.8     System ASP . . . . . . :        110.2 G
  Elapsed time . . . . . . :     00:00:01    % system ASP used . . :        86.1270
  Jobs in system . . . . . :        1195     Total . . . . . . . . :        114.4 G
  % perm addresses . . . . :         .018    Current unprotect used :         1529 M
  % temp addresses . . . . :         .541    Maximum unprotect . . :          1713 M

  Type changes (if allowed), press Enter.

  System    Pool    Reserved    Max    ---DB---   --Non-DB--
   Pool   Size (M)  Size (M)  Active  Fault Pages  Fault  Pages
    1      300.00    159.76   +++++    .0    .0     .0     .0
    2     1773.79      1.13    9999    .8    .8     .8    1.7
    3        2.20       .00      10    .0    .0     .0     .0
    4      100.00       .00    9999    .0    .0     .0     .0

                                                                    Bottom
  Command
  ===>
  F3=Exit    F4=Prompt           F5=Refresh   F9=Retrieve    F10=Restart
  F11=Display transition data    F12=Cancel   F24=More keys
```

Figure 12.5: The Work with System Status display contains information that can be used to determine if an IPL should be performed.

- You are applying PTFs that require an IPL to be activated. Note that not all PTFs require an IPL.

- You have installed new hardware that required you to power-off your system. Note that not all hardware changes require the system to be powered off.

- You experienced a system failure. The failure could have been caused by any number of conditions, such as a Power failure, operating system failure, or forced power-off. These situations will produce an abnormal IPL.

That's it! Contrary to myth, it is not necessary for you to sacrifice your machine to the IPL god on a weekly basis. In fact, many large customers who require continuous availability only IPL their machines quarterly, when they install new cumulative packages of PTFs.

In Review

For many people, IPL is a mysterious period in history. The most frustrating thing about an IPL is the factor of time unpredictability. However, recent improvements have made IPL times more predictable and faster. This chapter covers some of the basics of IPLs, as well as some of the steps pertinent to work management. When it comes to the steps in an IPL, however, you have just scratched the surface. A large number of steps in both LIC and OS/400 validate the condition of your database, the contents of your disk drives, accessibility to the objects that exist in your environment, etc. All of these steps are required to produce a complete IPL. There is no work left to do once you sign on. Your system is completely usable!

So, the next time you do an IPL, don't be frustrated. When you take your automobile to the shop, you want it to be checked out and in working order when you pick it up. Yes, it is inconvenient to be without it while it's being serviced, but it feels good to have it all done, and to know that it's in good working order. An IPL does the same thing, providing a "maintenance checkup" on your system and returning it in peak condition.

Afterword

Well, you've made it through everything this book covers and now you:

- Understand the parts of a subsystem and what it takes to get jobs initiated.

- Know how to customize work management to better fit the different jobs running in your environment. This includes adding additional job queues, pools, workstation entries, and job queue entries to the IBM-supplied subsystems.

- Are able to create a subsystem and provide the information necessary to have work initiated by the new subsystem.

- Are aware of the internal system mechanisms that differentiate shared and job-unique information in main storage.

- Know how the system schedules and dispatches jobs, and how you can apply runtime attributes of jobs to better utilize this function.

- Are able to determine the performance characteristics of your system, and understand how the performance adjust feature works.

- Understand the methods to find and manage jobs and their output.

- Are able to initiate more than one job at each workstation.

- Know the difference, or lack thereof, between the controlling subsystems QBASE and QCTL.

- Are aware of the system values used by work management, such as qtsepool, and how they can benefit your environment.

- Understand methods to reduce the overhead of job initiation and termination.

- Know the basics of a system IPL: the different types, modes, keylock positions, and function settings; the ways to initiate an IPL; and the difference between a normal and abnormal IPL.

Although there's always more to learn, with this information, you will have no trouble dealing with the work management structure at any iSeries installation anywhere in the world.

Index

Note: Boldface numbers indicate illustrations.